jQuery UI 1.10:
The User Interface Library for jQuery

Build highly interactive web applications with
ready-to-use widgets

Alex Libby

Dan Wellman

[PACKT] open source✱
PUBLISHING community experience distilled

BIRMINGHAM - MUMBAI

jQuery UI 1.10:
The User Interface Library for jQuery

First published: February 2009

Fourth published: December 2013

Production Reference: 1181213

Published by Packt Publishing Ltd.
Livery Place
35 Livery Street
Birmingham B3 2PB, UK.

ISBN 978-1-78216-220-9

www.packtpub.com

Cover Image by Aniket Sawant (aniket_sawant_photography@hotmail.com)

Credits

Authors
Alex Libby

Dan Wellman

Reviewers
Aamir Afridi

Islam AlZatary

Stephen Holsinger

Kristian Mandrup

Marjorie Roswell

Acquisition Editors
Joanne Fitzpatrick

Edward Gordon

Douglas Paterson

Lead Technical Editor
Akshay Nair

Technical Editors
Shashank Desai

Rosmy George

Jinesh Kampani

Manal Pednekar

Project Coordinator
Anugya Khurana

Proofreaders
Martin Diver

Samantha Lyon

Sandra Hopper

Indexers
Monica Ajmera Mehta

Priya Subramani

Graphics
Abhinash Sahu

Production Coordinator
Aparna Bhagat

Cover Work
Aparna Bhagat

About the Authors

Alex Libby is from an IT support background. He has been involved in supporting end users for the last 15 years in a variety of different environments, and currently works as a Technical Analyst, supporting a medium-sized SharePoint estate for an international parts distributor, based in the UK. Although Alex gets to play with different technologies in his day job, his first true love has always been with the Open Source movement, and in particular experimenting with CSS/CSS3 and HTML5. To date, Alex has written five books based on jQuery, HTML5 Video, and CSS for Packt Publishing, and has reviewed several more (including one on *Learning jQuery*). *jQuery UI 1.10: The User Interface Library for jQuery* is Alex's sixth book with Packt Publishing.

I would like to give a huge thanks to Dan Wellman for allowing me the opportunity to update one of his books; it has been a pleasure and a privilege. I just hope I've done justice to it! I also thank the reviewers for their help in reviewing the book, along with their constructive feedback. Thanks must also go to family and friends for their support and encouragement; it makes working the long hours all the more worthwhile.

Dan Wellman is an author and frontend engineer living on the South Coast of the UK and working in London. By day he works for Skype and has a blast writing application-grade JavaScript. By night he writes books and tutorials focused mainly on frontend web development. He is also a staff writer for the Tuts+ arm of the Envato network, and occasionally writes for .Net magazine. He's the proud father of four amazing children, and the grateful husband of a wonderful wife.

About the Reviewers

Aamir Afridi is a London-based frontend developer and has a passion for JavaScript and jQuery. He has been working on different projects for Google, YouTube, Facebook, and Apple. He is now helping TES in refactoring the frontend architecture. He is always keen in learning new JavaScript frameworks and wrote quite a few jQuery plugins and jQuery UI extensions. He can be found at `http://aamirafridi.com/` on the Web. He is `aamirafridi` on Twitter and GitHub.

Islam AlZatary graduated in Computer Information System from Jordan in 2008. He worked for two years as a PHP web developer, and then he was appointed as a frontend engineer at Bayt.com.

He deals with jQuery, jQuery UI, HTML/HTML5, CSS/CSS3, Bootstrap framework, Mailer engine, JavaScript frameworks (RequireJS, AngularJS), and with all design approaches (fixed, fluid, responsive, adaptive). He also likes the "mobile first approach".

Stephen Holsinger has been developing on the Web professionally for over seven years. He has worked for service companies and manufacturers, primarily focusing on e-commerce platform and website development. His experience stretches from backend system integration to frontend web development. He currently works as an independent contractor lending his expertise to clients implementing retail sites on the Demandware Commerce SaaS Platform.

Kristian Mandrup has a master's degree in Computer Science from Copenhagen University.

He has been developing software since he got his first computer at the age of 12 and has always been curious and always asks the hard questions: why? He likes to push the techs to the limits and live on the bleeding edge. He is always on the move, on new adventures and explorations, since the techs and tools never feel quite good enough.

He is a toolmaker and an architect more than a traditional software developer. He has crossed various platform boundaries over the year and has lately shifted from the Ruby on Rails platform to the new frontier of Node.js and the MEAN stack. He is currently exploring single-page, real-time applications. He likes to combine many of the best techs available into a high-powered stack. This is where jQuery UI fits in perfectly.

You can find Kristian on GitHub at `https://github.com/kristianmandrup` and his Twitter handle is `@kmandrup`.

Marjorie Roswell is a web developer from Baltimore, MD. She has been building websites that serve the community for more than a decade.

She wrote the *Drupal 5 Views Recipes* book for Packt Publishing. She has developed a GIS system for assisting citizen callers to the Baltimore Office of Recycling, and has taught professional classes in desktop publishing, AutoCAD, and Drupal. She currently serves clients as a NationBuilder website developer.

While in college, Marjorie received the Betty Flanders Thomson Prize for Excellence in Botany. Her `http://FarmBillPrimer.org` site is devoted to mapping and charting federal food and farm policy.

> The author of this book has a masterful knowledge of jQuery UI, and Packt Publishing staff Anugya Khurana and Prachi Bisht have been terrific to work with during the review process.

www.PacktPub.com

Support files, eBooks, discount offers and more

You might want to visit www.PacktPub.com for support files and downloads related to your book.

Did you know that Packt offers eBook versions of every book published, with PDF and ePub files available? You can upgrade to the eBook version at www.PacktPub.com and as a print book customer, you are entitled to a discount on the eBook copy. Get in touch with us at service@packtpub.com for more details.

At www.PacktPub.com, you can also read a collection of free technical articles, sign up for a range of free newsletters and receive exclusive discounts and offers on Packt books and eBooks.

http://PacktLib.PacktPub.com

Do you need instant solutions to your IT questions? PacktLib is Packt's online digital book library. Here, you can access, read and search across Packt's entire library of books.

Why Subscribe?

- Fully searchable across every book published by Packt
- Copy and paste, print and bookmark content
- On demand and accessible via web browser

Free Access for Packt account holders

If you have an account with Packt at www.PacktPub.com, you can use this to access PacktLib today and view nine entirely free books. Simply use your login credentials for immediate access.

Table of Contents

Preface

Modern web application user interface design requires rapid development and proven results. jQuery UI, a trusted suite of official plugins for the jQuery JavaScript library, gives you a solid platform on which you can build rich and engaging interfaces with maximum compatibility, stability, and minimum time and effort.

jQuery UI has a series of ready-made, great-looking user interface widgets and a comprehensive set of core interaction helpers designed to be implemented in a consistent and developer-friendly way. With all this, the amount of code that you need to write personally to take a project from conception to completion is drastically reduced.

Specially revised for Version 1.10 of jQuery UI, this book has been written to maximize your experience with the library by breaking down each component and walking you through examples that progressively build upon your knowledge, taking you from beginner to advanced usage in a series of easy-to-follow steps.

In this book, you'll learn how each component can be initialized in a basic default implementation and then see how easy it is to customize its appearance and configure its behavior to tailor it to the requirements of your application. You'll look at the configuration options and the methods exposed by each component's API to see how these can be used to bring out the best in the library.

Events play a key role in any modern web application if it is to meet the expected minimum requirements of interactivity and responsiveness. Each chapter will show you the custom events fired by the component covered and how these events can be intercepted and acted upon.

What this book covers

Chapter 1, Introducing jQuery UI, lets you find out exactly what the library is, where it can be downloaded from, and how the files within it are structured. We also look at ThemeRoller, which browsers support the library, how it is licensed, and how the API has been simplified to give the components a consistent and easy-to-use programming model.

Chapter 2, The CSS Framework and Other Utilities, looks in detail at the extensive CSS framework, which provides a rich environment for integrated theming through Themeroller and also allows developers to easily supply their own custom themes or skins. We also cover the new position utility and have a look at all the unique features and series of configuration options that it provides.

Chapter 3, Using the Tabs Widget, looks at the first widget, which is the tabs widget, a simple but effective means of presenting structured content in an engaging and interactive widget.

Chapter 4, The Accordion Widget, looks at the accordion widget, another component dedicated to the effective display of content. Highly engaging and interactive, the accordion makes a valuable addition to any web page and its API is exposed in full to show exactly how it can be used.

Chapter 5, The Dialog, focuses on the dialog widget. The dialog behaves in the same way as a standard browser alert, but it does so in a much less intrusive and more visitor-friendly manner. We look at how it can be configured and controlled to provide maximum benefit and appeal.

Chapter 6, The Slider and Progressbar Widgets, provides a less commonly used, but no less valuable user interface tool for collecting input from your visitors, and displaying the results of an action to them. We look closely at the APIs of both components throughout this chapter to see the variety of ways in which it can be implemented, and put to good use in our web applications.

Chapter 7, The Datepicker Widget, looks at the datepicker. This component packs a huge amount of functionality into an attractive and highly usable tool, allowing your visitors to effortlessly select dates. We look at the wide range of configurations that its API makes possible as well as seeing how easy common tasks such as skinning and localization are made.

Chapter 8, The Button and Autocomplete Widgets, looks at the brand new button, and recently revived autocomplete. Long-time users of the library will remember the autocomplete from a previous version of the library. The widget is now back, fully updated to fit in with the latest version of the library and in this chapter we get to see how it can be used to great effect.

Chapter 9, Creating Menus, takes us through how to create and add menus to our websites or application. We'll see how, with minimal code, we can turn a bunch of ordinary hyperlinks into an interactive system for navigating around your site, which will help engage your site's visitors and make it easy to find content.

Chapter 10, Working with Tooltips, will show us how, with minimal effort, we can easily provide a context-based system of support, by displaying important messages or feedback to the end user. This is particularly important in instances where visitors to your site may have inadvertently entered incorrect information; we can help get them back onto the right track!

Chapter 11, Drag and Drop, begins to look at the low-level interaction helpers, tackling first the related drag-and-droppable components. We look at how they can be implemented individually and how they can be used together to enhance your user interfaces.

Chapter 12, The Resizable Component, looks at the resizing component and how it is used with the dialog widget seen earlier in the book. We see how it can be applied to any element on the page to allow it to be resized in a smooth and attractive way.

Chapter 13, Selecting and Sorting with jQuery UI, looks at the final two interaction helpers in this chapter; the selectable and sortable components. We can use the components to select and sort elements in a website or application, although the sortable component really comes into its own when working with lists, as you can reorder them by dragging items to a new position in the list. Both components can help you add a high level of professionalism and interactivity to your site, while at the same time blurring the boundaries between desktop and browser-based applications.

Chapter 14, UI Effects, is dedicated solely to the special effects that are included with the library. We look at an array of different effects that allow you to show, hide, move, and jiggle elements in a variety of attractive and appealing animations.

Chapter 15, The Widget Factory, the downloadable chapter of the book provides an extensive look at the widget factory and how it allows us to quickly and easily create our very own jQuery UI plugins. The widget factory solves lots of common problems for you and can greatly improve productivity; it also extensively improves code reuse, making it a great fit for jQuery UI as well as many other stateful plugins. You can find this chapter at http://www.packtpub.com/sites/default/files/downloads/2209OS_Chapter_15.pdf.

Appendix, Help and Support, covers the basics of downloading the library. It provides the Getting Help section which helps readers with answers to all their queries throughout the book.

What you need for this book

All you need to work through most of the examples in this book is a simple text or code editor and a browser. One or two of the more advanced examples rely on PHP, but for convenience, I've included these examples in the code download that accompanies this book.

Who this book is for

The book is for frontend developers who need to quickly learn how to use jQuery UI, or designers who wish to see how jQuery UI functions, behaves, and looks. To get the most out of this book you should have a good working knowledge of HTML, CSS, and JavaScript, and ideally be comfortable using jQuery.

Conventions

In this book, you will find a number of styles of text that distinguish between different kinds of information. Here are some examples of these styles, and an explanation of their meaning.

Code words in text, database table names, folder names, filenames, file extensions, path names, dummy URLs, user input, and Twitter handles are shown as follows: "When prompted for a location to unpack the archive to, choose the `jqueryui` folder that we just created."

A block of code is set as follows:

```
<link rel="stylesheet"
href="development-bundle/themes/base/jquery.ui.tabs.css">
<link rel="stylesheet"
href="development-bundle/themes/base/jquery.ui.theme.css">
```

When we wish to draw your attention to a particular part of a code block, the relevant lines or items are set in bold:

```
$(".ui-positioned-element").position({
  of: ".ui-positioning-element",
  my: "right bottom",
  at: "right bottom"
});
```

New terms and **important words** are shown in bold. Words that you see on the screen, in menus or dialog boxes for example, appear in the text like this: "When we view the page and select the **Images** tab, after a short delay we should see six new images."

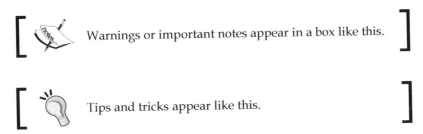

Warnings or important notes appear in a box like this.

Tips and tricks appear like this.

Reader feedback

Feedback from our readers is always welcome. Let us know what you think about this book – what you liked or may have disliked. Reader feedback is important for us to develop titles that you really get the most out of.

To send us general feedback, simply send an e-mail to feedback@packtpub.com, and mention the book title via the subject of your message.

If there is a topic that you have expertise in and you are interested in either writing or contributing to a book, see our author guide on www.packtpub.com/authors.

Customer Support

Now that you are the proud owner of a Packt book, we have a number of things to help you get the most from your purchase.

Downloading the example code

You can download the example code files for all Packt books you have purchased from your account at http://www.packtpub.com. If you purchased this book elsewhere, you can visit http://www.packtpub.com/support and register to have the files e-mailed directly to you.

Downloading the color images of this book

We also provide you a PDF file that has color images of the screenshots/diagrams used in this book. The color images will help you better understand the changes in the output. You can download this file from `http://www.packtpub.com/sites/default/files/downloads/2209OS_ColorImages.pdf`.

Errata

Although we have taken every care to ensure the accuracy of our content, mistakes do happen. If you find a mistake in one of our books – maybe a mistake in the text or the code – we would be grateful if you would report this to us. By doing so, you can save other readers from frustration and help us to improve subsequent versions of this book. If you find any errata, please report them by visiting `http://www.packtpub.com/support`, selecting your book, clicking on the **errata submission form** link, and entering the details of your errata. Once your errata are verified, your submission will be accepted and the errata will be uploaded on our website, or added to any list of existing errata, under the Errata section of that title. Any existing errata can be viewed by selecting your title from `http://www.packtpub.com/support`.

Piracy

Piracy of copyright material on the Internet is an ongoing problem across all media. At Packt, we take the protection of our copyright and licenses very seriously. If you come across any illegal copies of our works, in any form, on the Internet, please provide us with the location address or website name immediately so that we can pursue a remedy.

Please contact us at `copyright@packtpub.com` with a link to the suspected pirated material.

We appreciate your help in protecting our authors, and our ability to bring you valuable content.

Questions

You can contact us at `questions@packtpub.com` if you are having a problem with any aspect of the book, and we will do our best to address it.

1

Introducing jQuery UI

Welcome to *jQuery UI 1.10: The User Interface Library for jQuery*. This resource aims to take you from your first steps to an advanced usage of the JavaScript library of UI widgets and interaction helpers that are built on top of the hugely popular and easy-to-use jQuery.

jQuery UI extends the underlying jQuery library to provide a suite of rich and interactive widgets along with code-saving interaction helpers, built to enhance the user interfaces of your websites and web applications. Both jQuery Core and UI are built according to strict coding conventions, which are updated regularly, and follow the current best practice for JavaScript design. As the official UI library for jQuery, it's this strict adherence to current JavaScript standards that helps to make it one of the better UI libraries available for jQuery.

In this chapter we will cover the following topics:

- How to obtain a copy of the library
- How to set up a development environment
- The structure of the library
- ThemeRoller
- Browser support
- How the library is licensed
- The format of the API

jQuery has quickly become one of the most popular JavaScript libraries in use today, thanks to its ever-growing range of common UI widgets, high level of configurability, and its exceptional ease of implementation. The library is used and supported by some very well-known names, such as Microsoft, WordPress, Adobe, and Intel.

jQuery UI runs on top of jQuery, so the syntax used to initialize, configure, and manipulate the different components is in the same comfortable and easy-to-use style as jQuery. As jQuery forms the basis for UI, we can also take advantage of all the great jQuery functionality as well. The library is also supported by a range of incredibly useful tools, such as the CSS framework that provides a range of helper CSS classes, and the excellent ThemeRoller application that allows us to visually create our own custom themes for the widgets, or choose from a growing library of pre-existing themes. We will be taking a look at the ThemeRoller application later in this chapter.

Over the course of this book, we'll look at each of the existing components that make up the library. We will also be looking at their configuration options and trying out their methods in order to fully understand how they work and what they are capable of. By the end of the book, you'll be an expert in the configuration and use of each widget within the jQuery UI library. By the time we create a custom component, we'll already have a basic working knowledge of the components when we add a new widget or interaction helper, because of the consistency in how we implement the different components that make up the library. Therefore, we only need to learn any widget-specific functionality to master the particular component we wish to use.

Downloading the library

This book is specifically tailored towards Version 1.10 of jQuery UI and requires jQuery 1.6 or higher; throughout this book, we will be using jQuery 2.0.3 in our code samples.

 If you still need to support IE6 then the legacy Version 1.9.2 of the jQuery UI library is also available for download. You will also need to avail yourself of a copy of jQuery 1.10, as jQuery 2.0 does not support IE 6-8.

To obtain a copy of the library, we should visit the Download Builder at `http://www.jqueryui.com/download`. This tool gives us a range of different options for building a download package that is tailored to our particular requirements. The following screenshot shows the **Download Builder**:

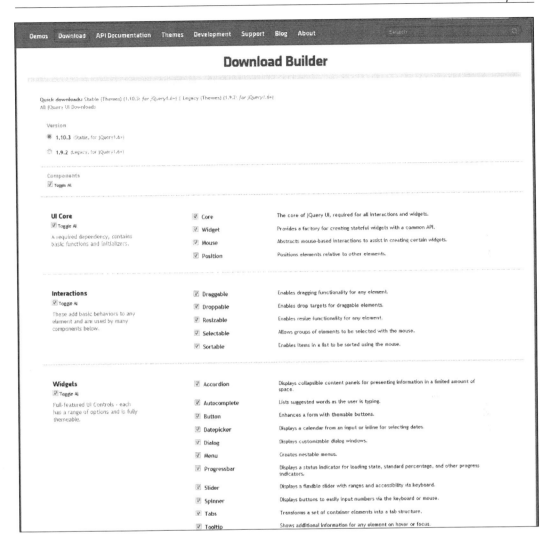

We can either download the complete current release or a complete package of a legacy version. We can also select just the components that we want and download a custom package—this is particularly recommended for production environments, where we are only using a subset of the UI library; this helps to reduce bandwidth used when viewing the page.

The page is laid out in a friendly and easy-to-use way. It lists all of the different components in their respective groupings (**UI Core**, **Interactions**, and **Widgets**) and allows us to choose from one of the 24 different predesigned themes (or no theme at all). The page also provides information about the package (including both its compressed and uncompressed size).

If as a developer you would like to see the latest snapshot of jQuery UI under source control, then you can download a copy from GitHub, which is available at https://github.com/jquery/jquery-ui.

We'll look at the different files found within the library in just a moment, but for now we should download the complete library. It will contain everything we need, including the JavaScript and CSS files, as well as any images from the current theme that rely on different components. It even contains the latest version of jQuery itself, so we don't need to worry about downloading this separately.

For now, just use the custom **Download** link at the top of the page then select **Smoothness** as the theme on the following page, and then click on **Download**. We'll look at downloading and using other themes in the next chapter.

The code download that accompanies this book includes a copy of jQuery 2.03 within each chapter's exercise folder. If you need to download a new copy, you can do so—the instructions for downloading a new copy are listed in *Appendix, Help and Support.*

Using the hosted versions of jQuery UI

We don't need to download the library in order to implement it in a production web application. Both jQuery and jQuery UI are hosted on **content delivery networks (CDN)** provided by Google, CDNJS, Microsoft, and MediaTemple (who provide the CDN for the jQuery UI).

On a live site that receives a lot of international traffic, using a CDN will help ensure that the library files are downloaded to a visitor's computer from a server that is geographically close to them. This helps in making the response quicker for them and saving our own bandwidth. This is not recommended for local development however!

 Hosted Files

If you would like to take advantage of using the CDN links, then these can be found at the following locations:

- Google's CDN: http://code.google.com/apis/libraries/
- CDNJS's CDN: http://cdnjs.com
- jQuery's CDN: http://code.jquery.com
- Microsoft's CDN: http://www.asp.net/ajaxlibrary/CDN.ashx

Setting up a development environment

We'll need a location to unpack the jQuery UI library in order to easily access the different parts of it within our own files. We should first create a `project` folder, into which all of our example files as well as all of the library, and other associated resources can be saved.

Create a new folder in your `C:` drive, or your home directory, and call it `jqueryui`. This will be the root folder of our project and will be the location where we store all of the example files that we'll make over the course of the book.

 The structure of the accompanying code download for this book will mirror the local environment we are creating.

To unpack the library, you can use Windows Explorer (if working on a PC), or a compression program such as 7-zip. When extracting the library, choose the `jqueryui` folder that we just created. If you are a Mac user, you may need to copy the contents of the `jqueryui-1.10.3.custom` folder into the new `jqueryui` folder we have just created. (We will go through the structure of the `jqueryui` folder later in this chapter.)

 7-zip is an open source archive application similar to WinZip or WinRAR; I personally find it better and easier to use. You can download it for free from at `http://www.7-zip.org`.

The code examples that we'll be looking at use other resources, mostly images, but occasionally some PHP files too. The accompanying code download available on the *Packt Publishing* website contains all of the images that we'll be using. You should download this if you can, from `http://www.packtpub.com/support/book/user-interface-library-for-jquery`. You'll need to create a new folder within the `jqueryui` project folder and call it `img`, then unpack all of the images within the image folder in the archive to this new folder.

Once you have unpacked the `jqueryui` folder and added any additional folders that are required, you will see something similar to the following screenshot—here I've used **Chapter 5** as an example, which requires an additional `img` folder to be created:

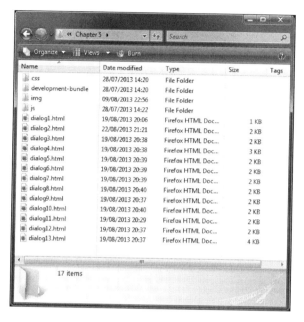

The code download also contains all the examples as well as the library itself. These files are provided in the hope that they will be used for reference purposes only. I'd recommend that you follow the examples in the book as you go along, manually creating each file as it is shown, instead of just referring to the files in the code download. The best way to learn code, is to code.

This is all that we need to do, no additional platforms or applications need to be installed and nothing needs to be configured or set up. As long as you have a browser and some kind of code or text editor, everything is in place to begin developing with the library.

There are plenty of editors available, any of which will be fine for use with jQuery UI, if you don't already have a preferred editor—for Windows users, you can try Notepad++ (freely available from `http://www.notepad-plus-plus.org`), or Sublime Text 2 (shareware, which can be downloaded from `http://www.sublimetext.com/2`). I would avoid using memory-hungry IDEs, as they tend to facilitate too much of the work and therefore impact on the learning curve when using jQuery UI.

For those of you who like to develop using a local web server, then you may use something like WAMP (for PC) or MAMP (for Mac), if you do not already have something set up as a part of your normal daily workflow. Linux users should find a suitable web server that is available from within their distro.

Understanding the structure of the library

Let's take a moment to look at the structure of the library once it has been unpacked, so that we know where to look for specific utilities and files. This will give us a feel for its composition and structure. Open up the `jqueryui` folder where we unpacked the library. The contents of this folder should be as follows:

- A `css` folder
- A `development-bundle` folder
- A `js` folder
- An `index.html` file

We can see what the structure looks like from the following screenshot:

For the purposes of using jQuery UI, it is sufficient to know that the `js` and `css` folders are the ones you will need to use within a production environment; these can be dropped into your site structure as they are, and the relevant compressed files referenced accordingly from within your code.

If however you are using the library in a development capacity, then I would recommend using the `development-bundle` folder instead; this contains the same code as the individual source files, but in uncompressed format.

Examining the folder structure in detail

For most people, it is not necessary to know how the jQuery UI library is made up; after all, the two key folders to use can simply be dropped in to your site and referenced accordingly. In this case, you may wish to skip this section and move onto *Working with ThemeRoller*.

If however your skills are more advanced and you want to learn more about the structure of the library, then please read on. I would recommend having a copy of the jQuery downloaded to hand as you work through this section, so that you can get to grips with how the library is made up.

The `css` folder is used to store the complete CSS framework that comes with the library. In this folder there will be a directory that has the name of the theme we chose when building the download package. Inside this is a single file that contains all of the CSS framework, and a folder that holds all the images used by the theme. We can also store the `css` files that we will be creating in this `css` directory.

The `js` folder contains minified versions of jQuery and the complete jQuery UI library, with all components rolled into one file. In a live project, it is the `js` and `css` folders that we'd want to drop into our site.

The index is an HTML file that gives a brief introduction to the library and displays all of the widgets along with some of the CSS classes. If this is the first time you've ever used the library, you can take a look at this file to see some of the things that we'll be working with throughout the course of this book.

The `development-bundle` directory contains a series of resources to help us develop with the library. It consists of the following subdirectories:

1. A `demos` folder
2. A `docs` folder
3. An `external` folder
4. A `themes` folder
5. A `ui` folder

The following screenshot shows how the folder structure should appear:

Also present in the directory are the license files, JSON source files, documents showing the version of the library and its main contributors, and an uncompressed version of jQuery.

The demos folder contains a series of basic examples, showing all of the different components in action. The docs folder contains API documents for each of the different components.

The external folder contains a set of tools that may be of use to developers. They are as follows:

- The globalize plugin
- The jshint plugin
- The mousewheel plugin
- The unit testing suite qunit (consisting of a JavaScript and a CSS file)

The globalize plugin provides localization support to jQuery, and can be used to format strings, dates, and numbers in over 350 cultures. The jshint plugin, a derivative of the jslint plugin, is a tool to detect errors and potential problems in JavaScript code while enforcing your own coding conventions. The mousewheel plugin, designed by Brandon Aaron, adds cross-browser mouse wheel support to your website or online application. The QUnit framework is jQuery's unit testing suite that we can use to run unit tests on our any code that we create.

For more information on QUnit, go to `http://docs.jquery.com/QUnit`.

The `themes` folder contains either the default theme or the theme that was selected during the download builder. Other themes that we download at a later point or themes that we create ourselves can also be stored here.

The `ui` folder contains the individual and uncompressed source files of each of the different components of the library.

 If you select the **Stable** download option from the main page, you will find that the contents appear different—the **Stable** download option contains the contents of the `development-bundle` folder only, and the theme included by default is called **Base**. This is visually similar to the **Smoothness** theme we've downloaded in the custom package.

Working with ThemeRoller

ThemeRoller is a custom tool written in jQuery and PHP. It allows us to visually produce our own custom jQuery UI theme and package it up in a convenient and downloadable archive, which we can then drop into our project with no further coding (other than using the stylesheet in an HTML `<link>` element, of course).

ThemeRoller, hosted at `http://ui.jquery.com/themeroller`, was created by Filament Group, Inc., and makes use of a number of jQuery plugins released into the open source community. It can be used to produce themes for jQuery UI 1.10 or the legacy Version 1.9 of jQuery UI.

 Hosted Themes

We don't even need to download a theme if we're using one of the themes available from the main site. In a production environment, you may prefer to use a CDN version of the theme, in the same way as you might use a CDN link to reference the main library.

You can import the base or smoothness theme using the following link: `http://code.jquery.com/ui/1.10.3/themes/smoothness/jquery-ui.css`. If you want to use one of the other themes, replace smoothness in the URL with your preferred theme.

ThemeRoller is certainly the most comprehensive tool available for creating your own jQuery UI themes. We can very quickly and easily create an entire theme comprised of all the styles needed for targeting the different widgets that make up the library, including the images we'll need.

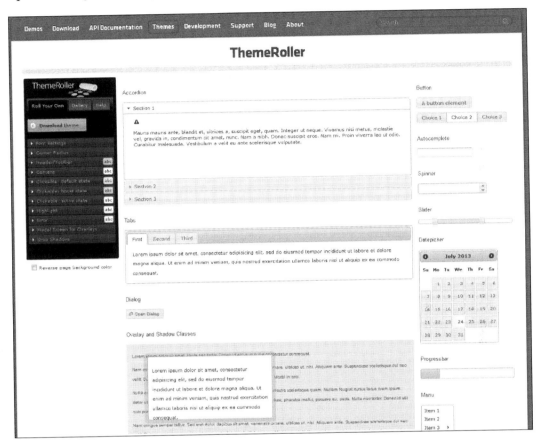

If you looked at the `index.html` file a little earlier, the ThemeRoller landing page will be instantly familiar, as it shows all the UI widgets on the page, skinned with the default **Smoothness** theme.

The ThemeRoller page features an interactive menu on the left that is used to work with the application. Each item within the menu expands to give you access to the available style settings for each part of the widget, such as the **Content** and **Clickable** areas, the **Header** and **Content** areas of the widget, and other associated things, such as warnings and **Error** messages.

Here we can create our custom theme with ease and see the changes as soon, as they are applied to the different visible parts of each widget on the page, as shown in the following screenshot:

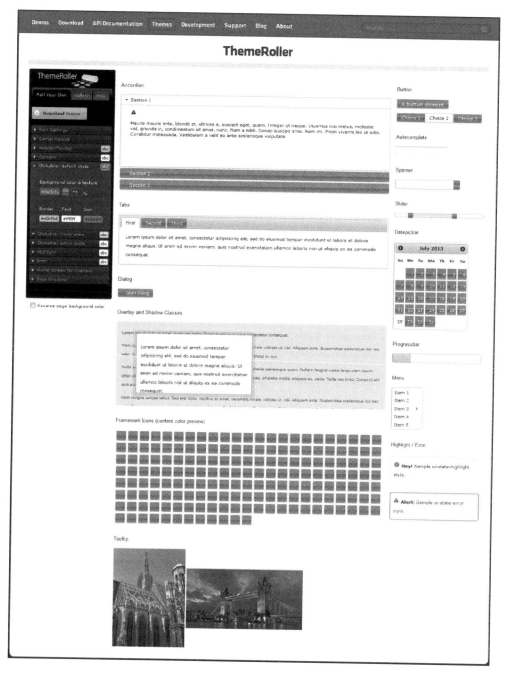

If you're not feeling particularly inspired while creating a theme, there is also a gallery of pre-configured themes that you can instantly use to generate a fully configured theme. Apart from convenience, the best thing about these pre-selected themes is that when you select one, it is loaded into the left menu. Therefore, you can easily make little tweaks as required.

This is an excellent way to create a visually appealing custom theme that matches the style of your existing site, and is the recommended method for creating custom skins.

Installing and using the new theme is as simple as selecting or creating it. The **Download theme** button in the above screenshot takes us back to the download builder that has the CSS and images for the new theme integrated into the download package.

If it's just the new theme we want, we can deselect the actual components and just download the theme. Once downloaded, the css folder within the downloaded archive will contain a folder that has the name of the theme. We can simply drag this folder into our own local css folder, and then link to the stylesheet from our pages.

We won't be looking at this tool in much detail in this book. We'll be focusing instead on the style rules that we need to manually override in our own custom stylesheets to generate the desired look of the examples manually.

Categorizing the component categories

There are three types of component found within the jQuery UI library, as follows:

- **Low-level interaction helpers**: These components are designed to work primarily with mouse events
- **Widgets**: These components produces visible objects on the page
- **Core components**: These are the components that the other parts of the library rely on

Let us take a moment to consider the components that make up each of these categories, beginning with the core components.

The core components consist of:

- Core
- Widget
- Mouse
- Position

The core file sets up the construct that all components use to function, and adds some core functionality that is shared by all of the library components, such as keyboard mappings, parent-scrolling, and a z-index manager. This file isn't designed to be used on its own, and exposes no functionality that can be used outside of another component.

The interaction helpers are comprised of the following components:

- Draggable
- Droppable
- Resizable
- Selectable
- Sortable

The interaction helpers add basic mouse-based behaviors to any element; this allows you to create sortable lists, resize elements (such as dialog boxes) on the fly or even build functionality (such as a drag-and-drop based shopping cart).

The higher-level widgets (at the time of writing) include:

- Accordion
- Autocomplete
- Button
- Datepicker
- Dialog
- Menu
- Progressbar
- Slider
- Tabs
- Menu
- Tooltips

The widgets are UI controls that bring the richness of desktop application functionality to the Web. Each of the widgets can be fully customized, appearance and their behavior.

Introducing the widget factory and effects

When working with jQuery UI's widgets, you will come across the widget factory. This literally creates the basis for all of the visible widgets exposed by the library. It implements the shared API common to all widgets, such as `create` and `destroy` methods, and provides the event callback logic. It also allows us to create custom jQuery UI widgets that inherit the shared API. We will cover the Widget Factory in detail later on in this chapter.

Apart from these components and interaction helpers, there are also a series of UI effects that produce different animations or transitions on targeted elements on the page. These are excellent for adding flair and style to our pages. We'll be looking at these effects in the final chapter of this book, *Chapter 14, UI Effects*.

The great thing about jQuery UI's simplified API is that once you have learned to use all of the existing components (as this book will show you), you'll be able to pick up any new components very quickly. There are plans for many more components in future versions, including a move to merge jQuery Mobile into the library!

Browser support

Like jQuery itself, this version of jQuery UI officially supports the current and the previous version of a browser, although the library works fine with older versions of major browsers, including the following: IE7+, Firefox 2+, Opera 9+, Safari 3+, and Chrome 1+.

Support for IE6 and IE7

As mentioned earlier, the jQuery UI team has dropped support for IE6 in UI 1.10; you can still use jQuery UI though, by downloading the legacy Version 1.9.2. Users of IE7 may note that there are plans to drop support for this browser too; at the time of writing, this is currently scheduled for Version 1.11, although this is yet to be confirmed.

The widgets are built from semantically correct HTML elements generated as needed by the components. Therefore, we won't see excessive or unnecessary elements being created or used.

Using the book examples

The library is as flexible as standard JavaScript. By this, I mean that there is often more than one way of doing the same thing, or achieving the same end. For example, the callback events used in the configuration objects for different components can usually take either references to functions or inline anonymous functions, and use them with equal ease and efficiency.

In practice, it is advisable to keep your code as minimal as possible (which jQuery can really help with anyway). But to make the examples more readable and understandable, we'll be separating as much of the code as possible into discrete modules. Therefore, callback functions and configuration options will be defined separately from the code that calls or uses them.

Throughout this book, we will separate JavaScript and CSS code into separate files; while this is overkill for the purposes of development work, it is advisable for production websites. Scripts that reside in external js files can be cached by the browser for vastly improved loading speeds; those written in-line (that is, directly into a `<script>` tags) are not cached by the browser.

I'd also just like to make it clear that the main aim throughout the course of this book is to learn how to use the different components that make up jQuery UI. If an example seems a little convoluted, it may be that this is the easiest way to expose the functionality of a particular method or property, as opposed to a situation that we would find ourselves coding for regular implementations.

I'd like to add here that the jQuery UI library is currently going through a rapid period of expansion, bug-fixing, and development. For this release, the jQuery team is focusing on bug-fixing to help make the library as stable as possible. Over the longer term, the jQuery UI team is focusing on complete redesigns of each widget's API, ahead of adding a host of new widgets in future releases, and completing a planned merger with jQuery Mobile.

Library licensing

Like jQuery, the jQuery UI library is licensed under the MIT open source license. This is a very unrestrictive license that allows the creators to take credit for its production and retain intellectual rights over it, without preventing us developers from using the library in any way that we like on any type of site.

The MIT license explicitly states that users of the software (jQuery UI in this case) are free to use, copy, merge, modify, publish, distribute, sublicense, and sell. This lets us do pretty much whatever we want with the library. The only requirement imposed by this license is that we must keep the original copyright and warranty statements intact.

This is an important point to make. You can take the library and do whatever you like with it. You can build applications on top of the library and then sell those applications or give them away for free. You can put the library in embedded systems such as cell phone OSes and sell them. But whatever you do, leave the original text file with John Resig's name present on it. You can also duplicate it word-for-word in the help files or documentation of your application.

The MIT license is very lenient, but because it is not copyrighted itself, we are free to change it. We can therefore demand that the users of our software give attribution to us instead of the jQuery team, or pass off the code as our own.

The license is not there to restrict us in any way and is not the same as the kind of license that comes with software that you might purchase and install on your own computer. In most cases, how the library is licensed will not be a consideration when using it. Plugin authors, however, will want to ensure that their plugins are released under a similar license.

Introducing the API

Once you've worked with one of the components from the library, you'll instantly feel at home when working with any of the other components, since the methods of each component are called in exactly the same way.

The API for each component consists of a series of different methods. While these are all technically methods, it may be useful to categorize them based on their particular function.

Method type	Description
The plugin method	This method is used to initialize the component and is simply the name of the component, followed by parentheses. I will refer to this throughout the book as the plugin method or the widget method.
Shared API methods	The `destroy` method can be used with any of the components to completely disable the widget being used and in most cases returns the underlying HTML to its original state.
	The `option` method is used by all components to get or set any configuration option after initialization.
	The `enable` and `disable` methods are used by most library components to enable or disable the component.
	The `widget` method, exposed by all widgets, returns a reference to the current widget.
Specialized methods	Each component has one or more methods unique to that particular component that perform specialized functions.

Methods are consistently called throughout each of the different components by passing the method that we'd like to call, as a simple string to the component's `plugin` method, with any arguments that the method accepts passed as strings after the method name.

For example, to call the `destroy` method of the accordion component, we would simply use the following code:

```
$("#someElement").accordion("destroy");
```

See how easy that was! Every single method that is exposed by all of the different components is called in this same simple way.

Some methods such as standard JavaScript functions accept arguments that trigger different behavior in the component. If we wanted to call the `disable` method on a particular tab in the tabs widget for example, we would use the following code:

```
$("#someElement").tabs("disable", 1);
```

The `disable` method, when used in conjunction with the tabs widget, accepts an integer that refers to the index of the individual tab within the widget. Similarly, to enable the tab again we would use the `enable` method as shown in the following code:

```
$("#someElement").tabs("enable", 1);
```

Again, we supply an argument to modify how the method is used. Sometimes the arguments that are passed to the method vary between components. The accordion widget, for example, does not enable or disable individual accordion panels, only the whole widget, so no additional arguments following the method name are required.

The `option` method is slightly more complex than the other common methods, but it's also more powerful and is just as easy-to-use. The method is used to either get or set any configurable option after the component has been initialized.

To use the option method in `getter` mode to retrieve the current value of an option, we could use the following code:

```
$("#someElement").accordion("option", "navigation");
```

The previous code would return the current value of the `navigation` option of the accordion widget. So to trigger the `getter` mode, we just supply the option name that we'd like to retrieve.

In order to use the `option` method in the `setter` mode instead, we can supply the option name and the new value as arguments:

```
$("#someElement").accordion("option", "navigation", true);
```

The previous code would set the value of the `navigation` option to `true`. Note that an object literal can also be passed to the `option` method in order to set several different options at once. For example:

```
$("#someElement").accordion("option", {
  animate: "bounceslide",
  heightStyle: "fill"
});
```

As you can see, although the `option` method gives us the power to use both the `get` and `set` configuration options, it still retains the same easy-to-use format of the other methods.

Events and callbacks

The API for each component also contains a rich event model that allows us to easily react to different interactions. Each component exposes its own set of unique custom events, yet the way in which these events are used is the same, regardless of which event is used.

We have two ways of working with events in jQuery UI. Each component allows us to add callback functions that are executed when the specified event is fired, as values for configuration options. For example, to use the `select` event of the tabs widget, which is fired every time a tab is selected, we could use the following code:

```
var options = {
  select: function() {
    ...
  }
};
$("#myTabs").tabs(options);
```

The name of the event is used as the `option` name and an anonymous function is used as the `option` value. We'll look at all of the individual events that are used with each component in later chapters.

The other way of working with events is to use the jQuery's `on()` method. To use events in this way, we simply specify the name of the component followed by the name of the event:

```
$("#someElement").on("tabsselect", function() {
  ...
});
```

Usually, but not always, callback functions used with the `on()` method are executed after the event has been fired, while callbacks that are specified using configuration options are executed directly before the event is fired. The callback functions are called in the context of the DOMElement that triggered the event. For example, in a tabs widget with several tabs, the `select` event will be triggered by the actual tab that is selected and not the tabs widget as a whole. This is extremely useful to us because it allows us to associate the event with a particular tab.

Some of the custom events fired by jQuery UI components are cancelable and if stopped, can be used to prevent certain actions from taking place. The best example of this (which we'll look at later in the book) is preventing a dialog widget from closing by returning `false` in the callback function of the `beforeClose` event:

```
beforeClose: function() {
  if (readyToClose === false) {
    event.preventDefault();
  }
}
```

If the arbitrary condition in this example was not met, `false` would be returned by the callback function and the dialog would remain open. This is an excellent and powerful feature that can give us fine-grained control over each widget's behavior.

Callback arguments

An important feature of using any widget is its ability to accept callbacks. We can use callbacks to run anonymous functions that perform a specific task. For example, we could fire an alert on screen each time a particular header is clicked in an Accordion widget.

Any anonymous functions that we supply as callback functions to the different events automatically pass two arguments: the original, extended or modified event object, and an object containing useful information about the widget. The information contained in the second object varies between components. As an example, let's take a look at a callback that could be implemented when using the Accordion widget:

```
$("#myAccordion").accordion({
  activate: function (event, ui) {
    if(ui.newHeader.length > 0){
      alert(ui.newHeader.attr("id"));
    } else {
      // closed
    }
  }
});
```

Here we've passed the arguments to the function and used them to determine which accordion heading is open, before displaying the result on screen. The same principle of passing these objects to any callback functions that we define applies to all components; we will cover this in detail in later chapters.

Summary

jQuery UI removes the difficulty of building engaging and effective user interfaces. It provides a range of components that can be used quickly and easily out of the box with little configuration. Each component exposes a comprehensive set of properties and methods for integration with your pages or applications that can be leveraged if a more complex configuration is required.

Each component is designed to be efficient, lightweight, and semantically correct, all while making use of the latest object-oriented features of JavaScript, and using a concise, well-tested framework. When combined with jQuery, it provides an awesome addition to any web developer's toolkit.

So far, we've seen how the library can be obtained, how your system can be set up to utilize it, and how the library is structured. We've also looked at how we can add or customize a theme for different widgets, how the API simply and consistently exposes the library's functionality, and the different categories of component. We've covered some important topics during the course of this chapter, but now we can get on with using the components of jQuery UI and get down to some proper coding, beginning with a look at the CSS framework.

2

The CSS Framework and Other Utilities

Added in Version 1.7, the jQuery UI library contains a refreshed CSS framework that can be used to effectively and consistently theme each widget available in the library. The framework is made up of many helper classes that we can use in our own code, even if we aren't using any of the library components.

In this chapter we'll be covering the following subjects:

- The files that make up the framework
- How to use the classes exposed by the framework
- How to switch themes quickly and easily
- Overriding the theme
- Using the position utility

Working with the files that make up the framework

There are two locations within the library's structure where the CSS files that make the framework reside, depending on which version of the library you choose to download.

They are as follows:

- `css`: This folder holds the complete CSS framework, including the theme that was selected when the download package was built. All the necessary CSS has been placed in a single, lean and mean stylesheet to minimize the HTTP requests in production environments. The CSS file is stored in a folder, named after the theme selected on the download builder. This version of the framework will contain styles for all the components that were selected in the download builder, so its size will vary depending on how much of the library is being used.

- `themes`: Another version of the framework exists within the `development-bundle` folder, within which you will find the `themes` folder. Two themes are provided in this folder—the base theme, and whichever theme that was selected when the library was downloaded. The base theme is a gray, neutral theme that is visually identical to the smoothness theme.

Within each of these theme folders, are the individual files that make up the framework. Each of the different components of the framework is split into its own respective files:

Component	Use
`jquery.ui.all.css`	All the required files for a theme can be linked by using this file in development. It consists of the `@import` directives that pull in the `ui.base.css` and the `ui.theme.css` files.
`jquery.ui.base.css`	This file is used by `ui.all.css`. It also contains `@import` directives that pull in the `ui.core.css file`, as well as each of the widget CSS files. However, it contains none of the theme styles that control each widget's appearance.
`jquery.ui.core.css`	This file provides core framework styles, such as the clear-fix helper and a generic overlay.

Component	Use

`jquery.ui.accordion.css`
`jquery.ui.datepicker.css`
`jquery.ui.button.css`
`jquery.ui.autocomplete.css`
`jquery.ui.dialog.css`
`jquery.ui.progressbar.css`
`jquery.ui.resizable.css`
`jquery.ui.selectable.css`
`jquery.ui.slider.css`
`jquery.ui.spinner.css`
`jquery.ui.tabs.css`
`jquery.ui.menu.css`
`jquery.ui.tooltip.css`
`jquery-ui.css`
	These files are the individual source files that control the layout and basic appearance of each widget.

`jquery.ui.theme.css`	This file contains the complete visual theme and targets of all the visual elements that make up each widget in the library.

Let's take a look at each of these files in more detail.

jquery.ui.all.css

The `jquery.ui.all.css` file makes use of CSS imports, using the `@import` rule to read in two files—the `jquery.ui.base.css` and the `jquery.ui.theme.css` file. This is all that is present in the file and all that is needed to implement the complete framework and the selected theme.

From the two directives found in this file, we can see the separations between the part of the framework that makes the widgets function and the theme that gives them their visual appearance.

jquery.ui.base.css

The `jquery.ui.base.css` file also consists of only `@import` rules, and imports the `jquery.ui.core.css` file along with each of the individual widget CSS files. At this point, I should mention that the resizable component has its own framework file, along with each of the widgets.

jquery.ui.core.css

The `jquery.ui.core.css` file provides generic styles for the framework that are used by all components. It contains the following classes:

Class	Use
`.ui-helper-hidden`	This class hides elements with `display: none.`
`.ui-helper-hidden-accessible`	This class hides elements by clipping them, so that the element remains fully accessible. The element is not hidden or positioned off-screen at all.
`.ui-helper-reset`	This is the reset mechanism for jQuery UI (it doesn't use a separate reset stylesheet), which neutralizes the margins, padding, and other common default styles applied to common elements by browsers. For an introduction to the importance of resetting default browser styling, visit: `http://sixrevisions.com/css/css-tips/css-tip-1-resetting-your-styles-with-css-reset/`.
`.ui-helper-clearfix`	The `.ui-helper-clearfix` styles are applied to the container itself.
`.ui-helper-zfix`	The `.ui-helper-zfix` class provides rules that are applied to `<iframe>` elements, in order to fix z-index issues when overlays are used.
`.ui-state-disabled`	This class sets the cursor to default for disabled elements and uses the important directive to ensure that it is not overridden.
`.ui-icon`	This rule is the library's method of replacing the text content of an element with a background image. The responsibility of setting the background images for the different icons found in the library is delegated to the `jquery.ui.theme.css` file.
`.ui-widget-overlay`	This class sets the basic style properties of the overlay that is applied to the page when dialogs and other modal pop ups are shown. As images are used by the overlay, some styles for this class are also found in the theme file.

The core file lays the foundation for the rest of the framework. We can also give these class names to our own elements, to clear floats or hide elements whenever we use the library, and especially when building new jQuery UI plugins for consistent theming with ThemeRoller.

Explaining the individual component framework files

Each widget in the library, as well as the resizable interaction helper, has a framework file that controls the CSS and makes the widget function correctly. For example, the tab headings in the tabs widget must be floated left in order to display them as tabs. The framework files set this rule. These styles will need to be presented when we are overriding the framework in a custom theme.

These files are brief, with each component using the smallest number of rules possible for it to function correctly. Generally the files are quite compact (usually not more than 15 style rules long). The Datepicker source file is the exception, as it requires a large number of rules to function correctly.

jquery.ui.theme.css

This file will be customized to the theme that was selected or created with ThemeRoller.

It sets all of the visual properties (colors, images, and so on) for the different elements that make up each widget.

Within the `jquery.ui.theme.css` file, there are many comments that contain descriptive labels, enclosed within curly braces. These are called **placeholders**, and the CSS styles that precede them are updated by ThemeRoller automatically when the theme is generated.

This is the file that will be generated for the complete theme and it contains styles for all the visible parts of each widget when creating or selecting a theme using ThemeRoller. When overriding the framework to create a custom theme, it is mostly rules in this file that will be overridden.

Each widget is constructed from a set of common elements. For example, the outer container of each widget has the class named `ui-widget`, while any content within the widget will be held in a container with the class named `ui-widget-content`. It is this consistent layout and classing convention that makes the framework so effective.

Downloading the example code

You can download the example code files for all Packt books you have purchased from your account at http://www. packtpub.com. If you purchased this book elsewhere, you can visit http://www.packtpub.com/support and register to have the files e-mailed directly to you.

This is the biggest stylesheet used by the framework and contains too many classes to list here in its entirety (but feel free to open it up at this point and take a look through it). The following table lists the different categories of classes:

Category	Use
Containers	This category sets style properties for widget, heading, and content containers.
Interaction states	These classes set the default, hover, and active states for any clickable elements.
Interaction cues	This category applies visual cues to elements including highlight, error, disabled, primary, and secondary styles.
States and images	These classes set the images used for icons displayed in the content and heading containers, as well as any clickable elements including default, hover, active, highlight, focus, and error states.
Image positioning	All of the icon images used by the theme are stored in a single sprite file, and are displayed individually by manipulating the background-position properties of the sprite file. This category sets the background positions for all individual icons.
Corner radius	CSS3 is used to give rounded corners to supporting browsers (such as Firefox 3+, Safari 3+, Chrome 1+, Opera 10+, and IE9+).
Overlays	The image used for the generic overlay defined in the core CSS file is set here, as it is a class that implements a semi-transparent overlay over specified elements.

The jQuery UI documentation features an extensive overview of the Theme API at: `http://api.jqueryui.com/category/theming/`.

Linking to the required framework files

For rapid theming of all jQuery UI widgets in a development environment, we can link to all of the individual files using `jquery.ui.all.css`:

```
<link rel="stylesheet"
href="development-bundle/themes/smoothness/jquery.ui.all.css">
```

To use each file individually when testing a component such as the tabs widget, for example, we would use the following `<link>` elements:

```
<link rel="stylesheet"
  href="development-bundle/themes/base/jquery.ui.core.css">
<link rel="stylesheet"
```

```
    href="development-bundle/themes/base/jquery.ui.tabs.css">
  <link rel="stylesheet"
    href="development-bundle/themes/base/jquery.ui.theme.css">
```

The CSS resources, when linked to separately, should be added to the HTML page in the following order: `core.css`, the widget's CSS file, and the `theme.css` file.

In a production environment, of course, we'd use the super-efficient combined file to minimize the number of HTTP requests for CSS files. We need to link to the combined `jquery-ui-x.x.x.min.css` stylesheet found in the `css/themename/` directory, where x.x.x is the version number of jQuery UI you have downloaded:

```
  <link rel="stylesheet"
    href="css/smoothness/jquery-ui-x.x.x.custom.css">
```

For easier coding and convenience, we'll be linking to the `development-bundle/themes/base/jquery.ui.all.css` file in all our examples. If you have unpacked the library as shown in the previous chapter, along with the `css`, `development-bundle`, and `js` folders, then the previous path to the CSS file will be correct. If you are using a different structure, please alter the path to the CSS file accordingly.

> **Creating the examples from this book**
>
> Throughout this book, you will note that we make reference to saving files in the `jqueryui` folder; you may wish to put a subfolder in for each chapter, so that the code is stored separately from other chapters. This is reflected in the code download that accompanies this book.

Using the framework classes

Along with using the framework while we're implementing official jQuery UI widgets, we can also use it when we're deploying our own custom plugins.

Working with containers

Containers are recommended because it means that widgets or plugins that we write will be ThemeRoller-ready and easier for end-developers to theme and customize. Let's look at how easy it is to use the framework with our own elements.

In your text editor, create a new file and add the following code:

```
<!DOCTYPE html>
<html>
<head>
  <meta charset="utf-8">
```

```
      <title>CSS Framework - Containers</title>
      <link rel="stylesheet"
        href="development-bundle/themes/base/jquery.ui.all.css">
  </head>
  <body>
    <div class="ui-widget">
      <div class="ui-widget-header ui-corner-top">
        <h2>This is a .ui-widget-header container</h2>
      </div>
      <div class="ui-widget-content ui-corner-bottom">
        <p>This is a .ui-widget-content container</p>
      </div>
    </div>
  </body>
  </html>
```

Save this page as `containers.html` within the `jqueryui` project folder that we created in *Chapter 1, Introducing jQuery UI*, when we unpacked the library. We're linking to the `jquery.ui.all.css` file from the base development theme in the library. If we were building a more complex widget, we'd probably want to link to the `jquery.ui.core.css` file as well.

Working with this file when creating widgets or plugins is essential, because it lets us verify that the class names we give our containers will pick up the appropriate styling, and reassures us that they will be ThemeRoller-ready. Any style that we need to apply ourselves would go into a separate stylesheet, just as each widget from the library has its own custom stylesheet.

We use only a couple of elements in this example. Our outer container is given the class name `ui-widget`.

Within the outer container, we have two other containers. One is the `ui-widget-heading` container and the other is the `ui-widget-content` container. We also give these elements variants of the corner-rounding classes: `ui-corner-top` and `ui-corner-bottom`, respectively.

Inside the header and content containers, we just have a couple of appropriate elements that we might want to put in, such as `<h2>` in the header and `<p>` in the content element. These elements will inherit some rules from their respective containers, but are not styled directly by the theme file.

When we view this basic page in a browser, we should see that our two container elements pick up the styles from the theme file as shown in the following screenshot:

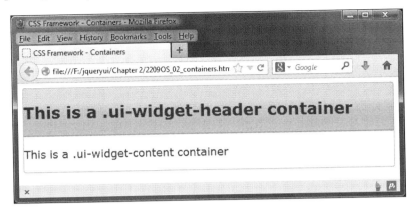

Using interactions

Let's look at some more of the framework classes in action. In `containers.html`, remove the markup with the `<body>` tags, and add the following:

```
<body>
  <div class="ui-widget">
    <div class="ui-state-default ui-state-active ui-corner-all">
      <a href="#">I am clickable and selected</a>
    </div>
    <div class="ui-state-default ui-corner-all">
      <a href="#">I am clickable but not selected</a>
    </div>
  </div>
</body>
```

Let's also alter the title too so it reflects what we are creating in the code—remove the existing `<title>`, and replace it with the following:

```
<title>CSS Framework - Interaction states</title>
```

Save this file as `interactions.html` in the `jqueryui` project folder. We've defined two clickable elements in these examples, which are comprised of a container `<div>` and an `<a>` element. Both containers are given the class names `ui-state-default` and `ui-corner-all`, but the first is also given the selected state `ui-state-active`.

This will give our clickable elements the following appearance:

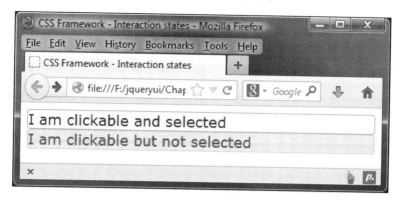

The CSS framework doesn't provide styles on the `:hover` CSS pseudo-class. Instead it applies a set of styles using a class name, which is added using JavaScript. To see this in action before the closing `</body>` tag, add the following code:

```
<script type="text/javascript" src="js/jquery-2.0.3.js"> </script>
<script>
  $(document).ready(function($){
    $(".ui-widget a").hover(function() {
      $(this).parent().addClass("ui-state-hover");
    }, function() {
      $(this).parent().removeClass("ui-state-hover");
    });
  });
</script>
```

Save this variation of the previous example file as `interactionsHovers.html`.

 The version number of jQuery will change as the library continues to evolve; we've used Version 2.03 throughout this book. You should replace it with whichever version you've downloaded, if it is different.

Our simple script adds the `ui-state-hover` class name to a clickable element when the mouse pointer moves on to it, and then removes it when the mouse pointer moves off. When we run the page in a browser and hover over the second clickable element, we should see the `ui-state-hover` styles:

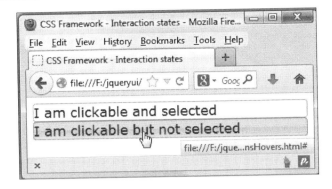

Adding icons

The framework also provides a series of images that we can use as icons. Change the contents of the ui-widget container in `interactionsHovers.html` so that it appears as follows:

```
<div class="ui-widget">
    <div class="ui-state-default ui-state-active ui-corner-all">
        <span class="ui-icon ui-icon-circle-plus"></span>

        <a href="#">I am clickable and selected</a>
    </div>
    <div class="ui-state-default ui-corner-all">
        <span class="ui-icon ui-icon-circle-plus"></span>

        <a href="#">I am clickable but not selected</a>
    </div>
</div>
```

Save this as `icons.html` in the `jqueryui` directory. In this example, our nested `<div>` elements, which have the classes `ui-icon` and `ui-icon-circle-plus`, are given the correct icon from a sprite file:

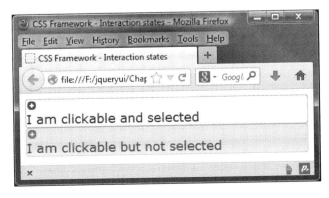

If you are not already familiar with how sprites work, then it is worth reading about this technique—have a look at `http://nerdwith.me/news/css-sprites-for-beginners/` for an example of how to create sprite images. If you need to create sprite images, then the CSS Sprites Generator at `http://csssprites.com/` is a good site to use.

As you can see, the `ui-state-active` icon differs slightly from the `ui-state-default` icon (as well as the `ui-state-hover` icon). We haven't positioned the icons at all in this example, because this would necessitate the creation of a new stylesheet.

The point of this example is to see how the icons can be automatically added using the class names from the framework, without having to add any extra CSS styling by default.

 If we wanted to adjust the positioning, we could have overridden the `.existing .ui-icon` class by adding an extra style, such as `span.ui-icon { float: left; }`, which would reposition the icons to the left of the text in each `<span>`.

Examining the icons in detail

Now that we have seen some of the icons in use, let's take a look at how you can use them in more detail.

The icons come in the form of a sprite image, which we download as part of the theme. In the main `css` folder in the library, you will find more than one theme folders. Depending on how many you need to download; each theme library contains a number of sprite images that are used by jQuery UI to produce the icons, such as the ones we've seen in the previous example.

When viewing the image sprites containing our icons, they will look something as follows:

If we examine the code within a DOM inspector such as Firebug, you will find at least two styles are added, such as:

```
<span class="ui-icon ui-icon-circle-plus"></span>
```

The format of the icon CSS will usually follow `.ui-icon-{icon type}-{icon sub description}-{direction}`; it should be noted that a third class will be added if you are using the `icon` option within widgets, such as the accordion.

Each icon element is given a base class of `.ui-icon`, which will set dimensions of the icon to a 16 px square block, hides inner text, and sets the background image with the chosen sprite image. The background sprite image used will depend on its parent container; for example a `ui-icon` element within a `ui-state-default` container will get colored according to the `ui-state-default`'s icon color.

Adding custom icons

Adding icons to widgets does not need to be limited to those within the library. It is possible to use your own custom icons.

To do this, we have two options—you can reference individual files, or use similar image sprites; the latter is preferable, particularly if you use multiple custom icons, as the sprite that contains them will be cached once loaded.

You can see a full list of icons available within the core jQuery UI library, along with their icon class names, at http://api.jqueryui.com/theming/icons/.

To reference the icons, you will need to add your own custom style, which overrides the `.ui-icon` class—this is to ensure that jQuery UI doesn't try to apply its own styles that cancel out your own. An example of such a custom class would look something as follows:

```
.ui-button .ui-icon.you-own-cusom-class {
    background-image: url(your-path-to-normal-image-file.png);
    width: your-icon-width;
    height: your-icon-height;
}
.ui-button.ui-state-hover .ui-icon.you-own-cusom-class {
    background-image: url(your-path-to-highlighted-image-file.png);
    width: your-icon-width;
    height: your-icon-height;
}
```

We can then apply our new style to our chosen widget, as illustrated using this example of a jQuery UI Button:

```
$('selector-to-your-button').button({
  text: false,
  icons: {
    primary: "you-own-cusom-class"    // Custom icon
  }
});
```

As long as the icon is of the right format, and is correctly referenced in our code, then we are free to add whichever icons we desire; it is worth researching options online, as there will be plenty of icons available for use, such as the Font Awesome library at `http://fortawesome.github.io/Font-Awesome/icons/`, or IcoMoon, which you can download from `http://icomoon.io/`.

Why does my icon appear on a new line?

In some instances, you may find that your icon appears on a new line above or below the text in your widget, as illustrated in our icons example earlier in this chapter. The reason for this is the `display: block` attribute in the `.ui-icon` class:

`.ui-icon { display: block; text-indent: -99999px;`
`overflow: hidden; background-repeat: no-repeat; }`
To get around it, you can use a float attribute, and set it to show the icon on the left, right, or center as appropriate.

Using custom icons – a note

If you decide to use custom icons, then there is nothing that will prevent you from doing so, this could open up a wealth of possibilities! You do need to note that using custom icons requires the use of two classes—the `base .ui-icon`, followed by your own custom class. This is to ensure the icons display correctly, and prevent jQuery UI from trying to override your own icon.

There is a risk that using your own icons may conflict with styles within the framework, if care is not taken in ensuring that the icons are of the right dimensions; it is strongly recommended that you look carefully through the existing icon library that is provided, as the jQuery UI team may have already converted something that could be of use. Alternatively a look online could help too; custom themes have been written for jQuery UI, and you may find one that contains the icon(s) you need.

Interaction cues

Another set of classes we can use is the interaction cues. We will look at another example using these. In a new page in your text editor, add the following code. This will create a form example, where we can see the cues in action:

```html
<!DOCTYPE html>
<html>
<head>
  <meta charset="utf-8">
  <title>CSS Framework - Interaction cues</title>
  <link rel="stylesheet" href="development-
    bundle/themes/base/jquery.ui.all.css">
  <link rel="stylesheet" href="css/jquery.ui.form.css">
</head>
<body>
  <div class="ui-widget ui-form">
    <div class="ui-widget-content ui-corner-all">
      <div class="ui-widget-header ui-corner-all">
        <h2>Login Form</h2>
      </div>
      <form action="#" class="ui-helper-clearfix">
        <label>Username</label>
        <div class="ui-state-error ui-corner-all">
          <input type="text">
          <div class="ui-icon ui-icon-alert"></div>
          <p class="ui-helper-reset ui-state-error-text">Required
            field</p>
```

```
        </div>
      </form>
    </div>
  </div>
</body>
</html>
```

Save this file as `cues.html` in the `jqueryui` folder. This time we link to a custom file, `jquery.ui.form.css` that we'll create in a moment.

On the page, we have the outer widget container, with the class names `ui-form` and `ui-widget`. The `ui-form` class will be used to pick up our custom styles from the `jquery.ui.form.css` stylesheet. Within the widget, we have `ui-widget-header` and `ui-widget-content` containers.

Within the content section, we've got a `<form>` with a single row of elements, a `<label>` element followed by a `<div>` element that has the `ui-state-error` and `ui-corner-all` class names hardcoded to it.

Within this `<div>` element, we have a standard `<input>`, a `<div>` with the `ui-icon`, and `ui-icon-alert` classes added, along with a `<p>` element with the `ui-state-error-text` class name added to it. Because the `<form>` will have child elements that are floated due to styles we will add in `jquery.ui.form.css`, we can make use of the `ui-helper-clearfix` class to clear the floats, which we add as a class name.

We should now create the custom `jquery.ui.form.css` stylesheet. In a new file in your text editor, add the following code:

```css
.ui-form { width: 470px; margin: 0 auto; }
.ui-form .ui-widget-header h2 { margin: 10px 0 10px 20px; }
.ui-form .ui-widget-content { padding: 5px; }
.ui-form label, .ui-form input, .ui-form .ui-state-error,
.ui-form .ui-icon, .ui-form .ui-state-error p { float: left; }
.ui-form label, .ui-state-error p { font-size: 12px; padding: 10px
  10px 0 0; }
.ui-form .ui-state-error { padding: 4px; }
.ui-form .ui-state-error p { font-weight: bold; padding-top: 5px;
  }
.ui-form .ui-state-error .ui-icon { margin:5px 3px 0 4px; }
.ui-helper-clearfix:before, .ui-helper-clearfix:after { margin-
  top: 10px; }
```

Within our `jqueryui` project folder, there is a folder called `css` that is used to store the single-file production version of the framework. All of the CSS files we create throughout the book will also be saved in here for convenience. Save this file as `jquery.ui.form.css` in the `css` folder.

Imagine we have more forms of elements and a submit button. By adding the `ui-state-error` class to the `<div>` element, we can use the error classes for form validation, which upon an unsuccessful submission would show the icon and text. The following screenshot shows how the page should look:

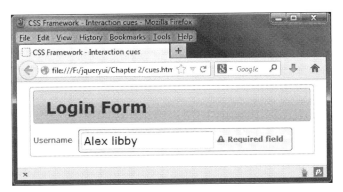

Switching themes quickly and easily

Once we have developed content using the base theme, we may decide to change the theme to something that fits in better with our overall site theme; thankfully, the CSS framework makes switching themes a painless task. Looking at the previous example, all we need to do to change the skin of the widget is choose a new theme using ThemeRoller (available at `http://www.jqueryui.com/themeroller`), and then download the new theme. We can download the new theme by selecting all of the components in the download builder and clicking on **Download** to obtain the theme.

Within the downloaded archive, there will be a directory with the name of the chosen theme, such as **redmond**. We drag the `theme` folder out of the archive into the `development-bundle\themes` folder and link the new theme file from our page, giving our form a completely new look as shown in the following screenshot:

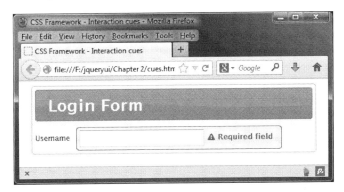

The theme I used to obtain this screenshot is redmond. This uses various shades of blue, either for the background or normal text; selected options, such as tab headings or selected items in a widget will appear either in orange text or with an orange background. We'll be using this theme, or themes of our own creation for the remainder of the book.

Overriding the theme

Using the ThemeRoller gallery and customization tools, we can generate an extraordinary number of unique themes. But there may be times when we need a deeper level of customization than we are able to reach using ThemeRoller; in this situation we have two options.

We can either create a complete theme file from scratch by ourselves, or we can create an additional stylesheet that overrides only those rules in the `jquery.ui.theme.css` file that we need. The latter is probably the easiest method and results in having to write less code.

We'll now take a look at this aspect of theming. Switch back to the base theme in `<head>` of `cues.html`, if you changed it for the previous example. Save the page as `cuesOverridden.html` and then create the following new stylesheet:

```
.ui-corner-all { border-radius: 4px; }
.ui-widget-header { font-family: Helvetica; background:
   #251e14; border-radius: 4px 4px 0 0; border: 1px solid #362f2d;
   color: #c7b299; }
.ui-form .ui-widget-header h2 { margin: 0; padding: 5px; font-
   style: italic; font-weight: normal; }
.ui-form .ui-widget-content { background: #eae2d8; border: 1px
   solid #362f2d; border-top: 0; width:  500px; padding: 0; }
.ui-widget-content form { padding: 20px; border: 1px solid
   #f3eadf; border-radius: 0 0 4px 4px; }
.ui-widget-content .ui-state-error-text { color: #9A1B1E; }
.ui-form .ui-state-error { border-radius:  4px 4px 4px 4px; }
```

Save this as `overrides.css` in the `css` folder. In this stylesheet we're mostly overriding rules from the `jquery.ui.theme.css` file. These are simple styles and we're just changing colors, backgrounds, and borders. Link to this stylesheet by adding the following line of code below the other stylesheet in `cuesOverridden.html`:

```
<link rel="stylesheet" href="css/overrides.css">
```

Our humble form should now appear as in the following screenshot:

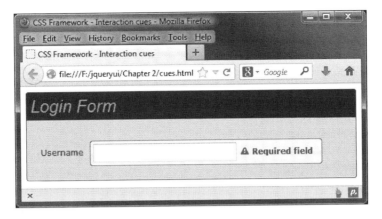

As long as our stylesheet appears after the `theme` file, and that we match or exceed the specificity of the selectors used in the `jquery.ui.theme.css` file, our rules will take precedence. A long discussion on CSS selector weight is beyond the scope of this book. However, a brief explanation of specificity may be beneficial as it is the key to overriding the selected theme. CSS specificity refers to how specific a CSS selector is—the more specific it is, the more weight it will have, and will subsequently override other rules that are applied to the element being targeted by other selectors. For example, consider the following selectors:

```
#myContainer .bodyText
.bodyText
```

The first selector is more specific than the second selector, because it not only uses the class name of the element being targeted, but also the ID of its parent container. It will therefore override the second selector, regardless of whether the second selector appears after it.

If you would like to learn more about CSS specificity, then there are lots of good articles on the Internet. As a start, you might like to look at `http://designshack.net/articles/css/what-the-heck-is-css-specificity/`, or `http://reference.sitepoint.com/ css/specificity`. Alternatively, you may like to work through Chris Coyier's example, at `http://css-tricks.com/specifics-on-css-specificity/`.

In this example, we have full control over the elements that we're skinning. But when working with any widgets from the library or with plugins authored by third parties, a lot of markup could be generated automatically, which we have no control over (without hacking the actual library files themselves).

Therefore, we may need to rely on overriding styles in this way. All we need to do to find which styles to override is open up the `jquery.ui.theme.css` file in a text editor and take a look at the selectors used there. Failing to do that, we can use Firebug's CSS viewer to see the rules that we need to override as in the following example:

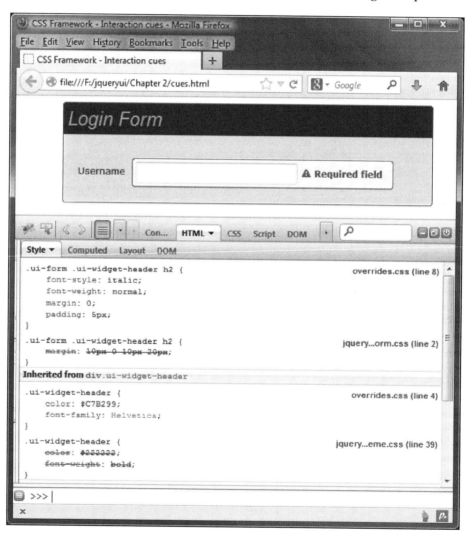

DOM Explorers

All modern browsers have DOM explorers and CSS inspectors like Firebug that can be used to see the order in which CSS rules are being applied. Using the browser's CSS inspector is usually the most convenient way of checking CSS order.

The position utility

The position utility is a powerful stand-alone utility that is used to position any element relative to the window, the document, a specific element, or the mouse pointer. It is unique among library components, in that it doesn't require `jquery.ui.core.js` or `jquery.effects.core.js` as dependencies.

It exposes no unique or custom methods (other than the `position()` method), and fires no events, but it does come with a series of configuration options that allow us to use it. These options are listed in the following table:

Option	Format	Used to
at	string	Specify the edges of the element that is being positioned against. Formatted as, for example, left bottom.
collision	string	Move the positioned element to an alternative position when the positioned element overflows its container.
my	string	Specify the edges of the element being positioned that are expected to be aligned to the element being positioned against, for example right top.
of	selector, jQuery, object, event object	Specify the element to position against the positioned element. When a selector or jQuery object is provided, the first matched element is used. When an event object is provided, the pageX and pageY properties are used
using	function	Accepts a function, which actually positions the positioned element. This function receives an object containing the top and left values of the new position.

Using the position utility

Using the position utility is easy. Let's look at a few examples; create the following page in your text editor:

```html
<!DOCTYPE html>
<html>
<head>
  <meta charset="utf-8">
  <title>Position Utility - position</title>
  <link rel="stylesheet" href="css/position.css">
  <script src="js/jquery-2.0.3.js"></script>
  <script src="development-bundle/ui/jquery.ui.position.js"> </script>
  <script>
    $(document).ready(function() {
      (function($) {
        $(".ui-positioned-element").position({
          of: ".ui-positioning-element"
        });
      })(jQuery);
    });
  </script>
</head>
<body>
  <div class="ui-positioning-element">I am being positioned against</div>
  <div class="ui-positioned-element">I am being positioned </div>
</body>
</html>
```

Save this as `position.html`. We also use a very basic stylesheet in this example, consisting of the following styles:

```css
.ui-positioning-element { width: 200px; height: 200px; border:
  1px solid #000; }
.ui-positioned-element { width: 100px; height: 100px; border:
  1px solid #f00; }
```

Save this file in the `css` folder as `position.css`. The element that we are positioning against, as well as the element that we are positioning itself, can be set to either relative, absolute, or static positioning, without affecting how the positioned element behaves. If the element we are positioning against is moved using its top, left, bottom, or right style properties, the element we are positioning will take account of this and still work correctly.

On the page we just have two `<div>` elements: one is what we will be positioning against, and the other is the actual element we will be positioning. jQuery itself is a requirement so we link to that within the `<head>` element, and we also link to the position utility's source file. As I mentioned earlier, we don't need to link to the `jquery.ui.core.js` file when using position by itself.

The minimum configuration we can use, as we have in this example, is to set the `of` option, against which we use to specify the element we are positioning. When we set just this one option, the element we are positioning is placed exactly in the center of the element we are positioning against, as shown in the following screenshot:

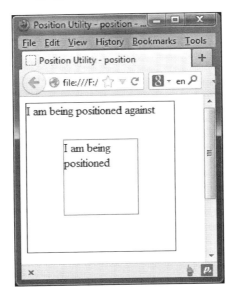

This alone is incredibly useful as the element is not only centered horizontally, but vertically too.

By using the `my` and `at` properties as well, we can place any edge of the positioned element against any edge of the element we are positioning against. Change the code within the outer function so that it appears as follows (new/altered code is shown in bold):

```
$(".ui-positioned-element").position({
    of: ".ui-positioning-element",
    my: "right bottom",
    at: "right bottom"
});
```

The following screenshot shows the output of this code:

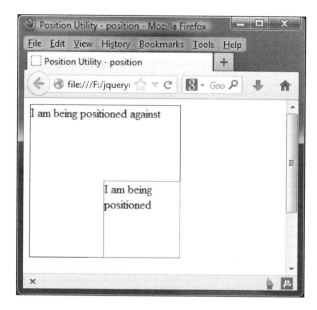

The `my` option refers to the element that is being positioned. The first part of the string, which is supplied as the value of this option, is the horizontal axis, and can be set to left, center, or right. The second part is the vertical axis, and can be set to top, center, or bottom.

The `at` option refers to the horizontal and vertical edges of the element being positioned against. It also accepts a string in the same format as the `my` configuration option.

Explaining collision avoidance

The position utility has a built-in collision detection system to prevent the element that is being positioned from overflowing the viewport. There are two different options that we can use to set what happens when a collision is detected. The default is `flip`, which causes the element to flip and align the opposite edges of those configured.

For example, if we position a `<div>` element's right edge to align to the left edge of another element, it will be flipped to have its right edge aligned to the positioning element's right edge instead, if it overflows the viewport.

Change the configuration in `position.html` to the following:

```
$(".ui-positioned-element").position({
  of: ".ui-positioning-element",
  my: "right",
  at: "left"
});
```

This would result in the following positioning:

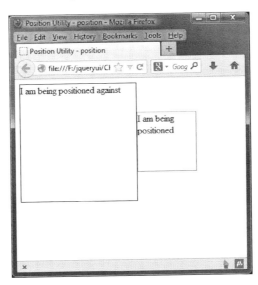

The other mode of collision avoidance is `fit`, which will honor the configured positioning as much as possible, but adjust the element's positioning, so that it stays within the viewport. Configure the collision option as follows:

```
$(".ui-positioned-element").position({
  collision: "fit",
  of: ".ui-positioning-element",
  my: "right",
  at: "left"
});
```

Save this file as `positionFit.html`. This time, the element is positioned as close as possible to its intended position:

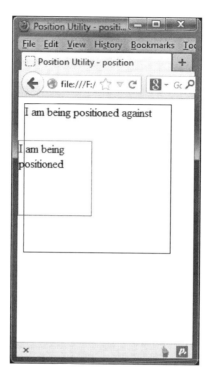

 We can also set the value of the `collision` option to `none` to disable collision detection entirely, and allow the positioned element to overflow the viewport.

Positioning with a function

We can set the `using` option to a function, and position the positioned element manually. Change the configuration so that it appears as follows:

```
$(".ui-positioned-element").position({
    of: ".ui-positioning-element",
    my: "right bottom",
    at: "right bottom",
    using: function(pos) {
        $(this).css({
```

```
        backgroundColor: "#fc7676",
        top: pos.top,
        left: pos.left
    });
  }
});
```

Save this change as `positionFunction.html`. We supply an anonymous function as the value of the `using` option. This function is passed as a single argument that is an object containing the properties top and left, which correspond to the values that the element we are positioning should be given.

As you can see from this code, we still need to position the element manually, but the function allows us to do any preprocessing of the element that may be required. Within the function, the `this` object is set to the element being positioned.

Using the position widget in a real-world example

So far, we've considered the theory behind using the position widget; before moving on to look at the widget factory, let us take a moment to consider how we can use the position widget in a real-world scenario.

A perfect example comes in the shape of jQuery UI's Dialog widget, configured to work as a modal dialog. Here we can use the position widget to place the dialog box on the page in relation to the button's current location.

To see how, add the following code to a new file in your text editor:

```html
<!DOCTYPE html>
<html>
<head>
  <meta charset="utf-8">
  <title>Dialog</title>
  <link rel="stylesheet" href="development-
    bundle/themes/redmond/jquery.ui.all.css">
  <script src="js/jquery-2.0.3.js"></script>
  <script src="development-bundle/ui/jquery.ui.core.js"></script>
  <script src="development-
    bundle/ui/jquery.ui.widget.js"></script>
  <script src="development-
    bundle/ui/jquery.ui.position.js"></script>
  <script src="development-
    bundle/ui/jquery.ui.dialog.js"></script>
```

```
  <script src="development-
    bundle/ui/jquery.ui.button.js"></script>
  <script></script>
</head>
<body></body>
</html>
```

We need some markup, so add the following code in between the `<body>` tags:

```
<div id="myDialog" title="This is the title!">
  Lorem ipsum dolor sit amet, consectetuer adipiscing elit.
  Aenean sollicitudin. Sed interdum pulvinar justo. Nam iaculis
  volutpat ligula. Integer vitae felis quis diam laoreet
  ullamcorper. Etiam tincidunt est vitae est.
</div>
Lorem ipsum dolor sit amet, consectetuer adipiscing elit.
Aenean sollicitudin. Sed interdum pulvinar justo. Nam iaculis
volutpat ligula. Integer vitae felis quis diam laoreet
ullamcorper. Etiam tincidunt est vitae est.
<button id="showdialog">Click me</button>
```

Finally, in order to tie it together and make it work, add the following script as the last entry before the closing `</head>` tag:

```
$(document).ready(function($){
  $("#showdialog").button();
  $("#myDialog").dialog({ autoOpen: false, modal: true, });
  $("#showdialog").click(function() {
    $("#myDialog").dialog("open");
  });
  $("#showdialog").position({
    my: "left+20 top+100",
    at: "left bottom",
    of: myDialog
  });
});
```

If we preview this in a browser, you'll see that we can't do anything with the text in the background when clicking on the button:

Here, we've instigated a UI dialog, and configured it to work as a modal; autopen has been set to `false`, so that the dialog doesn't show when displaying the page. We've then created a simple click handler to show the dialog on the click of a button; this is followed by a call to the position widget, where we set the `my` and `at` attributes, to correctly display the dialog in relation to the current position of the button.

The widget factory

Another tool within the jQuery UI library is the widget factory, which was introduced in Version 1.8 of jQuery UI, and has since undergone some important changes. This splits the functionality that allows widgets to be easily created into a separate and standalone utility file. This is the `jquery.ui.widget.js` file, and we can use it to create our very own jQuery UI plugins with ease. Like jQuery itself, which provides the `fn.extend()` method for easily creating plugins, jQuery UI also provides mechanisms to make plugin creation easier, and to ensure that the common API functionality is retained in new plugins. We will cover the Widget Factory in more detail in a separate chapter that can be downloaded with the book.

Summary

In this chapter, we've seen how the CSS framework consistently styles each of the library components. We've looked at the files that make it and how they work together to provide the complete look-and-feel of the widgets. We also saw how tightly integrated the ThemeRoller application is with the framework, and that it is easy to install or change a theme using ThemeRoller. We also looked at how we can override the theme file if we require a radical customization of a widget that we cannot obtain with ThemeRoller alone.

The chapter also covered building our own widgets or plugins in a way that is compatible with and can make use of the framework, as well as to ensure that our creations are ThemeRoller ready. We can also make use of the helper classes provided by the framework, such as the `ui-helper-clearfix` class, to quickly implement common CSS solutions.

We also looked at the position utility, which allows us to align any edge of one element with any edge of another element, giving us a powerful and flexible way of positioning elements that we create or manipulate.

In the next chapter, we'll move on to start looking at the widgets provided by the library, starting with the tabs widget.

3
Using the Tabs Widget

Now that we've been formally introduced to the jQuery UI library, the CSS framework, and some of the utilities, we can move on to begin looking at the individual components included in the library. Over the next seven chapters, we'll be looking at the widgets. These are a set of visually engaging, highly configurable user interface widgets.

The UI tabs widget is used to toggle visibility across a set of different elements, with each element containing content that can be accessed by clicking on its tab heading. Each panel of content has its own tab. The tab headings are usually displayed across the top of the widget, although it is possible to reposition them so that they appear along the bottom of the widget instead.

The tabs are structured so that they line up next to each other horizontally, whereas the content sections are all set to `display: none` except for the active panel. Clicking a tab will highlight the tab and show its associated content panel, while ensuring all of the other content panels are hidden. Only one content panel can be open at a time. The tabs can be configured so that no content panels are open.

In this chapter, we will look at the following topics:

- The default implementation of the widget
- How the CSS framework targets tab widgets
- How to apply custom styles to a set of tabs
- Configuring tabs using their options
- Built-in transition effects for content panel changes
- Controlling tabs using their methods
- Custom events defined by tabs
- AJAX tabs

The following screenshot is labeled with the different elements that a set of jQuery UI tabs consists of:

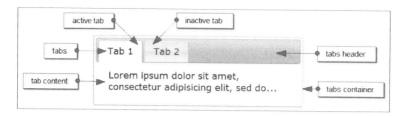

Implementing a tab widget

The structure of the underlying HTML elements on which tabs are based is fairly rigid, and widgets require a certain number of elements for them to work. The tabs must be created from a list element (ordered or unordered) and each list item must contain an `<a>` element. Each link will need to have a corresponding element with a specified `id` that is associated with the `href` attribute of the link. We'll clarify the exact structure of these elements after the first example.

In a new file in your text editor, create the following page:

```
<!DOCTYPE html>
<html>
<head>
  <meta charset="utf-8">
  <title>Tabs</title>
  <link rel="stylesheet" href="development-bundle/themes/base/jquery.
ui.all.css">
  <script src="js/jquery-2.0.3.js"></script>
  <script src="development-bundle/ui/jquery.ui.core.js"> </script>
  <script src="development-bundle/ui/jquery.ui.widget.js"> </script>
  <script src="development-bundle/ui/jquery.ui.tabs.js"> </script>
  <script>
    $(document).ready(function($){
    $("#myTabs").tabs();
  });
  </script>
</head>
<body>
  <div id="myTabs">
    <ul>
      <li><a href="#a">Tab 1</a></li>
      <li><a href="#b">Tab 2</a></li>
    </ul>
```

```
        <div id="a">This is the content panel linked to the first tab, it
    is shown by default.</div>
        <div id="b">This content is linked to the second tab and will be
    shown when its tab is clicked.</div>
      </div>
    </body>
    </html>
```

Save the code as `tabs1.html` in your `jqueryui` working folder. Let's review what was used. The following script and CSS resources are needed for the default tab widget configuration:

- `jquery.ui.all.css`
- `jquery-2.0.3.js`
- `jquery.ui.core.js`
- `jquery.ui.widget.js`
- `jquery.ui.tabs.js`

A tab widget is usually constructed from several standard HTML elements arranged in a specific manner:

- An outer container element, on which the tabs method is called
- A list element (`<ul>` or `<ol>`)
- An `<a>` element within an `<li>` element for each tab
- An element for the content panel of each tab

 These elements can be either hardcoded into the page, added dynamically, or can be a mixture of both, depending upon the requirements.

The list and anchor elements within the outer container make the clickable tab headings, which are used to show the content section that is associated with the tab. The `href` attribute of the link should be set to a fragment identifier, prefixed with #. It should match the `id` attribute of the element that forms the content section with which it is associated.

The content sections of each tab are created using `<div>` elements. The `id` attribute is required and will be targeted by its corresponding `<a>` element. We've used `<div>` elements in this example as the content panels for each tab, but other elements can also be used as long as the relevant configuration is provided and the resulting HTML is valid. The `panelTemplate` and `tabTemplate` configuration options can be used to change the elements used to build the widget (see the *Configuration* section, later in this chapter, for more information).

We link to several `<script>` resources from the library in the `<head>` section before its closing tag. Scripts can be loaded in the `<head>` section using the `document.ready()` command, or at the end after stylesheets and page elements. Loading them last is a proven technique for improving the apparent loading time of a page, although it is debatable as to how much benefit this really brings in performance.

After linking first to jQuery, we link to the `jquery.ui.core.js` file that is required by all components (except the effects, which have their own core file), and the `jquery.ui.widget.js` file. We then link to the component's source file, which in this case is `jquery.ui.tabs.js`.

After the three required script files from the library, we can turn to our custom `<script>` element in which we add the code that creates the tabs. We encapsulate the code used to create the tabs, within jQuery's DOMReady statement; this ensures the code is only executed when the page elements are loaded and ready to be manipulated. We also pass through the jQuery object ($) to help avoid conflicts with other JavaScript-based libraries.

Within the DOMReady function we simply call the `tabs()` widget method on the jQuery object, representing our tabs container element (the `<ul>` with an `id` of `myTabs`). When we run this file in a browser, we should see the tabs as they appeared in the first screenshot of this chapter (without the annotations of course).

Styling the Tabs widget

Using Firebug for Firefox (or another generic DOM explorer), we can see that a variety of class names are added to the different underlying HTML elements. Let's review these class names briefly and see how they contribute to the overall appearance of the widget. To the outer container `<div>`, the following class names are added:

Class name	Purpose
ui-tabs	Allows tab-specific structural CSS to be applied.
ui-widget	Sets generic font styles that are inherited by nested elements.
ui-widget-content	Provides theme-specific styles.
ui-corner-all	Applies rounded corners to the container.

The first element within the container is the `<ul>` element. This element receives the following class names:

Class name	Purpose
ui-tabs-nav	Allows tab-specific structural CSS to be applied.
ui-helper-reset	Neutralizes browser-specific styles applied to `<ul>` elements.
ui-helper-clearfi	Applies the clear-fix, as this element has children that are floated.
ui-widget-header	Provides theme-specific styles.
ui-corner-all	Applies rounded corners.

The individual `<li>` elements that form a part of the `tab` headings are given the following class names:

Class name	Purpose
ui-state-default	Applies the standard, non-active, non-selected, non-hovered state to the tab headings.
ui-corner-top	Applies rounded corners to the top edges of the elements.
ui-tabs-selected	This is only applied to the active tab. On page-load of the default implementation, this will be the first tab. Selecting another tab will remove this class from the currently selected tab and apply it to the newly selected tab.
ui-state-active	Applies theme-specific styles to the currently selected tab. This class name will be added to the tab that is currently selected, just like the previous class name. The reason there are two class names is that `ui-tabs-selected` provides the functional CSS, while `ui-state-active` provides the visual, decorative styles.

The `<a>` elements within each `<li>` are not given any class names, but they still have both structural and theme-specific styles applied to them by the framework.

Finally, the panel elements that hold each tab's content are given the following class names:

Class name	Purpose
ui-tabs-panel	Applies structural CSS to the content panels.
ui-widget-content	Applies theme-specific styles.
ui-corner-bottom	Applies rounded corners to the bottom edges of the content panels.

All of these classes are added to the underlying HTML elements automatically by the library. We don't need to manually add them when coding the page or adding the base markup.

Applying a custom theme to the tabs

In the next example, we can see how to change the tabs' basic appearance. We can override any rules used purely for display purposes with our own style rules for quick and easy customization, without changing the rules related to the tab functionality or structure.

In a new file in your text editor, create the following very small stylesheet:

```
#myTabs { min-width: 400px; padding: 5px; border: 1px solid
   #636363; background: #c2c2c2 none; }
.ui-widget-header { border: 0; background: #c2c2c2 none;
   font-family: Georgia; }
#myTabs .ui-widget-content { border: 1px solid #aaa; background:
   #fff none; font-size: 80%; }
.ui-state-default, .ui-widget-content .ui-state-default { border:
   1px solid #636363; background: #a2a2a2 none; }
.ui-state-active, .ui-widget-content .ui-state-active { border:
   1px solid #aaa; background: #fff none; }
```

This is all we need. Save the file as `tabsTheme.css` in your `css` folder. If you compare the class names with the tables on the previous pages, you'll see that we're overriding the theme-specific styles. Because we're overriding the theme file, we need to meet or exceed the specificity of the selectors in `theme.css`. This is why we target multiple selectors sometimes.

In this example, we override some of the rules in `jquery.ui.tabs.css`. We need to use the selector from `jquery.ui.theme.css` (`.ui-widget-content`), along with the ID selector of our container element in order to beat the double class selector `.ui-tabs .ui-tabs-panel`.

Add the following reference to this new stylesheet in the `<head>` of `tabs1.html` and resave the file as `tabs2.html`:

```
<link rel="stylesheet" href="css/tabsTheme.css">
```

Make sure the custom stylesheet we just created appears after the `jquery.ui.tabs.css` file, because the rules that we are trying to override will not be overridden by our custom theme file if the stylesheets are not linked in the correct order.

If we view the new page in a browser, it should appear as in the following screenshot:

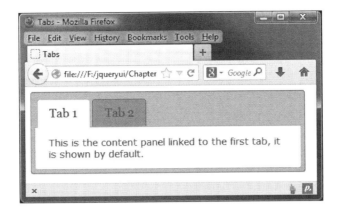

Our new theme isn't dramatically different from the default smoothness (as shown in the first screenshot), but we can see how easy it is, and how little code it requires to change the appearance of the widget to suit its environment.

Configuring the Tabs widget

Each of the different components in the library has a series of options that control which features of the widget are enabled by default. An object literal, or an object reference, can be passed in to the `tabs()` widget method to configure these options.

The available options to configure non-default behaviors are shown in the following table:

Option	Default value	Used to...
active	0	Indicate which panel is open.
collapsible	false	Allow an active tab to be unselected if it is clicked, so that all of the content panels are hidden and only the tab headings are visible.
disabled	false	Disable the widget on page load. We can also pass an array of tab indices (zero-based) in order to disable specific tabs.
event	"click"	Specify the event that triggers the display of content panels.
heightStyle	content	Control the height of the tabs widget and each panel. Possible values are auto, fill, and content.

Option	Default value	Used to...
hide	null	Control if or how to animate the hiding of the panel.
show	null	Control if or how to animate the showing of the panel.

Working with tabs

The Tabs widget provides a number of options we can use to perform actions, such as selecting or disabling tabs, or adding transition effects. Over the next few examples, we will take a look at some of these options, beginning with selecting tabs.

Selecting a tab

Let's look at how these configurable properties can be used. For example, let's configure the widget so that the second tab is displayed when the page loads. Remove the link for `tabsTheme.css` in the `<head>` of `tabs2.html` and change the final `<script>` element so that it appears as follows:

```
<script>
  $(document).ready(function($){
    var tabOpts = {
      active: 1
    };
    $("#myTabs").tabs(tabOpts);
  })
</script>
```

Save this as `tabs3.html`. The different tabs and their associated content panels are represented by a numerical index starting at zero. Specifying a different tab to open by default is as easy as supplying its index number as the value for the `active` property. When the page loads now, the second tab should be selected by default.

Along with changing which tab is selected, we can also specify that no tabs should be initially selected by supplying a value for `collapsible` in addition to the `active` property. Change the `<script>` element from `tabs4.html` so that it appears as follows:

```
<script>
  $(document).ready(function($){
    var tabOpts = {
      active: false,
      collapsible: true
    };
```

```
    $("#myTabs").tabs(tabOpts);
})
</script>
```

This will cause the widget to appear as follows on page load:

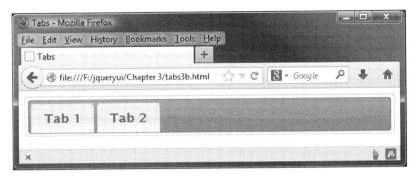

Disabling a tab

You may want a particular tab to be disabled until a certain condition is met. This is easily achieved by manipulating the `disabled` property of the tabs. Change the `tabOpts` configuration object in `tabs4.html` to this:

```
var tabOpts = {
    disabled: [1]
};
```

Save this as `tabs5.html` in your `jqueryui` folder. In this example, we remove the `active` property and add the index of the second tab to the disabled array. We could add the indices of other tabs to this array as well, separated by a comma, to disable multiple tabs by default.

When the page is loaded in a browser, the second tab has the class name `ui-widget-disabled` applied to it, and will pick up the disabled styles from `ui.theme.css`. It will not respond to mouse interactions in any way, as shown in the following screenshot:

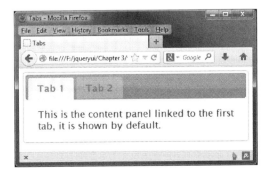

Adding transition effects

We can easily add attractive transition effects using the show property. These are displayed when tabs are opened or closed. This option is configured using another object literal (or an array) inside our configuration object, which enables one or more effects. We can enable fading effects, for example, using the following configuration object:

```
var tabOpts = {
   show: { effect: "toggle", duration: "slow" }
};
```

Save this file as `tabs6.html` in your `jqueryui` folder. The show object that we created has two properties. The first property is the animation to use when changing tabs. To use fading animations we specify `effect`, as this is what is adjusted. Toggling the effect simply reverses its current setting. If it is currently visible, it is made invisible and vice versa. You can use any one of the effects options, such as `toggle`, `fadeIn`, or `slideDown`; we will look at effects in more detail in *Chapter 14, UI Effects*.

The second property, `duration`, specifies the speed at which the animation occurs. The values for this property are `slow` or `fast`, which correspond to 200 and 600 milliseconds, respectively. Any other string will result in the default duration of 400 milliseconds. We can also supply an integer representing the number of milliseconds the animation should run for.

When we run the file we can see that the tab content slowly fades-out as a tab closes and fades-in when a new tab opens. Both animations occur during a single tab interaction. To only show the animation once, when a tab closes, for example, we would need to nest the show object within an array. Change the configuration object in `tabs6.html` so that it appears as follows:

```
var tabOpts = {
   show: [{ opacity: "toggle", duration: "slow" }, null]
};
```

The closing effect of the currently open content panel is contained within an object in the first item of the array, and the opening animation of the new tab is the second. By specifying null as the second item in the array, we disable the opening animations when a new tab is selected. Save this as `tabs7.html` and view the results in a browser.

We can also specify different animations and speeds for opening and closing animations, by adding another object as the second array item instead of `null`.

Collapsing a tab

By default when the currently active tab is clicked, nothing happens. But we can change this so that the currently open content panel closes when its tab heading is selected. Change the configuration object in `tabs7.html` so that it appears as follows:

```
var tabOpts = {
   collapsible: true
};
```

Save this version as `tabs8.html`. This option allows all of the content panels to be closed, much like when we supplied null to the `selected` property earlier on. Clicking a deactivated tab will select the tab and show its associated content panel. Clicking the same tab again will close it, shrinking the widget down so that only tab headings are visible.

Working with the Tab events

The Tabs widget defines a series of useful options that allow you to add callback functions to perform different actions, when certain events exposed by the widget are detected. The following table lists the configuration options that are able to accept executable functions on an event:

Event	Fired when...
add	A new tab is added.
disable	A tab is disabled.
enable	A tab is enabled.
load	A tab's remote data has loaded.
remove	A tab is removed.
select	A tab is selected.
show	A tab is shown.

Each component of the library has callback options (such as those in the previous table), which are tuned to look for key moments in any visitor interactions. Any functions we use within these callbacks are usually executed before the change happens. Therefore, you can return false from your callback and prevent the action from occurring.

In our next example, we will look at how easy it is to react to a particular tab being selected, using the standard non-bind technique. Change the final `<script>` element in `tabs8.html` so that it appears as follows:

```
$(document).ready(function($) {
  var handleSelect = function(e, tab) {
    $("<p></p>", {
      text: "Tab at index " + tab.newTab.index() + " selected",
      "class": "status-message ui-corner-all"
    }).appendTo(".ui-tabs-nav", "#myTabs").fadeOut(5000,
      function() {
        $(this).remove();
      });
  },
  tabOpts = {
    beforeActivate: handleSelect
  }
  $("#myTabs").tabs(tabOpts);
});
```

Save this file as `tabs9.html`. We also need a little CSS to complete this example. In the `<head>` of the page we just created, add the following `<link>` element:

```
<link rel="stylesheet" href="css/tabSelect.css">
```

Then in a new page in your text editor, add the following code:

```
.status-message { padding:11px 8px 10px; margin:0; border:1px
  solid #aaa; position: absolute; right: 10px; top: 9px; font-size:
  11px; background-color: #fff; }
.ui-widget-header { color: #2e6e9e; font-weight: bold; }
```

Save this file as `tabSelect.css` in the `css` folder. In this example, we've linked to multiple CSS files in a production environment; you may want to consider combining CSS into one file, to minimize CSS HTTP requests. Although this will help with performance on larger sites, it does come at the expense of not being able to drop in replacement jQuery UI CSS files, as you will lose any customizations you have added.

We made use of the `beforeActivate` callback in this example to create a new element in jQuery using the `<p>` tag, although the principle is the same for any of the other custom events fired by tabs. The name of our callback function is provided as the value of the `beforeActivate` property in our configuration object.

Two arguments will be passed automatically by the widget to the callback function we define, when it is executed. These are the original event object and custom object containing useful properties from the tab that was selected.

To find out which of the tabs was clicked, we can look at the `index()` property of the second object (remember these are zero-based indices). This is added, along with a little explanatory text, to a paragraph element that we create on the fly and append to the widget header:

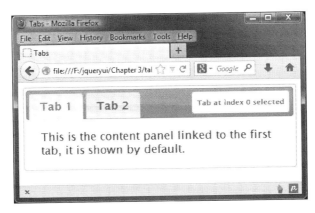

Whenever a tab is selected, the paragraph before it fades away. Note that the event is fired before the change occurs.

Binding to events

Using the event callbacks exposed by each component is the standard way of handling interactions. However, in addition to the callbacks listed in the previous table, we can also hook into another set of events fired by each component at different times.

We can use the standard jQuery `on()` method to bind an event handler to a custom event, fired by the Tabs widget in the same way that we could bind to a standard DOM event, such as a click.

The following table lists the tab widget's custom binding events and their triggers:

Event	Fired when...
tabsselect	A tab is selected.
tabsload	A remote tab has loaded.
tabsshow	A tab is shown.
tabsadd	A tab has been added to the interface.
tabsremove	A tab has been removed from the interface.
tabsdisable	A tab has been disabled.
tabsenable	A tab has been enabled.

The first three events are fired in succession, in the order of events in which they appear in the table. If no tabs are remote, then `tabsbeforeactivate` and `tabsactivate` are fired in that order. These events can be fired before or after the action has occurred, depending on which event is used.

Let's see this type of event usage in action; change the final `<script>` element in `tabs8.html` to the following:

```
<script>
    $(document).ready(function($){
      $("#myTabs").tabs();
      $("#myTabs").on("tabsbeforeactivate", function(e, tab) {
        alert("The tab at index " + tab.newTab.index() + " was
selected");
      });
    });
</script>
```

Save this change as `tabs10.html`. Binding to the `tabsbeforeactivate` in this way produces the same result as the previous example, using the `select` callback function. Like last time, the alert should appear before the new tab is activated.

All the events exposed by all the widgets can be used with the `on()` method, by simply prefixing the name of the widget to the name of the event.

> Although each callback name is spelled using camelCase format, each event name must be written in lowercase.

Using tab methods

The Tabs widget contains many different methods, which means it has a rich set of behaviors. It also supports the implementation of advanced functionality that allows us to work with it programmatically. Let's take a look at the methods, which are listed in the following table:

Method	Used to...
destroy	Completely remove the tabs widget.
disable	Disable all tabs.
enable	Enable all tabs.
load	Reload an AJAX tab's content, specifying the index number of the tab.
option	Get or set any property after the widget has been initialized.
widget	Return the element that the `tabs()` widget method is called on.

Enabling and disabling tabs

We can make use of the `enable` or `disable` methods to programmatically enable or disable specific tabs. This will effectively switch on any tabs that were initially disabled or disable those that are currently active.

Let's use the `enable` method to switch on a tab, which we disabled by default in an earlier example. Add the following new `<button>` elements directly after the existing markup for the tabs widget in `tabs5.html`:

```
<button type="button" id="enable">Enable</button>
<button type="button" id="disable">Disable</button>
```

Next, change the final `<script>` element so that it appears as follows:

```
<script>
$(document).ready(function($){
  $("#myTabs").tabs({
    disabled: [1]
  });
  $("#enable").click(function() {
    $("#myTabs").tabs("enable", 1);
  });
  $("#disable").click(function() {
    $("#myTabs").tabs("disable", 1);
  });
});
</script>
```

Save the changed file as `tabs11.html`. On the page, we've added two new `<button>` elements—one will be used to enable the disabled tab and the other is used to disable it again.

In the JavaScript, we use the `click` event of the **Enable** button to call the `tabs()` widget method. To do this, we pass the string `enable` to the `tabs()` method as the first argument. Additionally, we pass the index number of the tab we want to enable as a second argument. All methods in jQuery UI are called in this way. We specify the name of the method we wish to call as the first argument to the widget method. The `disable` method is used in the same way. Don't forget that we can use both of these methods without additional arguments, in order to enable or disable the entire widget.

Adding and removing tabs

Along with enabling and disabling tabs programmatically, we can also remove them or add completely new tabs on the fly. In `tabs11.html`, remove the existing `<button>` elements and add the following:

```
<label>Enter a tab to remove:</label>
<input for="indexNum" id="indexNum">
<button type="button" id="remove">Remove!</button>
<button type="button" id="add">Add a new tab!</button>
```

Then change the final <script> element as follows:

```
<script>
  $(document).ready(function($){
    $("#myTabs").tabs();
    $("#remove").click(function() {
      var indexTab = parseInt($("#indexNum").val(), 10);
      var tab = $("#myTabs").find(".ui-tabs-nav li:eq(" +
        indexTab + ")").remove();
      $("#myTabs").tabs("refresh");
    });
    $("#add").click(function() {
      $("<li><a href='remoteTab.txt'>New Tab</a></li>")
.appendTo("#myTabs .ui-tabs-nav");
      $("#myTabs").tabs("refresh");
    });
  });
</script>
```

We also need to provide some content that will be loaded into the tab remotely—in a new file, add `Remote tab content!`, and save it as `remoteTab.txt`.

Save this as `tabs12.html`—to preview this example, you will need to view it using a local webserver such as **WAMP** (for Windows), or **MAMP** (Apple Macs). The demo will not work if accessed using the filesystem.

On the page we've added a new instructional `<label>`, an `<input>`, and a `<button>` that are used to specify a tab to remove. We've also added a second `<button>`, which is used to add a new tab.

In `<script>`, the first of our new functions handle removing a tab, using the `remove` method. This method uses jQuery's `:eq()` function to find the index of the tab to be removed. We get the value entered into the textbox and use the index to identify which tab to remove, before using the `refresh` method to update the instance of Tabs.

The data returned by jQuery's `val()` method is in string format, so we wrap the call in the JavaScript `parseInt` function to convert it.

The `add` method, which adds a new tab to the widget, works using a similar process. Here, we create an instance of a list item, before using jQuery's `appendTo()` method to add it to the existing Tabs and updating them. In this example, we've specified that the content found in the `remoteTab.txt` file should be added as the content of the new tab. Optionally, we can also specify the index number of where the new tab should be inserted as a fourth argument. If the index is not supplied, the new tab will be added as the last tab.

After adding and perhaps removing some tabs, the page should appear something as follows:

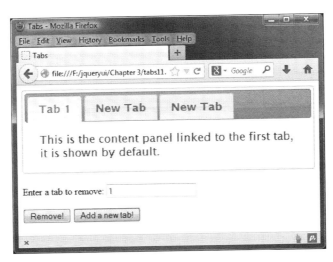

Simulating clicks

There may be times when you want to programmatically select a particular tab and show its content. This could happen as the result of some other interaction by the visitor.

We can use the `option` method to do this, which is completely analogous with the action of clicking a tab. Alter the final `<script>` block in `tabs12.html`, so that it appears as follows:

```
<script>
  $(document).ready(function($){
    $("#myTabs").tabs();
```

```
      $("#remove").click(function() {
        var indexTab = parseInt($("#indexNum").val(), 10);
        var tab = $( "#myTabs" ).find(".ui-tabs-nav li:eq(" + indexTab +
")").remove();
        $("#myTabs").tabs("refresh");
      });
      $("#add").click(function() {
        $("<li><a href='remoteTab.txt'>New Tab</a></li>").
appendTo("#myTabs .ui-tabs-nav");
        $("#myTabs").tabs("refresh");
        var tabCount = $("#myTabs ul li").length;
        $("#myTabs").tabs("option", "active", tabCount - 1);
      });
    });
</script>
```

Save this as `tabs13.html` in your `jqueryui` folder. Now when the new tab is added, it is automatically selected. The `option` method requires two additional arguments: the first is the name of the option to use, and the second is the ID of the tab to set as active.

As any tab that we add will, by default (although this can be changed), be the last tab in the interface, and as the tab indices are zero based, all we have to do is use the `length` method to return the number of tabs, and then subtract 1 from this figure to get the index. The result is passed to the `option` method.

Interestingly, selecting the newly added tab straight away fixes, or at least hides, the extra space issue from the last example.

Destroying tabs

As shown earlier, we can easily add tabs but there may be occasions when you need to completely destroy a set of tabs. This is possible using the `destroy` method, which is common to all the widgets found in jQuery UI. Let's see how it works. In `tabs13.html`, remove the existing markup immediately after the existing `<br>`, and add a new `<button>` as follows:

```
<br>
<button type="button" id="destroy">Destroy the tabs</button>
```

Next, change the final `<script>` element to this:

```
<script>
  $(document).ready(function($){
    $("#myTabs").tabs();
```

```
    $("#destroy").click(function() {
      $("#myTabs").tabs("destroy");
    });
  });
</script>
```

Save this file as `tabs14.html`. The `destroy` method, which that we invoke with a click on the button, completely removes the Tabs widget, returning the underlying HTML to its original state. After the button has been clicked, you should see a standard HTML list element and the text from each tab, similar to the following screenshot:

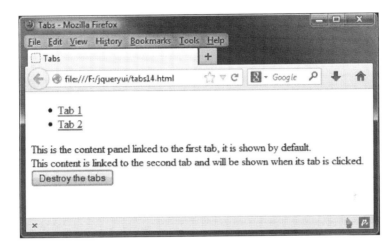

 Only the original tabs hard coded in the page will remain if the tabs are destroyed, not those added with the `add` method.

Getting and setting options

Like the `destroy` method, the `option` method is exposed by all the different components found in the library. This method is used to work with the configurable options and functions in both getter and setter modes. Let's look at a basic example; add the following `<button>` after the Tabs widget in `tabs9.html`:

```
<button type="button" id="show">Show Selected!</button>
```

Then change the final `<script>` element so that it is as follows:

```
<script>
$(document).ready(function($){
  $("#myTabs").tabs();
  $("#show").click(function() {
    $("<p></p>", {
      text: "Tab at index " + $("#myTabs").tabs("option", "active") +
" is active"
    }).appendTo(".ui-tabs-nav").fadeOut(5000);
  });
});
</script>
```

We also need to tweak the positioning of the text shown, so remove the link to `tabSelect.css` in the existing code, and add the following in the `<head>` section:

```
<style type="text/css">
  ul.ui-tabs-nav p { margin-top: 2px; margin-left: 210px;}
</style>
```

Save this file as `tabs15.html`. The `<button>` on the page has been changed, so that it shows the currently active tab. All we do is add the index of the selected tab to a status bar message, as we did in the earlier example. We get the `active` option by passing the string `active` as the second argument. Any value of any option can be accessed in this way.

> **Chaining UI methods**
>
> Chaining widget methods (either with other UI methods, or core jQuery ones) is possible because like the methods found in the underlying jQuery library, they almost always return the jQuery (`$`) object. Note that this is not possible when using getter methods that return data, such as the `length` method.

To trigger setter mode instead, we can supply a third argument containing the new value of the option that we'd like to set. Therefore, to change the value of the `active` option, in order to change the tab being displayed, we could use the following HTML instead,for this, alter the HTML as shown, at the bottom of `tabs15.html`:

```
<br>
<label for="newIndex">Enter a tab index to activate</label>
<input id="newIndex" type="text">
<button type="button2" id="set">Change Selected</button>
```

Next, append the click-handler as shown:

```
<script>
  $(document).ready(function($){
    $("#myTabs").tabs();
    $("#set").click(function() {
      $("#myTabs").tabs("option", "active", parseInt($("#newIndex").
val()));
    });
  });
</script>
```

Save this as `tabs16.html`. The new page contains a `<label>`, an `<input>`, as well as a `<button>` that is used to harvest the index number that the `active` option should be set to. When the button is clicked, our code will retrieve the value of the `<input>` and use it to change the selected index. By supplying the new value we put the method in setter mode.

When we run this page in our browser, we should see that we can switch to the second tab by entering its index number as 1 and clicking on the **Change Selected** button.

Working with AJAX tabs

We saw how we can use the `add` method to add an AJAX tab to the widget dynamically, but we can also add remote content to tabs using the underlying HTML. In this example, we want the tab that will display the remote content to be available all the time, not just after clicking on the button. This example will also only work correctly using a full web server with PHP installed and configured, such as WAMP (PC) or MAMP (Macs).

Add the following new <a> element to the underlying HTML for the widget in `tabs16.html`:

```
<li><a href="remoteTab.txt">AJAX Tab</a></li>
```

We should also remove the `<button>` from the last example.

The final `<script>` element can be used to call the `tabs` method; no additional configuration is required:

```
$("#myTabs").tabs();
```

Save this as `tabs17.html`. All we're doing is specifying the path to the remote file (the same one we used in the earlier example) using the `href` attribute of an `<a>` element in the underlying markup, from which the tabs are created.

Unlike static tabs, we don't need a corresponding `<div>` element with an `id` that matches the `href` of the link. The additional elements required for the tab content will be generated automatically by the widget.

If you use a DOM explorer, you can see that the file path that we added to link to the remote tab has been removed. Instead, a new fragment identifier has been generated and set as `href`. The new fragment is also added as the `id` of the new tab (minus the # symbol of course), so that the tab heading still shows the tab.

Along with loading data from external files, it can also be loaded from URLs. This is great when retrieving content from a database using query strings or a web service. Methods related to AJAX tabs include the `load` and `url` methods. The `load` method is used to load and reload the contents of an AJAX tab, which could come in handy for refreshing content that changes very frequently.

 There is no inherent cross-domain support built into the AJAX functionality of tabs widget. Therefore, unless additional PHP or some other server-scripting language is employed as a proxy, you may wish to make use of **JavaScript Object Notation (JSON)** structured data and jQuery's JSONP functionality. Files and URLs should be under the same domain as the page running the widget.

Changing the URL of a remote tab's content

The `url` method is used to change the URL that the AJAX tab retrieves its content from. Let's look at a brief example of these two methods in action. There are also a number of properties related to AJAX functionality.

Add the following new `<select>` element after the Tabs widget in `tabs17.html`:

```
<select id="fileChooser">
  <option value="remoteTab1.txt">remoteTab1</option>
  <option value="remoteTab2.txt">remoteTab2</option>
</select>
```

Then change the final `<script>` element to the following:

```
<script>
  $(document).ready(function($){
    $("#myTabs").tabs();
    $("#fileChooser").change(function() {
      $("#myTabs").tabs("option", "active", "2");
      $("#myTabs").find("ul>li a").attr("href", $(this).val());
      $("#myTabs").tabs("load", "active");
    });
  });
</script>
```

Save the new file as `tabs18.html`. We've added a simple `<select>` element to the page that lets you choose the content to display in the AJAX tab. In the JavaScript, we set a change handler for `<select>` and specified an anonymous function to be executed each time the event is detected.

This function first sets the active tab; in this instance, AJAX Tab, which has an ID of 2 – then uses jQuery's `find()` method to set the `href` attribute for the tab's panel, before using the `load()` method to insert the contents into the tab.

We'll also need a second local content file. Change the text in the `remoteTab1.txt` file and resave it as `remoteTab2.txt`.

Run the new file in a browser and use the `<select>` dropdown to choose the second remote file then switch to the remote tab. The contents of the second text file should be displayed.

Displaying data obtained via JSONP

For our final example, let's pull in some external content for our final tabs example. If we use the Tabs widget, in conjunction with the standard jQuery library `getJSON` method, we can bypass the cross-domain exclusion policy and pull-in a feed from another domain, to display in a tab. In `tabs19.html`, change the Tabs widget so that it appears as follows:

```
<div id="myTabs">
  <ul>
    <li><a href="#a"><span>Nebula Information</span></a></li>
    <li><a href="#flickr"><span>Images</span></a></li>
  </ul>
  <div id="a">
```

```
    <p>A nebulae is an interstellar cloud of dust, hydrogen gas, and
    plasma. It is the first stage of a star's cycle. In these regions
    the formations of gas, dust, and other materials clump together to
    form larger masses, which attract further matter, and eventually will
    become big enough to form stars. The remaining materials are then
    believed to form planets and other planetary system objects. Many
    nebulae form from the gravitational collapse of diffused gas in the
    interstellar medium or ISM. As the material collapses under its own
    weight, massive stars may form in the center, and their ultraviolet
    radiation ionizes the surrounding gas, making it visible at optical
    wavelengths.</p>
    </div>
    <div id="flickr"></div>
  </div>
```

Next, change the final `<script>` to the following:

```
<script>
  $(document).ready(function($){
    var img = $("<img/>", {
      height: 100,
      width: 100
    }),
  tabOpts = {
  beforeActivate: function(event, ui) {
    $('#myTabs a[href="#flickr"]').parent().index() != -1 ?
      getData() : null;
    function getData() {
      $("#flickr").empty();
      $.getJSON("http://api.flickr.com/services/feeds/
        photos_public.gne?tags=nebula&format=json&jsoncallback=?",
        function(data) {
          $.each(data.items, function(i,item){
            img.clone().attr("src", item.media.m)
            .appendTo("#flickr");
            if (i == 5) {
              return false;
            }
          });
        });
    }
  }
  };
  $("#myTabs").tabs(tabOpts);
});
</script>
```

Save the file as `tabs19.html` in your `jqueryui` folder. We first create a new `<img>` element and store it in a variable. We also create a configuration object and add the `select` event option to it. Every time a tab is selected, the function we set as the value of this option will check to see if it was the tab with an `id` of `flickr` that was selected. If it was, the jQuery `getJSON` method is used to retrieve an image feed from `http://www.flickr.com`.

Once the data is returned, first empty the contents of the **Flickr** tab to prevent a build-up of images, then use jQuery's `each()` utility method to iterate over each object within the returned JSON, and create a clone of our stored image.

Each new copy of the image has its `src` attribute set using the information from the current feed object, and is then added to the empty **Flickr** tab. Once iteration over six of the objects in the feed has occurred, we exit jQuery's `each` method. It's that simple.

When we view the page and select the **Images** tab, after a short delay we should see six new images, as seen in the following screenshot:

Summary

The Tabs widget is an excellent way of saving space on your page by organizing related (or even completely unrelated) sections of content that can be shown or hidden, with simple click-input from your visitors. It also lends an air of interactivity to your site that can help improve the overall functionality and appeal of the page on which it is used.

Let's review what was covered in this chapter. We first looked at how, with just a little underlying HTML and a single line of jQuery-flavored JavaScript, we can implement the default Tabs widget.

We then saw how easy it is to add our own basic styling for the Tabs widget so that its appearance, but not its behavior, is altered. We already know that in addition to this, we can use a predesigned theme or create a completely new theme using ThemeRoller.

We then moved on, to look at the set of configurable options exposed by the tabs' API. With these, we can enable or disable different options that the widget supports, such as whether tabs are selected by clicks or another event and whether certain tabs are disabled when the widget is rendered.

We took some time to look at how we can use a range of predefined callback options that allow us to execute arbitrary code, when different events are detected. We also saw that the jQuery on() method can listen for the same events if necessary.

Following the configurable options, we covered the range of methods that we can use to programmatically make the tabs perform different actions, such as simulating a click on a tab, enabling or disabling a tab, and adding or removing tabs.

We briefly looked at some of the more advanced functionalities supported by the Tabs widget such as AJAX tabs, and obtaining information using JSONP. Both these techniques are easy to use and can add value to any implementation.

In the next chapter, we'll move on to look at the **accordion** widget, which like the Tabs widget, is used to group content into related sections that are shown one at a time.

4
The Accordion Widget

The accordion widget is another UI widget that allows you to group the content into separate panels that can be opened or closed by visitor interaction. Therefore, most of its content is initially hidden from view, much like the tabs widget that we looked at in the previous chapter.

Each container has a heading element associated with it that is used to open the container and display the content. When you click on a heading, its content will slide into view (with an animation) below it. The currently visible content is hidden, while the new content is shown whenever we click on an accordion heading.

In this chapter, we are going to cover the following topics:

- The structure of an accordion widget
- The default implementation of an accordion
- Adding custom styling
- Using the configurable options to set different behaviors
- Working with methods for controlling the accordion
- The built-in types of animation
- Custom accordion events

The accordion widget is a robust and highly configurable widget that allows you to save the space on your web pages by displaying only a single panel of content at any time.

The following screenshot shows an example of an accordion widget:

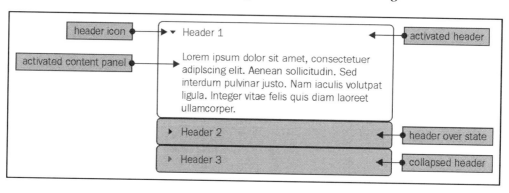

It's easy for our visitors to use and easy for us to implement. It has a range of configurable options that can be used to customize its appearance and behavior, and exposes a series of methods that allow you to control it programmatically. It also comes with a rich set of interaction events that we can use to hook into key interactions between our visitors and the widget.

The height of the accordion's container element will be set automatically so that there is room to show the tallest content panel in addition to the headers. Also, by default, the size of the widget will remain fixed so that it won't push other elements on the page around it out of the way when content panels open or close.

Structuring the accordion widget

Let's take a moment to familiarize ourselves with the underlying markup that an accordion is made of. Within the outer container is a series of links. These links are the headings within the accordion and each heading will have a corresponding content panel that opens when the header is clicked.

It's worth remembering that only one content panel can be open at a time when using the accordion widget. In a blank page in your text editor, create the following page:

```
<!DOCTYPE html>
<html>
<head>
  <meta charset="utf-8">
  <title>Accordion</title>
  <link rel="stylesheet" href="development-bundle/themes/redmond/
jquery.ui.all.css">
  <script src="js/jquery-2.0.3.js"></script>
```

```
  <script src="development-bundle/ui/jquery.ui.core.js"></script>
  <script src="development-bundle/ui/jquery.ui.widget.js"> </script>
  <script src="development-bundle/ui/jquery.ui.accordion.js"> </
script>
  <script>
    $(document).ready(function($) {
      $("#myAccordion").accordion();
    });
  </script>
</head>
<body>
  <div id="myAccordion">
    <h2><a href="#">Header 1</a></h2>
    <div>Lorem ipsum dolor sit amet, consectetuer adipiscing elit.
Aenean sollicitudin. Sed interdum pulvinar justo.
    Nam iaculis volutpat ligula. Integer vitae felis quis diam laoreet
ullamcorper.</div>

    <h2><a href="#">Header 2</a></h2>
    <div>Etiam tincidunt est vitae est. Ut posuere, mauris at sodales
rutrum, turpis tellus fermentum metus, ut
    bibendum velit enim eu lectus. Suspendisse potenti.</div>

    <h2><a href="#">Header 3</a></h2>
    <div>Donec at dolor ac metus pharetra aliquam. Suspendisse purus.
Fusce tempor ultrices libero. Sed
    quis nunc. Pellentesque tincidunt viverra felis. Integer elit
mauris, egestas ultricies, gravida vitae,
    feugiat a, tellus.</div>
  </div>
</body>
</html>
```

Save the file as accordion1.html in the jqueryui folder, and try it out in a browser.
The widget should appear as it did in the screenshot at the start of the chapter, fully
skinned and ready for action.

The following list shows the required dependencies of the widget:

- jquery.ui.all.css
- jquery-2.0.3.js
- jquery.ui.core.js
- jquery.ui.widget.js
- jquery.ui.accordion.js

As we saw with the tabs widget, each widget has its own source file (although it may be dependent on others to provide functionality); these must be referenced in the correct order for the widget to work properly. The jQuery library must always appear first, followed by the `jquery.ui.core.js` file. After that, the file that contains the required dependencies must follow. These files should be present before referencing the widget's on-script file. The library components will not function as expected if the files are not loaded in the correct order.

The underlying markup required for the accordion is flexible, and the widget can be constructed from a variety of different structures. In this example, the accordion headings are formed from links wrapped in the `<h2>` elements, and the content panels are the simple `<div>` elements.

For the accordion to function correctly, each content panel should appear directly after its corresponding header. All of the elements for the widget are enclosed within a `<div>` container that is targeted with the `accordion()` widget method.

After the required script dependencies from the library, we use a custom `<script>` block to transform the underlying markup into the accordion.

To initialize the widget, we use a simple ID selector `$("#myAccordion")`, to specify the element that contains the markup for the widget, and then chain the `accordion()` widget method after the selector to create the accordion.

In this example, we used an empty fragment (#) as the value of the `href` attribute in our tab heading elements, such as:

```
<h2><a href="#">Header 1</a></h2>
```

You should note that any URL supplied for the accordion headers will not be followed when the header is clicked in the default implementation.

Similar to the tabs widget that we looked at in the previous chapter, the underlying markup that is transformed into the accordion has a series of classnames added to it when the widget is initialized.

A number of different elements that make up the widget are given `role` and `aria-` attributes.

Accessible Rich Internet Applications (ARIA) is a W3C recommendation for ensuring that rich-internet applications remain accessible to assisted technologies.

The accordion panels that are initially hidden from view are given the `aria-expanded = "false"` attribute to ensure that screen readers don't discard or cannot access content that is hidden using `display: none`. This makes the accordion widget highly accessible; it stops the reader from having to wade through lots of content unnecessarily, that might be hidden, and tells the user that they can also expand or collapse the panel, depending on the current value of the `aria-expanded` attribute.

Styling the accordion

ThemeRoller is the recommended tool for choosing or creating the theme of the accordion widget, but there may be times when we want to considerably change the look and style of the widget beyond what is possible with ThemeRoller. In that case, we can just style our own accordion—in our example, we're going to flatten the styling effect, add a border, and remove the corners from some of the elements within the accordion widget.

In a new file in your text editor add the following code:

```
#myAccordion { width: 400px; border: 1px solid #636363; padding-
bottom: 1px; }
#myAccordion .ui-state-active { background: #fff; }
.ui-accordion-header { border: 1px solid #fff; font-family:
  Georgia; background: #e2e2e2 none; }
.ui-widget-content { font-size: 70%; border: none; }
.ui-corner-all { border-radius: 0; }
.ui-accordion .ui-accordion-header { margin: 0 0 -1px; }
```

Save this file as `accordionTheme.css` in the css folder, and link to it after the jQuery UI style sheet in the `<head>` element of `accordion1.html`:

```
<link rel="stylesheet" href="css/accordionTheme.css">
```

Save the new file as `accordion2.html` in the `jqueryui` folder and view it in a browser. It should appear something like as follows:

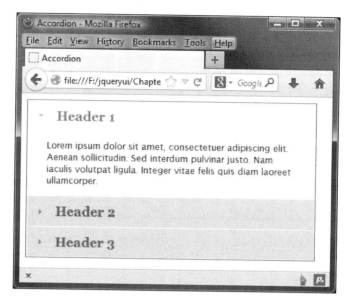

As you can see from the preceding screenshot, we've disabled the built-in rounded corners that are added by the theme file and have set alternative fonts, background colors, and border colors. We haven't changed the widget much, but we haven't used many style rules. It would be easy to continue overriding rules in this way to build a much more complex custom theme.

Configuring an accordion

The accordion has a range of configurable options that allow us to change the default behavior of the widget. The following table lists the available options, their default values, and gives a brief description of their usage:

Option	Default value	Use
active	first child (the first panel is open)	Sets the active heading on page load.
animate	{}	Controls the animation of panels.
collapsible	false	Allows all of the content panels to be closed at the same time.
disabled	false	Disables the widget.

Option	Default value	Use
event	`"click"`	Specifies the event on headers that trigger drawers to open.
header	`"> li >:first-child,>` `:not(li):even"`	Sets the selector for header elements. Although it looks complex, this is a standard jQuery selector that simply targets the first child within every odd `<li>` element.
heightStyle	`"auto"`	Controls the height of the accordion and each panel

icons	`'header': 'ui-icontriangle-1-e',`
	`'headerSelected':`
	`'uiicon- triangle-1-s'`
		Specifies the icons for the header elements and the selected state.

Changing the trigger event

Most of the options are self-explanatory, and the values they accept are usually Boolean, string, or element selectors. Let's put some of them to use, so that we can explore their functionality. Change the final `<script>` element in accordion2.html so that it appears as follows:

```
<script>
  $(document).ready(function($) {
    var accOpts = {
      event:"mouseover"
    }
    $("#myAccordion").accordion(accOpts);
  });
</script>
```

We no longer need the custom stylesheet added in accordion2.html, so go ahead and remove the following line from the code:

```
<link rel="stylesheet" href="css/accordionTheme.css">
```

Save these changes as accordion3.html. First, we create a new object literal called accOpts that contains the event key and the mouseover value, which is the event we wish to use to trigger the opening of an accordion panel. We pass this object to the accordion() method as an argument and it overrides the default option of the widget, which is click.

The `mouseover` event is commonly used as an alternative trigger event. Other events can also be used, for example, we can set `keydown` as the event, but in order for this to work, the accordion panel that we wish to open must already be focused. You should note that you can also set options using an inline object within the widget method, without creating a separate object. Using the following code would be equally as effective, and would often be the preferred way of coding, which we will use for the remainder of the book:

```
<script>
  $(function() {
    $("#myAccordion").accordion({
      event: "mouseover"
    });
  });
</script>
```

Changing the default active header

By default, the first header of the accordion will be selected when the widget is rendered with its content panel open. We can change which header is selected on page load using the `active` option. Change the configuration `<script>` block in `accordion3.html` so that it appears as follows:

```
<script>
  $(document).ready(function($) {
    $("#myAccordion").accordion({
      active: 2
    });
  });
</script>
```

Save this version as `accordion4.html`. We set the `active` option to the integer `2` to open the third content panel by default, and similar to the tab headers that we saw in the previous chapter, accordion's headers use a zero-based index. Along with an integer, this option also accepts a jQuery selector or raw DOM element.

We can also use the Boolean value of `false` to configure the accordion so that none of the content panels are open by default. Change the configuration object once again to the following:

```
<script>
  $(document).ready(function($) {
    $("#myAccordion").accordion({
      collapsible: true,
      active: false
```

```
        });
    });
</script>
```

 If you use the `active: false` option, as shown here, you must also include the `collapsible` option too, which must be set to true for `active` to work correctly.

Save this as `accordion5.html`. Now when the page loads, all of the content panels are hidden from view:

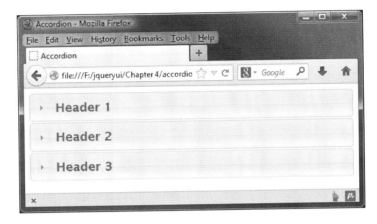

The accordion will remain closed until one of the headers is selected, which will remain open unless the active header is clicked; at this point, its associated content panel will close. For usability, it is best to avoid configuring both this and the `mouseover` event option together in the same implementation, as the open panels would close even when the user inadvertently moused off-and-back over them.

Filling the height of its container

If the `heightStyle` option is set, it will force the accordion to take the full height of its container. In our examples so far, the container of the accordion has been the body of the page, and the height of the body will only be the height of its largest element. We'll need to use a new container element with a fixed height to see this option in action.

In the `<head>` element of `accordion5.html`, add the following `<style>` element:

```
<style>
  #container { height: 600px; width: 400px; }
</style>
```

Then wrap all of the underlying markup for the accordion in a new container element as follows:

```
<div id="container">
  <div id="myAccordion">
    <h2><a href="#">Header 1</a></h2>
    <div>Lorem ipsum dolor sit amet, consectetuer adipiscing   elit.
Aenean sollicitudin. Sed interdum pulvinar justo. Nam iaculis volutpat
ligula. Integer vitae felis quis diam laoreet ullam corper.</div>
    <h2><a href="#">Header 2</a></h2>
    <div>Etiam tincidunt est vitae est. Ut posuere, mauris at
sodales rutrum, turpis tellus fermentum metus, ut bibendum
velit enim eu lectus. Suspendisse potenti.</div>
    <h2><a href="#">Header 3</a></h2>
    <div>Donec at dolor ac metus pharetra aliquam. Suspendisse purus.
Fusce tempor ultrices libero. Sed quis nunc. Pellentesque tincidunt
viverra felis. Integer elit mauris, egestas ultricies, gravida vitae,
feugiat a, tellus.</div>
  </div>
</div>
```

Finally, change the configuration `<script>` to use the `heightStyle` option:

```
<script>
  $(document).ready(function($) {
    $("#myAccordion").accordion({
      heightStyle: "fill"
    });
  });
</script>
```

Save the changes as `accordion6.html`. The new container is given a fixed height and width using the CSS specified in the `<head>` element of the page.

> In most cases, you'll want to create a separate style sheet. For our purposes, with just a single selector and two rules, using the style tag in our HTML file is most convenient.

The `heightStyle` option forces the accordion to take the entire height of its container, and restricting the width of the container naturally reduces the width of the widget too. This page should appear as follows:

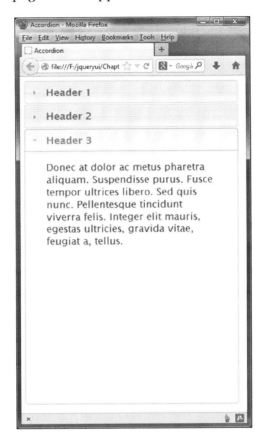

Using the accordion animation

The accordion widget comes with the built-in slide animation that is enabled by default, and has been present in all of our examples so far. Disabling this animation is as easy as supplying `false` as the value of the `animate` option. Remove the `<style>` tag from the `<head>` element of the page in `accordion6.html`, and remove the additional container `<div>`, then change the configuration object so that it appears as follows:

```
<script>
  $(document).ready(function($) {
    $("#myAccordion").accordion({
      animate: false
```

```
      });
    });
  </script>
```

Save this as `accordion7.html`. This will cause each content panel to open immediately instead of sliding-open nicely whenever a header is clicked.

An alternate animation has also been built into the widget—the `EaseOutBounce` animation. However, to use this alternate animation, we need to add a link to the `jquery.ui.effect.js` file.

Directly after the link to `jquery.ui.accordion.js` at the top of the `<head>` element, add the following line of code:

```
<script src="development-bundle/ui/jquery.ui.effect.js"></script>
```

Now, change the configuration object in our custom `<script>` element so that it appears as follows:

```
<script>
  $(document).ready(function($) {
    $("#myAccordion").accordion({
      animate: {
        duration: 600,
        down: {
          easing: "easeOutBounce",
          duration: 1000
        }
      }
    });
  });
</script>
```

Save these changes as `accordion8.html`. Although the accordion panels close in exactly the same way as they did in previous examples, when they open they bounce a few times at the end of the animation. It's a great way to make the animation more interesting, and as we saw in this example, it's easy to use.

In addition to the two preconfigured animations, we can also use any of the different easing effects defined within the `jquery.ui.effect.js` file, including the following:

- `easeInQuad`
- `easeInCubic`
- `easeInQuart`
- `easeInQuint`

- easeInSine

- easeInExpo

- easeInCirc

- easeInElastic

- easeInBack

- easeInBounce

Each of these easing methods is complimented by easeOut and easeInOut counterparts. For the complete list, see the jquery.ui.effect.js file, or refer to the easing table in *Chapter 14, UI Effects*.

 See the jQuery UI demo site for some great examples of the accordion effects at http://jqueryui.com/accordion/. The effects can be applied to any widget that can be animated, such as the accordion, tabs, dialog or datepicker.

The easing effects don't change the underlying animation, which will still be based on the slide animation. But they do change how the animation progresses. For example, we can make the content panels bounce both at the start and end of our animation by using the easeInOutBounce easing effect in our configuration object:

```
<script>
  $(document).ready(function($) {
    $("#myAccordion").accordion({
      animate: {
        duration: 600,
        down: {
          easing: "easeInOutBounce",
          duration: 1000
        }
      }
    });
  });
</script>
```

Save this file as accordion9.html and view it in a browser. Most of the easing effects have opposites, for example, instead of making the content panels bounce at the end of the animation, we can make them bounce at the start of the animation using the easeInBounce easing effect.

Another option that has an effect on animations is the `heightStyle` property, which resets `height` and `overflow` styles after each animation. Remember that animations are enabled by default, but this option isn't. Change the configuration object in `accordion9.html` to the following:

```
$(document).ready(function($) {
  $("#myAccordion").accordion({
    heightStyle: "content",
    animate: {
      duration: 600,
      down: {
        easing: "easeOutBounce",
        duration: 1000
      }
    }
  });
});
```

Save this as `accordion10.html`. Now when the page is run, the accordion will not keep to a fixed size; it will grow or shrink depending on how much content is in each panel. It doesn't make much of a difference in this example, but the property really comes into its own when using dynamic content, when we may not always know how much content will be within each panel when the panel content changes frequently.

Listing the accordion events

The accordion exposes three custom events, which are listed in the following table:

Event	Triggered when...
activate	The active header has changed.
beforeActivate	The active header is about to change
create	The widget has been created

The `activate` event is triggered every time the active header (and its associated content panel) is changed. It fires at the end of the content panel's opening animation, or if animations are disabled, immediately (but still after the active panel has been changed).

The `beforeActivate` event is fired as soon as the new header is selected, that is, before the opening animation (or before the active panel has changed, if animations are disabled). The `create` event is fired as soon as the widget has been initialized.

Using the change event

Let's see how we can use these events in our accordion implementations. In `accordion10.html`, change the configuration object so that it appears as follows:

```
$(document).ready(function($) {
  var statustext;
  $("#myAccordion").accordion({
    activate: function(e, ui) {
      $(".notify").remove();
      Statustext = $("<div />", {
        "class": "notify",
        text: [
          ui.newHeader.find("a").text(), "was activated,",
          ui.oldHeader.find("a").text(), "was closed"
        ].join(" ")
      });
      statusText.insertAfter("#myAccordion").fadeOut(2000, function(){
        $(this).remove();
      });
    }
  });
});
```

Save this as `accordion11.html`. In this example, we use the `activate` configuration option to specify an anonymous callback function that is executed every time the active panel is changed. This function will automatically receive two objects as arguments. The first object is the `event` object, which contains the original browser event object.

The second argument is an object, which contains useful information about the widget, such as the header element that was activated (`ui.newHeader`) and the header that was deactivated (`ui.oldHeader`). The second object is a jQuery object, so we can call jQuery methods directly on it.

In this example, we navigate down to the `<a>` element within the header and display its text content in an information box, which is appended to the page and then removed after a short interval with a fading animation.

For reference, the `ui` object also provides information on the content panels in the form of `ui.newPanel` and `ui.oldPanel` properties.

Once a header has been activated, and its content panel is shown, the notification will be generated:

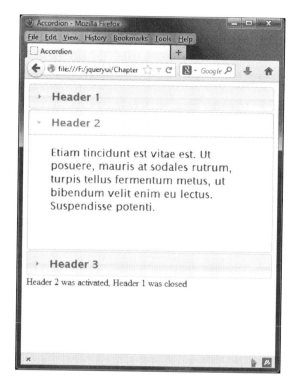

Configuring the beforeActivate event

The `beforeActivate` event can be used in exactly the same way, and any callback function we specify using this event also receives the `e` and `ui` objects to use.

Change the configuration object from the last example to as follows:

```
$(document).ready(function($) {
  var statusText;
  $("#myAccordion").accordion({
    beforeActivate: function(e, ui) {
      statusText = $("<div />", {
        "class": "notify",
```

```
        text: [ui.newHeader.find("a").text(),
          "was activated,", ui.oldHeader.find("a").text(),
          "was closed"].join(" ");
      });
      statusText.insertAfter("#myAccordion")
        .fadeOut(2000, function() {
          $(this).remove();
        });
    }
  });
});
```

Save this as `accordion12.html`. All that's changed is the property that we're
targeting with our configuration object. When we run the page, we should find that
everything is exactly as it was before, except that our notification is produced before
the content panel animation instead of after it.

There are also events such as `accordionactivate` and `accordionbeforeactivate`
for use with the standard jQuery `on()` method, so that we can specify a callback
function to execute outside of the accordion configuration. Using an event handler
in this manner allows us to fire it precisely in response to specific events, rather than
when the page is rendered on screen.

As an example, let's rework the script block for the demo we've just created, to use
the `accordionbeforeactivate` event handler. If you wanted to use this format
instead, simply replace the `<script>` block from `accordion12.html` with the
below script – you can see the main changes highlighted in the code:

```
<script>
  $(document).ready(function($) {
    var statusText;
    $("#myAccordion").accordion();

    $(document).on( "accordionbeforeactivate", function(e, ui) {
      statusText = $("<div />", {
        "class": "notify",
        text: [ui.newHeader.find("a").text(), "was activated, ",
ui.oldHeader.find("a").text(), "was closed"].join(" ")
      });
      statusText.insertAfter("#myAccordion")
        .fadeOut(2000, function() {
        $(this).remove();
      });
    });
  });
</script>
```

In this example, we've moved the beforeActivate event handler out of the main configuration call to Accordion, into its own event handler. Here, we've tied the event handler to the document object; we could equally have bound it to an object such as a button or hyperlink on the page.

Explaining the accordion methods

The accordion includes a selection of methods that allow you to control and manipulate the behavior of the widget programmatically. Some of the methods are common to each component of the library, such as the destroy method that is used by every widget. The following table lists the sole method for the accordion widget:

Method	Use
refresh	Recalculates the height of the accordion panels; the outcome is dependent on the content and the heightStyle options

Header activation

The option method can be used to programmatically show or hide different drawers. We can easily test this method using a textbox and a new button. In accordion12.html, add the following new markup directly after the accordion:

```
<label for="activateChoice">Enter a header index to activate    </label>
<input id="activateChoice">
<button type="button" id="activate">Activate</button>
```

Now change the <script> element so that it appears as follows:

```
<script>
  $(document).ready(function($) {
    var drawer = parseInt($("#activateChoice").val(), 10);

    $("#myAccordion").accordion();
    $("#activate").click(function() {
      $("#myAccordion").accordion("option", "active", drawer);
    });
  });
</script>
```

Save the new file as `accordion13.html`. The `option` method takes two additional arguments. It expects to receive the name of the option to use, as well as the index (zero-based) number of the header element to activate. In this example, we obtain the header to activate, by returning the value of the text input. We convert it to an integer using the `parseInt()` function of JavaScript because the `val()` jQuery method returns a string.

If an index number that doesn't exist is specified, nothing will happen. The first header will be activated if no index is specified. If a value other than an integer is specified, nothing will happen; the script will fail silently, without any errors, and the accordion will continue to function as normal.

Adding or removing panels

Prior to Version 1.10, the only way you could change the number of panels in an accordion was to destroy it and reinitialize a new instance. While this worked, it was not a satisfactory way to implement any changes, with this in mind the jQuery team have worked hard to introduce a new method, which brings it in line with other widgets, which don't require recreating in order to change any configured options. Let's test this method using an input button, to create our new panels.

In `accordion13.html`, change the markup immediately below the accordion to the following code:

```
<p>
  <button type="button" id="addAccordion">Add Accordion</button>
</p>
```

Alter the `<script>` block, so it appears as follows:

```
<script>
  $(document).ready(function($) {
    $("#myAccordion").accordion();
    $('#addAccordion').click( function() {
      var newDiv = "<h2><a ref='#'>New Header</a></h2><div>New
Content</div>";
      $("#myAccordion").append(newDiv).accordion("refresh");
    });
  });
</script>
```

Save the new file as `accordion14.html`. In this example, we've created the additional markup content for a new accordion panel, which we assign to the `newDiv` variable. This we append to the myAccordion `<div>`, which is then refreshed using accordion's `refresh` method. This does not require any arguments.

 We've specified the default text to be used within the markup for each accordion panel. This could easily be altered to include whatever text you need, as long as the same markup is maintained.

When the page loads, we can click on **Add Accordion** to add any number of new accordion panels, as shown in the following screenshot:

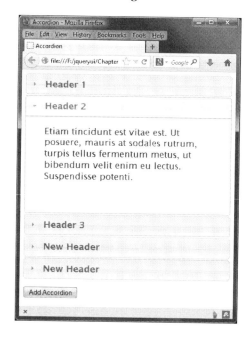

However, if we need to remove an accordion panel, this involves a little more work—the markup comes in two parts (header and panel), so we have to remove both separately. Alter the markup immediately below the accordion:

```
<p>
   <label>Enter a tab to remove:</label>
   <input for="indexNum" id="indexNum">
   <button type="button" id="remove">Remove!</button>
</p>
```

Now change the `<script>` block as follows:

```
<script>
  $(document).ready(function($) {
    function removeDrawer(removeIndex) {
      $("#myAccordion").find("h2").eq(removeIndex).remove();
      $("#myAccordion").find("div").eq(removeIndex).remove();
      $("#myAccordion").accordion("refresh");
    }
    $("#myAccordion").accordion();
    $("#remove").click(function(event, ui) {
      var removeIndex = $("#indexNum").val();
      removeDrawer(removeIndex);
    });
  });
</script>
```

Save the new file as `accordion15.html`; when the page loads, enter 1 and click on **Remove** to remove the middle header and its panel:

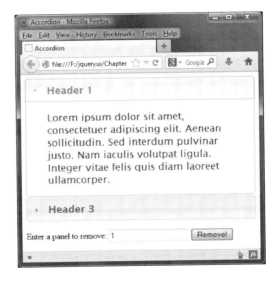

In this example, we obtain the accordion to remove by returning the value of the text input. If an index number that doesn't exist is specified, nothing will happen.

We then use `eq()` to find both the header and panel to remove, based on the given value, once found, they are then removed. The final stage is to `refresh` the accordion so a new header and panel can then be selected.

Resizing an accordion panel

Change the underlying markup for the accordion widget in `accordion10.html` so that the third header points to a remote text file and the third panel is empty. The heading element should also be given an `id` attribute:

```
<div id="myAccordion">
  <h2><a href="#">Header 1</a></h2>
  <div>Lorem ipsum dolor sit amet, consectetuer adipiscing elit.
Aenean sollicitudin. Sed interdum pulvinar justo. Nam iaculis volutpat
ligula. Integer vitae felis quis diam laoreet ullamcorper.</div>
  <h2><a href="#">Header 2</a></h2>
  <div>Etiam tincidunt est vitae est. Ut posuere, mauris at sodales
rutrum, turpis tellus fermentum metus, ut bibendum velit enim eu
lectus. Suspendisse poten-ti.</div>
  <h2 id="remote"><a href="remoteAccordion.txt">Remote</a></h2>
  <div></div>
</div>
```

You will see in the code that we've made reference to a text file, which will host our remote content. In a new file within your editor, add some dummy text, and save it with the name `remoteAccordion.txt`. (A copy of this file is available with the code download that accompanies this book).

Then change the final `<script>` element so that it appears as follows:

```
$(document).ready(function($) {
  $("#myAccordion").accordion({
    beforeActivate: function(e, ui) {
      if (ui.newHeader.attr("id") === "remote") {
        $.get(ui.newHeader.find("a").attr("href"),
        function(data) {
          ui.newHeader.next().text(data);
        });
      }
    },
    activate: function(e, ui) {
      ui.newHeader.closest("#myAccordion").accordion("refresh");
    }
  });
});
```

Save this file as `accordion16.html`. To view this example correctly, you will need to have installed a local web server, such as WAMP (for PC), or MAMP (Mac), otherwise the contents of the `remoteAccordion.txt` file will not be rendered.

In our configuration object, we use the `beforeActivate` event to check whether the `id` of the element matches the `id` we gave to our remote accordion heading.

If it does, we get the contents of the text file specified in the `href` attribute of the `<a>` element, using jQuery's `get()` method. If the request returns successfully, we add the contents of the text file to the empty panel after the header. This all happens before the panel opens.

We then use the `activate` event to call the `refresh` method on the accordion, after the panel has opened.

When we run the page in a browser, the contents of the remote text file should be sufficient to cause a scroll bar to appear within the content panel. Calling the `refresh` method allows the widget to readjust itself, so that it can contain all of the newly added content without displaying the scroll bar.

You will have seen from the code that we've used the `newHeader` property in two places; one as a part of loading the content, and the second to refresh the panel once content has been added. Let us explore this for a moment, as it is a key part of how we can access content in any accordion.

The `ui` object contains four properties that allow us to access the content within the header or panel of any accordion that has been added to a page. The full list is as follows:

Header	Access content in...
`ui.newHeader`	The header that was just activated
`ui.oldHeader`	The header that was just deactivated
`ui.newPanel`	The panel that was just activated
`ui.oldPanel`	The panel that was just deactivated

Once we've referenced the relevant panel or header, we are then free to manipulate the contents at our discretion.

Accordion interoperability

Does the accordion widget play nicely with other widgets in the library? Let's take a look and see whether the accordion can be combined with the widget from the previous chapter, the tabs widget.

Change the underlying markup for the accordion so that the third content panel now contains the markup for a set of tabs, and the third heading no longer points to the remote text file:

```
<div id="myAccordion">
  <h2><a href="#">Header 1</a></h2>
  <div>Lorem ipsum dolor sit amet, consectetuer adipiscing elit.
Aenean sollicitudin. Sed interdum pulvinar justo.Nam iaculis volutpat
ligula. Integer vitae felis quis diam laoreet ullamcorper.</div>
  <h2><a href="#">Header 2</a></h2>
  <div>Etiam tincidunt est vitae est. Ut posuere, mauris at sodales
rutrum, turpis tellus fermentum metus, ut bibendum velit enim eu
lectus. Suspendisse potenti.</div>
  <h2><a href="#">Header 3</a></h2>
  <div>
    <div id="myTabs">
      <ul>
        <li><a href="#0"><span>Tab 1</span></a></li>
        <li><a href="#1"><span>Tab 2</span></a></li>
      </ul>
      <div id="0">This is the content panel linked to the first tab,
it is shown by default.</div>
      <div id="1">This content is linked to the second tab and will be
shown when its tab is clicked.</div>
    </div>
  </div>
</div>
```

We should also link to the source file for the tabs widget after the accordion's source file; add this line immediately below the call to `jquery.ui.widget.js` in your code:

```
<script src="development-bundle/ui/jquery.ui.tabs.js"></script>
```

Next, change the final `<script>` element so that it appears as follows:

```
<script>
  $(document).ready(function($) {
    $("#myAccordion").accordion();
    $("#myTabs").tabs();
  });
</script>
```

Save this file as `accordion17.html`. All we've done with this file is to add a simple tab structure to one of the accordion's content panels. In the `<script>` element at the end of the page, we just call the accordion and tab's widget methods. No additional or special configuration is required.

When the third accordion heading is activated, the page should appear as follows:

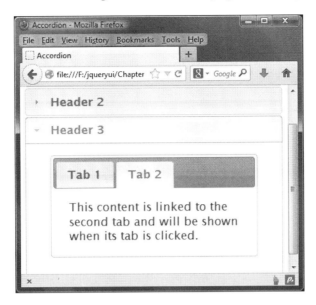

The widgets are compatible the other way round; that is, we can have an accordion within one of the tab's content panels without any adverse effects as well.

Using multiple accordions

We've seen how you can easily use the accordion with other widgets on the page. What about using multiple accordions on the same page? This is equally not a problem; we can have multiple accordions on the same page, as long as we configure the call(s) to the accordion properly.

In your text editor, add the following markup immediately below the existing block in `accordion1.html`:

```
<p>
<div class="myAccordion two">
   <h2><a href="#">Header 1</a></h2>
   <div>Lorem ipsum dolor sit amet, consectetuer adipiscing elit.
Aenean sollicitudin. Sed interdum pulvinar justo. Nam iaculis volutpat
ligula. Integer vitae felis quis diam laoreet ullamcorper.
   </div>
   <h2><a href="#">Header 2</a></h2>
```

```
    <div>Etiam tincidunt est vitae est. Ut posuere, mauris at sodales
rutrum, turpis tellus fermentum metus, ut bibendum velit enim eu
lectus. Suspendisse potenti.
</div>
    <h2><a href="#">Header 3</a></h2>
    <div>Donec at dolor ac metus pharetra aliquam. Suspendisse purus.
Fusce tempor ultrices libero. Sed quis nunc. Pellentesque tincidunt
viverra felis. Integer elit mauris, egestas ultricies, gravida vitae,
    feugiat a, tellus.</div>
  </div>
```

We need to allow for the second accordion widget in our code, so adjust the
<script> block as follows:

```
<script>
  $(document).ready(function($) {
    $(".myAccordion").accordion();
    $( ".two" ).accordion( "option", "icons", { "header": "ui-icon-
plus", "activeHeader": "ui-icon-minus" } );
  });
</script>
```

Save the file as accordion18.html. If we preview the results in our browser, you
should see something as follows:

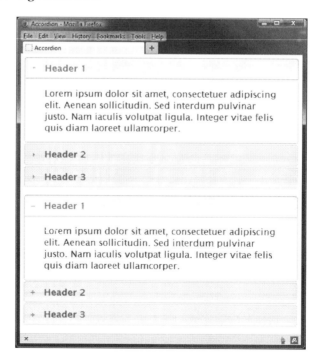

All we've done is to duplicate the existing markup for the first accordion; the trick is in how we initiate the second accordion functionality within our script.

Throughout this book, we've used selector IDs to initiate our accordions; this is perfect, particularly when there is only one accordion on the page. If we have multiple accordions on the same page (or even in the same website), this can become clumsy, as we are duplicating code unnecessarily.

We can get around this by switching to using classes, in place of selector IDs, accordion can easily use either method. In our example, we've assigned a classname of `.myAccordion` to both the accordions. We've then used this to initiate the call to `.accordion()` in our script. This allows us to share common functionality throughout multiple accordions, without duplicating code.

If we need to override the configuration for one or more of these accordions though, we can do this by adding a second separate class to our markup, in this instance, we want to change the second accordion to use + and − icons, in place of arrowheads.

To implement this, the second accordion has been assigned the `.myAccordion` `.two` classes. The second class is then used as the basis for the call to a second `accordion()` instance; this overrides the original configuration, but only for those accordions that have the additional `.two` class assigned to them. We can then extend this principle to apply to any other accordion that should have different functionality to the first by adding a second class to the accordion's markup.

Summary

We first looked at what the accordion does and how it is targeted by the CSS framework. We then moved on to look at the configurable options that can be used to change the behavior of the accordion, such as specifying an alternative heading to be open by default, or setting the event that triggers the opening of a content drawer.

Along with configurable options, we saw that the accordion exposes several custom events. Using them, we can specify callback functions during configuration, or bind to them after configuration to execute additional functionality, in reaction to different things happening to the widget.

Next, we looked at the accordion's default animation and how we can animate the opening of content panels, using easing effects. We saw that to make use of non-standard animations or easing effects, the `jquery.ui.effect.js` file needs to be included along with the requisite custom effect file.

In addition to looking at these options, we also saw that there are a range of methods which can be called on the accordion to make it do things programmatically. In the next chapter, we get to play with the dialog widget, which allows us to create a flexible, highly configurable overlay that floats above the page and displays any content we specify.

5
The Dialog

Traditionally, the way to display a brief message or ask a visitor a question would've been to use one of JavaScript's native dialog boxes (such as `alert` or `confirm`), or to open a new web page with a predefined size, styled to look like a dialog box.

Unfortunately, as I'm sure you're aware, neither of these methods is particularly flexible to us as developers or particularly engaging for our visitors. For every problem they solve, several new problems are usually introduced.

The dialog widget lets us display a message, supplemental content (such as images or text) or even interactive content (such as forms). It's also easy to add buttons, such as a simple **Ok** and **Cancel** to the dialog, and define the callback functions for them in order to react to their being clicked; the dialog can also be modal or nonmodal.

In this chapter, we will cover the following topics:

- Creating a basic dialog
- Working with the dialog options
- Modality
- Enabling the built-in animations
- Adding buttons to the dialog
- Working with the dialog callbacks
- Controlling a dialog programmatically

The following screenshot shows a dialog widget and the different elements it is made of:

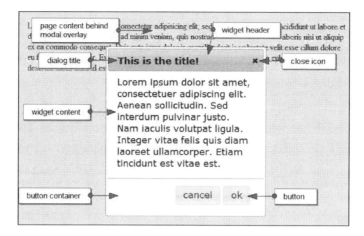

Creating a basic dialog

A dialog has a lot of built-in default behavior, but few methods are needed to control it programmatically, making this an easy-to-use widget, which is also highly configurable and powerful.

Generating the widget is simple and requires a minimal underlying markup structure. The following page contains the minimum markup that's required to implement the dialog widget:

```
<!DOCTYPE html>
<html>
<head>
  <meta charset="utf-8">
  <title>Dialog</title>
  <link rel="stylesheet" href="development-bundle/themes/redmond/
jquery.ui.all.css">
  <script src="js/jquery-2.0.3.js"></script>
  <script src="development-bundle/ui/jquery.ui.core.js"></script>
  <script src="development-bundle/ui/jquery.ui.widget.js"> </script>
  <script src="development-bundle/ui/jquery.ui.position.js"> </script>
  <script src="development-bundle/ui/jquery.ui.dialog.js"> </script>
  <script src="development-bundle/ui/jquery.ui.button.js"> </script>
  <script>
    $(document).ready(function($){
      $("#myDialog").dialog();
    });
```

```
    </script>
  </head>
  <body>
    <div id="myDialog" title="This is the title!">
    Lorem ipsum dolor sit amet, consectetuer adipiscing elit.
Aenean sollicitudin. Sed interdum pulvinar justo. Nam iaculis volutpat
ligula. Integer vitae felis quis diam laoreet ullamcorper. Etiam
tincidunt est vitae est.
    </div>
  </body>
</html>
```

Save this file as `dialog1.html` in the `jqueryui` project folder. To use the dialog, the following dependencies are required:

- `jquery.ui.all.css`
- `jquery.ui.core.js`
- `jquery.ui.widget.js`
- `jquery.ui.position.js`
- `jquery.ui.dialog.js`
- `jquery.ui.button.js`

Optionally, we can also include the following files to make the dialog draggable and resizable:

- `jquery.ui.mouse.js`
- `jquery.ui.draggable.js`
- `jquery.ui.resizable.js`

The dialog widget is initialized in the same way as the other widgets, which we have already looked at by calling the widget's plugin method.

When you run this page in your browser, you should see the default dialog widget, as shown in the following screenshot:

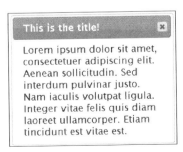

As with the previous widgets that we've covered, a variety of classnames from the CSS framework are added to different elements within the widget to give them the appropriate styling for their respective elements, and any additional elements that are required are created on the fly.

The dialog in the first example is fixed both in size and position and will be positioned in the center of the viewport. We can easily make the widget draggable, resizable, or both. All we need to do is include the draggable and resizable component's source files, as well as the mouse utility, with the other `<script>` resources at the end of `<head>`.

It's not important that the draggable and resizable files are included in the page before the dialog's source file. They can come before or after, and the widget will still inherit these behaviors. Any styling that is required, such as the resize indicator that appears in the bottom-left of the dialog, will be picked up automatically from the master CSS file.

Add the following three `<script>` elements directly before the closing `</head>` tag in `dialog1.html`:

```
<script src="development-bundle/ui/jquery.ui.mouse.js">
</script>
<script src="development-bundle/ui/jquery.ui.draggable.js">
</script>
<script src="development-bundle/ui/jquery.ui.resizable.js">
</script>
```

Save this as `dialog2.html` and view it in a browser. The dialog should now be draggable and can be moved to any part of the viewport, but will not cause it to scroll if the widget is moved to an edge.

The dialog should also be resizable—by clicking and holding any corner and dragging, the widget can be made bigger or smaller. If the dialog is made bigger than the viewport, it will cause the window to scroll.

Listing the dialog options

An option object can be used in a dialog's widget method to configure various dialog options. Let's look at the available options:

Option	Default value	Description
appendTo	"body"	Determines which element the dialog (and overlay, if modal) should be appended to.
autoOpen	true	Shows the dialog as soon as the dialog() method is called, when set to true.
buttons	{}	Supplies an object containing buttons to be used with the dialog. Each key becomes the text on the `<button>` element, and each value is a callback function, which is executed when the button is clicked.
closeOnEscape	true	If set to true, the dialog will close when the *Esc* key is pressed.
dialogClass	""	Sets additional classnames on the dialog for theming purposes.
draggable	true	Makes the dialog draggable (requires use of jquery.ui.draggable.js).
height	auto	Sets the starting height of the dialog.
hide	null	Sets an effect to be used when the dialog is closed.
maxHeight	false	Sets a maximum height for the dialog.
maxWidth	false	Sets a maximum width for the dialog.
minHeight	150	Sets a minimum height for the dialog.
minWidth	150	Sets a minimum width for the dialog.
modal	false	Enables modality while the dialog is open.
position	center	Sets the starting position of the dialog in the viewport. It can accept a string, an array of strings, or an array containing the exact coordinates of the dialog offset from the top and left of the viewport use (requires use of jquery.ui.position.js).
resizable	true	Makes the dialog resizable (also requires jquery.ui.resizable.js).
show	null	Sets an effect to be used when the dialog is opened.
title	""	Alternative to specifying the title attribute on the widget's underlying container element.
width	300	Sets the starting width of the dialog.

As you can see, we have a wide range of configurable options to work with while implementing the dialog. Many of these options are Boolean, numerical, or string-based, making them easy to get and set within your code.

Showing the dialog

In our examples so far, the dialog has been displayed as soon as the page is loaded. The autoOpen option is set to true by default, so the dialog will be displayed as soon as it is initialized.

We can change this so that the dialog is opened when something else occurs, like a button being clicked by setting the autoOpen option to false. Change the final <script> element at the bottom of dialog2.html to the following one:

```
<script>
  $(document).ready(function($){
    $("#myDialog").dialog({
      autoOpen: false
    });
  });
</script>
```

Save this as dialog3.html. The widget is still created; the underlying markup is removed from the page, transformed into the widget, and then reappended to the end of <body>. It will remain hidden until the open method is called on it. We'll come back to this option when we look at the open method a little later in this chapter.

Setting a dialog title

The options table shows a title option, which we can use to control how the title is displayed on the widget; this can be made selectable if the draggable attribute is set to false. Although it is possible to set it directly in code, it is far easier to set it within the configuration options, as this gives us a greater control over how the title is displayed in the widget.

By default, the title text of the dialog widget will be shown in plain text; we can override this by adding a custom style to the .ui-dialog-title class.

In your browser, alter the <script> block for dialog in dialog3.html as follows:

```
<script>
  $(document).ready(function($){
    $("#myDialog").dialog({
      draggable: false,
      open: function() {
```

```
        $(".ui-dialog-title").addClass("customtitle");
      }
    });
  });
</script>
```

Save the file as `dialog4.html`. We can now add some styling to our dialog's title bar – in a separate file add the following code, saving it as `dialogOverrides.css` after the link to the jQuery UI stylesheet:

```
.customtitle { color: #800080; }
```

If we preview the results in our browser, you can clearly see the title now shows in a different color:

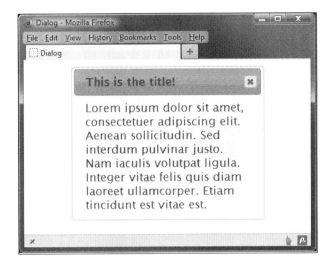

To see the effect on the code, we can see how the script has overridden the base code, using a DOM inspector such as Firebug:

```
<span id="ui-id-1" class="ui-dialog-title customtitle">This is the
title!</span>
```

We could manually style the dialog elements within our stylesheet, but it would be through trial and error; it is much easier to simply add a new class using jQuery, which we can then style to our heart's content!

If a value is not provided to the `title` attribute, the attribute on the dialog source element will be used.

Configuring the modality option

One of the dialog's greatest assets is modality. This feature creates an overlay that covers the underlying page beneath the dialog while it is open. The overlay is removed as soon as the dialog is closed. None of the underlying page content can be manipulated within anyway while the dialog is open.

The benefit of this feature is that it ensures the dialog is closed before the underlying page becomes interactive again, and gives a clear visual indicator to the visitor that the dialog must be interacted with before they can proceed.

Change the configuration object in `dialog4.html` to the following:

```
$(document).ready(function($){
  $("#myDialog").dialog({
    modal: true
  });
});
```

This file can be saved as `dialog5.html`. The following screenshot shows the modal effect (you may like to add some fake content to the page to fully appreciate the effect of the modal):

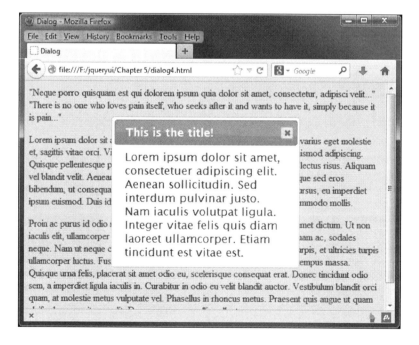

Only a single property is required while adding modality and that is the `modal` option. When you view the page in a browser, you'll see the modal effect immediately. The repeated background image that is used to create the overlay is styled completely by the CSS framework and is therefore fully themeable through the **ThemeRoller** tool. We can also use our own image if we need to. The class name `ui-widget-overlay` is added to the overlay, so this is the selector to override if customization is required.

Adding buttons

The `button` option accepts an object literal that is used to specify the different `<button>` elements that should be present on the dialog. Each `property: value` pair represents a single button. Let's add a couple of `<button>` elements to our dialog.

Modify the final `<script>` element in `dialog5.html` so that it appears as follows:

```
<script>
  $(document).ready(function($){
    $("#myDialog").dialog({
      buttons: { Ok: function() { }, Cancel: function() { } },
      draggable: false
    });
  });
</script>
```

Save the file as `dialog6.html`. The key for each property in the `buttons` object is the text that will form the `<button>` label, and the value is the name of the callback function to execute when the button is clicked. The `buttons` option can take either an object, as in this example, or an array of objects. In this example the `execute()` and `cancel()` functions don't do anything; we'll come back to this example shortly and populate them.

The following screenshot shows how our new `<button>` elements would appear:

The widget will add our new buttons to their own container at the foot of the dialog, and if the dialog is resized, this container will retain its original dimensions. The `<button>` elements are fully themable and will be styled according to the theme in use.

Adding icons to the dialog buttons

Until now, closing a dialog usually meant having to click on the cross icon in the title bar – it works well for this purpose, but doesn't offer us any opportunity to get a response from the person browsing our website or online application.

The addition of buttons in the previous example helps remove this constraint, and allows us to accept a varied response from the end user – we can take this a step further by adding icons to provide visual support to the buttons.

In your text editor, alter the `<script>` block in `dialog6.html` as follows:

```
<script>
  $(document).ready(function($){
    $("#myDialog").dialog({
      buttons: [ {
          text: "Ok",
          icons: { primary: "ui-icon-check", secondary: "ui-icon-
circle-check" },
          click: function() { }
        }, {
          text: "Cancel",
          icons: { primary: "ui-icon-closethick", secondary: "ui-icon-
circle-close" },
          click: function() { }
        } ],
      draggable: false
    });
  });
</script>
```

Save this as `dialog7.html`. Here, we've used the buttons option to specify the text, icons, and the action that should be taken when the button is clicked. You will notice that we've also used a different way to specify each option, compared to the previous example. Both work equally well; we need to use this method while adding icons, otherwise you may find you have buttons with no text appearing!

If we preview the results in a browser, we can now see the buttons with added icons appearing, at the foot of our dialog:

The icons will be styled according to the theme in use. In our example we've specified both primary and secondary icons; the former sits to the left of the button text, whilst the latter sits to the right. It is likely though you would only need to specify one or the other in your application or website, according to your requirements.

Enabling dialog animations

The dialog provides us with a built-in effect that can be applied to the opening or closing (or both) phases of the widget. There is only a single effect that we can use, which is an implementation of the scale effect (we'll look at this in more detail in *Chapter 13, Selecting and Sorting with jQuery UI*). Change the final `<script>` element in `dialog7.html` to the following one:

```
<script>
  $(document).ready(function($){
    $("#myDialog").dialog({
      show: true,
      hide: true
    });
  });
</script>
```

Save this as `dialog8.html`. We set both the `hide` and `show` options to the Boolean value `true`. This enables the built-in effect, which gradually reduces the dialog's size and opacity until it gracefully disappears. The following screenshot shows an effect in motion:

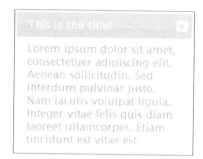

We can enable or disable either the show or hide animations individually using Booleans, as we have in this example. We could also specify the type of animation to be used by supplying a string specifying the name of the effect to use:

```
<script>
  $(document).ready(function($){
    $("#myDialog").dialog({
      show: {effect: "fadeIn", duration: 1000},
      hide: {effect: "fadeOut", duration: 1000}
    });
  });
</script>
```

We can even take this a step further, using some of the effects such as bounce or explode, although these should only be added if appropriate! We will cover the use of effects in jQuery UI later, in *Chapter 14, UI Effects*. You can also see more details at `http://api.jqueryui.com/category/effects/`.

Configuring the dialog's dimensions

There are several options related to the dialog's size, and the minimum and maximum size that it can be resized to. We can add all of these options to the next example as they're all related, to save looking at them individually. Change the configuration object in `dialog8.html` to the following:

```
$("#myDialog").dialog({
  width: 500,
  height: 300,
  minWidth: 150,
```

```
    minHeight: 150,
    maxWidth: 600,
    maxHeight: 450
});
```

Save this file as `dialog9.html`. The effect these options have on the widget is simple; the `width` and `height` options define how big the dialog is when it is first opened, while the `min-` and `max-` options define how small or large the dialog can be resized to respectively.

 As an additional note, assistive technologies and keyboard users may find the content difficult to navigate if the dialog is made too small. There is a usability tenet that insists dialog boxes should always be non-resizable, whereas the windows should always be resizable.

While I don't think this is a black and white, set in granite rule, it may be wise to keep small, informational, text-based dialogs at a fixed size, while allowing dialogs richer in content, composed of both images and text to be resizable. We will cover how you can add resize handles to any suitable element (such as dialogs), later in *Chapter 12, The Resizable Component*.

Setting the z-index order of dialogs

The dialog is made so that it appears above any of the existing page content. We can alter its z-index setting using CSS, or by ensuring it is correctly appended to its parent element using the `appendTo` option, in case we need to raise it slightly to cover our existing content. But what if we have two dialogs on the page? Do we need to separately define `zIndex` for each dialog? How is focus taken into consideration?

Let's see if we can answer these questions by looking at another example; change the `<body>` tag of `dialog7.html` so that it has two dialog boxes on it:

```
<div id="dialog1" title="Dialog 1">
    Lorem ipsum dolor sit amet, consectetuer adipiscing elit.
Aenean sollicitudin. Sed interdum pulvinar justo. Nam aculis
volutpat ligula. Integer vitae felis quis diam laoreet ullamcorper.
Etiam tincidunt est vitae est.
</div>
<div id="dialog2" title="Dialog 2">
    Lorem ipsum dolor sit amet, consectetuer adipiscing elit. Aenean
sollicitudin. Sed interdum pulvinar justo. Nam iaculis volutpat
ligula. Integer vitae felis quis diam laoreet ullamcorper. Etiam
tincidunt est vitae est.
</div>
```

Now change the final `<script>` element so that it appears as follows:

```
<script>
  $(document).ready(function($){
    $("#dialog1, #dialog2").dialog();
  });
</script>
```

Save this file as `dialog10.html`. We've added another dialog to the page, which is basically just a clone of the original with different `id` and `title` attributes. In the `<script>`, we simply call the `widget` method on both of our underlying dialog containers.

As the `widget` method is called last on the second dialog and therefore it receives the focus, the second dialog will automatically have a higher z-index value. This means we don't need to worry about configuring it separately. The order in which the dialogs appear in the underlying markup doesn't matter; it's the order of the widget methods that dictates each dialog's z-index value.

Overriding the z-index value

If you need to override the z-index value, you can (and should) do this using CSS – you will need to use the `!important` attribute to override the existing value.

Because neither dialog has its position explicitly set, only the second dialog will be visible when our example page loads. However, both are draggable and we can align them so that they overlap slightly by dragging the second dialog away. If we click on the first dialog box, it will receive focus and so it will be shown above the second box.

Controlling the focus

While opening a dialog, the element that receives focus is determined by whichever item matches the following:

- The first element within the dialog with the autofocus attribute
- The first `:tabbable` element within the dialog's content
- The first `:tabbable` element within the dialog's buttonpane
- The dialog's close button
- The dialog itself

This can best be illustrated by the following code excerpt, where we've added the `autofocus` attribute to the `yes` radio button:

```
<div id="myDialog" title="Best Widget Library">
  <p>Is jQuery UI the greatest JavaScript widget library?</p>
  <label for="yes">Yes!</label>
  <input type="radio" autofocus="autofocus" id="yes" value="yes"
name="question" checked="checked"><br>
  <label for="no">No!</label>
  <input type="radio" id="no" value="no" name="question">
</div>
```

The `yes` radio button will receive the focus first; we can then tab away from that element to others within the widget. As soon as the dialog is closed, the focus will automatically return to the element that had it prior to the dialog being opened.

Handling the dialog's event callbacks

The dialog widget gives us a wide range of callback options that we can use to execute arbitrary code at different points, in any dialog interaction. The following table lists the options available to us:

Event	Description
beforeClose	This is fired when the dialog is about to be closed
close	This is fired when the dialog is closed
create	This is fired when the dialog is initialized
drag	This is fired when the dialog is being dragged
dragStart	This is fired when the dialog starts being dragged
dragStop	This is fired when the dialog stops being dragged
focus	This is fired when the dialog receives focus
open	This is fired when the dialog is opened
resize	This is fired when the dialog is being resized
resizeStart	This is fired when the dialog starts to be resized
resizeStop	This is fired when the dialog stops being resized

Some of these callbacks are only available in certain situations, such as the `drag` and `resize` callbacks, which will only be available when the draggable and resizable jQuery UI components are included. We won't be looking at these callback options in this chapter, as they'll be covered in detail in *Chapters 11, Drag and Drop* and *Chapter 12, The Resizable Component*, respectively.

Other callbacks, such as the `beforeClose`, `create`, `open`, `close`, and `focus` will be available in any implementation. Let's look at an example in which we make use of some of these callback options.

Remove the second dialog from the page in `dialog10.html` and add the following new markup directly after the first dialog:

```
<div id="status" class="ui-widget ui-dialog ui-corner-all ui-widget-
content">
  <div class="ui-widget-header ui-dialog-titlebar ui-corner-
all">Dialog Status</div>
  <div class="ui-widget-content ui-dialog-content"></div>
</div>
```

Now change the final `<script>` element so that it appears as follows:

```
<script>
  $(document).ready(function($){
    $("#dialog1").dialog({
      open: function() {
        $("#status").children(":last").text("The dialog is open");
      },
      close: function() {
        $("#status").children(":last").text("The dialog is closed");
      },
      beforeClose: function() {
        if ($(".ui-dialog").css("width") > "300") {
          return false;
        }
      }
    });
  });
</script>
```

Save this as `dialog11.html`. The page contains a new status box, which will be used to report whether the dialog is open or closed. We've given the elements that make up the status box of several CSS framework classes, to make them fit with the theme in use.

Our configuration object uses the `open`, `close`, and `beforeClose` options to specify simple callback functions. The `open` and `close` callbacks simply set the text of the status box accordingly. The `beforeClose` callback that is fired after the **Close** button on the dialog has been clicked (but before it is actually closed) is used to determine whether or not to close the dialog.

We use a simple `if` statement to check the width of the dialog; if the dialog is greater than 300 pixels wide, we return `false` from the callback and the dialog remains open. This kind of behavior is of course usually a big no in terms of usability, but it does serve to highlight how we can use the `beforeClose` callback to prevent the dialog being closed.

When the page loads and the dialog is shown, the `open` callback will be executed and the status box should display a message. When the dialog is closed, as shown in the following screenshot, a different message is displayed:

One thing I should make clear is that the dialog widget only passes a single object (the original event object) to the callback functions. It does pass a second `ui` object into the handler function, although in this release of the library, this object contains no properties.

Controlling a dialog programmatically

The dialog is intuitive and easy-to-use, and like the other components in the library, it comes with a range of methods that are used to programmatically control the widget after it has been initialized. The full list of the methods we can call on a dialog is as follows:

Method	Description
close	This is used to close or hide the dialog.
destroy	This is used to permanently disable the dialog. The `destroy` method for a dialog works in a slightly different way than it does for the other widgets we've seen so far. Instead of just returning the underlying HTML to its original state, the dialog's `destroy` method also hides it.
isOpen	This is used to determine whether a dialog is open or not.

Method	Description
moveToTop	This is used to move the specified dialog to the top of the stack.
open	This is used to open the dialog.
option	This is used to get or set any configurable option after the dialog has been initialized.
widget	This is used to return the outer element that the dialog() widget method is called on.

Toggling the dialog

We first take a look at opening the widget, which can be achieved with the simple use of the open method. Let's revisit dialog3.html in which the autoOpen option was set to false, so that the dialog didn't open when the page was loaded. Add the following <button> to the page:

```
<button type="button" id="toggle">Toggle dialog!</button>
```

Then add the following click handler to the <script> block at the top of the code:

```
$("#toggle").click(function() {
  if(!$("#myDialog").dialog("isOpen")) {
    $("#myDialog").dialog("open");
  } else {
    $("#myDialog").dialog("close");
  }
});
```

Save this file as dialog12.html. To the page, we've added a simple <button> that can be used to either open or close the dialog depending on its current state. In the <script> element, we've added a click handler for the <button> element that checks the return value of the isOpen method; the use of the exclamation mark means we are looking to see if the dialog box isn't open. If the statement returns true, the dialog is not open so we call its open method, otherwise we call the close method.

The open and close methods both trigger any applicable events; for example, the #toggle click handler method first fires the beforeClose and then the close events. Calling the close method is analogous to clicking the close button on the dialog.

Getting data from the dialog

Because the widget is a part of the underlying page, passing data to and from it is simple. The dialog can be treated as any other standard element on the page. Let's look at a basic example.

We looked at an example earlier in the chapter, which added some `<button>` elements to the dialog. The callback functions in that example didn't do anything, but the following example gives us the opportunity to use them. Replace the existing dialog markup in `dialog8.html` with the following:

```
<div id="myDialog" title="Best Widget Library">
  <p>Is jQuery UI the greatest JavaScript widget library?</p>
  <label for="yes">Yes!</label>
  <input type="radio" id="yes" value="yes" name="question"
checked="checked"><br>
  <label for="no">No!</label>
  <input type="radio" id="no" value="no" name="question">
</div>
```

Now change the final `<script>` element as follows:

```
<script>
$(document).ready(function($){
  var execute = function(){
    var answer = $("#myDialog").find("input:checked").val();
    $("<p>").text("Thanks for selecting " + answer).
      appendTo($("body"));
    $("#myDialog").dialog("close");
  }
  var cancel = function() {
    $("#myDialog").dialog("close");
  }
  $("#myDialog").dialog({
    buttons: {
      "Ok": execute,
      "Cancel": cancel
    }
  });
});
</script>
```

Save this as `dialog13.html`. Our dialog widget now contains a set of radio buttons, some `<label>` elements, and some text. In this example, we're going to get the result of the selected radio button, and then do something with it, when the dialog closes.

We start the `<script>` element by filling out the `execute` function that will be attached as the value of the `Ok` property in the buttons object, later in the script. It will therefore be executed each time the **Ok** button is clicked.

In this function, we use the `:checked` filter to determine which of the radio buttons is selected. We set the value of the `answer` variable to the radio button's value, and then create a short message along with appending it to the `<body>` element of the page. The callback mapped to the **Cancel** button is simple; all we do is close the dialog using the `close` method.

The point of this example was to see that getting data from the dialog is as simple as getting data from any other element on the page. If you preview it in your browser, you will first see the dialog on the left; clicking on a button gives the appropriate response, as shown in the following screenshot:

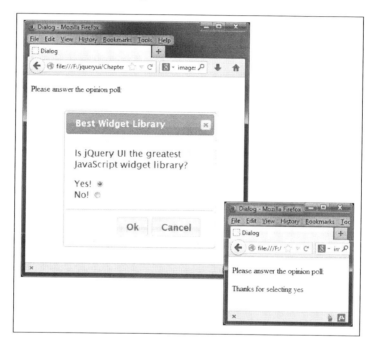

Exploring dialog interoperability

In the previous chapters, we've combined multiple widgets so that we can see how well they work together, and this chapter will be no exception. We can easily place other UI widgets into the dialog such as the accordion widget that we looked at in the previous chapter. In a new file in your text editor, create the following page:

```
<!DOCTYPE html>
<html>
<head>
  <meta charset="utf-8">
  <title>Dialog</title>
```

```html
<link rel="stylesheet" href="development-bundle/themes/redmond/
jquery.ui.all.css">
  <script src="js/jquery-2.0.3.js"></script>
  <script src="development-bundle/ui/jquery.ui.core.js"></script>
  <script src="development-bundle/ui/jquery.ui.widget.js"></script>
  <script src="development-bundle/ui/jquery.ui.position.js"></script>
  <script src="development-bundle/ui/jquery.ui.dialog.js"></script>
  <script src="development-bundle/ui/jquery.ui.button.js"></script>
  <script src="development-bundle/ui/jquery.ui.accordion.js">
  </script>
  <script src="development-bundle/ui/jquery.ui.mouse.js"></script>
  <script src="development-bundle/ui/jquery.ui.draggable.js"></script>
  <script src="development-bundle/ui/jquery.ui.resizable.js"></script>
  <script>
    $(document).ready(function($){
      $("#myDialog").dialog();
        $("#myAccordion").accordion();
    });
  </script>
</head>
<body>
  <div id="myDialog" title="An Accordion Dialog">
    <div id="myAccordion">
      <h2><a href="#">Header 1</a></h2>
      <div>Lorem ipsum dolor sit amet, consectetuer adipiscing elit.
Aenean sollicitudin.</div>
      <h2><a href="#">Header 2</a></h2>
      <div>Etiam tincidunt est vitae est. Ut posuere, mauris at so
dales rutrum, turpis.</div>
      <h2><a href="#">Header 3</a></h2>
      <div>Donec at dolor ac metus pharetra aliquam. Suspendisse pu
rus.</div>
    </div>
  </div>
</body>
</html>
```

Save this file as `dialog14.html`. The underlying markup for the accordion widget is placed into the dialog's container element, and we just call each component's widget method in the `<script>` element.

In this example, we use quite a few separate `<script>` resources. It is worth remembering that for production, we should use the combined and minified script file, which contains all of the components we selected in the download builder.

The combined widget should appear like this:

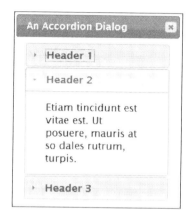

Creating a dynamic image-based dialog

The class behind the dialog widget is compact and caters to a small range of specialized behavior, much of which we have already looked at. We can still have some fun with a dynamic dialog box, which loads different content depending on which element triggers it.

In a new page in your text editor, add the following code:

```
<!DOCTYPE html>
<html>
<head>
  <meta charset="utf-8">
  <title>Dialog</title>
  <link rel="stylesheet" href="development-bundle/themes/redmond/
jquery.ui.all.css">
  <link rel="stylesheet" href="css/dialogTheme.css">
  <script src="js/jquery-2.0.3.js"></script>
  <script src="development-bundle/ui/jquery.ui.core.js"></script>
  <script src="development-bundle/ui/jquery.ui.widget.js"></script>
  <script src="development-bundle/ui/jquery.ui.position.js"></script>
  <script src="development-bundle/ui/jquery.ui.dialog.js"></script>
  <script src="development-bundle/ui/jquery.ui.button.js"></script>
```

```
    <script src="development-bundle/ui/jquery.ui.accordion.js"></script>
    <script src="development-bundle/ui/jquery.ui.mouse.js"></script>
    <script src="development-bundle/ui/jquery.ui.draggable.js"></script>
    <script src="development-bundle/ui/jquery.ui.resizable.js"></script>
</head>
<body>
    <div id="thumbs" class="ui-corner-all">
        <div class="ui-widget-header ui-corner-top">
            <h2>Some Common Flowers</h2>
            </div>
            <p>(click a thumbnail to view a full-size image)</p>
            <div class="thumb ui-helper-clearfix ui-widget-content">
                <a href="img/haFull.jpg" title="Helianthus annuus"><img
src="img/haThumb.jpg" alt="Helianthus annuus"></a>
                <h3>Helianthus annuus</h3>
                <p>Sunflowers (Helianthus annuus) are annual plants native to
the Americas, that possess a large flowering head</p>
            </div>
            <div class="thumb ui-helper-clearfix ui-widget-content">
                <a href="img/lcFull.jpg" title="Lilium columbianum"> <img
src="img/lcThumb.jpg" alt="Lilium columbianum"></a>
                <h3>Lilium columbianum</h3>
                <p>The Lilium columbianum is a lily native to western North
America. It is also known as the Columbia Lily or Tiger Lily</p>
            </div>
            <div class="thumb ui-helper-clearfix ui-widget-content">
                <a href="img/msFull.jpg" title="Myosotis scorpioides"> <img
src="img/msThumb.jpg" alt="Myosotis scorpioides"></a>
                <h3>Myosotis scorpioides</h3>
                <p>The Myosotis scorpioides, or Forget-me-not, is a
herbaceous perennial plant of the genus Myosotis.</p>
            </div>
            <div class="thumb ui-helper-clearfix ui-widget-content last">
                <a href="img/nnFull.jpg" title="Nelumbo nucifera"><img
src="img/nnThumb.jpg" alt="Nelumbo nucifera"></a>
                <h3>Nelumbo nucifera</h3>
                <p>Nelumbo nucifera is known by a number of names including;
Indian lotus, sacred lotus, bean of India, or simply lotus.</p>
            </div>
        </div>
        <div id="dialog"></div>
</body>
</html>
```

Save this file as `dialog15.html`. The following screenshot shows the result when previewed in a browser:

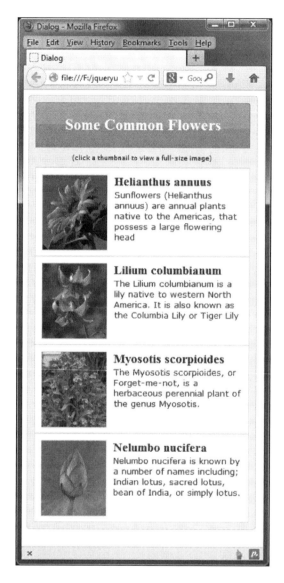

The page is relatively straightforward—we've got an outer container, which encloses everything and an element, which we've given the class name `ui-widget-header`. We've used the latter in order to pick up some of the default styling from the theme in use.

Following this, we have some explanatory text followed by a series of containers. Several classnames are given to these containers, some of which are so that we can style them, and others (such as `ui-helper-clearfix`), in order to pick up the framework or theme styles.

Within each of these containers is an image, wrapped in an anchor, a subheading, and some descriptive text. After the outer container, comes the empty `<div>` element, which is used to create the dialog. In this example, we don't use the resizable feature. Each of the thumbnail images is wrapped in an anchor, in order for the page to function even with JavaScript disabled. The dialog widget won't display in this situation, but the visitor will still be able to see a full-sized version of each image. This form of progressive enhancement is essential in this kind of application, where we can always view the content. Adding in the call to the dialog widget is enhancing the overall view to the visitor, whilst ensuring content will always display something, even with JavaScript disabled!

Now add the following `<script>` block directly before the closing `</head>` tag:

```
<script>
  $(document).ready(function($){
    var filename, titleText, dialogOpts = {
      modal: true,
      width: 388,
      height: 470,
      autoOpen: false,
      open: function() {
        $("#dialog").empty();
        $("<img />", { src: filename }).appendTo("#dialog");
        $("#dialog").dialog("option", "title", titleText);
      }
    };
    $("#dialog").dialog(dialogOpts);
    $("#thumbs").find("a").click(function(e) {
      e.preventDefault();
      filename = $(this).attr("href");
      titleText = $(this).attr("title");
      $("#dialog").dialog("open");
    });
  });
</script>
```

The first thing we do is define three variables; the first variable is used to add the path to the full-sized image of whichever thumbnail was clicked, the second is to store the image title to use as the text for the widget's title, and the third is the configuration object for the dialog. We've seen the entire configuration options in action already, so I won't go over most of them in much detail.

The `open` callback, called directly before the dialog is opened, is where we add the full-sized image to the dialog. We first empty the dialog, then create a new `<img>` element, and set its `src` to the value of the `filename` variable. The new `<img>` is then appended to the inner content area of the dialog.

We then use the `option` method to set the title option to the value of the `titleText` variable. Once the `open` callback has been defined, we call the dialog's widget method as normal.

We can use the wrapper `<a>` elements as the triggers to open the dialog. Within our click handler, we first call `e.preventDefault()` to stop the default action of the click, before setting the contents of our `filename` and `titleText` variables using the `href` and `title` attributes of the link that was clicked. We then call the dialog's `open` method to display the dialog, which in turn triggers the callback function specified in the `open` option.

 If we omit `e.preventDefault()`, this will override the dialog and the browser will render each image as if it were a link that had been clicked.

We'll also need a new stylesheet for this example. In a new page in your text editor, add the following code:

```
#thumbs { width:342px; padding: 10px 0 10px 10px; border:1px
   solid #ccc; background-color:#eee; }
#thumbs p { width: 330px; font-family: Verdana; font-size: 9px;
   text-align: center; }
.thumb { width: 310px; height: 114px; padding: 10px;
   border:1px solid #ccc; border-bottom: none; }
.last { border-bottom: 1px solid #ccc; }
.thumb img { border: 1px solid #ccc; margin-right: 10px;
   float: left; cursor: pointer; }
.thumb h3 { margin: 0; float: left; width:198px; }
#thumbs .thumb p { width: 310px; margin:0; font-family:
   Verdana; font-size: 13px; text-align: left; }
#thumbs .ui-widget-header { width: 330px; text-align: center; }
```

Many of these styles have been used in the previous examples, but adding some new rules for the other page elements lets us see the dialog in a real-world context. Save this as `dialogTheme.css` in the `css` folder. We also use some images in this example, which can be found in the `img` folder of the accompanying code download for this book.

This should now give us the page that we saw in the previous screenshot and when a thumbnail is clicked, the full size version of the same image will be displayed:

Summary

The dialog widget is specialized and caters to the display of a message or question in a floating panel that sits above the page content. Advanced functionality such as dragging and resizing is directly built-in and require just the inclusion of an additional script file for each feature. Other features such as the excellent modality and overlay are easy to configure.

We started out by looking at the default implementation, which is as equally simple to configure as the other widgets we have looked at so far. We then examined the range of configurable options exposed by the dialog's API. We can make use of them to enable or disable built-in behavior such as modality, or set the dimensions of the widget. It also gives us a wide range of callbacks that allow us to hook into custom events fired by the widget during an interaction.

We then took a brief look at the built-in opening and closing effects that can be used with the dialog, before moving on to see the basic methods we can invoke, in order to make the dialog do things, such as open or close.

In the next chapter, we'll move on to look at the slider and progress bar widgets, which allow us to create interactive form widgets used to select from a predefined range of values and display the results on screen.

6
The Slider and Progressbar Widgets

The slider component allows us to implement an engaging and easy-to-use widget that our visitors should find attractive and intuitive to use. Its basic function is simple. The slider track represents a series of values that are selected by dragging the handle along the track.

The progressbar widget is used to show the percentage complete for any arbitrary process. It's a simple and easy-to-use component with an extremely compact API that provides excellent visual feedback to visitors.

In this chapter we will cover the following topics:

- The default slider implementation
- Custom styling for sliders
- Changing the configuration options
- Creating a vertical slider
- Setting minimum, maximum, and default values
- Enabling multiple handles and ranges
- The slider's built-in event callbacks
- Slider methods
- The default implementation for a progressbar
- The configurable options
- The event API exposed by the widget
- The single unique method exposed by the progressbar
- Some real-world examples of a progressbar

Before we roll up our sleeves and begin creating a slider, let's look at the different elements that it is made from. The following diagram shows a typical slider widget:

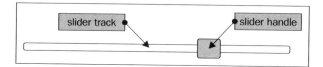

It's a simple widget, as you can see, comprised of just two main elements — the **slider handle** (sometimes called the thumb), and the **slider track**.

Introducing the slider widget

Creating the default, basic slider takes no more code than any of the other widgets that we have looked at so far. The underlying HTML markup required is also minimal. Let's create a basic one now. In a new page in your text editor, add the following code:

```html
<!DOCTYPE html>
<html>
<head>
  <meta charset="utf-8">
  <title>Slider</title>
  <link rel="stylesheet" href="development-bundle/themes/redmond/
  jquery.ui.all.css">
  <script src="js/jquery-2.0.3.js"></script>
  <script src="development-bundle/ui/jquery.ui.core.js"></script>
  <script src="development-bundle/ui/jquery.ui.widget.js">
  </script>
  <script src="development-bundle/ui/jquery.ui.mouse.js"></script>
  <script src="development-bundle/ui/jquery.ui.slider.js">
  </script>
  <script>
    $(document).ready(function($){
      $("#mySlider").slider();
    });
  </script>
</head>
<body>
  <div id="mySlider"></div>
</body>
</html>
```

Save this file as `slider1.html` and view it in your browser. On the page is a simple container element; this will be transformed by the widget into the slider track. In `<script>` within the `<head>` section of the code, we select this element and call the `slider` method on it. The `<a>` element that is used for the slider handle will be automatically created by the widget.

When we run the `slider1.html` file in a browser, we should see something similar to the previous diagram. We've used several library resources for the default implementation, including the following files:

- `jquery.ui.all.css`
- `jquery-2.0.3.js`
- `jquery.ui.core.js`
- `jquery.ui.widget.js`
- `jquery.ui.mouse.js`
- `jquery.ui.slider.js`

The default behavior of a basic slider is simple but effective. The thumb can be moved horizontally along any pixel of the track on the x axis by dragging the thumb with the mouse pointer, or using the left/down or right/up arrow keys on the keyboard. Clicking anywhere on the track with the left button will instantly move the handle to that position.

Custom styling

Because of its simplicity, it is easy to create a custom theme for the slider widget. Using ThemeRoller is one method of theming: we can simply download a new theme, then put it into the theme folder and change the reference within our code to the name of the new theme. Like all other widgets, the slider will be restyled to use the new theme.

To completely change the look and feel of the widget though, we can easily create our own theme file. In your text editor create the following stylesheet:

```
.background-div {
  height: 50px; width: 217px; padding: 36px 0 0 24px;
  background:  url(../img/slider_outerbg.gif) no-repeat;
}
#mySlider {
```

```
    background: url(../img/slider_bg.gif) no-repeat; height: 23px;
    width: 184px; border: none; top: 4px; position: relative;
    left: 4px;
}
#mySlider .ui-slider-handle {
    width: 14px; height: 30px; top: -4px;
    background: url(../img/slider_handle.gif) no-repeat;
}
```

Save this file as `sliderTheme.css` in the `css` directory. In `slider1.html`, add a link to the stylesheet in the `<head>` of the page (after the jQuery UI stylesheet), and wrap the underlying slider element in a new container:

```
<div class="background-div">
    <div id="mySlider"></div>
</div>
```

Save this file as `slider2.html`. With a minimum of CSS and a few images (these can be found in the code download), we can easily but considerably modify the widget's appearance, as shown in the following screenshot:

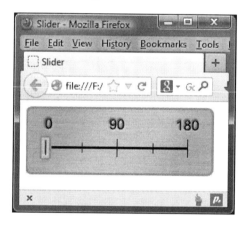

Let us turn our attention to how we can configure the slider widget, using some of its options.

Configuring a basic slider

Additional functionality, such as vertical sliders, multiple handles, and stepping can also be configured using an object literal, passed into the widget method when the slider is initialized. The options that can be used in conjunction with the slider widget are listed in the following table:

Option	Default value	Usage
animate	false	Enables a smooth animation of the slider handle when the track is clicked.
disabled	false	Disables the widget when it is initialized.
max	100	Sets the maximum value of the slider.
min	0	Sets the minimum value of the slider.
orientation	auto	Sets the axis along which the slider thumb is moved. This can accept the strings vertical or horizontal.
range	false	Creates a styleable range of elements between them.
step	1	Sets the distance of the step that the handle will take along the track. The max value must be equally divisible by the supplied number.
value	0	Sets the value of the slider thumb when the widget is initialized.
values	null	Accepts an array of values. Each supplied integer will become the value of a slider handle.

Creating a vertical slider

To make a vertical slider, all we need to do is set the orientation option to vertical; the widget will do the rest for us.

In slider1.html, change the final <script> element so that it appears as follows:

```
<script>
  $(document).ready(function($){
    $("#mySlider").slider({
      orientation: "vertical"
    });
  });
</script>
```

Save this file as `slider3.html`. We just need to set this single option to put the slider into `vertical` mode. When we launch the page, we see that the slider operates exactly as it did before, except that it now moves along the y axis, as in the following screenshot:

The widget defaults to `100px` in height, unless we provide our own CSS rule for `.ui-slider-vertical` in the stylesheet.

Setting the maximum and minimum values

By default, the minimum value of the slider is `0` and the maximum value is `100`, but we can change these values easily using the `min` and `max` options. Change the configuration object in `slider3.html` to the following code:

```
$("#mySlider").slider({
  min: -50,
  max: 50
});
```

Save this file as `slider4.html`. We simply specify the integers that we'd like to set as the start and end values. The `value` and `values` methods are exclusive to the slider, and are used to get or set the value of single or multiple handles. As the `value` option is set to `0` by default, when we run the `slider4.html` file, the slider thumb will start in the middle of the track, half way between `-50` and `50`.

When the slider handle, in this example, is at the minimum value, the `value` method will return to `-50`, as we would expect. To prove this, we could adapt `slider4.html` to show this value in an alert. Add the following code immediately below the slider configuration object:

```
$("#getValue").click(function(){
  var value = $("#mySlider").slider("value");
  alert("Value of slider is " + value);
});
```

In the markup within <body>, change it as follows:

```
<div id="mySlider"></div>
<p>
<button id="getValue">Get value of slider</button>
```

If we now try previewing changes in a browser, you will get an alert that will appear when clicking on the button, once you've moved the handle to the far left of the slider. We will explore the value option later in the *Using the slider methods* section of this chapter.

Stepping with the slider widget

The step option refers to the number and position of steps along the track that the slider's handle jumps, when moving from the minimum to the maximum positions on the track. The best way to understand how this option works is to see it in action, so change the configuration object in slider4.html to the following code:

```
$("#mySlider").slider({
  step: 25
});
```

Save this file as slider5.html. We set the step option to 25 in this example. We haven't set the min or max options, so they will take the default values of 0 and 100 respectively. Hence, by setting step to 25, we're saying that each step along the track should be a quarter of the track's length, because 100 (the maximum) divided by 25 (the step value) is 4. The handle will therefore take four steps along the track, from beginning to end.

The max value of the slider should be equally divisible by whatever value we set as the step option; other than that, we're free to use whatever value we wish. The step option is useful to confine the value selected by the visitors to one of a set of predefined values.

If we were to set the value of the step option, in this example, to 27 instead of 25, the slider would still work, but the points along the track that the handle stepped to would not be equal.

Animating the slider widget

The slider widget comes with a built-in animation that moves the slider handle smoothly to a new position, whenever the slider track is clicked. This animation is disabled by default, but we can easily enable it by setting the `animate` option to `true`. Change the configuration object in `slider5.html`, so that it is as follows:

```
$("#mySlider").slider({
  animate: true
});
```

Save this file as `slider6.html`. This simple change can give a slider a more polished feel; instead of the slider handle just moving instantly to a new position when the track is clicked, it smoothly slides there.

If the `step` option is configured to a value other than `1`, and the `animate` option is enabled, the thumb will slide to the nearest step mark on the track. This may mean that the slider thumb moves past the point that was clicked.

Setting the slider's value

The `value` option, when set to `true` in a configuration object, determines the starting value for the slider thumb. Depending on what we want the slider to represent, the starting value of the handle may not be `0`. If we wanted to start at half-way across the track instead of at the beginning, we can use the following configuration object:

```
$("#mySlider").slider({
  value: 50
});
```

Save this file as `slider7.html`. When the file is loaded in a browser, we see that the handle starts halfway along the track instead of at the beginning, exactly as it did when we set the `min` and `max` options earlier. We can also set this option after initialization, to programmatically set a new value.

Using multiple handles

I mentioned earlier that a slider may have multiple handles; additional handles can be added using the `values` option. It accepts an array where each item in the array is a starting point for a handle. We can specify as many items as we wish, up to the `max` value (taking step into account):

```
$("#mySlider").slider({
  values: [25, 75]
});
```

Save this file as `slider8.html`. This is all we need to do; we don't need to supply any additional underlying markup. The widget has created both new handles for us, and as you'll see, they both function exactly as a standard single handle does.

The following screenshot shows our dual-handled slider:

We could make use of a double-handled slider to create a time window for a schedule. A good example would be on a travel booking form. Normally you would enter dates manually, which could be a bit clunky.

Instead, you could use a double-handled slider to select dates; the user would simply slide each handle to the left or right to change the date window. We can then use the method described in *Setting the minimum and maximum values* section earlier in this chapter to obtain the position values of each slider's handle.

> When a slider has two or more handles, each handle may move past the other handle(s) without issue; you may want to consider setting a `range`, if you need to prevent this from happening.

Working with the range option

When working with multiple handles, we can set the `range` option to `true`. This adds a styled range element between two handles. In `slider8.html`, change the configuration object so that it is as follows:

```
$("#mySlider").slider({
  values: [25, 75],
  range: true
});
```

Save this file as `slider9.html`. When the page loads, we should see that a styled `<div>` element now connects our two handles, as shown in the following screenshot:

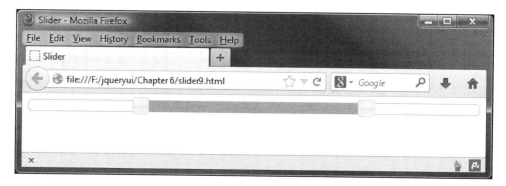

When using two handles and a range, the two handles will not be able to cross each other on the track.

A maximum of two handles can be used in conjunction with the `range` option, but we can also enable it with a single handle change the configuration object in the previous example to the following:

```
$("#mySlider").slider({
    range: "min"
});
```

Save this file as `slider10.html`. Along with the Boolean value `true`, we can also supply one of the string values `min` or `max`, but only when a single handle is in use.

In this example, we set it to `min`, so when we move the slider handle along the track, the range element will stretch from the start of the track to the slider handle. If we set the option to `max`, the range will stretch from the handle to the end of the track.

If you want to capture the value of where the handle is on the scale, we can do this by using the `slide` event handler. In this instance, we only need to get one value (as we only have one handle), but the same principle applies if a second handle had been configured.

In `slider4.html`, add the following function in just above our slider's configuration object:

```
function slideValues(event, ui){
  var val0 = $("#mySlider").slider("values", 0),
    endValue = parseInt(val0, 10);

  $("#rangeValues").text("Range: 0 - " + endValue);
}:
```

We need to then modify the configuration object, to call our `slideValues` event handler at the appropriate time:

```
$("#mySlider").slider({
  range: "min",
  slide: slideValues
});
```

So we can display the results on screen, add this in below the existing markup in the `<body>` section:

```
<div id="rangeValues"></div>
```

We can then do as we wish with the value; if you preview the results, you will see the value on the right change; the left value will always remain at `0`, as this is the default value for the `min` option in our code.

Using the slider's event API

In addition to the options we saw earlier, there are another five options used to define functions that are executed at different times during a slider interaction. Any callback functions that we use are automatically passed the standard event object, and an object representing the slider. The following table lists the event options we can use:

Event	Fired when...
change	The slider's handle stops moving and its value has changed.
create	The slider is created
slide	The slider's handle moves.
start	The slider's handle starts moving.
stop	The slider's handle stops moving.

Hooking into these built-in callback functions is easy. Let's put a basic example together to see. Change the configuration object in `slider10.html` so that it appears as follows:

```
$("#mySlider").slider({
  start: function() {
    $("#tip").fadeOut(function() {
      $(this).remove();
    });
  },
  change: function(e, ui) {
```

```
$("<div></div>", {
  "class": "ui-widget-header ui-corner-all",
  id: "tip",
  text: ui.value + "%",
  css: { left: e.pageX-35 }
}).appendTo("#mySlider");
  }
});
```

Save this file as `slider11.html`. We use two of the callback options in this example—`start` and `change`. In the `start` function, we select the tooltip element if it exists, and fade it out with jQuery's `fadeOut()` method. Once hidden from view, it is removed from the page.

The `change` function will be executed each time the value of the slider handle changes; when the function is called, we create the tool tip and append it to the slider. We position it so that it appears above the center of the slider handle and give it some of the framework class names in order to style it with the theme in use.

In several places we use the second object passed to the callback function, the prepared `ui` object that contains useful information from the slider. In this example, we use the `value` option of the object to obtain the new value of the slider handle.

We also need a very small custom stylesheet for this example. In your text editor, add the following code:

```
#mySlider { margin: 60px auto 0; }
#tip { position: absolute; display: inline; padding: 5px 0;
  width: 50px; text-align: center; font: bold 11px Verdana;
  top: -40px }
```

Save this file as `sliderTheme2.css` in the `css` folder and add a link to it from the `<head>` of `slider11.html`. When displayed, our tool tip should appear as shown in the following screenshot:

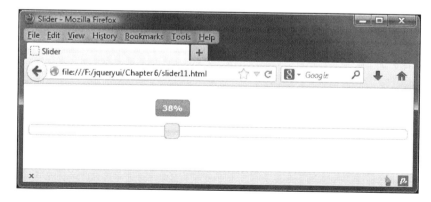

When all of the event options are used together, the events will be fired in the following order:

- `create`
- `start`
- `slide`
- `stop`
- `change`

The `slide` callback can be quite an intensive event as it is fired on every mouse move while the handle is selected, but it can also be used to prevent a slide in certain situations by returning `false` from the callback function. When using the `stop` and `change` callbacks together, the `change` callback may override the `stop` callback.

As with all library components each of these events can also be used with the jQuery's `on()` method by prefixing the word `slider` to the event name, for example, `sliderstart`.

Using slider methods

The slider is intuitive, and like the other components in the library it comes with a range of methods that are used to programmatically control the widget after it has been initialized. The methods specific to the slider are shown in the following table:

Method	Usage
`value`	Sets a single slider handle to a new value. This will move the handle to the new position on the track automatically. This method accepts a single argument which is an integer representing the new value.
`values`	Sets the specified handle to move to a new value when multiple handles are in use. This method is the same as the value method, except that it takes two arguments—the index number of the handle followed by the new value.

The `destroy`, `disable`, `enable`, `option`, and `widget` methods are common to all components, and work in the same way with a slider that we would expect them to.

As we saw earlier in this chapter, the `value` and `values` methods are exclusive to the slider, and can be used to get or set the value of single or multiple handles. Of course, we can also do this using the `option` method, so these two methods are merely shortcuts to cater for common implementation requirements. Let's take a look at them in action. First of all let's see how the `value` method can be used.

In `slider11.html`, remove the `<link>` to `sliderTheme2.css` and add a new `<button>` element to the page, directly after the slider container:

```
<p><button type="button" id="setMax">Set to max value</button></p>
```

Now, change the final `<script>` element so that it is as follows:

```
<script>
  $(document).ready(function($){
    $("#mySlider").slider();
    $("#setMax").click(function() {
      var maxVal = $("#mySlider").slider("option", "max");
      $("#mySlider").slider("value", maxVal);
    });
  });
</script>
```

Save this file as `slider12.html`. We add a click handler for our new `<button>`; whenever it is clicked, this method will first determine what the maximum value for the slider is, by setting a variable to the result of the `option` method, specifying `max` as the option we'd like to get. Once we have the maximum value, we then call the `value` method, passing in the variable that holds the maximum value as the second argument; our variable will be used as the new value. Whenever the button is clicked, the slider handle will instantly move to the end of the track.

Using value as an option or method

In a number of examples throughout this chapter, we've made reference to `value` (or `values`) as an option or method. This can be a little confusing; think of `value`'s method as being a shortcut for using the value option as a getter in your code.

Working with multiple handles is just as easy but involves a slightly different approach.

Remove the `setMax` button in `slider12.html` and add the following two buttons directly after the slider element:

```
<p>
<button type="button" class="preset" id="low">Preset 1 (low) </button>
<button type="button" class="preset" id="high">Preset 2 (high) </
button>
```

Now change the final `<script>` element at the end of the `<head>` to the following code:

```
<script>
  $(document).ready(function($){
```

```
    $("#mySlider").slider({
      values: [25, 75]
    });

    $(".preset").click(function() {
      if (this.id === "low") {
        $("#mySlider").slider("values", 0, 0).slider("values", 1,
        25);
      } else {
        $("#mySlider").slider("values", 0, 75).slider("values" ,
        1, 100);
      }
    });
  });
</script>
```

Save this file as `slider13.html`. To trigger multiple handles, we specify the values of two handles in our configuration object. When either of the two `<button>` elements on the page are clicked, we work out whether **Preset 1** or **Preset 2** was clicked and then set the handles to either low values or high values, depending on which button was clicked.

You can also use the array notation method for setting the values in a slider; this will set the same value for all the handles, irrespective of how many are present.

The `values` method takes two arguments. The first argument is the index number of the handle we'd like to change, and the second argument is the value that we'd like the handle to be set to. The following screenshot shows how the page should appear after the second button is clicked:

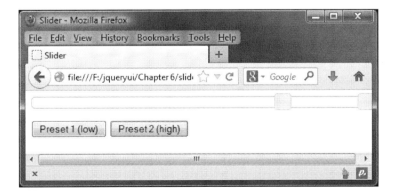

Practical uses

An HTML5 element that may lend itself particularly well to implementations of the slider widget is the `<audio>` element. This element will automatically add controls that enable the visitor to play, pause, and adjust the volume of the media being played.

The default controls, however, cannot be styled; if we wish to change their appearance, we need to create our own controls. A slider widget, of course, makes an excellent substitution for the default volume control. Let's take a look at how you can add one, as a basis that you can take further in your own projects.

Create the following new code in your text editor:

```
<!DOCTYPE html>
<html>
<head>
  <meta charset="utf-8">
  <title>Slider</title>
  <link rel="stylesheet" href="development-bundle/themes/redmond/
  jquery.ui.all.css">
  <link rel="stylesheet" href="css/sliderTheme3.css">
  <script src="js/jquery-2.0.3.js"></script>
  <script src="development-bundle/ui/jquery.ui.core.js"></script>
  <script src="development-bundle/ui/jquery.ui.widget.js"></script>
  <script src="development-bundle/ui/jquery.ui.mouse.js"></script>
  <script src="development-bundle/ui/jquery.ui.slider.js"></script>
  <script>
    $(document).ready(function($){
      var audio = $("audio")[0];
      audio.volume = 0.5;
      audio.play();
      $("#volume").slider({
        value: 5,
        min: 0,
        max: 10,
        change: function() {
          var vol = $(this).slider("value") / 10;
          audio.volume = vol;
        }
      });
    });
  </script>
</head>
<body>
  <audio id="audio" controls="controls" src="uploads/prelude.mp3">
```

```
       Your browser does not support the <code>audio</code> element.
    </audio>
    <div id="volume"></div>
</body>
</html>
```

Save this file as `slider14.html`. We also need to add a couple of styles to tweak the display. In a new page in your text editor, add the following, and save it as `sliderTheme3.css`:

```
#volume { padding-top: 5px; }
#volume.ui-slider { width: 300px; }
.ui-slider-horizontal .ui-slider-handle { margin-left: -0.6em;
   top: -0.1em; }
```

Don't forget to add a link to `sliderTheme3.css` from your main page:

```
<link rel="stylesheet" href="css/sliderTheme3.css">
```

On the `slider14.html` page, we have the `<audio>` tag that has its `src` attribute set to an audio clip available from the Internet Archive. We also have the empty container element for our volume control.

> This example uses one of the music soundtrack files created by Jan Morgenstern for the Big Bunny Movie; you can download it, and others in the collection at `https://archive.org/details/JanMorgenstern-BigBuckBunny`.

In the script, we first select the `<audio>` element using the standard jQuery syntax and retrieve the actual DOM element from the jQuery object, so that we can call methods from the `<audio>` API.

Next, we define the configuration object for our slider and set the initial minimum and maximum values. We then add a handler for the `change` event that is used to change the volume of the currently playing audio track, using the `volume` property method. Whenever the slider is changed, we get a new slider value and convert it to the required format for the `volume` property, by dividing the slider value by `10`. Once our variables are defined, we set the volume of the audio clip and begin playing the clip immediately with the `play()` method.

When we run this example in a supporting browser, we can pause or play the audio clip; if the slider handle is moved, the volume of the clip should increase or decrease as shown in the following screenshot:

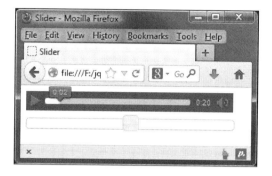

Creating a color slider

A fun implementation of the slider widget, which can be very useful in certain applications, is the color slider. Let's put what we've learned about this widget into practice to produce a basic color-choosing tool. The following screenshot shows the page that we'll be making:

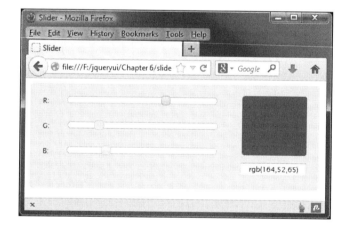

In your text editor, alter the `<body>` markup in `slider1.html` to the following code:

```
<div id="container" class="ui-widget ui-corner-all ui-widget-content
ui-helper-clearfix">
  <label>R:</label>
  <div id="rSlider"></div><br>
  <label>G:</label>
  <div id="gSlider"></div><br>
```

```
    <label>B:</label>
    <div id="bSlider"></div>
    <div id="colorBox" class="ui-corner-all ui-widget-content"></div>
    <label for="output" id="outputLabel">Color value:</label>
    <input id="output" type="text" value="rgb(255,255,255)">
</div>
```

Let's now add in the `script` functionality for our demo, so go ahead and remove the contents of the last `<script>` element, and add the following code:

```
<script>
  $(document).ready(function($){
    $("#rSlider, #gSlider, #bSlider").slider({
      min:0,
      max: 255,
      value: 255,
      slide: function() {
        var r = $("#rSlider").slider("value"),
        g = $("#gSlider").slider("value"),
        b = $("#bSlider").slider("value");
        var rgbString = ["rgb(", r, ",", g, ",", b, ")"].join("");
        $("#colorBox").css({
          backgroundColor: rgbString
        });
        $("#output").val(rgbString);

      }
    });
  });
</script>
```

Save this file as `slider15.html`. The page itself is simple enough. We've got some elements used primarily for displaying the different components of the color slider, as well as the individual container elements that will be transformed into slider widgets. We use three sliders for our color chooser, one for each RGB channel.

We'll need some CSS as well to complete the overall appearance of our widget. In a new page in your text editor, create the following stylesheet:

```
#container { width: 426px; height: 146px; padding: 20px 20px
   0; position: relative; font-size: 11px; background: #eee; }
#container label { float: left; text-align: right; margin: 0
   30px 26px 0; clear: left; }
.ui-slider { width: 240px; float: left; }
.ui-slider-handle { width: 15px; height: 27px; }
#colorBox { width: 104px; height: 94px; float: right; margin:
   -83px 0 0 0; background: #fff; }
```

```
#container #outputLabel { float: right; margin: -14px 34px 0 0; }
#output { width: 100px; text-align: center; float: right; clear: both;
margin-top: -17px; }
```

Save this file as `colorSliderTheme.css` in the `css` folder; don't forget to add a link to this in your main file immediately after the call to the jQuery UI stylesheet:

```
<link rel="stylesheet" href="css/colorSliderTheme.css">
```

In our code, we give the container and color box elements class names from the CSS framework, so that we can take advantage of effects such as the rounded corners, so that we can cut down on the amount of CSS we need to write ourselves.

Turning our attention to the JavaScript code, we first set the configuration object. As RGB color values range from `0` to `255`, we set the `max` option to `255` and the `value` option to `255` as well, so that the widget handles start in the correct location (the color box will have a white background on page load).

The `slide` callback is where the action happens. Every time a handle is moved, we update each of the `r`, `g`, and `b` variables, by using the `value` method, and then construct a new RGB string from the values of our variables. This is necessary as we can't pass the variables directly into jQuery's `css()` method. We also update the value in the `<input>` field.

When we run the example, we should find that everything works as expected. As soon as we start moving any of the slider handles, the color box begins to change color and the `<input>` updates.

 The slide event is fired on every mouse move as soon as the handle is selected; this is a potentially intensive event that may cause issues in older browsers or on slow computers. Care should therefore be taken when used in a production environment to keep any unnecessary actions in the event handler to a minimum.

Introducing the progressbar widget

The widget is made up of just two nested `<div>` elements—an outer `<div>` container and an inner `<div>` container, which is used to highlight the current progress. The following diagram shows a progressbar that is 50 percent complete:

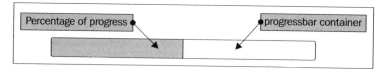

Let's take a look at the most basic progressbar implementation. In a new file in your text editor, create the following code:

```
<!DOCTYPE html>
<html>
<head>
  <meta charset="utf-8">
  <title>Progressbar</title>
  <link rel="stylesheet" href="development-bundle/themes/redmond/
jquery.ui.all.css">
  <script src="js/jquery-2.0.3.js"></script>
  <script src="development-bundle/ui/jquery.ui.core.js"></script>
  <script src="development-bundle/ui/
jquery.ui.widget.js"></script>
  <script src="development-bundle/ui/
jquery.ui.progressbar.js"></script>
  <script>
    $(document).ready(function($){
      $("#myProgressbar").progressbar();
    });
  </script>
</head>
<body>
  <div id="myProgressbar"></div>
</body>
</html>
```

Save this file as `progressbar1.html` in the `jqueryui` project folder. With no configuration, the progressbar is, of course, empty. Our example should appear like the first screenshot but without any progress displayed (the container is empty).

The progress bar depends on the following components:

- `jquery.ui.all.css`
- `jquery-2.0.3.js`
- `jquery-ui.core.js`
- `jquery-ui.progressbar.js`

All we need on the page is a simple container element. In this case we've used a `<div>` element, but other block-level elements, such as a `<p>` for example, can also be used. The widget will add a nested `<div>` element to the specified container element at initialization that represents the value of the progressbar.

This widget, like some of the other widgets, such as the accordion, will naturally fill the width of its container. Other widgets that also work in a similar way are tabs, accordion, slider, and menu—each of these equally need some form of container to restrict their size on screen. Both the container and the inner `<div>` element are given a series of attributes and class names by the component. The class names pick up styling from the theme file in use, and the component is fully ThemeRoller-ready. Being ThemeRoller-ready means that your chosen theme can easily be changed with another jQuery ThemeRoller theme, and that widgets will still function without any changes required to styling.

The additional attributes added to the widget are ARIA compliant, making the widget fully accessible to visitors using assisted technologies. **ARIA (Accessible Rich Internet Applications)** defines ways of making web content more accessible to those with assistive technologies such as screen the readers. All jQuery widgets have varying levels of support for ARIA, including a progressbar; this is provided through the use of additional tags that appear in your code, such as these (highlighted in the following code):

```
<div id="myProgressbar" class="ui-progressbar ui-widget ui-widget-
content ui-corner-all" role="progressbar" aria-valuemin="0" aria-
valuemax="100" aria-valuenow="20">
```

These help translate code into content that assistive technologies will understand; without them, the code is effectively hidden, which will affect what the end user will see or hear.

Listing the progressbar's options

The progressbar has three configuration options at the time of writing:

Option	Default Value	Usage
disabled	false	Disable the widget
Max	100	The maximum value of the progressbar
Value	0	Set the value (in percent) of the widget

Setting the progressbar's value

Change the final `<script>` element in `progressbar1.html`, so that it appears as follows:

```
<script>
  $(document).ready(function($){
    $("#myProgressbar").progressbar({
```

```
            value: 50
        });
    });
</script>
```

Save this file as `progressbar2.html`. The `value` option takes an integer and sets the width of the inner `<div>` of the widget to the corresponding percentage. This change will make the widget appear as it did in the first screenshot of this chapter, with the progressbar half-filled.

The progressbar's event API

The progressbar exposes three custom events as shown in the following table:

Event	Fired when...
create	The widget is initialized
change	The widget's value changes
complete	The value of the widget reaches 100 percent

As with the other widgets, we can supply an anonymous callback function as the value of these events in a configuration object, and the component will automatically call the function for us, each time the event fires.

To see this event in action add the following `<button>` to the page in `progressbar2.html`:

```
<p><button id="increase">Increase by 10%</button>
```

Next, change the final `<script>` block to the following:

```
<script>
    $(document).ready(function($){
        var progress = $("#myProgressbar"),
            progressOpts = {
                change: function() {
                    var val = $(this).progressbar("option", "value");
                    if (!$("#value").length) {
                        $("<span />", { text: val + "%", id: "value"})
                    .appendTo(progress);
                } else {
                    $("#value").text(val + "%");
                }
            }
        }
    };
```

```
      progress.progressbar(progressOpts);
      $("#increase").click(function() {
        var currentVal = progress.progressbar("option", "value"),
      newVal = currentVal + 10;
      progress.progressbar("option", "value", newVal);
      });
    });
  </script>
```

Save this file as `progressbar3.html`. We also need to add some styling for our progressbar, so add the following to a new file, saving it as `progressIncrease.css`:

```
#value { margin-top: -28px; margin-right: 10px; float: right; }
```

Don't forget to add a link to the new stylesheet from the `<head>` of our page (after the link to the standard jQuery UI stylesheet):

```
<link rel="stylesheet" href="css/progressIncrease.css">
```

In our example, we first cache the selector for the progressbar, then define an event handler for the `change` event. Within this callback function, we first obtain the current value of the progressbar, which will correspond to the value after its last update. We can select the progressbar using `$(this)` when inside the event handler.

Provided the value is less than or equal to 100 (percent), we check whether there is already an element with an `id` of `value` on the page. If the element doesn't exist (that is, its value has no length), we create a new `<span>` element and set its text to the current value. We also give it an `id` attribute and position it, so that it appears inside the progressbar. If the element already exists, we just update its text to the new value.

> **Use of self-closing shortcut tag selectors**
>
> You may have seen the use of `$("<span />")` in the code; this is a shortcut that jQuery uses to produce the full version of the tags; in this instance, it would encapsulate any content it is passed within `<span>`...`</span>` tags.

We also add a click-handler for the button that we added to the page. Whenever the button is clicked, we first get the current value of the progressbar by using the `option` method in `getter` mode. We then add `10` to the value before using the `option` method in `setter` mode to increase the value of the inner `<div>` by `10` percent. The value is added to a `<span>` element to indicate the progress.

The following screenshot shows the result of clicking on the button:

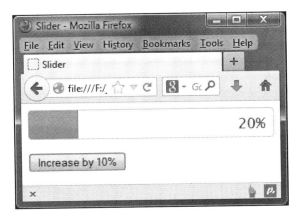

In this example, we set the value of the progressbar manually whenever the **Increase by 10%** button is clicked; we use the standard `option` method, common to all UI library components, to retrieve information about the current state of the progressbar.

Don't forget that like the other library components, this event can be used with jQuery's `on()` method by prefixing the name of the widget onto the event name, for example, `progressbarchange`.

Using progressbar methods

In addition to the common API methods that are exposed by all library components, such as `destroy`, `disable`, `enable`, `widget`, and `option`, the slider API also exposes the `value` method, which is a shortcut for using the `option` method to set the value of the progressbar.

We can do exactly the same as we did in the last example, but with less code, using the `value` method. Change the final `<script>` element in `progressbar3.html`, so that it is as follows:

```
<script>
  $(document).ready(function($){
    var progress = $("#myProgressbar");
    progress.progressbar();
    $("#increase").click(function() {
      var currentVal = progress.progressbar("option", "value"),
      newVal = currentVal + 10;
      progress.progressbar("value", newVal);
      if (!$("#value").length) {
        $("<span />", { text: newVal + "%", id: "value"
```

```
        }).appendTo(progress);
      } else {
        $("#value").text(newVal + "%");
      }
    });
  });
</script>
```

Save this file as `progressbar4.html`. We lose the configuration object in this example, as it isn't required.

The logic for increasing the value using the `value` method has been moved into the click handler for the `<button>` element. Within the event handler, we get the value of `currentVal`, then add `10` to it, and assign that to `newVal`. The `value` attribute of the progressbar widget is updated with the new value; a check is performed to see if the percentage count text exists. If it doesn't (that is, the length of `#value` is zero), then we add a new instance, with the updated figure and display this on screen.

You will notice though, with the move of the update code into the event handler, that this has allowed us to perform the same action as in the previous example, but in a more concise format.

Adding indeterminate support

So far, we've looked at how you can control the percentage value that a progressbar should use, when updating its results. However, there may be instances where this isn't always possible—to allow for this, an indeterminate option can be used. Added in jQuery UI 1.10, this allows for those instances where the value can't be updated, as the final value is not known.

Let's take a look at a couple of examples to compare the difference between setting a known value and an indeterminate one. In `progressbar4.html`, change the `<script>` element to the following code:

```
<script>
  $(document).ready(function($) {
    $("#myprogressbar").progressbar({ value: false });
    $("button").on("click", function(event) {
    var target = $(event.target), progressbar = $("#myprogressbar"),
  progressbarValue = progressbar.find(".ui-progressbar-value");
      if (target.is("#numButton")) {
        progressbar.progressbar("option", { value: Math.floor(Math.
  random() * 100) });
      } else if (target.is("#falseButton")) {
        progressbar.progressbar("option", "value", false);
```

```
    }
  });
});
</script>
```

In the `<body>` element of the code, alter the HTML to the following code:

```
<div id="myprogressbar"></div>
<p>
<button id="numButton">Random Value - Determinate</button>
<button id="falseButton">Indeterminate</button>
```

Save this file as `progressbar5.html`. The following screenshot shows the results of clicking on the **Indeterminate** button:

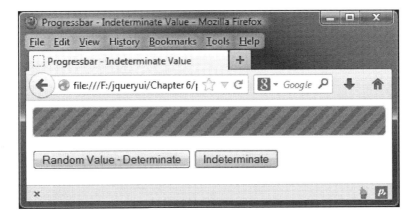

Although it's hard to see it in action in print, the previous example shows a continually moving progressbar at 100 percent; clicking on the **Indeterminate** button sets the value attribute to `false`, which tells the progressbar to assume 100 percent as the value. The automatic setting to 100 percent in this instance is an indicator that we are making progress. As we are unable to get an accurate figure for how much progress has been made at each point, the progressbar widget automatically assumes that the value is 100 percent.

In comparison, if we know the value that the progressbar should use, we can set that value instead. Clicking on the **Random Value - Determinate** button shows the effect of setting such a value as shown in the following screenshot, in a similar fashion to previous examples throughout this chapter:

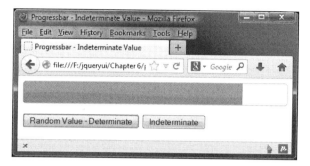

Responding to user interaction

At its most basic level, we can manually update the progressbar in response to user interaction. For example, we could specify a wizard-style form, which has several steps to complete. In this example, we'll create a form as shown in the following screenshot:

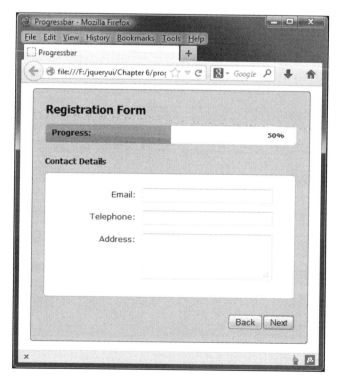

During each step, we can increment the progressbar manually to let the user know how far through the process they are. In `progressbar5.html`, replace the progressbar container and buttons with the following code:

```
<div class="form-container ui-helper-clearfix ui-corner-all">
  <h1>Registration Form</h1>
  <p>Progress:</p>
  <div id="myProgressbar"></div>
  <label id="amount">0%</label>
  <form action="serverScript.php">>
    <div class="form-panel">
      <h2>Personal Details</h2>
      <fieldset class="ui-corner-all">
        <label for="name">Name:</label>
        <input id="name" type="text">
        <label for="dob">D.O.B:</label>
        <input id="dob" type="text">
        <label for="passwrd1">Choose password:</label>
        <input id="passwrd1" type="password">
        <label for="passwrd2">Confirm password:</label>
        <input id="passwrd2" type="password">
      </fieldset>
    </div>
    <div class="form-panel ui-helper-hidden">
      <h2>Contact Details</h2>
      <fieldset class="ui-corner-all">
        <label for="email">Email:</label>
        <input id="email" type="text">
        <label for="tel">Telephone:</label>
        <input id="tel" type="text">
        <label for="address">Address:</label>
        <textarea id="address" rows="3" cols="25"></textarea>
      </fieldset>
    </div>
    <div class="form-panel ui-helper-hidden">
      <h2>Registration Complete</h2>
      <fieldset class="ui-corner-all">
        <p>Thanks for registering!</p>
      </fieldset>
    </div>
  </form>
  <button id="next">Next</button>
  <button id="back" disabled="disabled">Back</button>
</div>
```

Save this file as `progressbar6.html`. In the `<head>` section, we add a link to the framework theme files, as we have done with the other examples in this chapter, and will need to add a link to a custom stylesheet that we'll add in a moment:

```
<link rel="stylesheet" href="css/progressTheme.css">
```

The `<body>` element of the page contains a few layout elements and some text nodes, but the main elements are the container for the progressbar and the `<form>`. The `<form>` section is separated into several different sections using the `<div>` and `<fieldset>` elements. The reason for this is that we can hide the parts of the form to make it appear as if it spans several pages.

We've added a paragraph and a `<label>` parameter next to the progressbar. We'll position these so that they appear inside the widget. The paragraph contains a simple text string. The label will be used to show the current progress value.

The outer container is given several class names; the first is that we can apply some custom styling to the element, but the next two are to target different features of the jQuery UI CSS framework. The `ui-helper-clearfix` class is used to automatically clear floated elements and is a great way of reducing the clutter of additional and unnecessary clearing of the `<div>` elements. Don't forget to make explicit use of this and other framework classes when creating your own widgets.

We covered some of the core CSS classes back in *Chapter 2, The CSS Framework and Other Utilities*; more details of the CSS framework API are available at `http://learn.jquery.com/jquery-ui/theming/api/`.

The `ui-corner-all` class is used to give the container element (as well as the progressbar itself, which has them automatically, and our `<fieldset>` elements) rounded corners, using several proprietary style rules. These are now supported by most modern browsers. We also have a **Next** button to move forward through each panel, and a **Back** button that is disabled by default.

We use another class from the CSS framework within the form. Several panels need to be hidden when the page first loads; we can therefore make use of the `ui-helper-hidden` class to ensure that they are set to `display: none`. When we want to show them, all we have to do is remove this class name.

Now let's add the JavaScript. Change the final `<script>` element at the bottom of the page, so that it appears as follows:

```
$(document).ready(function($){
   var prog = $("#myProgressbar"), progressOpts = {
     change: function() {
```

```
        prog.next().text(prog.progressbar("value") + "%");
      }
    };
    prog.progressbar(progressOpts);
    $("#next, #back").click(function() {
      $("button").attr("disabled", true);
      if (this.id == "next") {
        prog.progressbar("option", "value",
        prog.progressbar("option", "value") + 50);
        $("form").find("div:visible").fadeOut().next()
          .fadeIn(function(){
          $("#back").attr("disabled", false);
          if (!$("form").find("div:last").is(":visible")) {
            $("#next").attr("disabled", false);
          }
        });
      } else {
        prog.progressbar("option", "value", prog.progressbar
        ("option", "value") - 50);
        $("form").find("div:visible").not(".buttons").fadeOut()
        .prev().fadeIn(function() {
          $("#next").attr("disabled", false);
          if (!$("form").find("div:first").is(":visible")) {
            $("#back").attr("disabled", false);
          }
        });
      }
    });
  });
```

We first cache a selector for the progressbar and define our configuration object, making use of the change event to specify an anonymous callback function. Each time the event is fired we'll grab the current value of the progressbar using the value method, and set it as the text of the <label> parameter directly after the progressbar element. The event is fired after the change takes place, so the value we obtain will always be the new value.

Once the progressbar is initialized, we add a click handler for the buttons after the form. Within this handler function, we first disable both of the buttons to prevent the form from breaking if a <button> is repeatedly clicked. We then use an if statement to run the slightly different code branches, depending on the button that was clicked.

If the **Next** button was clicked, we increase the value of the progressbar by 50 percent by setting the `value` option to the current value plus 50 percent. We then fade out the currently visible panel and fade in the next panel. We use a callback function as an argument to the `fadeIn()` method, which will be executed once the animation ends.

Within this function, we re-enable the **Back** button (as it was **Next** that was clicked, it is not possible for the first panel to be visible, and so this button should be enabled) and determine whether to enable the **Next** button, which can be done, provided the last panel is not visible.

The second branch of the outer `if` statement deals with the **Back** button being clicked. In this case, we reduce the progressbar by 50 percent, enable the **Next** button, and check whether the **Back** button should be enabled.

This is now all of the JavaScript that we'll need. All we have to do now is add some basic CSS to lay the example out; in a new file in your text editor add the following code:

```
h1, h2 { font-family: Tahoma; font-size: 140%; margin-top: 0;}
h2 { margin: 20px 0 10px; font-size: 100%; text-align: left; }
p { margin: 0; font-size: 95%; position: absolute; left: 30px;
   top: 60px; font-weight: bold; }
#amount { position: absolute; right: 30px; top: 60px; font-      size:
80%; font-weight: bold; }
#thanks { text-align: center; }
#thanks p { margin-top: 48px; font-size: 160%; position:
   relative; left: 0; top: 0; }
form { height: 265px; position: relative; }
.form-container { width: 400px; margin: 0 auto; position:
   relative; font-family: Verdana; font-size: 80%; padding:
   20px; background-color: #C5DBEC; border: 1px solid #2E6E9E; }
.form-panel { width: 400px; height: 241px; position: absolute;
   top: 0; left: 0; }
fieldset { width: 397px; height: 170px; margin: 0 auto; padding: 22px
0 0; border: 1px solid #abadac; background-color: #ffffff; }
label { width: 146px; display: block; float: left; text-align:
   right; padding-top: 2px; margin-right: 10px; }
   input, textarea { float: left; width: 200px; margin-bottom:
   13px; }
button { float: right; }
```

Save this as `progressTheme.css` in the `css` directory. We should now have a working page with a wired-up progressbar. When we run the page, we should find that we can navigate through each panel of the form, and the progressbar will update itself accordingly.

We're still relying on user interaction to set the value of the progressbar in this example, which is driven by the visitor navigating through each of the panels.

Implementing rich uploads with a progressbar

Instead of relying on user interaction to increase the value of the progressbar and therefore the completion of the specified task, we can instead rely on the system to update it, as long as something is available that can be used to update it accurately.

In our final progressbar example, we can incorporate the HTML5 file API, in order to upload a file asynchronously, and can use the onprogress event to update the progressbar, while the file is uploading.

 At this point, you may like to obtain a copy of the code download that accompanies this book, so that you can work through the code at the same time as you study the example.

This example will only work correctly using a full web server with PHP installed and configured. We won't be looking at the server-side part of the upload process in this example; we're not interested in what happens to the file once it's been uploaded, only in updating the progressbar based on feedback received from the system, while it is uploading.

Change the <body> in progressbar6.html, so that it contains the following elements:

```
<div id="container">
  <h1>HTML5 File Reader API</h1>
  <form id="upload" action="upload.php" method="POST"
  enctype="multipart/form-data">
    <fieldset>
      <legend>Image Upload</legend>
      <input type="hidden" id="MAX_FILE_SIZE" name="MAX_FILE_SIZE"
      value="300000" />
      <div>
        <label for="fileselect">Image to upload:</label>
        <input type="file" id="fileselect" name="fileselect[]"
        multiple="multiple" />
      </div>
      <div id="progress"></div>
    </fieldset>
  </form>
  <div id="messages"></div>
</div>
```

On the page, we have an `<input>` element of the `file` type, followed by the container for the progressbar as usual. Next, let's add the script; change the final `<script>` element at the end of `<head>` to the following code:

```
$("document").ready(function($) {
  if (window.File && window.FileList && window.FileReader) {
    $("#fileselect").on("change", function(e) {
      var files = e.target.files || e.dataTransfer.files;
      for (var i = 0, f; f = files[i]; i++) {
        ParseFile(f);
        UploadFile(f);
      }
    });
  }
});
```

Save this file as `progressbar7.html`. Add the following code to a new document, and save it as `uploads.js`:

```
function ParseFile(file) {
  $("#messages").html(
    "<p>File information: <strong><br>" +
    "</strong> type: <strong>" + file.type + "<br>" +
    "</strong> size: <strong>" + file.size +
    "</strong> bytes</p>"
  );

  if (file.type.indexOf("image") === 0) {
    var reader = new FileReader();
    reader.onload = function(e) {
      $("#messages").prepend(
        "<br>Image:<br><strong>" + file.name + "</strong><br />" +
        '<img class="preview" src="' + e.target.result + '"
        /></p>'
      );
    };
    reader.readAsDataURL(file);
  }
}

function UploadFile(file) {
  $("#progress").progressbar();
  var xhr = new XMLHttpRequest();
  xhr.upload.onprogress = function updateProgress(e) {
    var fileloaded = (e.loaded / e.total);
```

```
  $("#progress").progressbar("value", Math.round(fileloaded *
    100));
};

xhr.upload.onload = function() {
  $("#progress").progressbar("value", 100);
};

xhr.open("POST", $("#upload").action, true);
xhr.setRequestHeader("X_FILENAME", file.name);
xhr.send(file);
}
```

Finally, add the following immediately below the links to jQuery UI in the `<head>` element of your document:

```
<script type="text/javascript" src="js/uploads.js"></script>
```

First of all, in `progressbar7.html` we perform a check to confirm if the browser supports the File API; if it can, then we instigate an event handler that fires as soon as the `fileselect` button is clicked.

Within the change handler, we get details of the files selected and save them to an array; we then call out to the `ParseFile()` function (in `uploads.js`) to first initiate the output messages, then to load and read a copy of the image using `FileReader()`, and output a copy of the image to screen. At the same time, we display details of the image name.

Moving on to `uploads.js`, we then shell out to the `UploadFile` function, which is where the real magic happens. We begin by initiating an instance of the progressbar, give it the `progress` ID, and using a `<div>` element as its container. The code then sets up an instance of `XMLHttpRequest()` and opens a `POST` connection in order to upload the file. In this instance, the file is actually only uploaded to a test folder on the server (or in this case, your PC), called uploads; it's at this point where you would create an upload script that would redirect the file to the appropriate location on the remote server.

Each time the `XMLHttpRequest` parameter is updated, it fires the `onprogress` event handler to update the progressbar; we calculate the difference between the total file size and the uploaded content, then convert it to a percentage and use this to update the progressbar. Once the upload is completed, we fire the `onload()` event handler to ensure it shows 100 percent completion.

We also need a bit of CSS for this example; in a new text file add the following code:

```
body { font-family: "Segoe UI", Tahoma, Helvetica, Freesans,
    sans-serif; font-size: 90%; margin: 10px; color: #333;
    background-color: #fff; }
#container { margin-left: auto; margin-right: auto; width: 430px;  }
#messages { padding: 0 10px; margin: 1em 0; border: 1px solid #999;
width: 400px; clear: both; height: 275px; }
#messages p { position: absolute; float: left; margin-left:
    275px; width: 150px; }
#progress { margin-top: 3px; width: 390px; left: -2px; }
h1 { font-size: 1.5em; font-weight: normal; }
legend { font-weight: bold; color: #333; }
.preview { height: 60%; width: 60%; float: left; }
fieldset { width: 400px; }
```

This file can be saved in the css folder as uploads.css. Mostly the styles just position the various elements and set the width of the progressbar. We also don't need the link to progressTheme.css, so this can be removed as well.

When we run this file, we should see that once a file has been selected, it will automatically begin to upload, and the progressbar will begin to fill up. If testing locally, it will be pretty quick, so it's best tested with reasonably large files.

The following screenshot shows the page once the upload has completed:

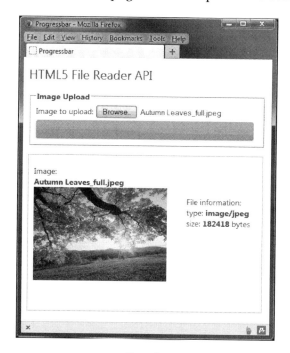

Summary

In this chapter, we've looked at two interface widgets that can both provide some form of visual feedback, either as result of an operation, or to set a particular value. We saw how quickly and easily it can put a slider widget on the page, and that it requires minimal underlying markup and just a single line of code to initialize.

We explored the different options that we can set, to control how the slider behaves and how it is configured once it's initialized, while providing callbacks that can be used to execute code at important times during an interaction. We also covered the range of methods that can be used to programmatically interact with the slider, including methods for setting the value of the handle(s), or getting and setting configuration options after initialization.

We also looked at the progressbar widget with a compact API that provides essential visitor feedback when processes are in progress. We then looked into the various options that can be used to configure the widget, prior to initialization, or once the widget is in use. We also examined the methods available for working with the progressbar widget, to see how we can easily react to changes in progress, or once the widget has completed.

We also looked at how the progressbar includes support for an indeterminate progress indicator, for use when the current status of the process cannot be accurately determined.

In the next chapter, we will look at the datepicker widget, which has the biggest, most feature-packed API of any widget in the library and includes full internationalization.

7
The Datepicker Widget

The jQuery UI datepicker widget is probably the most refined and documented widget found in jQuery library. It has the biggest **Application programming interface (API)** and probably provides the most functionality out of all the widgets. It not only works completely out of the box, but is also highly configurable and robust.

Quite simply, the datepicker widget provides an interface that allows visitors of your site or application to select dates. Wherever a form field is required that asks for a date to be entered, the datepicker widget can be added. This means your visitors get to use an attractive and engaging widget, and you get dates in the format in which you expect them.

In this section, we will look at the following topics:

- The default datepicker implementation
- Exploring the configurable options
- Implementing a trigger button
- Configuring alternative animations
- The `dateFormat` option
- Easy localization
- Multiple month datepickers
- Data-range selection
- Datepicker widget's methods
- Using AJAX with the datepicker

Additional functionality built into the datepicker includes automatic opening and closing animations along with the ability to navigate the interface of the widget using the keyboard. While holding down the *Ctrl* key (or command key on Mac), the arrows on the keyboard can be used to choose a new day cell, which can then be selected using the return key.

While easy to create and configure, the datepicker is a complex widget made up of a wide range of underlying elements, as shown in the following figure:

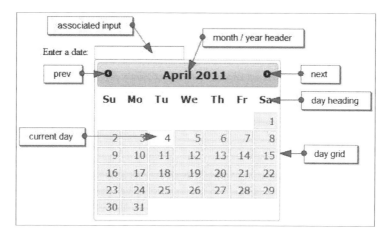

 Despite this complexity, we can implement the default datepicker with just a single line of code, much like the other widgets in the library that we have covered so far.

Implementing the datepicker widget

To create the default datepicker, add the following code to a new page in your text editor:

```
<!DOCTYPE html>
<html>
<head>
  <meta charset = "utf-8">
  <title>Datepicker</title>
  <link rel="stylesheet" href="development-bundle/themes/redmond/
jquery.ui.all.css">
  <script src="js/jquery-2.0.3.js"></script>
  <script src="development-bundle/ui/jquery.ui.core.js"></script>
  <script src="development-bundle/ui/jquery.ui.widget.js"></script>
```

```
<script src="development-bundle/ui/jquery.ui.datepicker.js"> </script>
  <script>
    $(document).ready(function($){
      $("#date").datepicker();
    });
  </script>
</head>
<body>
  <label for="date">Enter a date:</label>
  <input id="date" />
</body>
</html>
```

Save this as `datePicker1.html` in the `jqueryui` project folder. All we have on the page is a `<label>` and a standard text `<input>` element. We don't need to specify any empty container elements for the datepicker widget to be rendered into, as the markup required to create the widget is automatically added by the library.

 Although it might be tempting to use the HTML5 `type="date"` attribute in your `<input>` statements, it is not recommended—this can cause conflicts where it shows both jQuery UI datepickers at the same time as the native HTML5 version.

When you run the page in your browser and focus on the `<input>` element, the default datepicker should appear beneath the input. Along with an `<input>` element, the datepicker can also be attached to a `<div>` element.

Apart from looking great, the default datepicker also comes with a lot of built-in functionality. When the datepicker opens, it is smoothly animated from zero to full size, and it will automatically be set to the present date. Selecting a date will automatically add the date to the `<input>` and close the calendar (again with a nice animation).

With no additional configuration and a single line of code, we now have a perfectly usable and attractive widget that makes date selection easy. If all you want is to let people pick a date, this is all that you need. The source files required for the default datepicker are as follows:

- `jquery-2.0.3.js`
- `jquery.ui.core.js`
- `jquery.ui.widget.js`
- `jquery.ui.datepicker.js`

Selecting dates using inline calendars

We've created a basic datepicker widget, which we've linked into a normal text `<input>` box. While this will work perfectly fine, there may be instances where you don't want to use a normal input box, and just need to display the calendar already open within your page.

Fortunately this is easy to achieve using the datepicker widget. Change the HTML code to use `<div>` elements as shown in the following code:

```
<body>
   Enter a date: <div id="date"></div>
</body>
```

If we preview the results in a browser, you will notice that the input textbox has disappeared, and that the calendar is already displayed in full:

Configurable options of the datepicker

The datepicker has a large range of configurable options (currently 50 to be exact). The following table lists the basic options, their default values, and gives a brief description of their usage:

Option	Default value	Usage
altField	" "	Specifies a CSS selector for an alternative `<input>` field to which the selected date is also added.
altFormat	" "	Specifies an alternative format for the date added to the alternative `<input>`. See the `dateFormat` option in the later section for clarification on the value this option takes.
appendText	" "	Adds text after datepicker `<input>` to show the format of the selected date.
autoSize	false	Automatically sets the width of the `<input>` element so that it can accommodate a date according to the specified `dateFormat`.
beforeShow	null	Allows the datepicker configuration object to update the datepicker just before it is called.
beforeShowDay	null	Takes a date as a parameter, and returns values to indicate if the date is selectable, the class name to add to the date's cell, and an (optional) pop-up tooltip for the date. The function is called for each day in the datepicker, before it is displayed.
buttonImage	" "	Specifies a path to the image to use for the trigger `<button>`.

Option	Default value	Usage
buttonImageOnly	false	Sets to `true` to use an image instead of a trigger button.
buttonText	"..."	Provides text to display on a trigger <button> (if present).
calculateWeek	$.datepicker. iso8601Week	Accepts a function, used to calculate the week of the year for a specified date.
changeMonth	false	Show the month change dropdown.
changeYear	false	Show the year change dropdown.
closeText		
constrainInput	true	Constrains the <input> element to the format of the date, specified by the widget.
currentText	"Today"	The text to display for the current day link. This option must be used in conjunction with the showButtonPanel attribute to display this button.
dateFormat		The format to use for parsed and displayed dates. A full list of formats is displayed in the *Changing the date format* section later in this chapter.
dayNames	["Sunday", "Monday", "Tuesday", "Wednesday", "Thursday", "Friday", "Saturday"]	The list of long day names to be used in conjunction with the dateFormat attribute.
dayNamesMin	["Su", "Mo", "Tu", "We", "Th", "Fr", "Sa"]	An array that contains the minimized date names that show on the column headers in the datepicker widget. This can be localized, as we will see later in this chapter.

Option	Default value	Usage
dayNamesShort	["Sun", "Mon", "Tue", "Wed", "Thu", "Fri", "Sat"]	The list of abbreviated day names, for use with the dateFormat attribute of the widget.
defaultDate	null	Sets the date that will be highlighted when the datepicker opens and the <input> element is empty.
duration	"normal"	Sets the speed at which the datepicker opens.
firstDay	0	Sets the first day of the week, beginning with 0 for Sunday, through to 6 for Saturday.
gotoCurrent	false	Sets the current day link to move the datepicker widget to the currently selected date instead of today.
hideIfNoPrevNext	false	Hides the previous/next links when not needed, instead of disabling them.
isRTL	false	Controls whether the language used is drawn from right to left.
maxDate	null	Sets the maximum date that can be selected. Accepts a date object or a relative number. For example: +7, or a string such as +6m.
minDate	null	Sets the minimum date that can be selected. Accepts a number, date object, or string.
monthNames	Array of month names, for example ["January", "February", "March"...]	Sets the full list of month names, for use with the dateFormat attribute in the widget.
monthNamesShort	Array of abbreviated month names, such as ["Jan", "Feb", "Mar"...]	Sets the list of abbreviated month names for use in each month header within the datepicker widget, as specified by the dateFormat attribute.

Option	Default value	Usage
navigationAsDateFormat	false	Allows us to specify month names using the previous, next, and current links.
nextText	"Next"	Sets the text to display for the next month link.
numberOfMonths	1	Sets the number of months shown on a single datepicker widget.
onChangeMonthYear	Function	Called when datepicker moves to a new month or year.
onClose	Function	Called when the datepicker widget is closed, irrespective of whether a date has been selected.
onSelect	Function	Called when the datepicker widget has been selected.
prevText	"Prev"	Sets the text to display for the previous month link.
selectOtherMonths	false	Allows days in previous or following months that are shown on the current month's panel (see the showOtherMonths option) to be selected.
shortYearCutoff	"+10"	Determines the current century while using the year representation; numbers less than this are deemed to be in the current century.
showAnim	"show"	Sets the animation used when the datepicker widget is displayed.
showButtonPanel	false	Shows a panel of buttons for the datepicker widget, consisting of close and current links.
showCurrentAtPos	0	Sets the position of the current month in multiple-month datepickers
showOn	"focus"	Sets the event that triggers displaying the datepicker.

Option	Default value	Usage
showOptions	{}	An object literal containing options to control the configured animation.
showOtherMonths	false	Shows the last and first days of the previous and next months.
showWeek	false	Displays a column showing the week of the year. The week is determined using the calculateWeek option.
stepMonths	1	Sets how many months are navigated with the previous and next links.
weekHeader	"Wk"	Sets the text to display for the week of the year column heading.
yearRange	"-10:+10"	Specifies the range of years in the year dropdown.

We will explore some of these options in detail throughout this chapter.

Using the basic options

Change the final `<script>` element in `datepicker1.html` to the following:

```
<script>
  $(document).ready(function($){
    $("#date").datepicker({
      appendText: "  (mm/dd/yy)",
      defaultDate: "+5",
      showOtherMonths: true
    });
  });
</script>
```

Save this as `datePicker2.html`. The following screenshot shows how the widget will look after configuring these options:

We've used a number of options in this example simply because there are so many options available. The appearance of the initial page, before the datepicker is even shown, can be changed using the `appendText` option. This adds the specified text string using a `<span>` element directly after the `<input>` field, which is associated with the picker. This helps visitors to clarify the format that will be used for the date.

For styling purposes, we can target the new `<span>` element using the `.ui-datepicker-append` class name.

The `defaultDate` option sets which date is highlighted in the datepicker when it opens initially and the `<input>` element is empty. We've used the relative `+5` string in this example, so that when the datepicker widget opens initially, the date five days from the current date is selected. Pressing the *Enter* key on the keyboard will select the highlighted date.

Along with a relative string, we can also supply `null` as the value of `defaultDate` to set it to the current date (today subjectively), or a standard JavaScript date object.

As we can see in the previous screenshot, the styling of the datepicker widget date for the current date is different from the styling used to show the default date. This will vary between themes, but for reference, the current date is shown in bold against a light shade (orange), while the selected date has a darker border than normal dates with the default theme.

Once a date has been selected, subsequent openings of the datepicker widget will show the selected date as the default date, which again has different styling (a preselected date with the redmond theme will be light blue).

By setting the `showOtherMonths` option to `true`, we've added grayed-out (nonselectable) dates from the previous and next months to the empty squares that sit at the beginning and end of the date grid, before and after the current month. These are visible in the previous screenshot and are rendered in a much lighter color than the selectable dates.

Minimum and maximum dates

By default, the datepicker will go forward or backward infinitely, there are no upper or lower boundaries. If we want to restrict the selectable dates to a particular range, we can do it easily using the `minDate` and `maxDate` options. Change the configuration object in `datePicker2.html` to the following:

```
$("#date").datepicker({
  minDate: new Date(),
  maxDate: "+10"
});
```

Save this as `datePicker3.html`. In this example, we supply a standard, unmodified JavaScript date object to the `minDate` option, which will set the minimum date to the current date. This will make any dates in the past unselectable.

For the `maxDate` option, we use a relative text string of +10, which will make only the current date and the next 10 dates selectable. You can see how these options affect the appearance of the widget in the following screenshot:

The `minDate` and `maxDate` options can also take strings such as `+6w`, `-10m`, or `1y`, which represent weeks, months, and years respectively. You can find more details on how to set these options at `http://api.jqueryui.com/datepicker/#option-minDate` and `http://api.jqueryui.com/datepicker/#option-maxDate`.

Changing the elements in the datepicker UI

The datepicker API exposes a number of options directly related to adding or removing additional UI elements within the datepicker. To show `<select>` elements that allow the visitor to choose the month and year, we can use the `changeMonth` and `changeYear` configuration options:

```
$("#date").datepicker({
    changeMonth: true,
    changeYear: true
});
```

Save this as `datePicker4.html`. Using the month and year `<select>` elements, gives the user a much quicker way to navigate to dates that may be far in the past or future. The following screenshot shows how the widget will appear with these two options enabled:

By default, the year select box will include the previous and next 10 years, covering a total range of 20 years. We can navigate further than this using the previous/next arrow links, but if we know beforehand that visitors may be choosing dates very far in the past or future, we can change the range of years using the `yearRange` option:

```
$("#date").datepicker({
  changeMonth: true,
  changeYear: true,
  yearRange: "-25:+25"
});
```

Save this as `datePicker5.html`. This time when we run the page, we should find that the year range now covers 50 years in total.

Another change we can make to the UI of the datepicker is to enable the button panel, which adds two buttons to the footer of the widget. Let's see it in action.

Change the configuration object in `datepicker5.html`, so that it appears as follows:

```
$("#date").datepicker({ showButtonPanel: true })
```

Save this as `datePicker6.html`. The buttons added to the foot of the widget appear exactly as the buttons in a dialog widget, as you can see in the following screenshot:

The **Today** button will instantly navigate the datepicker back to the month showing the current date, while the **Done** button will close the widget without selecting a date.

We could also change the **Today** button so that it goes to the selected date instead of the current date using the `gotoCurrent` option; we can achieve this by adding it into the configuration object for the widget, as follows:

```
$("#date").datepicker({
    showButtonPanel: true,
    gotoCurrent: true
});
```

If you select a date, then scroll through a number of months, you can then return to the selected date by clicking on the **Today** button.

Adding a trigger button

By default, the datepicker is opened when the `<input>` element that it is associated with receives focus. However, we can change this very easily, so that the datepicker opens when a button is clicked instead. The most basic type of `<button>` can be enabled with just the `showOn` option. Change the configuration object in `datePicker6.html`, so that it is as follows:

```
$("#date").datepicker({
    showOn: "button"
});
```

Save this as `datePicker7.html`. Setting the `showOn` option to `true` in our configuration object will automatically add a simple `<button>` element directly after the associated `<input>` element. We can also set this option to both, so that it opens when the `<input>` is focused as well as when the `<button>` is clicked.

The datepicker will now open only when the `<button>` is clicked, rather than when the `<input>` is focused. This option also accepts the string value "both", which opens the widget when the `<input>` is focused and when the `<button>` is clicked. The new `<button>` is shown in the following screenshot:

The default text shown on the `<button>` (an ellipsis) can easily be changed by providing a new string as the value of the `buttonText` option; change the previous configuration object to this:

```
$("#date").datepicker({
  showOn: "button",
  buttonText: "Open Calendar"
});
```

Save this as `datePicker8.html`. Now, the text on the `<button>` should match the value that we set as the `buttonText` option:

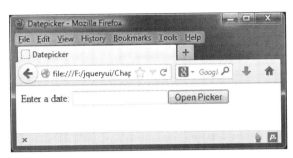

Instead of using text as the label of the `<button>` element, we can use an image. This is configured using the `buttonImage` option:

```
$("#date").datepicker({
  showOn: "button",
  buttonText: "Open Calendar",
  buttonImage: "img/cal.png"
});
```

Save this as `datePicker9.html`. The value of the `buttonImage` option is a string, consisting of the path to the image that we'd like to use on the button. Notice that we also set the `buttonText` option in this example too. The reason for this is that the value of the `buttonText` option is automatically used as the `title` and `alt` attributes of the `<img>` element, that is, added to the `<button>`.

Our trigger button should now look as shown in the following screenshot:

In this example, we've deliberately not styled the button at this point, and concentrated on just adding a logo. You could however style it using jQuery UI, as we will see in *Chapter 8, The Button and Autocomplete Widgets*.

We don't need to use a button at all if we don't want to; we can replace the `<button>` element with an `<img>` element instead. Change the configuration object in `datePicker9.html`, so that it appears as follows:

```
$("#date").datepicker({
  showOn: "button",
  buttonImage: "img/date-picker/cal.png",
  buttonText: "Open Calendar",
  buttonImageOnly: true
});
```

Save this as `datePicker10.html`. This should give you a nice image-only button, as illustrated in the following screenshot:

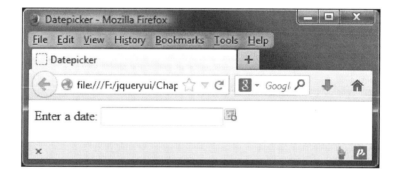

Configuring alternative animations

The datepicker widget comes with an attractive built-in opening animation that makes the widget appear to grow from nothing to full size. Its flexible API also exposes several options related to animations. These are the `duration`, `showAnim`, and `showOptions` configuration options.

The simplest animation configuration that we can set is the speed at which the widget opens and closes. To do this, all we have to do is change the value of the `duration` option. This option requires a simple string that can take a string value of either `slow`, `normal` (the default), or `fast`, or a number representing a duration in milliseconds.

Change the configuration object in `datePicker10.html` to the following:

```
$("#date").datepicker({
  duration: "fast"
});
```

Save this variation as `datePicker11.html`. When we run this page in a browser, we should find that the opening animation is visibly faster.

Along with changing the speed of the animation, we can also change the animation itself using the `showAnim` option. The default animation used is a simple show animation, but we can change this so that it uses any of the other show/hide effects included with the library (refer to *Chapter 14, UI Effects*). Change the configuration object from the previous example to the following:

```
$("#date").datepicker({
  showAnim: "drop",
  showOptions: {direction: "up"}
});
```

Save this as `datePicker12.html`. We also need to use two new `<script>` resources to use alternative effects. These are the `jquery.ui.effect.js` and the source file of the effect we wish to use, in this example, `jquery.ui.effect-drop.js`. We'll look at both of these effects in more detail in *Chapter 14, UI Effects*, but they are essential for this example to work. Make sure you add these to the file, directly after the source file for the datepicker:

```
<script src="development-bundle/ui/jquery.ui.datepicker.js">
</script>
<script src="development-bundle/ui/jquery.ui.effect.js"></script>
<script src="development-bundle/ui/jquery.ui.effect-drop.js"></script>
```

Our simple configuration object configures the animation to drop using the `showAnim` option, and sets the `direction` option of the effect using `showOptions`, which is required due to the datepicker's absolute positioning. When you now run this example, the datepicker should drop down into position instead of opening. Other effects can be implemented in the same way.

Displaying multiple months

So far, all of our examples have looked at single-month datepickers, where only one month was shown at a time. However, we can easily adjust this to show a different number of months, if we wish using a couple of configuration options. Remove the effect source files before the configuration object in `datePicker12.html`, and change the configuration object so that it appears as follows:

```
$("#date").datepicker({
  numberOfMonths: 3
});
```

Save this as `datePicker13.html`. The `numberOfMonths` option takes an integer representing the number of months that we would like to be displayed in the widget at any point. Our datepicker should now appear like this:

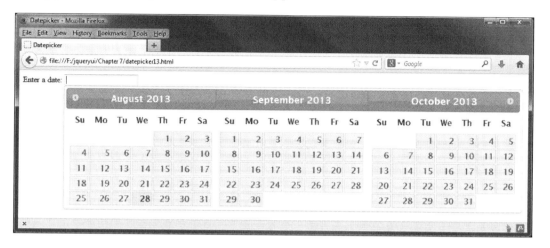

 There is no upper limit to the number of months that will be displayed; however, the performance of the widget decreases with each additional month shown. There is also a noticeable lag between focusing the `<input>` and the widget being displayed.

Also, the individual month panels are floated side-by-side, and due to their size, they will soon overflow the viewport causing a horizontal scroll bar to appear. However, as soon as the scroll bar is used, the datepicker will close, making any months that go beyond the boundary of the screen unusable. For these reasons, it's best to keep the number of months displayed to a minimum.

There are several other configuration options related to multiple-month datepickers. The `stepMonths` option controls how many months are changed when the previous or next links are used.

The default value of `stepMonths` is 1, so in our previous example, the widget starts with the current month displayed first and the next two months after it. Each time the **Previous** or **Next** icons are clicked; the panels move one space left or right.

If we set `stepMonths` to 3, the same as the number of months shown, each month will move three spaces left or right when the previous or next links are clicked, so entirely new panels are shown on each click.

The `showCurrentAtPos` option specifies where the current month is shown when the datepicker is displayed. In our previous example, the current month is shown as the first month panel. Each month panel has a zero-based index number, so if we want the current month to be in the middle of the widget, we would set this option to `1` instead.

Displaying the datepicker vertically

In the previous example, it was noted that the use of multiple months should be kept to a minimum, as we cannot change the styling used for the width, if the calendar goes too far to the right.

We can mitigate this to an extent, by adapting the `numberofMonths` option. It takes two attributes: the first is to control the number of months we display, and the second is for the number of columns that should be used. If we set the example from `datepicker13.html` accordingly, this is how it could look when set to show two months in a single column:

To achieve this effect, all we need to do is to change the configuration object in datepicker13.html as follows:

```
$("#date").datepicker({
  numberOfMonths: [2, 1]
});
```

You will see that the datepicker now only displays two calendar months, and that these are now in a vertical format. We could then use a little jQuery to get the size of the window, and set the numberOfMonths attribute depending on the size returned:

```
function responsive(){
  var winWidth = $(window).width();
   if((winWidth < 991)&&(winWidth >= 768)) {
    // tablet
    $("#date").datepicker("option", "numberOfMonths", [ 2, 1 ]);
  } else {
    //desktop
    $("#date").datepicker("option", "numberOfMonths", 2 );
  }
}
```

 It isn't possible to achieve the same effect manually using CSS; while most styles can be altered, the container width is hardcoded into the library and cannot be altered.

Changing the date format

The dateFormat option is one of the localization options at our disposal for advanced datepicker locale configuration. Setting up this option allows you to quickly and easily set the format of selected dates (as displayed in the <input>) using a variety of short-hand references. The format of dates can be a combination of any of the following characters (they are case sensitive):

- **d**: This is the day of month (single digit where applicable)
- **dd**: This is the day of month (two digits)
- **m**: This is the month of year (single digit where applicable)
- **mm**: This is the month of year (two digits)
- **y**: This is the year (two digits)
- **yy**: This is the year (four digits)
- **D**: This is the short day name

- **DD**: This is the full day name
- **M**: This is the short month name
- **MM**: This is the long month name
- **'...'**: This is any literal text string
- **@**: This is the UNIX timestamp (milliseconds since January 1, 1970)

We can use these shorthand codes to quickly configure our preferred date format, as in the following example. Change the configuration object in `datePicker13.html` to the following:

```
$("#date").datepicker({
    dateFormat:"d MM yy"
});
```

Save the new file as `datePicker14.html`. We use the `dateFormat` option to specify a string containing the shorthand date code for our preferred date format. The format we set is the day of the month (using a single digit if possible) with `d`, the full name of the month with `MM`, and the full four-digit year with `yy`.

When dates are selected and added to the associated `<input>`, they will be in the format specified in the configuration object, as shown in the following screenshot:

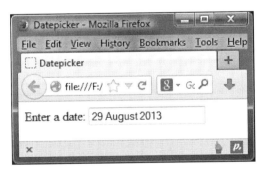

While using a string as the value of this option to configure dates, we can also specify whole strings of text. However, if we do and any letters in the string are those used as shorthand, they will need to be escaped using single quotes.

For example, to add the string `Selected:` to the start of the date, we would need to use the string `Selecte'd':` to avoid having the lowercase `d` picked up as the short day of month format:

```
$("#date").datepicker({
    dateFormat:"Selecte'd': d MM yy"
});
```

Save this change as `datePicker15.html`. Notice how we escape the lowercase `d` in the string `Selected` by wrapping it in single quotes. Now when a date is selected, our text string is prefixed to the formatted date:

Styling the <input> tag

You may want to add `width: 15em` as a style for the input box, so you can see the whole text clearly. I've added this into the code file available in the download that accompanies this book.

There are also a number of built-in preconfigured date formats that correspond to common standards or RFC notes. These formats are added to the components as constants and can be accessed via the `$.datepicker` object. As an example, let's format the date according to the ATOM standard:

```
$("#date").datepicker({
    dateFormat: $.datepicker.ATOM
});
```

Save this as `datePicker16.html`. When a date is selected in this example, the value entered into the `<input>` should be in the format as shown in the following screenshot:

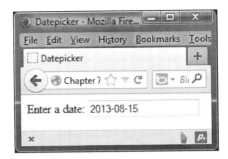

 The ATOM format or RFC 3339/ISO 8601 as it is technically known, is an international standard designed to provide a clear format for dates and times to avoid misinterpretation, especially when data is transferred between countries that use different date formats.

The complete set of predefined date formats is listed in the following table:

Option value	Shorthand	Formatted as...
`$.datepicker.ATOM`	`"yy-mm-dd"`	**2013-07-25**
`$.datepicker.COOKIE`	`"D, dd M y"`	**Wed, 25 Jul 2013**
`$.datepicker.ISO_8601`	`"yy-mm-dd"`	**2013-07-25**
`$.datepicker.RFC_822`	`"D, d M y"`	**Wed, 25 Jul 11**
`$.datepicker.RFC_850`	`"DD, dd-M-y"`	**Wednesday, 25-Jul-11**
`$.datepicker.RFC_1036`	`"D, d M y"`	**Wed, 25 Jul 11**
`$.datepicker.RFC_1123`	`"D, d M yy"`	**Wed, 25 Jul 2013**
`$.datepicker.RFC_2822`	`"D, d M yy"`	**Wed, 25 Jul 2013**
`$.datepicker.RSS`	`"D, d M y"`	**Wed, 25 Jul 13**
`$.datepicker.TIMESTAMP`	`@ (UNIX timestamp)`	**1302649200000**
`$.datepicker.W3C`	`"yy-mm-dd"`	**2013-07-25**

Updating an additional input element

There may be times when we want to update two `<input>` elements with the selected date, perhaps to show a different date format. The `altField` and `altFormat` options can be used to cater to this requirement. Add a second `<input>` element to the page in `datepicker16.html` with an `id` attribute of `dateAltDisplay`, and then change the configuration object to the following:

```
$("#date").datepicker({
  altField: "#dateAltDisplay",
  altFormat: $.datepicker.TIMESTAMP
});
```

Save this as `datePicker17.html`. The `altField` option accepts a standard jQuery selector as its value, and allows us to select the additional `<input>` element that is updated when the main `<input>` is updated. The `altFormat` option can accept the same formats as the `dateFormat` option. The following screenshot shows how the page should appear, once a date has been selected using the datepicker:

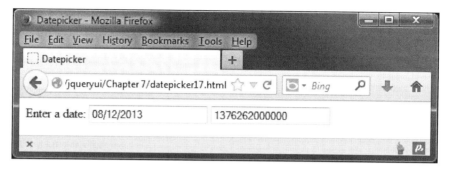

Changing the date format

While using the datepicker widget, you may have noticed that dates returned programmatically through the `getDate` method (see the *Datepicking methods* section) are in the default GMT date and time standard. In order to change the format of the date returned by the API, the `$.datepicker.formatDate()` utility method should be used. Let's take a look at how we can use this function.

In `datePicker17.html`, alter the date configuration object as follows:

```
$("#date").datepicker({
  dateFormat: 'yy-mm-dd',
  onSelect: function(dateText, inst) {
    var d = new Date(dateText);
    var fmt2 = $.datepicker.formatDate("DD, d MM, yy", d);
    $("#selecteddate").html("Selected date: " + fmt2);
  }
});
```

Save this as `datePicker18.html`. We need to add an additional CSS style rule, so that we can see the results of selecting a date within the widget. Add the following to the `<head>` of our file:

```
<style type="text/css">
  #selecteddate { margin-top: 250px; }
</style>
```

If we preview the results in a browser, you will see that the date format used in the initial `<input>` field is set using the `dateFormat` attribute in the configuration object; this was set to `dd-mm-yy`. In the `onSelect` event handler, we use `$.datepicker.` `formatDate` to change the selected date to that shown in the following screenshot:

Localizing the datepicker widget

In addition to the options already listed, there are also a range of localization options. They can be used to provide custom locale support in order to display a datepicker with all the text shown in an alternative language, or to change the default values of words in English.

Those options that are used specifically for localization are listed in the following table:

Option	Default	Usage
closeText	"Close"	Text to display on the close button.
currentText	"Today"	The text to display for the current day link.
dateFormat	"mm/dd/yy"	The format selected dates should take when added to the `<input>`.

Option	Default	Usage
dayNames	["Sunday", "Monday","Tuesday", "Wednesday", "Thursday", "Friday","Saturday"]	An array of names of days in a week.
dayNamesMin	["Su", "Mo", "Tu","We", "Th", "Fr", "Sa"]	An array of two-letter names of days in a week.
dayNamesShort	["Sun", "Mon", "Tue", "Wed", "Thu", "Fri", "Sat"]	An array of abbreviated names of days in a week.
firstDay	0	Specify the first column of days in the datepicker.
isRTL	false	Set the calendar to right-to-left format.
monthNames	["January", "February", "March", "April", "May", "June", "July, "August", "September", "October", "November", "December"]	An array of month names.
monthNamesShort	["Jan", "Feb", "Mar", "Apr", "May", "Jun", "Jul", "Aug", "Sep", "Oct", "Nov", "Dec"]	An array of abbreviated month names.
nextText	"Next"	Text to display on the next link.
prevText	"Prev"	Text to display on the previous link.
showMonthAfterYear	false	Shows the month after the year in the header of the widget.
yearSuffix	""	An additional text string to display after the year in the month header.

A wide range of different translations have already been provided and reside within the `i18n` folder in the `development-bundle/ui` directory. Each language translation has its own source file and to change the default language, all we have to do is include the source file of the alternative language.

In `datePicker17.html`, add the following new `<script>` element directly after the link to `jquery.ui.datepicker.js`:

```
<script src="development-bundle/ui/i18n/jquery.ui.datepicker-fr.js">
</script>
```

Remove the `altField` and `altFormat` attributes of the configuration object:

```
$("#date").datepicker();
```

Save this as `datePicker19.html` and view the results in a browser:

With just a single link to one new resource, we've changed all of the visible text in the datepicker to an alternative language, and we don't even need to set any configuration options. If we wanted to truly internationalize the datepicker, there is even a roll-up file containing all of the alternative languages that we can use, and which avoids the need to include multiple language files.

In `datepicker19.html`, alter the link for `jquery.ui.datepicker-fr.js` in the `<head>` to the following code:

```
<script src="development-bundle/ui/i18n/jquery-ui-i18n.js">
</script>
```

Next, change the configuration object for datepicker as follows:

```
$(document).ready(function($){
  $("#date").datepicker();
  $("#date").datepicker("option", $.datepicker.regional["ar"]);
});
```

Save the file as `datepicker20.html`. If we preview the results in our browser, you will see that it displays the widget in Arabic. We've used datepicker's option attribute to set `$.datepicker.regional` to `ar`, which is jQuery UI's code for the Arabic language:

We will revisit the localization roll-up file later in this chapter, in the *Localizing a datepicker dynamically* example.

Implementing custom localization

Custom localization is also very easy to implement. This can be done using a standard configuration object containing the configured values for the options from the previous table. In this way, any alternative language not included in the roll-up file can be implemented.

For example, to implement a `Lolcat` datepicker, remove the existing configuration object of `datePicker20.html`, and add the following code:

```
$("#date").datepicker({
  closeText: "Kthxbai",
  currentText: "Todai",
  nextText: "Fwd",
  prevText: "Bak",
  monthNames: ["January", "February", "March", "April", "Mai", "Jun",
"July", "August", "Septembr", "Octobr", "Novembr", "Decembr"],
  monthNamesShort: ["Jan", "Feb", "Mar", "Apr", "Mai", "Jun", "Jul",
"Aug", "Sep", "Oct", "Nov", "Dec"],
  dayNames: ["Sundai", "Mondai", "Tuesdai", "Wednesdai", "Thursdai",
"Fridai", "Katurdai"],
  dayNamesShort: ["Sun", "Mon", "Tue", "Wed", "Thu", "Fri", "Kat"],
  dayNamesMin: ["Su", "Mo", "Tu", "We", "Th", "Fr", "Ka"],
  dateFormat: 'dd/mm/yy',
  firstDay: 1,
  isRTL: false,
  showButtonPanel: true
});
```

Save this change as `datePicker21.html`. Most of the options are used to provide simple string substitutions. However, the `monthNames`, `monthNamesShort`, `dayNames`, `dayNamesShort`, and `dayNamesMin` options require arrays.

Notice that the `dayNamesMin` option and other day-related arrays should begin with `Sunday` (or the localized equivalent); here, we've set `Monday` to appear first in this example using the `firstDay` option. Our datepicker should now appear like this:

For those of you curious about the term Lolcat, it is a term dating from 2006, but based on a series of images created in the early twentieth century. It is used to signify a series of cat images that had (albeit grammatically incorrect or idiosyncratic) phrases, intended to create humor. You can learn more about this unique form of humor at `http://en.wikipedia.org/wiki/Lolcat`.

Implementing callbacks

The final set of configuration options is related to the event model exposed by the widget. It consists of a series of callback functions that we can use to specify the code to be executed at different points during an interaction with the datepicker.

These are listed in the following table:

Event	Fired when...
beforeShow	The datepicker is about to open.
beforeShowDay	Each individual date is rendered in the datepicker. Can be used to determine whether the date should be selectable or not.
onChangeMonthYear	The current month or year changes.
onClose	The datepicker is closed.
onSelect	A date is selected.

To highlight how useful these callback properties are, we can extend the previous internationalization example to create a page that allows visitors to choose any available language found in the i18n roll-up file.

Localizing a datepicker dynamically via rollup

Earlier in the book, we took a brief look at how you can use the roll-up file to change the language displayed by the datepicker. This avoids the need to reference multiple language files, which helps reduce HTTP requests to the server; the downside though is that the datepicker widget will always be displayed in the language that has been hardcoded into the widget's attributes.

We can change that though. Let's take a look at how you can use the beforeShow callback by adding a language selection dropdown that displays the datepicker in whichever language is selected.

In datePicker21.html, add the following new <select> box to the page with the following <option> elements. For reasons of brevity, I've only included a few here; you can see the full list in the code download that accompanies this book:

```
<select id="language">
<option id="en-GB">English</option>
<option id="ar">Arabic</option>
<option id="ar-DZ">Algerian Arabic</option>
<option id="az">Azerbaijani</option>
<option id="bg">Bulgarian</option>
<option id="bs">Bosnian</option>
<option id="ca">Catalan</option>
<option id="cs">Czech</option>
...
<option id="en-NZ">English/New Zealand</option>
```

```
<option id="en-US">English/United States</option>
<option id="eo">Esperanto</option>
<option id="es">Spanish</option>
<option id="et">Estonian</option>
<option id="zh-HK">Chinese</option>
<option id="zh-TW">Taiwanese</option>
</select>
```

Next, link to the `i18n.js` roll-up file as follows:

```
<script src="development-bundle/ui/i18n/jquery-ui-i18n.js">
</script>
```

Now change the final `<script>` element so that it appears as follows:

```
<script>
  $(document).ready(function($){
    $("#date").datepicker({
      beforeShow: function() {
        var lang = $(":selected", $("#language")).attr("id");
        $.datepicker.setDefaults($.datepicker.regional[lang]);
      }
    });
    $.datepicker.setDefaults($.datepicker.regional['']);
  });
</script>
```

Save this file as `datePicker22.html`. We use the `beforeShow` callback to specify a function that is executed each time the datepicker is displayed on the screen.

Within this function, we obtain the `id` attribute of the selected `<option>` element, and then pass this to the `$.datepicker.regional` option. This option is set using the `$.datepicker.setDefaults()` utility method.

When the page first loads, the `<select>` element won't have a selected `<option>` child, and because of the order of the `i18n` roll-up file, the datepicker will be set to Taiwanese. In order to set it to default English, we can set the regional utility to an empty string after the datepicker has been initialized.

The following screenshot shows the datepicker after an alternative language has been selected in the `<select>` element:

We can take this a step further; you may have noticed that the language doesn't change until you click inside the `<input>` field to display the widget.

The code works, but feels a little clunky; instead, if we make a change to how we display the widget, we can remove the need to click inside the `<input>` field. I've included an example of how to do this in the code download, as `datepickerXX.html`.

Introducing the utility methods

We used one of the utility methods available in a datepicker in the previous example, `setDefaults` is used to set configuration options on all datepicker instances. In addition to this, there are several other utility methods that we can use; these are shown in the following table:

Utility	Used to...
formatDate	Transform a `date` object into a string in a specified format.
	While using the `dateFormat` option, dates are returned in this specified format using the `formatDate` method. This method accepts three arguments—the format to convert the date to (see `dateFormat` in configurable options of the picker), the `date` object to convert, and an optional configuration object containing additional settings. The following options can be provided: `dayNamesShort`, `dayNames`, `monthNamesShort`, and `monthNames`.

Utility	Used to...
iso8601Week	Return the week number that a specified date falls on according to the ISO 8601 date and time standard. This method accepts a single argument—the date to show the week number.
noWeekends	Make weekend dates unselectable. It can be passed to the beforeShowDay event.
parseDate	Do the opposite of formatDate, converting a formatted date string into a date object. It also accepts three arguments—the expected format of the date to parse, the date string to parse, and an optional setting object containing the following options: shortYearCutoff, dayNamesShort, dayNames, monthNamesShort, and monthNames.
regional	Set the language of the datepicker.
setDefaults	Set configuration options on all datepickers. This method accepts an object literal containing the new configuration options.

All of these methods are called on the singleton instance of the $.datepicker manager object, which is created automatically by the widget on initialization and used to interact with instances of the datepicker. Irrespective of the number of datepickers that have been created on the page as jQuery objects, they will always reference the properties and methods of the first instance of the datepicker widget created on that page.

Listing the datepicker methods

Along with the wide range of configuration options at our disposal, there are also a number of useful methods defined that make working with the datepicker a breeze.

In addition to the shared API methods discussed in *Chapter 1, Introducing jQuery UI*, such as destroy, disable, enable, option, and widget. The datepicker API also exposes the following unique methods:

Method	Used to...
dialog	Open the datepicker in a dialog widget.
getDate	Get the currently selected date.
hide	Programmatically close a datepicker.
isDisabled	Determine whether a datepicker is disabled.
refresh	Redraw the datepicker.
setDate	Programmatically select a date.
show	Programmatically show a datepicker.

Let's take a look at some of these methods in more detail, beginning with selecting dates programmatically.

Selecting a date programmatically

There may be times (such as on dynamic, client-server sites), when we want to be able to set a particular date from within our program logic, without the visitor using the datepicker widget in the usual way. Let's look at a basic example.

Remove the `<select>` element in `datePicker22.html` and directly after the `<input>` element add the following `<button>`:

```
<button id="select">Select +7 Days</button>
```

Now change the final `<script>` element so that it appears like this:

```
<script>
  $(document).ready(function($){
    $("#date").datepicker();
    $("#select").click(function() {
      $("#date").datepicker("setDate", "+7");
    });
  });
</script>
```

Save this as `datePicker23.html`. The `setDate` function accepts a single argument, which is the date to set. As with the `defaultDate` configuration option, we can supply a relative string (as we do in this example) or a date object.

> You can see some of the options available to set the date object at
> `http://api.jqueryui.com/datepicker/#utility-formatDate`.

If we're forced to work with strings as the source for our datepicker, we can easily convert them to a date object; to achieve this, we can use one of the many date JavaScript libraries available such as `Moment.js`. I've included a simple example of how to use this library to generate our date object in the code download that accompanies this book.

Showing the datepicker in a dialog box

The `dialog` method produces the same highly usable and effective datepicker widget, but it displays it in a floating dialog box. The method is easy to use, although it affects the placement of the datepicker dialog; the dialog will appear disconnected from the date input field, as we shall see.

Remove the `<button>` from the page and change the final `<script>` element in `datePicker23.html` to the following code:

```
<script>
  $(document).ready(function($){
    function updateDate(date) {
      $("#date").val(date);
    }
    $("#date").focus(function() {
      $(this).datepicker("dialog", null, updateDate);
    });
  });
</script>
```

Save this as `datePicker24.html`. First we define a function called `updateDate`. This function will be called whenever a date is selected in the datepicker. All we do within this function is to assign the date that is selected, which will be passed to the function automatically to our `<input>` element on the page.

We use the `focus` event to call the `dialog` method, which takes two arguments. In this example, we've supplied `null` as the first argument, so the datepicker defaults to the current date.

The second argument is a callback function to execute when a date is selected, which is mapped to our `updateDate` function.

We can also supply additional third and fourth arguments; the third is the configuration object for the datepicker, and the fourth is used to control the position of the dialog containing the datepicker. By default, it will render the dialog in the center of the screen.

 You can learn more about how to configure these options at
`http://api.jqueryui.com/datepicker/#method-dialog`.

Implementing an AJAX-enabled datepicker

For our final datepicker example, we'll work a little magic into the mix and create a datepicker, which will communicate with a remote server to see if there are any dates that cannot be selected. These dates will then be styled as such within the datepicker widget.

Change the `<body>` of `datepicker24.html`, so that it contains the following markup:

```
<div id="bookingForm" class="ui-widget ui-corner-all">
  <div class="ui-widget-header ui-corner-top">
    <h2>Booking Form</h2>
  </div>
  <div class="ui-widget-content ui-corner-bottom">
    <label for "date">Appointment date:</label>
    <input id="date">
  </div>
</div>
<script>
  $(document).ready(function($){
    var months = [], days = [], x;
    $.getJSON("http://www.danwellman.co.uk/bookedDates.php?
     jsoncallback=?", function(data) {
      for (x = 0; x < data.dates.length; x++) {
        months.push(data.dates[x].month);
        days.push(data.dates[x].day);
      }
    });

    function disableDates(date) {
      for (x = 0; x < days.length; x++) {
        if (date.getMonth() == months[x] - 1 && date.getDate() ==
days[x]) {
          return [false, "preBooked"];
        }
      }
      return [true, ""];
    }

    function noWeekendsOrDates(date) {
      var noWeekend = jQuery.datepicker.noWeekends(date);
      return noWeekend[0] ? disableDates(date) : noWeekend;
    }
```

```
    $("#date").datepicker({
        beforeShowDay: noWeekendsOrDates,
        minDate: "+1"
    });
});
</script>
```

The first part of our script initially declares two empty arrays, and then performs a request to obtain the JSON object from a PHP file. The JSON object contains a single option called dates. The value of this option is an array, where each item is also an object.

Each of these subobjects contain month and day properties, representing one date that should be made unselectable. The months or days array are populated with the values from the JSON object for later use in the script.

Next, we define the `noWeekendsOrDates` callback function that is invoked on the `beforeShowDay` event. This event occurs once for each of the 35 individual day squares in the datepicker. Even the empty squares are included!

The date of each day square is passed to this function, which must determine first if the selected date is not a weekend using jQuery UI's `$.datepicker.noWeekends()` function. If yes, it is automatically passed to the `disableDates` function, otherwise it is marked as being disabled.

If the value is passed to the `disableDates` function, it is passed the date of each square sent to it from the `noWeekendsOrDates` function, and must return an array containing up to two items.

The first is a Boolean indicating whether the day is selectable, and the second is optionally a class name to give the date. Our function loops through each item in our months and days arrays to see if any of the dates passed to the callback function match the items in the arrays. If both the month and day items match a date, the array returns with `false` and a custom class name as its items. If the date does not match, we return an array containing `true` to indicate that the day is selectable. This allows us to specify any number of dates that cannot be selected in the datepicker.

Finally we define a configuration object for the datepicker. The properties of the object are simply the callback function to make the dates specified in the JSON object unselectable, and the `minDate` option, which will be set to the relative value +1, as we don't want people to select dates in the past, or the current day.

In addition to the HTML page, we'll also need a little custom styling. In a new page in your editor, create the following stylesheet:

```
#date { width: 302px; }
#bookingForm { width: 503px; }
#bookingForm h2 { margin-left: 20px; }
#bookingForm .ui-widget-content { padding: 20px 0; border-top:  none;
}
label { margin: 4px 20px 0; font-family: Verdana; font-size: 80%;
float: left; }
.ui-datepicker .preBooked span { color: #ffffff;
background: url(../img/red_horizon.gif) no-repeat; }
```

Save this as `datepickerTheme.css` in the `css` folder. We use PHP to provide the JSON object in response to the request made by our page. If you don't want to install and configure PHP on your web server, you can use the file that I have placed at the URL specified in the example. For anyone that is interested, the PHP used is as follows:

```
<?php
   header('Content-type: application/json');
   $dates = "({
     'dates':[
       {'month':12,'day':2},
       {'month':12,'day':3},
       etc...
     ]
   })";
   $response = $_GET["jsoncallback"] . $dates;
   echo $response;
?>
```

This can be saved as `bookedDates.php` in the main `jqueryui` project folder.

The pre-booked dates are just hardcoded into the PHP file. Again, in a proper implementation, you'd probably need a more robust way of storing these dates, such as in a database.

When we run the page in a browser and open the datepicker, the dates specified by the PHP file should be styled according to our `preBooked` class, and should also be completely nonresponsive, as shown in the following screenshot:

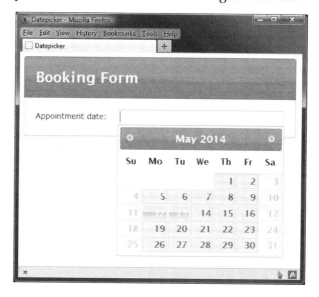

Summary

In this chapter, we looked at the datepicker widget that is supported by one of the biggest APIs in the jQuery UI library. This gives us a huge number of options to work with and methods to receive data from. We first looked at the default implementation and how much behavior is added to the widget automatically.

We looked at the rich API exposed by the datepicker, which includes more configurable options than any other component. We also saw how we can use the utility functions that are unique to the datepicker manager object.

We saw how easy the widget makes implementing internationalization. We also saw that there are 34 additional languages the widget has been translated into. Each of these is packed into a module that is easy to use in conjunction with the datepicker for adding support for alternative languages. We also saw how we create our own custom language configuration.

We covered some of the events that are fired during a datepicker interaction, and looked at the range of methods available for working with and controlling the datepicker from our code.

In the next chapter, we'll look at two of the more recent additions to the library, the button widget and the autocomplete widget.

8
The Button and Autocomplete Widgets

The button and autocomplete widgets are two of the more recent additions to the library, and were released with Version 1.8.

Traditionally, it has been tricky to style the form elements consistently across all browsers and platforms, and to confound this, most browsers and platforms render the form controls uniquely. Both of the widgets covered in this chapter are used to improve some of the traditional form elements that are used on the web.

The button widget allows us to create visually appealing and highly configurable buttons from elements, including the `<button>`, `<input>`, and `<a>` elements that can be styled with themes generated using ThemeRoller. The types of the `<input>` element that are supported include `submit`, `radio`, and `checkbox`. Additional features, such as icons, button sets, and split buttons can be used to further enhance the underlying controls.

The autocomplete widget is attached to a standard text `<input>` and is used to provide a menu of contextual selections. When the visitor begins typing in the `<input>` element, the suggestions that match the characters entered into the control are displayed.

Autocomplete is fully accessible through the keyboard input, allowing the list of suggestions to be navigated with the arrow keys, a selection made with the **Enter** key, and the menu closed with the *Esc* key. When the arrow keys are used to navigate the list of suggestions, each suggestion will be added to the `<input>` element before a selection is made. If the *Esc* key is used to close the menu after the list has been navigated, the value of the `<input>` element will revert to the text entered by the visitor.

In this chapter we will cover the following topics:

- Standard button implementations
- Configurable options
- Adding icons
- Button events
- Button sets
- Button methods
- Using local data sources with autocomplete
- The configurable options of autocomplete
- Autocomplete events
- Unique methods of autocomplete
- Using remote data sources with autocomplete
- Using HTML in the autocomplete suggestions menu

Introducing the button widget

The button widget is used to provide a consistent, fully-themed styling to a range of elements and input types. The widget can be created from several different elements and the resulting DOM of the widget, as well as the features that can be used, will vary slightly depending on which element is used.

A standard button widget, built from either a `<button>`, `<a>`, or `<input>` element with a type of `button`, `submit`, or `reset` will appear as follows:

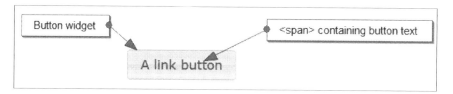

Implementing the standard buttons

As the button can be built from several different elements, there are some minor variations of the underlying code that we can use. When creating buttons using the `<a>`, `<button>`, or `<span>` element will be created automatically by the widget and nested within the underlying element. This new `<span>` will contain the text label of the button.

To create a link button, use the following code:

```
<!DOCTYPE html>
<html>
<head>
  <meta charset="utf-8">
  <title>Button</title>
  <link rel="stylesheet" href="development-bundle/themes/redmond/
jquery.ui.all.css">
  <script src="js/jquery-2.0.3.js"></script>
  <script src="development-bundle/ui/jquery.ui.core.js"></script>
  <script src="development-bundle/ui/jquery.ui.widget.js">
  </script>
  <script src="development-bundle/ui/jquery.ui.button.js">
  </script>
</head>
<body>
  <a href="some_other_page.html" id="myButton">A link button</a>
</body>
</html>
```

Save this file as `button1.html`. The script required to create a button, when using an `<a>` element as the underlying HTML can be as simple as this, which should be added after the last `<script>` element in the previous code:

```
<script>
  $(document).ready(function($){
    $("#myButton").button();
  });
</script>
```

In this case, no special behavior is added to the resulting button; the `<a>` element will simply send the visitor to the new page or anchor specified in the `href` attribute of the anchor. In this case, the widget is simply themed consistently with other jQuery UI widgets that we may be using in the page or site. Markup is automatically added by the widget when compiled in the browser—if you use a DOM inspector such as Firebug, you will see the following code for `button1.html`:

```
<a href="some_other_page.html" id="myButton" class="ui-button
ui-widget ui-state-default ui-corner-all ui-button-text-only"
role="button" aria-disabled="false"><span class="ui-button-text">A
link button</span></a>
```

The button widget requires the following library resources:

- `jquery.ui.all.css`
- `jquery-2.0.3.js`
- `jquery.ui.core.js`
- `jquery.ui.widget.js`
- `jquery.ui.button.js`

Creating buttons using the <input> or <button> tags

We are not limited to just using hyperlinks to create buttons; the button widget will also work with the `<input>` or `<button>` tags.

It is imperative that the `type` attribute of the element is set when using `<input>`, so that the appearance of the button matches that of other buttons created from other underlying elements. For a standard, single button widget, the `type` attribute can be set to be `submit`, `reset`, or `button`.

Creating a button from a `<button>` element is identical to the code used in `button1.html` (except that we don't add a `href` attribute to the `<button>` tag):

```
<button id="myButton">A &lt;button&gt; button</button>
```

Creating a button from an `<input>` element is also very similar except that we use the `value` attribute to set the text on the button instead of adding text content to the `<input>` tag:

```
<input type="button" id="myButton" value="An &lt;input&gt; button">
```

Theming

Like all widgets, the button has a variety of class names added to it, which contribute to its overall appearance. Of course, we can use the theme's class names in our own stylesheets to override the default appearance of the theme in use, if we wish to provide custom styling. ThemeRoller is still usually the best tool for theming buttons.

Exploring the configurable options

The button widget has the following configuration options:

Option	Default Value	Usage
disabled	false	Disables the button instance.
icons	{primary: null, secondary: null}	Sets the icons for the button instance.
label	The content of the underlying element or value attribute	Sets the text of the button instance.
text	true	Hides the text of the button when using an icon-only instance.

In our first example, the text content of the `<a>` element was used as the button's label. We can easily override this using the `label` option. Change the final `<script>` element in `button1.html`, so that it appears as follows:

```
<script>
  $(document).ready(function($){
    $("#myButton").button({
      label: "A configured label"
    });
  });
</script>
```

Save this file as `button2.html`. As we'd expect, when we run this file in a browser, we see that the `<span>` within the button widget takes the configured text as its label, instead of the text content of the `<a>` element.

Adding the button icons

We can easily configure our buttons, so that they have up to two icons in most cases. Whenever an `<a>` or `<button>` element is used as the underlying element for the button, we can use the icons' configuration option to specify one or two icons.

To see icons in action, change the configuration object in `button2.html`, so that it appears as follows:

```
$("#myButton").button({
  icons: {
    primary: "ui-icon-disk",
    secondary: "ui-icon-triangle-1-s"
  }
});
```

Save this file as `button3.html`. The `icons` property accepts an object with up to two keys; `primary` and `secondary`. The values of these options can be any of the `ui-icon-` classes found in the `jquery.ui.theme.css` file. The icons that we set are displayed as shown in the following screenshot:

The icons are added to the widget using additional `<span>` elements, which are automatically created and inserted by the widget. The `primary` icon is displayed to the left of the button text, while the `secondary` icon is displayed to the right of the text.

To generate an icon-only button that has no text label, change the configuration object in `button3.html` to the following code:

```
$("#myButton").button({
   icons: {
      primary: "ui-icon-disk",
      secondary: "ui-icon-triangle-1-s"
   },
   text: false
});
```

Save this file as `button4.html`. When we view this variation in a browser, we see that the button displays only two icons as shown in the following screenshot:

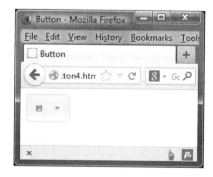

Input icons

As child `<span>` elements are used to display the specified icons, we cannot use icons when using an `<input>` element as an underlying markup for a button instance. We can add our own icons when using the `<input>` elements, by adding an extra container, the required `<span>` elements, and some custom CSS.

Change the `<body>` of `button4.html`, so that it contains the following elements:

```
<div class="iconic-input ui-button-text-icons ui-state-default
uicorner-all">
  <span class="ui-button-icon-primary ui-icon ui-icon-disk">
  </span>
  <input id="myButton" type="button" value="Input icons"
  class="ui-button-text">
  <span class="ui-button-icon-secondary ui-icon ui-icon-triangle-
  1-s"></span>
</div>
```

Save this file as `button5.html`. We'll also need to override some of the button's styling for this example. Create a new stylesheet and add to it the following basic styles:

```
.iconic-input { display: inline-block; position: relative; }
.ui-icon { z-index: 2; }
.iconic-input input { border: none; margin: 0; }
```

 In older versions of Internet Explorer, the `display: inline-block` style will not be applied. To prevent the button taking up the full width of its container, we would need to float it, or set a width explicitly.

Save this file in the `css` directory as `buttonTheme.css`. Don't forget to link to the new stylesheet from the `<head>` element of our page (after the link to the standard jQuery UI stylesheet):

```
<link rel="stylesheet" href="css/buttonTheme.css">
```

Visually our custom `<input>` based widget is complete, but practically it's not quite there; the icons do not pick up the correct hover states (the reason for this is that the widget has applied the required class names to the underlying `<input>` element instead of our custom container). We can add the required behavior, like we have added the container and `<span>` elements, using jQuery. Change the code in the final `<script>` element, so that it appears as follows:

```
$(document).ready(function($){
  $("#myButton").button().hover(function() {
```

```
    $(this).parent().addClass("ui-state-hover");
  }, function() {
    $(this).parent().removeClass("ui-state-hover");
  });
});
```

Now our button should work as intended. As the previous example shows, although it's technically feasible to manually add the elements, the styling and the behavior required to add icons to a button built from an `<input>` element, in most cases, it will be easier and more efficient to simply use an `<a>` or `<button>` element.

Adding the Button events

Buttons that are built from `<a>` elements will work as intended with no further intervention from us—the browser will simply follow the `href` as we would expect—provided the `<button>` or `<input>` elements are within a `<form>` element and have the relevant type attribute set. These elements will submit the form data in the standard way.

If more modern AJAX submission of any `<form>` data is required, or if the button is to trigger some other action or process, we can use standard jQuery click event handlers to react to the button being clicked.

In the next example, we use the following underlying markup for the button widget:

```
<button type="button" id="myButton">A button</button>
```

The button widget exposes a single event, the `create` event, which is fired when the button instance is initially created. We could use this event to run additional code each time a button instance is created. For example, if we wanted the button to be initially hidden from view (in order to display later, after something else has occurred), we could use `.css()` to set the `display` property to `none`.

Replace the `document.ready()` code in `button5.html`, with the following code:

```
$(document).ready(function($){
  $("#myButton").button({
    create: function() {
      $(this).css("display", "none")
    }
  });
});
```

Save this file as `button6.html`. Within the event handler, `$(this)` refers to the button instance, which is hidden from view using jQuery's `css()` method.

In order for the button to fulfill its primary purpose, that is, to do something when clicked, we should attach a handler to the button manually. We might want to collect some registration information from our visitors, for example, and use a button to send this information to the server.

Replace the <button> in button6.html with the following code:

```
<form method="post" action="serverscript.php">
  <label for="name">Name:
    <input type="text" id="name" name="name">
  </label>
  <label for="email">Email:
    <input type="text" id="email" name="email">
  </label>
  <p>
    <input type="submit" id="myButton" value="Register" />
  </p>
</form>
```

Change the final <script> element to the following code:

```
<script>
  $(document).ready(function($){
    var form = $("form"), formData = {
      name: form.find("#name").val(),
      email: form.find("#email").val()
    };

    $("#myButton").button();
    $("#myButton").click(function(e) {
      e.preventDefault();
      form.find("label").remove();
      $("#myButton").button("option", "disabled", true);

      $.post("register.php",$.post("register.php", formData,
      function() {
        $("<label />", { text: "Thanks for registering!"
        }).prependTo(form);
      });
    });
  });
</script>
```

Save this file as `button7.html`. The underlying `<button>` element is now part of a simple `<form>`, which simply provides text inputs for the visitor, their name, and an e-mail address. In the script, we first initialize the button widget, before creating a `click` event handler. This prevents the default action of the browser, which would be to post the form in a traditional non-AJAX way.

We then collect the name and e-mail address entered into the fields, and post the data to the server asynchronously using jQuery's `post()` method. In the success handler for the request, we use the widget's `option` method to disable the button, then create and display a thanks message.

We're not interested in the server-side of things in this example, and we don't include any validation (although the latter should be included in production use), but you can see how easy it is to react to the button being clicked using standard jQuery functionality. To see the example work, we'll need to run the page through a web server, and should add a PHP file of the name specified in the request in the same directory as the page (which doesn't need to contain anything for the purposes of this example). The following screenshot shows how the page should appear after the button has been clicked:

Creating button sets

The button widget can also be used in conjunction with radio buttons and checkboxes. The button component is unique in jQuery UI, in that it has not one but two widget methods. It has the `button()` method that we have already looked at, and it has the `buttonset()` method, which is used to create groups of buttons based on radio buttons and checkboxes.

Checkbox button sets

Change the `<body>` element of `button7.html`, so that it contains the following code:

```
<div id="buttons">
  <h2>Programming Languages</h2>
  <p>Select all languages you know:</p>
  <label for="js">JavaScript</label>
  <input id="js" type="checkbox">
  <label for="py">Python</label>
  <input id="py" type="checkbox">
  <label for="cSharp">C#</label>
  <input id="cSharp" type="checkbox">
  <label for="jv">Java</label>
  <input id="jv" type="checkbox">
</div>
```

Now change the final `<script>` element, so that it appears as follows:

```
$(document).ready(function($){
  $("#buttons").buttonset();
});
```

Save this file as `button8.html`. All we need to do is call the `buttonset()` method on the container in which the `<label>` and `<input>` elements reside.

When we run this file in a browser, we see that the checkboxes are hidden from view and the `<label>` elements are converted into buttons and grouped visually in a horizontal set as shown in the following screenshot:

Although the actual checkboxes themselves are hidden from view behind the buttons, whenever a button is selected, the underlying checkbox will have its `checked` attribute updated, so we can still harvest the states from script with ease.

When a checkbox button is clicked, it will have a selected state applied to it by the widget, so that the visitor can easily see that it has been selected. As we would expect, multiple buttons may be selected at once.

There are a couple of rules that we need to adhere to when creating buttons from checkboxes. In HTML5, it is common to nest form controls within their associated `<label>` elements (we did this in an earlier example), but this is not allowed when using the button widget. Using the `for` attribute with the `<label>` element is required.

Radio button sets

Buttons based on radio buttons are visually the same as those based on checkboxes; they differ only in their behavior. Only one button can be selected at any one time, whereas multiple buttons can be selected when using checkboxes.

Let's see this behavior in action in `button8.html`; change the elements in `<body>` to the following code:

```
<div id="buttons">
  <h2>Programming Languages</h2>
  <p>Select your most proficient languages:</p>
  <label for="js">JavaScript</label>
  <input id="js" type="radio" name="lang">
  <label for="py">Python</label>
  <input id="py" type="radio" name="lang">
  <label for="cSharp">C#</label>
  <input id="cSharp" type="radio" name="lang">
  <label for="jv">Java</label>
  <input id="jv" type="radio" name="lang">
</div>
```

Save this file as `button9.html`. The script to initialize radio buttons is the same: we simply call the `buttonset()` method on the container. The only difference to the underlying markup, other than specifying `radio` as the type, is that these `<input>` elements must have the `name` attribute set.

Working with button methods

The button widget comes with the default `destroy`, `disable`, `enable`, `widget`, and `option` methods common to all widgets. In addition to these methods, the button widget exposes one custom method, which is the `refresh` method. This method is used for changing the state of checkbox and radio buttons, if they are changed programmatically. By combining some of the previous examples, we can see this method in action.

Change the `<body>` of `button8.html`, so that it includes two new `<button>` elements as shown in the following code:

```
<div id="buttons">
  <h2>Programming Languages</h2>
  <p>Select all languages you know:</p>
  <label for="js1">JavaScript</label>
  <input id="js1" type="checkbox">
  <label for="py1">Python</label>
  <input id="py1" type="checkbox">
  <label for="cSharp1">C#</label>
  <input id="cSharp1" type="checkbox">
  <label for="jv1">Java</label>
  <input id="jv1" type="checkbox">
</div>
<p>
  <button type="button" id="select">Select All</button>
  <button type="button" id="deselect">Deselect All</button>
</p>
```

In this example, we have reverted to the checkboxes, so that we can programmatically select or deselect them as a group. Now change the final `<script>` element, so that it appears as follows:

```
$("#buttons").buttonset();
function buttonSelected(buttonState){
  $("#buttons").find("input").prop("checked", buttonState);
  $("#buttons").buttonset("refresh");
}

$("#select").click(function() {
  buttonsSelected(true);
});

$("#deselect").button().click(function() {
  buttonsSelected(false);
});
```

Save this file as `button10.html`. If we preview the results in a browser, you can see the effect by clicking on the **Select All** button as shown in the following screenshot:

In this example, we have a **Select All** button and a **Deselect All** button. When the **Select All** button is clicked, we set the checked attribute of the checkboxes to `true`. This will check the underlying (and hidden) checkboxes, but it won't do anything to the `<label>` elements that are styled to appear as buttons. To update the state of these buttons, so that they appear selected, we call the `refresh` method.

The **Deselect All** button sets the `checked` attribute to `false`, and then calls the `refresh` method again to remove the selected states from each button.

Introducing the autocomplete widget

The autocomplete widget, reintroduced in jQuery UI 1.8, is back and looking better than ever. This is one of my favorite widgets in the library, and although it doesn't yet have the full set of behavior that it had in its first incarnation, it still provides a rich set of functionality to enhance simple text inputs that expect data from a predefined range.

A good example is cities; you have a standard `<input type="text">` on the page, which asks for the visitor's city. When they begin typing in the `<input>` element, all of the cities that contain the letter that the visitor has typed are displayed. The range of cities that the visitor can enter is finite and constrained to the country in which the visitor lives (this is either assumed by the developer or has already been selected previously by the visitor).

The following screenshot shows how this widget appears:

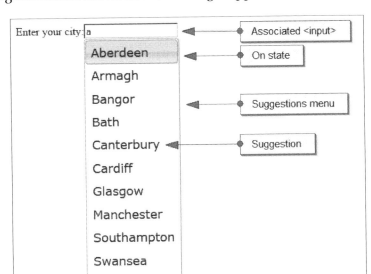

Like other widgets, a range of elements and class names are added programmatically when the widget is initialized.

Working with local data sources

To implement a basic autocomplete with a local array as its data source, create the following code in a new file:

```html
<html>
  <head>
  <meta charset="utf-8">
  <title>Autocomplete</title>
    <link rel="stylesheet" href="development-bundle/
    themes/redmond/jquery.ui.all.css">
    <script src="js/jquery-2.0.3.js"></script>
    <script src="development-bundle/ui/jquery.ui.core.js">
    </script>
    <script src="development-bundle/ui/jquery.ui.widget.js">
    </script>
    <script src="development-bundle/ui/jquery.ui.position.js">
    </script>
    <script src="development-bundle/ui/jquery.ui.menu.js">
    </script>
```

```
      <script src="development-bundle/ui/jquery.ui.autocomplete.js">
      </script>
    </head>
    <body>
      <label>Enter your city:</label>
      <input id="city">
    </body>
</html>
```

All we need on the page is a standard `<input>` element of the `text` type. The initialization required for autocomplete is slightly larger than that required for other components; add the following `<script>` element, after the autocomplete source file:

```
<script>
  $(document).ready(function($){
    $("#city").autocomplete({ source: [ "Aberdeen", "Armagh",
    "Bangor", "Bath", "Canterbury", "Cardiff", "Derby", "Dundee",
    "Edinburgh", "Exeter", "Glasgow", "Gloucester", "Hereford",
    "Inverness", "Leeds", "London", "Manchester", "Norwich",
    "Newport", "Oxford", "Plymouth", "Preston", "Ripon",
    "Southampton", "Swansea", "Truro", "Wakefield", "Winchester",
    "York" ]});
  });
</script>
```

Save this file as `autocomplete1.html`. In our configuration object for the autocomplete, we use the `source` option to specify a local array of strings. The `source` option is mandatory and must be defined. The object is then passed to the `autocomplete` method, which is called on the city `<input>` that the autocomplete is to be associated with.

When we run this file in a browser, we should find that as we begin to type into the `<input>` element, a list of the cities defined in our source array that contain the letter(s) that we have typed is displayed in a drop-down menu attached to the `<input>`.

The autocomplete widget requires the following files in order to function:

- `jquery.ui.all.css`
- `jquery-2.0.3.js`
- `jquery.ui.core.js`
- `jquery.ui.widget.js`
- `jquery.ui.position.js`
- `jquery.ui.menu.js`
- `jquery.ui.autocomplete.js`

Using an array of objects as the data source

In addition to providing an array of strings, we can also supply an array of objects as the data source, which gives us more flexibility over the text added to the `<input>` when a suggestion from the menu is selected. Change the configuration object in `autocomplete1.html`, so that it appears as follows:

```
$("#city").autocomplete({
  source: [
    { value: "AB", label: "Aberdeen" },
    { value: "AR", label: "Armagh" },
    { value: "BA", label: "Bangor" },
    { value: "BA", label: "Bath" },
    { value: "CA", label: "Canterbury" },
    { value: "CD", label: "Cardiff" },
    { value: "DE", label: "Derby" },
    { value: "DU", label: "Dundee" },
    { value: "ED", label: "Edinburgh" },
    { value: "EX", label: "Exeter" },
    { value: "GL", label: "Glasgow" },
    { value: "GO", label: "Gloucester" },
    { value: "HE", label: "Hereford" },
    { value: "IN", label: "Inverness" },
    { value: "LE", label: "Leeds" },
    { value: "LO", label: "London" },
    { value: "MA", label: "Manchester" },
    { value: "NO", label: "Norwich" },
    { value: "NE", label: "Newport" },
    { value: "OX", label: "Oxford" },
    { value: "PL", label: "Plymouth" },
    { value: "PR", label: "Preston" },
    { value: "RI", label: "Ripon" },
    { value: "SO", label: "Southampton" },
    { value: "SW", label: "Swansea" },
    { value: "TR", label: "Truro" },
    { value: "WA", label: "Wakefield" },
    { value: "WI", label: "Winchester" },
    { value: "YO", label: "York" }
  ]
});
```

Save this file as `autocomplete2.html`. Each item in the array that we are using as the data source is now an object, instead of a simple string. Each object has two keys: `value` and `label`. The value of the `value` key is the text that is added to the `<input>` element when a suggestion is selected from the list. The value of `label` is what is displayed in the suggestion list. Other keys, which store custom data can also be used.

If each object in the array contains only a single property, the property will be used as both the `value` and `label` key. In this case, we might as well use an array of strings instead of an array of objects, but it is worth noting the alternative format of the local data.

Configurable autocomplete options

The following options can be set in order to modify the behavior of the widget:

Option	Default Value	Usage
appendTo	"body"	Specifies which element to append the widget to.
autofocus	false	Focuses the first suggestion in the list when displaying the list of suggestions.
delay	300	Specifies the number of milliseconds the widget should wait before displaying the list of suggestions, after the visitor has started typing in the `<input>`.
disabled	false	Disables the widget.
minLength	1	Specifies the number of characters the visitor needs to enter in the `<input>` before the list of suggestions is displayed. Can be set to `0` to make the widget display all suggestions in the menu.
position	`{ my: "left top", at: "left bottom", collision: "none" }`	Specifies how the list of suggestions should be positioned relative to the `<input>` element. This option is used in the exact same way, and accepts the same values as the position utility that we looked at earlier in the book.
source	Array, String or Function	Specifies the data source used to fill the list of suggestions. This option is mandatory and must be configured. It accepts an array, string, or function as its value.

Configuring minimum length

The minLength option allows us to specify the minimum number of characters that need to be typed into the associated <input> element before the list of suggestions is displayed. By default, the suggestions that are displayed by the widget only contain the letters typed into the <input> element, rather than just those starting with the entered letters, which can result in many more suggestions being displayed than is necessary.

Setting the minLength option to a number higher than the default value of 1 can help narrow the list of suggestions, which may be much more important when dealing with large remote data sources.

Change the configuration object that we used in autocomplete1.html (we'll revert to using an array of strings as the data source for the time being), so that it appears as follows:

```
$("#city").autocomplete({
  minLength: 2,
  source: [
    "Aberdeen", "Armagh", "Bangor", "Bath", "Canterbury",
    "Cardiff", "Derby", "Dundee", "Edinburgh", "Exeter",
    "Glasgow", "Gloucester", "Hereford", "Inverness", "Leeds",
    "London", "Manchester", "Norwich", "Newport",
    "Oxford", "Plymouth", "Preston", "Ripon", "Southampton",
    "Swansea", "Truro", "Wakefield", "Winchester", "York"
  ]
});
```

Save this file as autocomplete3.html. When we run this file in a browser, we should find that we need to type two characters into the <input>, and only cities that contain the characters in consecutive order are displayed, which vastly reduces the number of suggestions.

Although the benefits are not obvious in this basic example, this can greatly reduce the data returned by a remote data source.

Appending the suggestion list to an alternative element

By default, the suggestion list is appended to the <body> of the page, when using their autocomplete widget. We can change this, and specify that the list should be added to another element on the page. The autocomplete widget then uses the position utility to position the list, so that it appears to be attached to the <input> element it is associated with. We can change this and specify that the list should be added to another element on the page, by using the appendTo option.

Wrap the underlying `<label>` and `<input>` in a container `<div>` in
`autocomplete3.html`:

```
<div id="container">
  <label>Enter your city:</label>
  <input id="city">
</div>
```

Then change the configuration object in the final `<script>` element to the
following code:

```
$("#city").autocomplete({
  appendTo: "#container",
  source: [ "Aberdeen", "Armagh", "Bangor", "Bath", "Canterbury",
    "Cardiff", "Derby", "Dundee", "Edinburgh", "Exeter",
    "Glasgow", "Gloucester", "Hereford", "Inverness", "Leeds",
    "London", "Manchester", "Norwich", "Newport", "Oxford",
    "Plymouth", "Preston", "Ripon", "Southampton", "Swansea",
    "Truro", "Wakefield", "Winchester", "York" ]
});
```

Save this file as `autocomplete4.html`. Usually, the suggestion list is added right at
the bottom of the `<body>` element of the code. The `appendTo` option accepts a jQuery
selector or an actual DOM element as its value.

In this example, we see that the list is appended to our `<div>` container instead of
the `<body>` element, which we can verify using Firebug, or another DOM explorer.

Working with autocomplete events

The autocomplete widget exposes a range of unique events that allow us to react
programmatically to the widget being interacted with. These events are listed
as follows:

Event	Fired when...
change	A suggestion from the list is selected. This event is fired once the list has closed and the `<input>` has lost focus.
close	The suggestion list is closed.
create	An instance of the widget is created.
focus	The keyboard is used to focus a suggestion in the list.
open	The suggestion menu is displayed.
search	The request for the suggestions is about to be made.
select	A suggestion from the list is selected.

The `select` event is useful when we are working with an array of objects as the data source and have additional data other than the `label` and `value` properties that we used earlier. For the next example, remove the `<div>` container that we used in the last example and then change the configuration object, so that it appears as follows:

```
$("#city").autocomplete({
  source: [
    { value: "AB", label: "Aberdeen", population: 212125 },
    { value: "AR", label: "Armagh", population: 54263 },
    { value: "BA", label: "Bangor", population: 21735 },
    { value: "BA", label: "Bath", population: 83992 },
    { value: "CA", label: "Canterbury", population: 43432 },
    { value: "CD", label: "Cardiff", population: 336200 },
    { value: "DE", label: "Derby", population: 233700 },
    { value: "DU", label: "Dundee", population: 152320 },
    { value: "ED", label: "Edinburgh", population: 448624 },
    { value: "EX", label: "Exeter", population: 118800 },
    { value: "GL", label: "Glasgow", population: 580690 },
    { value: "GO", label: "Gloucester", population: 123205 },
    { value: "HE", label: "Hereford", population: 55700 },
    { value: "IN", label: "Inverness", population: 56660 },
    { value: "LE", label: "Leeds", population: 443247 },
    { value: "LO", label: "London", population: 7200000 },
    { value: "MA", label: "Manchester", population: 483800 },
    { value: "NO", label: "Norwich", population: 259100 },
    { value: "NE", label: "Newport", population: 137011 },
    { value: "OX", label: "Oxford", population: 149300 },
    { value: "PL", label: "Plymouth", population: 256700 },
    { value: "PR", label: "Preston", population: 114300 },
    { value: "RI", label: "Ripon", population: 15922 },
    { value: "SO", label: "Southampton", population: 236700 },
    { value: "SW", label: "Swansea", population: 223301 },
    { value: "TR", label: "Truro", population: 17431 },
    { value: "WA", label: "Wakefield", population: 76886 },
    { value: "WI", label: "Winchester", population: 41420 },
    { value: "YO", label: "York", population: 182000 }
  ],
  select: function(e, ui) {
    if ($("#pop").length) {
      $("#pop").text(ui.item.label + "'s population is: " +
      ui.item.population);
    } else {
      $("<p></p>", {
        id: "pop",
```

```
            text: ui.item.label + "'s population is: " + ui.item.
              population
          }).insertAfter("#city");
      }
    }
  });
```

Save this file as `autocomplete5.html`. We've added an extra property to each object in our array data source—the population of each city. We use the `select` event to obtain the label and our extra property, and write them to the page whenever a city is selected.

The event handler that we pass to the `select` event accepts the `event` object and the object from the data source that was selected. The `.length` test is used to determine if the `pop` element exists on the page. If it does, we simply replace the text within it, with the updated statement. If not, we create a new `<p>` element, with an `id` of `pop`, and insert this immediately after the `city` input field. We can access any property defined within our object in the standard way.

Once a city has been selected, the page should appear as shown in the following screenshot:

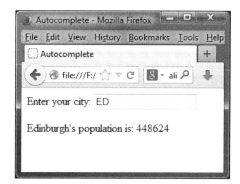

The autocomplete methods

In addition to the standard methods that all widgets share, the autocomplete gives us two unique methods that allow us to initiate certain actions. The unique methods are listed as follows:

Method	Usage
close	Close the suggestion menu.
search	Request the list of suggestions from the data source specifying the search term as an optional argument

The `close` method is extremely easy to use, we simply call the `autocomplete` widget method and specify `close` as an argument:

```
$("#associated_input").autocomplete("close");
```

This will cause the suggestions menu to be closed, and the `close` event to be triggered. A possible use for the close event handler is to alert the user if there is a problem with the entry they have selected; if it doesn't match an entry in a predefined list, then this can be flagged to the user.

The `search` method is slightly more complex, in that it can accept an additional argument, although this is not mandatory. If the search method is called without passing an argument (which is likely to be the default behavior), the value of the associated `<input>` element is used as the search term. Alternatively, the term can be provided to the method as the argument.

Working with remote data sources

So far in this example, we've worked with a rather small local array of data. The autocomplete widget really comes into its own when working with remote data sources, which is the recommended way of using the widget when the data source is large.

Retrieving content based on input

In the next example, we'll use a web service to retrieve the list of countries instead of using our local array. Change the `<input>` element in `autocomplete5.html`, so that it appears as follows:

```
<label>Enter your country:</label>
<input id="country">
```

Then change the final `<script>` element, so that the configuration object is defined as follows:

```
$("#country").autocomplete({
  source: "http://danwellman.co.uk/countries.php?callback=?"
});
```

Save this file as `autocomplete6.html`. We changed the `<input>` element in this example, as we are requesting the visitor's country instead of a city.

We have specified a string as the value of the source configuration object in this example. When a string is supplied to this option, the string should contain a URL that points to a remote resource. The widget assumes that the resource will output JSON data, and it assumes that the JSON data will be in the format that we saw earlier when using an array of objects as the source.

Therefore, when using a simple string as the value of the `source` option, the data that is returned should be an array of objects, where each object contains at least a key called `label`. The data can be in JSON or JSONP format for cross-domain requests. The widget will automatically add the query string `term=`, followed by whatever was typed into the `<input>` element.

In this example, I have specified a URL of my own website. The resource at this URL will output the data in the correct format, so you can run this example from your desktop computer (without even needing a web server) and see the correct behavior as shown in the following screenshot:

One important point that I should make is about the PHP file that I have used. It will only return entries from the database that start with the letter(s) typed into the `<input>` element, and do not contain the letters as is the default for the widget. I wanted to clarify that this is a change that I implemented at the server level, and not behavior exhibited by the widget.

So, using a string as the value of the `source` option is useful and convenient when we have a data source that outputs data in the exact format we require, which is usually when we are in control of the web service that returns the data, as well as the data itself. This may not be the case if we are trying to extract data from a public web service over which we have no control. In these situations, we will need to use a function as the value of the `source` option and parse out the data manually.

Passing a function as a source option

Passing a function to the `source` option, instead of a local array or a string, is the most powerful way of working with the widget. In this scenario, we have complete control over the request and how the data is processed before being passed to the widget to display in the suggestion menu.

In this example, we'll use a different PHP file that returns different data which is not in the format that autocomplete expects. We'll use the function to request and process the data before passing it to the widget. The context of the example will be the frontend for a messaging system similar to Facebook's, in which the autocomplete suggests possible message recipients, but can also be removed after they have been selected and added to the `<input>` element. The page we will end up with will appear as in the following screenshot:

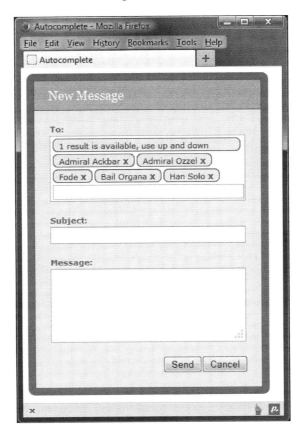

To start with, change the `<body>` of `autocomplete6.html`, so that it contains the following markup:

```html
<div id="formWrap">
  <form id="messageForm" action="#">
  <fieldset>
    <legend>New message form</legend>
    <span>New Message</span>
    <label id="toLabel" for="friends">To:</label>
    <div id="friends" class="ui-helper-clearfix">
    <input id="to" type="text">
    </div>
    <label>Subject:</label>
    <input id="subject" name="subject" type="text">
    <label>Message:</label>
    <textarea id="message" name="message" rows="5" cols="50">
    </textarea>
    <button type="button" id="cancel">Cancel</button>
    <button type="submit" id="send">Send</button>
    </fieldset>
  </form>
</div>
```

Then change the final `<script>` element, so that it appears as follows:

```javascript
$(document).ready(function($){
  var suggestions = [];

  var getData = function(req, resp){
    $.getJSON("http://danwellman.co.uk/contacts.php?callback=?",
    req, function(data) {
      var suggestions = [];
      $.each(data, function(i, val){
        suggestions.push(val.name);
      });
      resp(suggestions);
    });
  };

  var selectEmail = function(e, ui) {
    var removeLink = $("<a>").addClass("remove")
    .attr({href: "javascript:", title: "Remove " + friend});
    var friend = ui.item.value,
    span = $("<span>").text(friend),
    a = removeLink.text("x").appendTo(span);
```

```
      span.insertBefore("#to");
    }

  $("#to").autocomplete({
    source: getData,
    select: selectEmail,
    change: function() {
        $("#to").val("").css("display", 2);
    }
  });

  $("#friends").click(function(){
    $("#to").focus();
  });

  $("#to").click(function(){
    if (this.length != 0) {
      $("#to").val('');
    }
  });

  $(".remove", document.getElementById("friends")).on("click",
function(){
  $(this).parent().remove();
  if($("#friends span").length === 0) {
    $("#to").css("top", 0);
    }
  });
});
```

Save this file as autocomplete7.html. On the page, we've got some basic markup for a form and the necessary elements to recreate the Facebook-style message dialog. To test the effect, try entering Admiral Ozzel, Fode, or Han Solo into the textbox, then selecting their name when the autocomplete displays their entry.

> The autocomplete parameter will only display certain names; if you would like to see possible options, then I would recommend browsing to http://danwellman.co.uk/contacts.php.

We use a <div> element that is styled to look just like an <input> element, with a totally unstyled actual <input> within this.

The actual `<input>` is needed, so that the visitor can type into it and so that it can be associated with the autocomplete. We use the `<div>` element because we can't insert the `<span>` elements that will make up each contact into the `<input>` element. We also have a hidden `<input>` element, which will be used to store the actual e-mail addresses.

In the script, we use the `getData` function as the value of our `source` option; this is called every time the text in the `<input>` field is updated. We first make a JSON request to the PHP file containing the data and then iterate over each item in the JSON object returned by the request.

Each newly created object is added to the `suggestions` array, and once each item in the returned data has been processed, the `suggestions` array is passed to the `resp` callback function, which is passed to the `source` function as the second argument.

We then define the `selectEmail` handler for the autocomplete's `select` event; this function is automatically passed to two arguments, which are the `event` object and a `ui` object containing the suggestion that was selected. We use this function to create a `<span>` element to format and hold the text and an anchor element that can be used to remove the recipient. The formatted `<span>` is then inserted directly before the camouflaged `<input>` element.

Lastly, we added a click handler for the `#friends` field, so that this gains focus when anyone clicks inside it. A click handler has also been added to the `#to` field, so that if you click inside it, it will automatically remove the contents of the previous entry.

We'll also need a stylesheet to go with this example; add the following CSS to a new file:

```
#formWrap { padding: 10px; position: absolute; float: left;
    background-color: #000; background: rgba(0,0,0,.5); -moz-border-
    radius: 10px; -webkit-border-radius: 10px; border-radius: 10px; }
#messageForm { width: 326px; border: 1px solid #666; background-
    color: #eee; }
#messageForm fieldset { padding: 0; margin: 0; position: relative;
    border: none; background-color: #eee; }
#messageForm legend { visibility: hidden; height: 0; }
#messageForm span { display: block; width: 326px; padding: 10px 0;
    margin: 0 0 20px; text-indent: 20px; background-color: #bbb;
    border-bottom: 1px solid #333; font: 18px Georgia, Serif; color:
#fff; }
#friends { width: 274px; padding: 3px 3px 0; margin: 0 auto;
    border: 1px solid #aaa; background-color: #fff; cursor: text; }
#messageForm #to { margin: 0 0 2px 0; padding: 0 0 3px; position:
    relative; top: 0; float: left; }
```

```
#messageForm input, #messageForm textarea { display: block; width:
  274px; padding: 3px; margin: 0 auto 20px; border: 1px solid #aaa;
}
#messageForm label { display: block; margin: 20px 0 3px; text-
  indent: 22px; font: bold 11px Verdana, Sans-serif; color: #666; }
#messageForm #toLabel { margin-top: 0; }
#messageForm button { float: right; margin: 0 0 20px 0; }
#messageForm #cancel { margin-right: 20px; }
#friends span { display: block; width: auto; height: 10px; margin:
  0 3px 3px 0; padding: 3px 20px 4px 8px; position: relative; float:
  left; text-indent: 0; background-color: #eee; border: 1px solid
#333; -moz-border-radius: 7px; -webkit-border-radius: 7px; border-
  radius: 7px; color: #333; font: normal 11px Verdana, Sans-serif; }
#friends span a { position: absolute; right: 8px; top: 2px; color:
#666; font: bold 12px Verdana, Sans-serif; text-decoration: none;
}
#friends span a: hover { color: #ff0000; }
.ui-menu .ui-menu-item { white-space: nowrap; padding: 0 10px 0 0;
}
```

Save this file as `autocompleteTheme.css` in the `css` folder, and link to the new file from the `<head>` of our new page:

```
<link rel="stylesheet" href="css/autocompleteTheme.css">
```

When we run the page in a browser, we should find that we can type into the `<input>` element, select a name from the suggestions menu, and get a nicely formatted and styled name added to the fake input.

Displaying HTML in the list of suggestions

By default, the autocomplete widget will only display plain text for each suggestion in the list. Of course, this plain text is within HTML elements created by the widget, but nevertheless, if we try to use HTML within our data source, then it will be stripped out and ignored. However, Scott González, the current project leader for jQuery UI, has written an extension that allows us to use HTML for each suggestion in the list instead of plain text, if the need arises.

This could be handy if we wanted to highlight to the visitor the parts of the suggestion that matched with what they had typed in the `<input>` element. We will need the extension for this example, which can be found at https://github. com/scottgonzalez/jquery-ui-extensions/blob/master/src/autocomplete/ jquery.ui.autocomplete.html.js.

The file can be saved in our local `js` directory and a reference to it should be included on the page, after the source file for the autocomplete:

```
<script src="js/jquery.ui.autocomplete.html.js"></script>
```

Before we make a start on our code, let's take a look at how it will appear, when previewed in a browser:

In our next example, we're going to make use of Scott's plugin with the autocomplete widget, to allow a user to search for some city names. If there is a match, each letter in the selection drop-down will begin to change color, if the letter matches the characters entered in the textbox.

Change the final `<script>` element in `autocomplete5.html`, so that it appears as follows:

```
$(document).ready(function($){
  var data = [
    { value: "Aberdeen", label: "Aberdeen" },
    { value: "Armagh", label: "Armagh" },
    { value: "Bangor", label: "Bangor" },
    { value: "Bath", label: "Bath" },
    { value: "Canterbury", label: "Canterbury" },
    { value: "Cardif", label: "Cardif" },
    { value: "Derby", label: "Derby" },
    { value: "Dundee", label: "Dundee" },
    { value: "Edinburgh", label: "Edinburgh" },
    { value: "Exeter", label: "Exeter" },
    { value: "Glasgow", label: "Glasgow" },
    { value: "Gloucester", label: "Gloucester" },
    { value: "Hereford", label: "Hereford" },
    { value: "Inverness", label: "Inverness" },
    { value: "Leeds", label: "Leeds" },
```

```
        { value: "London", label: "London" },
        { value: "Manchester", label: "Manchester" },
        { value: "Norwich", label: "Norwich" },
        { value: "Newport", label: "Newport" },
        { value: "Oxford", label: "Oxford" },
        { value: "Plymouth", label: "Plymouth" },
        { value: "Preston", label: "Preston" },
        { value: "Ripon", label: "Ripon" },
        { value: "Southampton", label: "Southampton" },
        { value: "Swansea", label: "Swansea" },
        { value: "Truro", label: "Truro" },
        { value: "Wakefield", label: "Wakefield" },
        { value: "Winchester", label: "Winchester" },
        { value: "York", label: "York" }
    ];

    $("#city").autocomplete({
      html: true,
      source: function(req, resp) {
        var suggestions = [],
          chosenTerm = "<span>" + req.term + "</span>",
          regEx = new RegExp("^" + req.term, "i");

        $.each(cityList, function(i, val){
          if (val.label.match(regEx)) {
            var obj = {};
            obj.value = val.value;
            obj.label = val.label.replace(regEx, chosenTerm);
            suggestions.push(obj);
            }
          });
          resp(suggestions);
        }
      });
    });
```

Save this file as `autocomplete8.html`. We also need to add a styling rule to our code; add this to the `<head>` of your file:

```
<style>
  span { color:green !important; }
</style>
```

Although this appears as a short example, there are some key points here to note; let's explore the code we've used in more detail.

In this example, we've gone back to using a local array of objects, called `cityList`. Both the `value` and `label` properties in each object hold the same data to begin with.

In our configuration object, we specify a new `html` option, which is used in conjunction with the HTML extension. We set the value of this option to `true` as in the following code:

```
$("#city").autocomplete({
    html: true,
```

We've used a function as the value of the `source` option in this example. Within the function, we first create a new empty array and define a new regular expression object. This will case-insensitively match whatever is typed into the `<input>`, at the start of a string:

```
source: function(req, resp) {
  var suggestions = [],
  chosenTerm = "<span>" + req.term + "</span>",
  regEx = new RegExp("^" + req.term, "i");
```

We then iterate over each object in our data array and test whether our regular expression matches any of the `label` values in the objects in our array. If any items do match, we create a new object and give it `value` and `label` properties. The `value` property (which is added to the `<input>` element when a suggestion is selected) is simply the corresponding value from our data array, and the `label` (what is displayed in the suggestion menu) is a new string that contains a `<span>` element wrapping the text entered into the `<input>` element:

```
$.each(cityList, function(i, val){
  if (val.label.match(regEx)) {
    var obj = {};
    obj.value = val.value;
    obj.label = val.label.replace(regEx, chosenTerm);
    suggestions.push(obj);
  }
```

Finally, we call the `resp` callback, passing in the newly constructed suggestions array. We should always ensure that this callback is called, as this is required by the widget. It doesn't matter if the suggestions array is empty, the important thing is that the callback is called.

```
resp(suggestions);
```

So now, each item in the suggestions menu will have a `<span>` element, wrapping the text that was typed into the `<input>` element. We can use it to style this text slightly differently, such as with the green text `<style>` that we have added to our example.

Summary

We covered two widgets in this chapter; both of them are relatively new to the library and both work with `<form>` elements of some description. The button widget can be used to turn `<a>`, `<button>`, and `<input>` (of the `button`, `submit`, or `reset` type) into attractively and consistently styled-rich widgets.

The autocomplete widget is attached to an `<input>` element of the `text` type and is used to show a list of suggestions when the visitor begins typing into the `<input>` element. The widget is preconfigured to work with a local array of data or a URL that outputs data in the expected format. It can also be configured to work with data that is not in the expected format. We must first process the data being displayed before passing it to the widget, making this an extremely versatile and powerful widget.

We're almost at the end of the section covering the visible widgets, before focusing on the interaction helpers available with jQuery UI; let's take a look at the two newest additions to the library over the next couple of chapters, beginning with the menu widget.

9
Creating Menus

The menu widget, previously a part of the autocomplete widget, became a standalone plugin in its own right from Version 1.9 of the library, which allows for its re-use in other components. It can be used on its own to transform a list of hyperlinks into a themeable menu that can be controlled using the keyboard or mouse, although it really comes into its own when used with other components such as buttons.

Each menu has a number of menu items associated with it, which when selected will direct the visitor to any part of your site. When you click on the top level, a number of submenu items will slide into view; these may have extra decoration in the form of icons, or be disabled if access is to be prevented at the time of accessing the menu option.

In this chapter, we will cover the following topics:

- How to turn a list into a menu, with or without submenus
- The options available for configuring a menu
- Adding style to menus
- Manipulating menu items with icons and dividers
- Using methods
- Enabling and disabling menu options programmatically
- Responding to events
- Creating horizontal and context menus
- Extending a `<select>` box using jQuery UI's menu

Implementing a basic menu widget

Navigation is a crucial element of the web design; a poorly designed menu will always detract from good content. Good navigation must be both aesthetically pleasing and usable. Using the jQuery UI menu widget, we can create the perfect navigation for your website.

Although it is possible to use a variety of different elements to create our menu, the <ul> element is by far the most common one to use. Menus can be created from any valid markup, as long as the elements have a strict parent-child relationship, with each menu having its own anchor. Following the first example, where we will take a series of European towns and convert them into a basic menu we will further explore the structure.

In a new file in your text editor, create the following page:

```
<!DOCTYPE HTML>
<html>
  <head>
    <meta charset="utf-8">
    <title>Menu</title>
    <link rel="stylesheet" href="development-bundle/themes/redmond/
jquery.ui.all.css">
    <style>
      .ui-menu { width: 150px; }
    </style>
    <script src="js/jquery-2.0.3.js"></script>
    <script src="development-bundle/ui/jquery.ui.core.js"></script>
    <script src="development-bundle/ui/jquery.ui.widget.js"></script>
    <script src="development-bundle/ui/jquery.ui.position.js"></
script>
    <script src="development-bundle/ui/jquery.ui.menu.js"></script>
    <script>
      $(document).ready(function($){
        $("#myMenu").menu();
      });
    </script>
  </head>
  <body>
    <ul id="myMenu">
      <!-- Top level menu -->
      <li class="ui-state-disabled"><a href="#">London</a></li>
      <li><a href="#">Antwerp</a></li>
      <li><a href="#">Belgium</a>
        <ul>
```

```
        <!-- Second level menu -->
        <li class="ui-state-disabled"><a href="#">Antwerp </a></li>
        <li><a href="#">Brussels</a></li>
        <li><a href="#">Bruges</a></li>
      </ul>
    </li>
    <!-- Top level menu -->
    <li><a href="#">Brussels</a></li>
    <li><a href="#">Bruges</a>
      <ul>
        <li><a href="#">Belgium</a>
          <ul>
            <li><a href="#">Antwerp</a></li>
            <li><a href="#">Brussels</a></li>
            <li><a href="#">Bruges</a></li>
          </ul>
        </li>
        <!-- Second level menu -->
        <li><a href="#">Belgium</a>
        <ul>
          <!--Third level menu -->
          <li><a href="#">Antwerp</a></li>
          <li><a href="#">Brussels</a></li>
          <li><a href="#">Bruges</a></li>
        </ul>
      </li>
      <li><a href="#">Paris</a></li>
    </ul>
  </li>
  <li class="ui-state-disabled"><a href="#">Amsterdam</a> </li>
  </ul>
  </body>
</html>
```

Save the code as menu1.html in your jqueryui working folder. Let's take a moment to familiarize ourselves with the code that goes into making the markup required for a menu.

We need the following files from the library to create a menu from our chosen elements:

- jquery-2.0.3.js
- jquery.ui.core.js
- jquery.ui.widget.js

- `jquery.ui.position.js`
- `jquery.ui.menu.js`

When you view the page in a browser, you'll see that we've turned our unordered list into a simple menu. We've added an additional style in our example, unlike other library components, the menu widget needs some additional styling, otherwise it will consume 100 percent of the width of its container by default, which will be the screen. You can see the results in the following screenshot:

A menu widget is normally constructed from several standard HTML elements arranged in a specific manner:

- An outer container element, on which the `menu()` method is called (this can be either a `<ul>` or `<ol>` element)
- An `<a>` element within an `<li>` element for each menu item
- An element for the title of each menu item

 These elements can be either hardcoded into the page, added dynamically, or can be a mixture of both, depending upon the requirements.

All we need on the page is a list, using either the `<ul>` or `<ol>` tags. In our example we've created a more complex example, which jQuery UI uses to turn into a menu with two levels of submenus.

After linking first to the jQuery core library, we link to the `jquery.ui.core.js` and `jquery.ui.widget.js` files that are required by all UI-based components, the file, and finally `jquery.ui.position.js`. We then link to the component's source file, which in this case is `jquery.ui.menu.js`. We can then turn to our custom `<script>` element in which we add the code that creates the menu. This is then executed as soon as the Document Object Model (DOM) is loaded and ready.

Within this function we simply call the `menu()` widget method on the jQuery object, representing our menu container element (the `<ul>` element with an id of `myTabs`). When we run this file in a browser, we should see the tabs as they appeared in the first screenshot of this chapter (without the annotations of course).

Exploring the menu CSS framework classes

Using Firebug for Firefox (or another generic DOM explorer), we can see that a variety of classnames are added to the different underlying HTML elements that go to make up a menu widget.

Let's review these classnames briefly and see how they contribute to the overall appearance of the widget. To the outer container `<ul>`, the following classnames are added:

Classname	Applies/Applied to
ui-menu	The outer container of the menu.
ui-widget	The outer container of all widgets. It sets font family and font size to widgets.
ui-widget-content	Applies content container styles to an element and its child text, links, and icons (applicable to a parent or sibling of the header).
ui-corner-all	Applies corner radius to all four corners of the element
ui-menu-icons	The submenu icons set via the `icons` option when initiating the menu.

The first element within the container is the `<li>` element. This element receives the following classnames:

Classname	Purpose
ui-state-disabled	Applies a dimmed opacity to the disabled UI elements. This should be added in addition to an already-styled element.
ui-menu-item	The container for individual menu items.
ui-menu-divider	Applies a divider between the menu items, if added to a `<li>` element.

Finally, the `<a>` elements within each of the `<li>` element are given the following classnames:

Classname	Purpose
ui-state-focus	Applies a clickable focus container style to an element and its child text, links, and icons.
ui-state-active	Applies a clickable active container style to an element and its child text, links, and icons.
ui-icon	Applies a base class to an icon element. Sets dimensions to a 16 px square block, hides inner text, and sets the background image to the content state sprite image. The background image for this class will be influenced by the parent container; if for example, the `ui-icon` element within a `ui-state-default` container will get colored according to the icon color of `ui-state-default`.
ui-icon-xxx-xxx	Applied as a second class to describe the type of the icon. The syntax for the icon classes generally follows the format of `.ui-icon-{icon type}-{icon sub description}-{direction}`. For a single triangle icon pointing to the right, the format would be `.ui-icon-triangle-1-e`. For more examples of icon names, hover over the icons in the ThemeRoller at `http://jqueryui.com/themeroller/`.

Most of these classnames are added to the underlying HTML elements automatically by the library, with the exception of the classes used for displaying icons or menu dividers; the latter should be added as part of designing your menu structure. For more examples of CSS classnames, it is worth taking a look at `http://api.jqueryui.com/theming/css-framework/`, this details all of the CSS classes available within the framework, which can be applied to most (if not all) widgets within the jQuery UI library.

You may like to take a look at the link, which details some good practices for building menus: `https://developer.apple.com/library/mac/documentation/UserExperience/Conceptual/AppleHIGuidelines/Menus/Menus.html#//apple_ref/doc/uid/TP30000356-TP6`

Configuring menu options

Each of the different components in the library has a series of options that control which features of the widget are enabled by default. An object literal, or an object reference, can be passed in to the `menu()` widget method to configure these options.

The available options to configure non-default behaviors are shown in the following table:

Option	Default value	Use
disabled	false	Disables the menu if set to `true`.
icons	{submenu: "ui-icon-carat-1-e"}	Sets the icons to use for submenus, matching an icon provided by the jQuery UI CSS framework.
menus	"ul"	Assigns the selector for the elements that serve as the menu container, including submenus.
position	{ my: "left top", at: "right top" }	Identifies the position of submenus in relation to the associated parent menu item. The of option defaults to the parent menu item, but you can specify another element to position against. There are more details on how to use the positioning widget, in *Chapter 2, The CSS Framework and Other Utilities*.
role	"menu"	Customizes the **Accessible Rich Internet Application (ARIA)** roles used for the menu and menu items. Roles cannot be changed once they have been initialized: any existing menus, submenus, or menu items will not be updated once they have been created.

Styling menus

All of the UI-based widgets in the jQuery UI library—and the menu widget is no different—can be customized using either one of the prebuilt themes available from `http://jqueryui.com/download/` or by customizing one using the ThemeRoller tool available at `http://jqueryui.com/themeroller/`. All you need to do is to download your theme, and then alter the following line in the code, to reflect the name of the new theme in use:

```
<link rel="stylesheet" href="development-bundle/themes/redmond/jquery.ui.all.css">
```

You can even change to using a theme hosted on a CDN connection, if preferred. The key to this is to choose whichever best suits your development workflow and environment.

Displaying the state of the selected menu options using icons

In our next example, we'll see how we can enhance the appearance of selected menu items by adding icons.

In your text editor, remove the existing markup between the `<body>` tags, and replace it with this:

```
<body>
  <ul id="myMenu">
    <li><a href="#">File</a></li>
    <li><a href="#"><span class="ui-icon ui-icon-zoomin"></span>Read email</a></li>
    <li><a href="#"><span class="ui-icon ui-icon-zoomout"></span>Move to folder...</a></li>
    <li class="ui-state-disabled"><a href="#"><span class="ui-icon ui-icon-print"></span>Print...</a></li>
    <li><a href="#"><span class="ui-icon ui-icon-contact"></span>Address Book</a></li>
    <li>
      <a href="#">Edit</a>
      <ul>
    <li><a href="#"><span class="ui-icon ui-icon-pencil"></span>Compose email</a></li>
    <li><a href="#"><span class="ui-icon ui-icon-bookmark"></span>Mark email</a></li>
    <li><a href="#"><span class="ui-icon ui-icon-trash"></span>Send to trash</a></li>
```

```
        </ul>
      </li>
    </ul>
  </body>
```

We need to tweak the styling slightly, so in a separate file, add the following, and save it as `menuIcons.css` — don't forget to add a link to it from your page:

```
.ui-menu { width: 150px; }
.ui-widget { font-size: 1em; }
```

Add the following reference to this new stylesheet in the `<head>` tag of `menu1.html` and re-save the file as `menu2.html`. We can remove the existing styling too, as this is no longer required. When the page is loaded in a browser, we can now see the icons that have been applied to selected menu items, as shown in the following screenshot:

We can take this a step further, let's say we didn't like the icon used to indicate the presence of submenus, and wanted to change it. This is easy enough to do. Alter the `<script>` block from our last example, as shown:

```
<script>
  $(document).ready(function($){
    $("#menu").menu({
      icons: { submenu: "ui-icon-circle-triangle-e" }
    });
  });
</script>
```

Save this as `menu3.html`. If you load this into a browser now, you will find the icon has changed to an arrow inside a circle. While this works perfectly, it could benefit from a slight adjustment to its position. Add the following to the `menuIcons.css` stylesheet, and save it as `menuIconsOverrides.css`:

```
.ui-menu-icon { margin-top: 5px; }
```

Don't forget to update the CSS link in your code too:

```
<link rel="stylesheet" type="text/css" href="css/menuIconsOverrides.css">
```

Let's preview this in a browser. You should find the icon is now better placed, as shown in this screenshot:

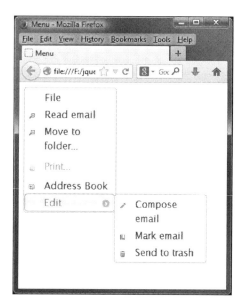

Adding dividers to menus

So far we've seen how to set up a basic menu and add icons, one feature that you may often see, but which is so far lacking, is the use of dividers. Menu dividers help group related items together, or can act to separate fixed menu items from those that may change, such as a recent items list.

There are two ways you can achieve this:

- Addition of `class="ui-menu-divider"` to a `<li>` item.
- Insertion of `<li>-</li>` between menu items. These should not be wrapped in any other tags, such as the `<a>` link tags.

Either option will work perfectly and produce the same results, but they work on different principles and have different merits. The CSS option is perhaps the most descriptive, but requires more markup with the body of your code.

In a copy of menu2.html, alter the markup as shown:

```
<ul id="menu">
  <li><a href="#">File</a></li>
  <li class="ui-menu-divider"></li>
  <li><a href="#"><span class="ui-icon ui-icon-zoomin"></span>Read
email</a></li>
```

Save this as menu4.html. When loading this into your browser, you will see a menu separator appear, immediately after the **File** menu option:

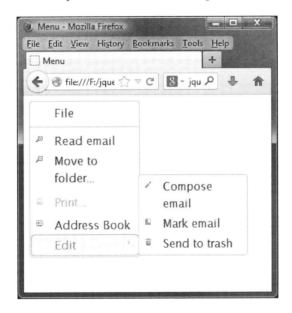

You can also achieve this using the `<li>-</li>` route; this requires less markup and is more akin to the method used by those used to programming in code, such as C#. Alter the code immediately after the Address Book option, as follows:

```
<li><a href="#"><span class="ui-icon ui-icon-contact"></span>Address
Book</a></li>
<li>-</li>
<li><a href="#">Edit</a>
```

The styling will be applied by jQuery UI automatically to turn this into a separator.

Using menu methods

The menu widget contains a host of different methods, in addition to the core methods such as `destroy`, `disable`, `enable`, `option`, and `widget`, which means that it has a rich set of different behaviors. It also supports the implementation of advanced functionality that allows us to work with it programmatically. Let's take a look at the methods, which are listed in the following table:

Option	Use
blur	Removes focus from a menu, resets any active element styles, and triggers the menu's `blur` event.
collapse	Closes the currently active submenu.
collapseAll	Closes all open submenus.
expand	Opens the submenu below the currently active item, if one exists.
focus	Activates a particular menu item, begins opening any submenu, if present, and triggers the menu's `focus` event.
isFirstItem	Returns a Boolean value stating whether or not the currently active item is the first item in the menu.
isLastItem	Returns a Boolean value stating whether or not the currently active item is the last item in the menu.
next	Moves active state to the next menu item.
nextPage	Moves active state to the first menu item below the bottom of a scrollable menu or the last item if not scrollable.
option	Gets or sets any property after the widget has been initialized.
previous	Moves the active state to the previous menu item.
previousPage	Moves the active state to the first menu item above the top of a scrollable menu or the first item if not scrollable.
refresh	Initializes submenus and menu items that have not already been initialized, once new items or content have been added.
select	Selects the currently active menu item, collapses all submenus, and triggers the menu's `select` event.

Let's take a look at some of these options over the next few sections, beginning with enabling and disabling menu options.

Enabling and disabling menu options programmatically

A common requirement when working with menus is to either enable or disable an option based on whether it matches a particular set of conditions, for example, you might disable the printing option if printing is not available.

One would hope that there would be an option available to do this within the menu widget. Alas! there isn't. The only method available is to either disable or enable the whole menu, not a specific menu item. It's not a problem though, as we can achieve the same effect using the `ui-state-disabled` class and a little jQuery magic.

Add the following new `<button>` elements directly after the existing markup for the menu widget in `menu2.html`:

```
<p>
  <form>
    <input type="button" id="disableprint" value="Disable printing" />
    <input type="button" id="enableprint" value="Enable printing" />
  </form>
<p>
```

Next, change the `<script>` element so that it appears as follows:

```
<script>
  $(document).ready(function($){
    $("#myMenu").menu();

    $("#disableprint").click(function() {
      $("ul li:nth-child(4)").addClass("ui-state-disabled ui-menu-
item");
    });

    $("#enableprint").click(function() {
      $("ul li:nth-child(4)").removeClass("ui-state-disabled");
    });
  });
</script>
```

Save the changed file as `menu5.html`. In jQuery, we've used a pseudo-selector to find the fourth element (not the third—the count starts from 0, not 1), and then add or remove the `ui-state-disabled` class using `removeClass` or `addClass` whichever is appropriate.

You will notice that we remove all of the classes when disabling the menu item, this is purely so that when we add the CSS styles to mark the item as disabled, it adds the CSS styles in the correct order. You could easily just use the `.removeClass()` option in both cases, but then the CSS markup order will not match that of the already disabled **Print...** option!

Adding and removing menu items

Along with enabling or disabling menu items programmatically, we can also add or remove menu items on the fly. In `menu2.html`, add the following code immediately after the existing markup:

```
<p>
  <form>
    <input type="button" id="additem" value="Add menu item" />
  </form>
</p>
```

Then change the final `<script>` element to this:

```
<script>
  $(document).ready(function($){
    $("#myMenu").menu();
    $("#additem").click(function() {
      $("<li><a href='#'>New item</a></li>").appendTo("#myMenu");
```

```
        $("#myMenu").menu("refresh");
    });
});
</script>
```

Save the changes as `menu6.html`. On this page, we've added a new `<input>` element, which we will use to add a new menu item.

In the `<script>` element, our function handles the addition of a menu item by first building the required markup. We then append this to the `myMenu` menu, before calling menu's `refresh()` method to update the display. After adding a few menu items, the page should appear something like this:

Not to be outdone, we can use the same `refresh()` method to remove a menu item, although the process we need to use to find the item to remove will change. Let's take a look at how to achieve this, alter the `<form>` tag contents, as shown:

```
<form>
    <input type="button" id="removeitem" value="Remove menu item" />
</form>
```

Next, change the `<script>` element in `menu6.html` as shown:

```
<script>
    $(document).ready(function($){
```

```
$("#myMenu").menu();
$("#removeitem").click(function() {
    $("#ui-id-3").remove();
    $("#myMenu li:nth-child(3)").remove();
    $("#myMenu").menu("refresh");
});
});
</script>
```

Save the changes as `menu7.html`. If we load the page in the browser, and hit the **Remove menu item** button, you will find the **Move to folder...** menu option has been removed:

Working with menu events

The menu widget defines a series of useful options that allow you to add callback functions to perform different actions when certain events exposed by the widget are detected. The following table lists the configuration options that are able to accept executable functions on an event:

Event	Triggered when...
blur	The menu loses focus
create	The menu is created
focus	The menu gains focus or when any menu item is activated
select	A menu item is selected

Each component of the library has callback options (such as those in the previous table), which are tuned to look for key moments in any visitor interactions. Any functions we use within these callbacks are usually executed before the change happens. Therefore, you can return `false` from your callback and prevent the action from occurring.

In our next example, we will look at how easy it is to react to a particular menu item being selected, using the standard non-bind technique. Remove the final `<script>` element in `menu1.html` and replace it with this:

```
<script>
  $(document).ready(function($){
    var menuarray;
    $("#myMenu").menu({
      select: function(event, ui) {
        $('.selected', this).removeClass('selected');
        ui.item.addClass('selected');
        menuarray = ui.item.text().split(" ");
        $("#menutext").").text("You clicked on: " + menuarray[0]);
      },
      focus: function(event, ui) {
        if ($("#menutext").text() != "") {
          $("#menutext").removeClass("normaltext").
addClass("hilitetext");
        }
      },
      blur: function(event, ui) {
        $("#menutext").removeClass("hilitetext").
addClass("normaltext");
      }
    });
  });
</script>
```

Below the final `</ul>` tag, add the following:

```
<div id="menutext"></div>
```

Save this file as `menu8.html`. We also need a little CSS to complete this example; in a new page in your text editor, add the following code:

```
#menutext { width: 150px; font-family: Lucida Grande,Lucida
   Sans,Arial,sans-serif; text-align: center; }
.ui-menu { width: 150px; }
.hilitetext { background-color:  #a6c9e2; padding: 3px;
border-radius: 4px; margin-top: 6px; }
```

```
.normaltext { background-color: #fff; padding: 3px; margin-
  top: 6px; }
.selected { background-color : #313c43;  border-radius: 4px; }
.selected a { color: #fff; }
```

Save this file as `menuEvents.css` in the `css` folder. In the `<head>` element of the page we just created, add the following `<link>` element:

```
<link rel="stylesheet" href="css/menuEvents.css">
```

If we preview our results, we will see something like the following screenshot when navigating around the menu. Notice the selected menu item being displayed below the menu:

We made use of three callbacks in our example— `select`, `focus`, and `blur`; the principle is largely the same for any other callback fired by other widgets in the library.

Two arguments will be passed automatically by the widget to the callback function we define when it is executed. These are the original event object and the custom object containing useful properties from the menu it which was selected.

In our example, we've used the `select` callback to determine the title of the selected menu item, before assigning a `.selected` class to it to indicate when it has been selected; the `blur` and `focus` callbacks are used to provide a hover functionality while navigating around our menu.

Binding to events

Using the event callbacks exposed by each component is the standard way of handling interactions. However, in addition to the callbacks listed in the previous table, we can also hook into another set of events fired by each component at different times.

We can use the standard jQuery on() method to bind an event handler to a custom event, fired by the menu widget in the same way that we could bind to a standard DOM event, such as a click.

The following table lists the menu's custom binding events and their triggers:

Event	Fired when...
Menucreate	The menu is created
Menuselect	A menu item is selected
Menufocus	A menu gains focus or when any menu item is activated
Menublur	The menu loses focus

The first event menucreate is fired, as soon as the menu object is initialized; the next three will be fired depending on whether a menu item has been selected by the user.

Let's see this type of event usage in action; change the final <script> element in menu8.html to the following:

```
<script>
  $(document).ready(function($){
    var menuarray;
    $("#myMenu").menu();

    $("#myMenu").on("menuselect", function( event, ui ) {
      $('.selected', this).removeClass('selected');
      ui.item.addClass('selected');
      menuarray = ui.item.text().split(" ");
      $("#menutext").text("You clicked on: " + menuarray[0]);
    });

    $("#myMenu").on("menufocus", function( event, ui ) {
      if ($("#menutext").text() != "") {
        $("#menutext").removeClass("normaltext")
.addClass("hilitetext");
      }
    });

    $("#myMenu").on("menublur", function( event, ui ) {
```

```
        $("#menutext").removeClass("hilitetext")
   .addClass("normaltext");
       });
     });
   </script>
```

Save this change as `menu9.html`. Binding to the `menuselect` event in this way produces the same result as the previous example, using the `select` callback function. Like last time, the confirmation text should appear when selecting a menu item.

All the events exposed by all of the widgets can be used with the `on()` method, by simply prefixing the name of the widget to the name of the event.

Creating horizontal menus

Have you noticed one thing? Throughout this chapter all of the menu examples are vertical. This is not through pure chance, but simply because the menu widget, at the time of writing, doesn't yet have an option to create a horizontal menu.

It's not a problem though, as it is easy enough to create one using the power of the position widget and a little extra styling. In this example, we'll take a look at how to achieve this effect, while updating it for jQuery Version 2.

 Lots of people have attempted doing it, with varying degrees of success—my personal favorite is the version produced by *Aurélien Hayet*, and which we will use in this example. If you want to see the original article by *Aurélien Hayet* (in French language), then it is available at `http://aurelienhayet.com/2012/11/03/comment-realiser-un-menu-horizontal-a-laide-de-jquery-ui/`.

Remove the existing menu markup in `menu2.html`, and replace it with the following, saving it as `menu10.html`:

```
<body>
  <ul id="menu">
    <li><a href="#">Item A</a></li>
    <li><a href="#">Item B</a></li>
    <li><a href="#">Item C</a>
      <ul>
        <li><a href="#">Item C-1</a></li>
        <li><a href="#">Item C-2</a></li>
        <li><a href="#">Item C-3</a></li>
        <li><a href="#">Item C-4</a>
```

```
          <ul>
            <li><a href="#">Item C-4-1</a></li>
            <li><a href="#">Item C-4-2</a></li>
            <li><a href="#">Item C-4-3</a></li>
            <li><a href="#">Item C-4-4</a></li>
            <li><a href="#">Item C-4-5</a></li>
          </ul>
        </li>
        <li><a href="#">Item C-5</a></li>
      </ul>
    </li>
    <li><a href="#">Item D</a></li>
    <li><a href="#">Item E</a></li>
  </ul>
</body>
```

Alter the final `<script>` element as follows:

```
<script>
  $(document).ready(function($){
    $("#menu").menu({ position: { using: setSubMenu} });
    $("#menu > li > a > span.ui-icon-carat-1-e").removeClass("ui-icon-
carat-1-e").addClass("ui-icon-carat-1-s");
    function setSubMenuposition, elements) {
      var options = { of: elements.target.element };
      if (elements.element.element.parent().parent().attr("id") ===
"menu") {
        options.my = "center top";
        options.at = "center bottom";
      } else {
        options.my = "left top";
        options.at = "right top";
      }
      elements.element.element.position(options);
    };
  });
</script>
```

We need to tweak the styling a little to turn it into a horizontal menu, so add the following to a new document, and save it as `menuHorizontal.css` in the `css` folder. Don't forget to add a link to it from the main document:

```
.ui-menu { width: 100px; font-size: 12px; min-height: 22px; }
ul#menu { width: 500px; }
ul#menu > li { width: 100px; float: left; }
```

When loading it into a browser, the page should appear something like this:

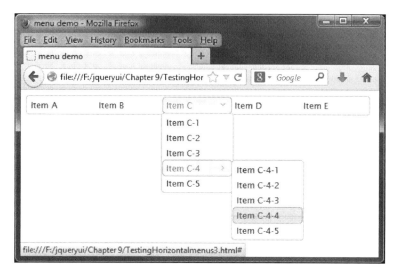

It should be noted that a MenuBar widget is in the works at the time of writing; you can see a version at `http://view.jqueryui.com/menubar/demos/menubar/default.html`. There are still some bugs to iron out and features to complete on this development version, but it is nonetheless still a usable widget that you can download and try at your own risk.

Combining with other widgets

Let's switch tracks now and take a look at some more in-depth examples of how you can use the menu widget, beginning with using it with a button.

An odd combination I hear you say, but not in reality; we can use both to build a nice little split button with a drop-down menu!

Fortunately for us, a plugin has already been created by *Mike Cantrell*; we'll use this in our example. You can download a copy of this plugin from Github (`https://gist.github.com/mcantrell/1255491`); I've updated the version in the code download for use with jQuery 2.0 and UI 1.10.3.

Immediately after the link to `jquery.ui.menu.js` in `menu2.html`, add the following:

```
<script src="development-bundle/ui/jquery.ui.button.js"></script>
<script src="js/jquery.ui.splitbutton.js"></script>
```

Alter the final `<script>` element as follows:

```
<script>
  $(document).ready(function($){
    $("#split-button").splitButton();
  });
</script>
```

Replace the existing markup between the `<body>` tags with the following:

```
<div>
  <a href="http://www.packtpub.com" id="split-button">Edit</a>
  <a href="#">Menu</a>
</div>
<ul style="display:none;">
  <li><a href="#">Print</a></li>
  <li><a href="#">Copy</a></li>
  <li><a href="#">Delete</a></li>
</ul>
```

Save the document as `menu11.html`. We need to add in our jQuery some magic that will combine our menu and document together, so in a new document add the following, and save it as `jquery.ui.splitbutton.js` within the `js` folder:

```
(function($) {
  $.fn.splitButton = function(options) {
    var menu = null;
    var settings = {
      selected: function(event, ui) {
        document.location = ui.item.children()[0];
      },
      showMenu: function() {
        if (menu) menu.hide();
        menu = $(this).parent().next().show().position({
          my: "left top", at: "left bottom", of: $(this).prev()
        });
        $(document).one("click", function() { menu.hide(); });
        return false;
      }
    };
    if (options) { $.extend(settings, options); }
    var buttonConfig = { text: false, icons: { primary: "ui-icon-
triangle-1-s" }};
    return this.button().next().button(buttonConfig).click(settings
      .showMenu).parent().buttonset().next().menu({select: settings.
selected});
```

```
    };
}) (jQuery);
```

To complete the effect, we need to adjust the CSS styling a little, so add the following into a new document and save it as `menuSplit.css` within the `css` folder:

```
#menutext { width: 150px; font-family: Lucida Grande, Lucida
Sans, Arial, sans-serif; text-align: center; }
.ui-menu { width: 150px; }
```

Don't forget to add a link into your code, pointing to `menuSplit.css`. If we load the page into a browser, you should see something similar to the following screenshot:

While the **Edit** text won't change in this example, you could easily adapt it to your own needs, adding valid links to each of the options in the drop-down menu list.

Designing context menus

One menu format that isn't, at present, available with jQuery UI is that of a context menu; more and more applications rely on the use of context menus for quick access to options, such as formatting content.

It is however a relatively easy configuration to replicate in jQuery. In our next example, we've reused some of the standard HTML markup from the main UI website and turned it into a context menu. It goes to show that, with a little jQuery magic, the markup doesn't actually need to change—a bargain!

 For this exercise and the next, you will need a copy of the code download that accompanies this book. We will be using some of the files in the code download.

Once we have created our page, we can view the results in a browser by right-clicking on the image. It should resemble the following screenshot:

 The image can be found at `http://upload.wikimedia.org/wikipedia/commons/2/25/Coffee_Roasting.jpg`.

Let's begin by extracting a copy of `menu2.html` from the code download and saving it to the `jqueryui` folder. Next, change the final `<script>` element so that it appears as follows:

```
<script>
  $(document).ready(function($){
    $("#myMenu").menu({
      select: function (event, ui) {
        $("#myMenu").hide();
        alert("Menu element clicked!");
      }
    });
    $("#contextMenu").on("contextmenu", function (event) {
      $("#myMenu").show();
      $("#myMenu").position({ collision: "none", my: "left top",
        of: event });
      return false;
    });
    $("#contextMenu").click(function (event) {
      $("#myMenu").hide();
```

```
        });
        $("#myMenu").on("contextmenu", function (event) { return false;
    });
        });
    </script>
```

Save the changed file as `menu12.html` in the `jqueryui` folder. We need to tweak the styling a little, so add the following to a new document, and save it in the `css` folder as `menuContext.css`:

```
body { color: #fff; font-family: 'Doppio One', sans-serif; text-
shadow: 0 1px 0 rgba(0,0,0,.3); line-height: 1.5; -webkit-font-
smoothing: antialiased; }
.ui-menu { width: 150px; }
#menu { position: absolute; display: none; }
#contextMenu { color: #000; }
```

Save this file as `menuContext.css` in the `css` folder, and link to it after the jQuery UI stylesheet in the `<head>` section of `menu12.html`:

```
<link rel="stylesheet" type="text/css" href="menuContext.css">
```

With use of menu's position attribute and a little extra jQuery magic, I am sure you will agree that this produces a very nice result!

Enhancing a select menu

In our final menu example, let's look at how you can use the power of a menu widget to enhance a `<select>` menu. The original author of this book, *Dan Wellman*, produced an excellent example of how to achieve this using some additional jQuery and techniques we've already covered earlier in this book. I've updated it to work with jQuery 2.03 and UI 1.10.3.

Replace the existing markup in `menu2.html` with the following:

```
<body>
    <select id="selectmenu">
        <option>Option 1</option>
        <option>Option 2</option>
        <option>Option 3</option>
        <option>Option 4</option>
        <option>Option 5</option>
    </select>
</body>
```

From the code download that accompanies this book, extract a copy of the
`menuSelect.js` file, then save it in the the `js` folder, and link it to immediately
below the last jQuery UI library reference to `jquery.ui.menu.js`.

In `menu2.html`, change the second `<link>` to point to a new stylesheet as follows:

```
<link rel="stylesheet" href="css/menuSelect.css">
```

In `menuSelect.css`, add the following:

```
.ui-menu-container { width: 200px; height: 26px; padding: 4px 0 0
    4px; position: relative; cursor: pointer; }
.ui-menu { position: absolute; right: 0; top: 100%; }
.ui-menu .ui-menu-item a { padding: 2px 20px; }
.ui-menu-trigger { padding: 0 3px; margin: -1px 3px; float: right;
text-decoration: none; }
```

Save the page as `menu13.html`. If we load the page into a browser and preview it,
you will see something akin to this screenshot:

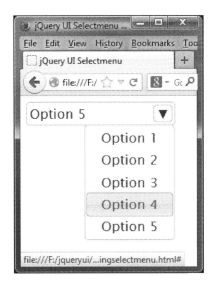

We've used a fair bit of jQuery in this example; this would lend itself to being
turned into a plugin that could be included on a page and used to enhance the
existing `<select>` menus. If written correctly, it would work using a progressive
enhancement technique, while still maintaining the original base code, in the event of
jQuery not being available.

Summary

The menu widget is an excellent way of saving space on your page by organizing related (or even completely unrelated) sections of content that can be shown or hidden with simple click input from your visitors.

Let's review what was covered in this chapter. We first looked at how, with just a little underlying HTML and a single line of jQuery-flavored JavaScript, we can implement the default menu widget. We then took a look at the CSS classes and menu options that are available for you to use to customize the menu to your needs, and how you can use some of these attributes to great effect when styling the menu. We also covered the range of methods and events that we can use to perform actions or react to events triggered by the menu widget.

We finished with a look at some examples of how you can completely alter the look of the menu, while still maintaining the original markup. We used three examples of customizing a `<select>` menu, enhancing a button, as well as turning a menu into a context menu.

In the next chapter, we'll move on to look at the Tooltips widget, which we can use to point out points of note on elements such as fields or images, or set up to work as a mini-menu of options for visitors to your site.

10
Working with Tooltips

Introduced as a part of the HTML 3 standard, and using the title attribute as its text, tooltips are a common element used to provide context within a page. You could find them in use in a variety of situations, although it is most likely that they will be found when providing assistance in correcting errors as part of the submission of a form (particularly when it concerns payment for products!).

The jQuery team introduced their version of the **tooltip** as part of changes to Version 1.9 of the library; it was designed to act as a direct replacement for the standard tooltip used in all browsers. The difference here, though, was that whilst you can't style the standard tooltip, jQuery UI's replacement is intended to be accessible, themeable, and completely customizable. It has been set to display not only when a control receives focus, but also when you hover over that control, which makes it easier to use for keyboard users.

In this chapter, we'll look at the following topics:

- The default implementation of the widget
- How the CSS framework targets tooltip widgets
- How to apply custom styles
- Configuring tooltips using their options
- Controlling tooltips using their methods
- Displaying tooltips programmatically
- Displaying different types of content in the tooltip
- Built-in transition effects for tooltips
- AJAX tooltips

Implementing a default tooltip

Tooltips were built to act as direct replacements for the browser's native tooltips. They will recognize the default markup of the title attribute in a tag, and use it to automatically add the additional markup required for the widget. The target selector can be customized though using tooltip's items and content options; you'll see an example of this later in this chapter. Let's first have a look at the basic structure required for implementing tooltips.

In a new file in your text editor, create the following page:

```
<!DOCTYPE HTML>
<html>
  <head>
    <meta charset="utf-8">
    <title>Tooltip</title>
    <link rel="stylesheet" href="development-bundle/themes/redmond/
jquery.ui.all.css">
    <style>
    p { font-family: Verdana, sans-serif; }
    </style>
    <script src="js/jquery-2.0.3.js"></script>
    <script src="development-bundle/ui/jquery.ui.core.js"></script>
    <script src="development-bundle/ui/jquery.ui.widget.js"></script>
    <script src="development-bundle/ui/jquery.ui.position.js">
</script>
    <script src="development-bundle/ui/jquery.ui.tooltip.js"></script>
    <script>
      $(document).ready(function($){
      $(document).tooltip();
      });
    </script>
  </head>
  <body>
 <p>Lorem ipsum dolor sit amet, consectetur adipiscing elit. Nulla
blandit mi quis imperdiet semper. Fusce vulputate venenatis fringilla.
Donec vitae facilisis tortor. Mauris dignissim nibh ac justo
ultricies, nec vehicula ipsum ultricies. Mauris molestie felis ligula,
id tincidunt urna consectetur at. Praesent <a href="http://www.
ipsum.com" title="This was generated from www.ipsum.com">blandit</a>
faucibus ante ut semper. Pellentesque non tristique nisi. Ut hendrerit
tempus nulla, sit amet venenatis felis lobortis feugiat. Nam ac
facilisis magna. Praesent consequat, risus in semper imperdiet, nulla
lorem aliquet nisi, a laoreet nisl leo rutrum mauris.</p>
  </body>
</html>
```

Save the code as `tooltip1.html` in your `jqueryui` working folder. Let's review what was used. The following script and CSS resources are needed for the default tooltip widget configuration:

- `jquery.ui.all.css`
- `jquery-2.0.3.js`
- `jquery.ui.core.js`
- `jquery.ui.widget.js`
- `jquery.ui.tooltip.js`

The script required to create a tooltip, when using the title element in the underlying HTML can be as simple as this, which should be added after the last `<script>` element in your code, as shown in the previous example:

```
<script>
  $(document).ready(function($){
    $(document).tooltip();
  });
</script>
```

In this example, when hovering over the link, the library adds in the requisite aria described by the code for screen readers into the HTML link. The widget then dynamically generates the markup for the tooltip, and appends it to the document, just before the closing `</body>` tag. This is automatically removed as soon as the target element loses focus.

> **ARIA**, or **Accessible Rich Internet Applications**, provides a way to make content more accessible to people with disabilities. You can learn more about this initiative at `https://developer.mozilla.org/en-US/docs/Accessibility/ARIA`.

It is not necessary to only use the `$(document)` element when adding tooltips. Tooltips will work equally well with classes or selector IDs; using a selector ID, will give a finer degree of control, as we will see later in this chapter.

Exploring the tooltip CSS framework classes

Using Firebug for Firefox (or another generic DOM explorer), we can see that specific class names are added to the underlying HTML elements that the Tooltip widget is created from. Let's review these class names briefly and see how they contribute to the overall appearance of the widget.

Classname	Purpose
ui-tooltip	The outer container for the tooltip
ui-tooltip-content	The content of the tooltip
ui-widget-content	Applies content container styles to an element and its child text, links, and icons
ui-corner-all	Applies a corner-radius to all four corners of element

Unlike other widgets, little in the way of styling is added by tooltip—the majority of the styles are added when the tooltip is created, as shown in the following screenshot:

```html
<!DOCTYPE html>
<html>
    <head>
    <body>
        <p>
            Lorem ipsum dolor sit amet, consectetur adipiscing elit. Nulla blandit mi quis imperdiet
            semper. Fusce vulputate venenatis fringilla. Donec vitae facilisis tortor. Mauris
            dignissim nibh ac justo ultricies, nec vehicula ipsum ultricies. Mauris molestie felis
            ligula, id tincidunt urna consectetur at. Praesent
            <a title="This was generated from
            www.ipsum.com" href="http://www.ipsum.com">blandit</a>
            faucibus ante ut semper. Pellentesque non tristique nisi. Ut hendrerit tempus nulla, sit
            amet venenatis felis lobortis feugiat. Nam ac facilisis magna. Praesent consequat, risus
            in semper imperdiet, nulla lorem aliquet nisi, a laoreet nisl leo rutrum mauris.
        </p>
        <div id="ui-tooltip-17" class="ui-tooltip ui-widget ui-corner-all ui-widget-
        content" role="tooltip" style="top: 85px; left: 86px; display: block; opacity: 0;">
            <div class="ui-tooltip-content">This was generated from www.ipsum.com</div>
        </div>
    </body>
</html>
```

Overriding the default styles

When styling the Tooltip widget, we are not limited to merely using the prebuilt themes on offer (about which we will cover in the next section), we can always elect to override existing styles with our own. In our next example, we'll see how easy this is to accomplish, by making some minor changes to the example from tooltip1.html.

In a new document, add the following styles, and save it as `tooltipOverride.css`, within the `css` folder:

```
p { font-family: Verdana, sans-serif; }
.ui-tooltip { background: #637887; color: #fff; }
```

Don't forget to link to the new style sheet from the `<head>` element of your document:

```
<link rel="stylesheet" href="css/tooltipOverride.css">
```

Before we continue, it is worth explaining a great trick for styling tooltips before committing the results to code.

If you are using Firefox, you can download and install the **Toggle JS** add-on for Firefox, which is available from `https://addons.mozilla.org/en-US/firefox/addon/toggle-js/`. This allows us to switch off JavaScript on a per-page basis; we can then hover over the link to create the tooltip, before expanding the markup in Firebug and styling it at our leisure.

Save your HTML document as `tooltip2.html`. When we run the page in a browser, you should see the modified tooltip appear when hovering over the link in the text:

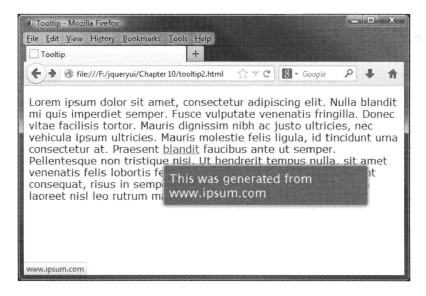

Using prebuilt themes

If creating completely new styles by hand is overkill for your needs, you can always elect to use one of the prebuilt themes that are available for download from the jQuery UI site.

This is a really easy change to make. We first need to download a copy of the replacement theme; in our example, we're going to use one called **Excite Bike**. Let's start by browsing to `http://jqueryui.com/download/`, then deselecting the **Toggle All** option:

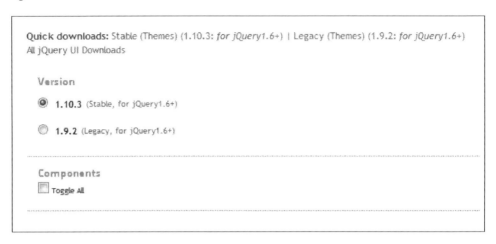

We don't need to download the whole library, just the theme at the bottom, change the theme option to display **Excite Bike** then click on **Download**:

Next, open a copy of `tooltip2.html` then look for this line:

```
<link rel="stylesheet" href="development-bundle/themes/redmond/jquery.
ui.all.css">
```

You will notice the highlighted word in the above line. This is the name of the existing theme. Change this to `excite-bike` then save the document as `tooltip3.html`, then remove the `tooltipOverride.css` link, and you're all set. The following is our replacement theme in action:

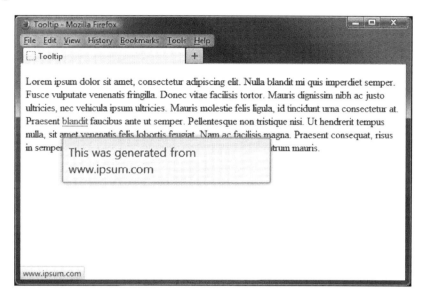

With a single change of word, we can switch between any of the prebuilt themes available for use with jQuery UI (or indeed even any of the custom ones that others have made available online), as long as you have downloaded and copied the theme into the appropriate folder.

There may be occasions, though, where we need to tweak the settings. This gives us the best of both worlds, where we only need to concentrate on making the required changes. Let's take a look at how we can alter an existing theme using ThemeRoller.

Creating custom themes with ThemeRoller

If we browse to `http://jqueryui.com/themeroller/`, we can alter some of the settings used to style the **Tooltip** example on this page. Alter the **Background color & texture** option under **Content**, then change the **Border** option to #580000, as shown in the following screenshot:

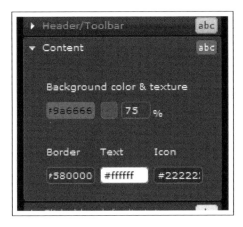

Move down to the **Clickable: active state** section, then change the **Background color & texture** option to **#ccb2b2** at **100%**, and the **Border** option to **#580000**. Leave the rest unchanged:

If you scroll down to the **Tooltip** example at the foot of the page, then hover over either image, you should see the effects of our changes:

Whilst I know the colors may not win any style awards, you can see how easy it is to alter the colors. When you've finished choosing your colors, you can then download the final version from the download page. A copy of the custom theme is also available in the code download that accompanies this book; take a look at `tooltip4.html` in the `jquery` folder to see an example of our new stylesheet in action.

We can take it even further with the use of HTML. Beware though, as this will introduce a security risk to your pages and should be used with care! Have a look at the section marked *Working with HTML in tooltips*, later in this chapter, for an example of how you can really go to town in altering the styles of your tooltips.

Configuring tooltip options

Each of the different components in the library has a series of options that control which features of the widget are enabled by default. An object literal, or an object reference, can be passed into the `tooltip()` widget method to configure these options.

The available options to configure non-default behaviors are shown in the following table:

Option	Default value	Used to...
`content`	`function returning the title attribute`	Set the content of the tooltip—if setting this option, then it is likely you will also need to change the items option as well.
`disabled`	`false`	Disable the tooltip.
`hide`	`null`	Determine if or how to animate the hiding of the tooltip.
`items`	`[title]`	Set a selector that indicates which items should show tooltips. This can be customized if you are planning to use something other than the title attribute for the tooltip content, or need to set a different selector for event delegation.
`position`	`{ my: "left top+15", at: "left bottom", collision: "flipfit" }`	Identify the position of the tooltip in relation to the associated target element.
`show`	`null`	Determine if or how to animate the showing of the tooltip.
`tooltipClass`	`null`	Add a class to a widget that can display different tooltip types, such as errors or warnings.
`track`	`false`	Determine whether the tooltip should track (follow) the mouse.

Positioning tooltips accurately

One of the most useful features of jQuery UI's tooltips is the ability to fine-tune where they appear on screen. There may be instances where you need them to appear, but not at the expense of hiding an important feature on your website or application! Let's have a look at how the `position` attribute works, using a custom styled tooltip with pointer as an example.

In your text editor, alter the final `<script>` block of `tooltip4.html`, as shown in the following code:

```
<script>
  $(document).ready(function($){
    $('a').tooltip({
      position: {
```

```
            my: 'center+30 bottom',
            at: 'center top-8',
            of: '#tip'
          }
        });
        $('a').tooltip('option', 'tooltipClass', 'top');
      });
</script>
```

We need to alter the markup so it includes the selector ID we've just referenced in the tooltip call:

```
<p>Lorem ipsum dolor sit amet, consectetur adipiscing elit. Nulla
blandit mi quis imperdiet semper. Fusce vulputate venenatis fringilla.
Donec vitae facilisis tortor. Mauris dignissim nibh ac justo
ultricies, nec vehicula ipsum ultricies. Mauris molestie felis ligula,
id tincidunt urna consectetur at. Praesent <a href="http://www.ipsum.
com" id="tip" title="This was generated from www.ipsum.com">blandit
</a> faucibus ante ut semper. Pellentesque non tristique nisi. Ut
hendrerit tempus nulla, sit amet venenatis felis lobortis feugiat. Nam
ac facilisis magna. Praesent consequat, risus in semper imperdiet,
nulla lorem aliquet nisi, a laoreet nisl leo rutrum mauris.</p>
```

In a new file in your text editor, create the following small style sheet:

```
body { margin-top: 75px; }
.ui-tooltip { background: #c99; color: white; border: none; padding:
0; opacity: 1; border-radius: 8px; border: 3px solid #fff; width:
245px; }
.ui-tooltip-content { position: relative; padding: 1em; }
.ui-tooltip-content::after { content: ''; position: absolute; border-
style: solid; display: block; width: 0; }
.right .ui-tooltip-content::after { top: 18px; left: -10px; border-
color: transparent #c99; border-width: 10px 10px 10px 0; }
.left .ui-tooltip-content::after { top: 18px; right: -10px; border-
color: transparent #c99; border-width: 10px 0 10px 10px; }
.top .ui-tooltip-content::after { bottom: -10px; left: 72px; border-
color: #c99 transparent; border-width: 10px 10px 0; }
.bottom .ui-tooltip-content::after { top: -10px; left: 72px; border-
color: #c99 transparent; border-width: 0 10px 10px; }
```

Save this as `tooltipPointer.css`. Remove the existing styling from `tooltip4.html`, then add the following references into the <head> and resave it as `tooltip5.html`:

```
<link rel="stylesheet" href="development-bundle/themes/redmond/jquery.
ui.all.css">
<link rel="stylesheet" href="css/tooltipPointer.css">
```

In this example, we've used a number of pseudo-selectors to style our tooltip; this has the added advantage that it doesn't require any images as part of producing the tooltip. If we view the new page in a browser, it should appear similar to the following screenshot:

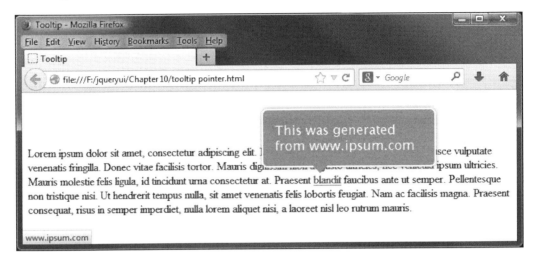

Using the position widget

In our example, you will have noticed that we've resized the window to achieve the effect shown in the previous screenshot. If you expand that window to full size, the tooltip is very likely to shift; to prevent this from happening, it's important to use the of attribute, so that the tooltip (in this instance) remains next to the original link we added to our markup.

Using the position attribute (and indeed the widget) can be a little tricky to master, but it is worth the effort to ensure that your widgets are positioned just where you need them to appear.

 Chris Coyier of CSS Tricks (http://www.css-tricks.com) has produced a nice example of how the position utility works, which you can see at http://css-tricks.com/jquery-ui-position-function/.

In a nutshell, an example use of the position widget such as the following code:

```
$("#move-me").position({
    "my": "right top",
    "at": "left bottom",
    "of":  $("#thing")
```

```
});
```

...would translate in the following illustration:

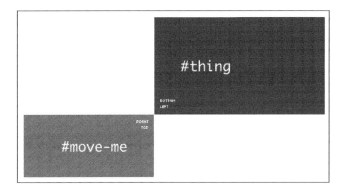

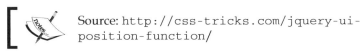

Source: `http://css-tricks.com/jquery-ui-position-function/`

Tracking mouse movement with tooltips

So far, we've had a look at how to add tooltips to your page, and covered some of the possibilities for styling and positioning them on screen. One small enhancement we can make to our tooltips is to set them so that they can follow your cursor, when activated.

This is a simple change to make; change the body of `tooltip5.html` so it contains the following elements:

```
<div id="content">
  <p>Lorem ipsum dolor sit amet, consectetur adipiscing
elit. Nulla blandit mi quis imperdiet semper. Fusce vulputate
venenatis fringilla. Donec vitae facilisis tortor. Mauris <a
href="#" rel="tooltip1"title="This is a tooltip hovering over
a link">dignissim</a> nibh ac justo ultricies, nec vehicula
ipsum ultricies. Mauris molestie felis ligula, id tincidunt urna
consectetur at. Praesent blandit faucibus ante ut semper. <a href="#"
rel="tooltip2" title="Here is another tooltip">Pellentesque non
tristique</a> nisi. Ut hendrerit tempus nulla, sit amet venenatis
felis lobortis feugiat. Nam ac facilisis magna. Praesent consequat,
risus in semper imperdiet, nulla lorem aliquet nisi, a laoreet nisl
leo rutrum mauris.
  <p>Tooltips are also useful for form elements, to show some
additional information in the context of each field.</p>
  <p>
```

```
        <label for="textinput">First text input:</label>
        <input id="test" title="Please enter text in this field." />
    </p>
</div>
<p>Hover over the input field or links to see the tooltips in
action.</p>
```

We need to add the tracking facility, so update the final `<script>` block as follows:

```
<script>
  $(document).ready(function($){
    $(document).tooltip({ track: true });
  });
</script>
```

Save the updated document as `tooltip6.html`. Let's now add in some final tweaks to our styling so the content appears properly on screen. Add the following to a new document, saving it as `tooltipTrack.css`, in the `css` folder:

```
p { font-family: Verdana, sans-serif; font-size: 0.8em; font-style:
italic; }
label { display: inline-block; width: 8.5em; }
#content { border: 2px solid #42505a; padding: 5px; border-radius:
4px; }
#content p { font-style: normal; }
```

Don't forget to link to the new style sheet from the `<head>` of our page (by replacing the existing reference to `tooltipPointer.css`):

```
<link rel="stylesheet" href="css/tooltipTrack.css">
```

The following screenshot shows how the page should appear when previewing our results:

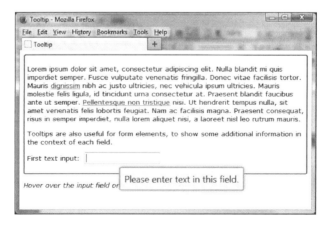

We've now set the tooltip to follow our cursor anytime we are hovering over a target element. In our example, this includes either of the two links or the input element. We're not limited to either of those elements when setting up tracking; this can be used on any valid HTML element, such as radio buttons, buttons, or even labels.

Although we can't easily show it in print, you should find that when you move your cursor around, the tooltip will follow it as long as the cursor is still hovering over its target element.

Displaying certain tooltips

So far, we've assigned all of our tooltips to work using the $(document) object; whilst this will work perfectly well, it does mean that our tooltips will always follow the same format, and work in the same manner, as the configuration will apply to all tooltips on that page.

We can easily change this, though; jQuery UI's Tooltip will work equally fine with any jQuery selectors, as it does with the document object. To prove this, let's take a look at how you would configure tooltip to work with a specific element.

In tooltip2.html, change the final <script> element to the following:

```
<script>
  $(document).ready(function($){
    $("#input").tooltip();
  });
</script>
```

We don't need the CSS override styles, so remove this line from the <head> of the document:

```
<link rel="stylesheet" href="css/tooltipOverride.css">
```

We also need to add the following code below the existing markup:

```
<p>Tooltips are also useful for form elements, to show some additional
information in the context of each field.</p>
<label for="input">Please enter some text:</label>
<input type="text" id="input" title="I am a tooltip!">
```

Save this as `tooltip7.html` in your `jqueryui` folder. In this example, we've removed the reference to document, and replaced it with the `id` assigned to the textbox, as shown in the following screenshot:

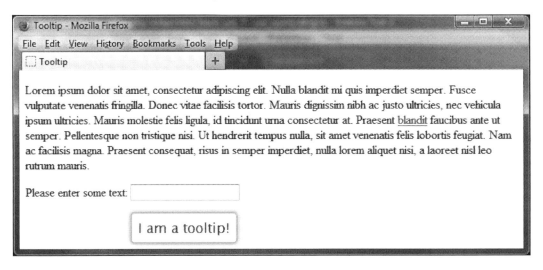

The same style classes that we've seen earlier will still be applied, but this time they will only appear when hovering over the textbox, and not the link in the text.

Displaying AJAX content in tooltips

Throughout most of this chapter, we've used the standard technique of displaying content in our tooltips, which is to reference the text stored in the title attribute of any tags that can be found on the page.

However, jQuery UI's Tooltips are able to reference content using AJAX; this allows you to generate tooltips dynamically, rather than being limited to what is displayed in your markup. In our example, we will use the content attribute to pass plain text to the widget; you could equally pass a callback function as the content's value to the tooltip.

In your text editor, remove the existing final `<script>` block in `tooltip7.html`, and replace it with the following code:

```
$(document).ready(function($){
  var url = "ajax.html";
  $("#ajaxTip").load(url);
  $('a').tooltip({
    content: '... waiting on ajax ...',
    open: function(evt, ui) {
      var elem = $(this);
```

```
        var data = $("#ajaxTip").text();
        $.ajax().always(function(event, ui) {
          elem.tooltip('option', 'content', data);
        });
      }
    });
  });
```

Next, remove the `<label>` and `<input>` code, then add the following immediately below your markup in the `<body>` section:

```
<div id="ajaxTip" style="display:none;"></div>
```

We also need to create some content that will be imported into the page using AJAX, so in a new document, add the following code and save it as `ajax.html`:

```
Lorem ipsum dolor sit amet, consectetur adipiscing elit.
```

Save the file as `tooltip8.html`. In this instance, you will need to view this through a web server, in order for the AJAX effect to work correctly; if you don't have access to some online web space, you can use WAMP Server(for PC, available from `http://www.wampserver.com/en/`) or MAMP locally (for Macs, downloadable from `http://www.mamp.info/en/mamp/`), which will work equally as well.

When hovering over the link, a tooltip will appear but with the content of the HTML file that it has imported, as shown in the following screenshot:

As we are pulling in HTML-based content, you should ensure that content is handled correctly, to minimize risks of attacks to your site. In this example, we've just imported plain text from our test HTML file, but using this method does allow you to import any HTML (within reason) to great effect.

 Later in this chapter, we will look at using HTML in tooltips in more detail; you could potentially use the styling and content from that method, but import it all using AJAX instead.

How can we tell if it has worked?

The easiest way to tell if your content has successfully been imported is by inspecting it in the **Console** tab of a DOM inspector, such as Firebug.

 DOM Inspectors can be used to inspect, browse, and edit the **Document Model Object (DOM)** of any webpage, for a number of purposes, such as establishing slow-loading objects or sources, or previewing changes to CSS styling before committing them to code.

Here you can clearly see the call to `test.html` (taken from Firebug), which has returned a value of `200`, indicating success:

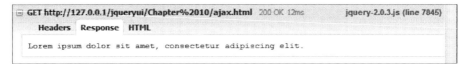

Using effects in tooltips

You will have hopefully noticed that, from each of the examples demonstrated in this chapter, each tooltip will fade in and out gradually, by default. Tooltips are not limited to using only this fade in or out effect; you may prefer to use something that shows a little more impact when displayed on screen.

In our next example, we will look at how you can alter your code to use different effects, to achieve this effect. Add the following lines of code immediately below the last call to the jQuery UI library in `tooltip7.html`:

```
<script src="development-bundle/ui/jquery.ui.effect.js"></script>
<script src="development-bundle/ui/jquery.ui.effect-bounce.js">
</script>
<script src="development-bundle/ui/jquery.ui.effect-explode.js">
</script>
```

Next, remove these two lines from the existing markup:

```
<label for="input">Please enter some text:</label>
<input type="text" id="input" title="I am a tooltip!">
```

Alter the final `<script>` element to include the new effects, as shown:

```
<script>
  $(document).ready(function($){
    $(document).tooltip({
      show: { effect: "bounce", duration: 800 },
      hide: { effect: "explode", duration: 800 }
    });
  });
</script>
```

Save the document as `tooltip9.html`. If we load the page into a browser and hover over the link in the text, you will see the tooltip explode when moving away, as shown in the following screenshot:

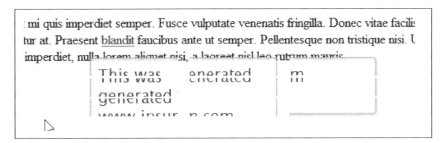

Working with HTML in tooltips

So far, we've covered how you can set up tooltips to appear on your pages, as well as style them. The latter presents us with a slight dilemma, though, as we have to rely on jQuery to add in CSS styles programmatically, which can be detrimental if we're aiming to maintain a progressive style of enhancement for our tooltips. There is a way around this; whilst it involves an element of jQuery, it does allow us to use HTML to generate our tooltips, making it far more flexible for our needs.

> **Use of HTML in your tooltips**
>
> Before we go any further, I should point out that use of this method introduces a security risk to your code; it is for this reason that the default usage of content was switched from allowing HTML to just plain text. Please use this at your own risk!

Remove the contents of the markup in `tooltip9.html`, and add in the following:

```
<p>Lorem ipsum dolor sit amet, consectetur adipiscing elit.
Nulla blandit mi quis imperdiet semper. Fusce vulputate venenatis
fringilla. Donec vitae facilisis tortor. Mauris <a href="#"
rel="tooltip1">dignissim</a> nibh ac justo ultricies, nec vehicula
ipsum ultricies. Mauris molestie felis ligula, id tincidunt urna
consectetur at. Praesent blandit faucibus ante ut semper. Pellentesque
non tristique nisi. Ut hendrerit tempus nulla, sit amet venenatis
felis lobortis feugiat. Nam ac facilisis magna. Praesent consequat,
risus in semper imperdiet, nulla lorem aliquet nisi, a laoreet nisl
leo rutrum mauris.
</p>
```

Next, alter the final `<script>` block, as shown in the following code:

```
<script>
  $(document).ready(function($){
    var tooltiptext = "<div id='tooltip'><div id='title'>Test Tooltip
</div><div id='content'>This is a random tooltip with some text</
div></div>";
    $("a[rel=tooltip]").tooltip({
      items: "a",
      content: function() {
        return tooltiptext;
      }
    });
  });
</script>
```

Save this as `tooltip10.html`. We now have a working tooltip, but it won't look very attractive. Create a new style sheet and add to it the following basic styles:

```
p { font-family: Verdana, sans-serif; }
#tooltip { width: 100px; border: 1px solid #F1D031; font-family:
Verdana, sans-serif; font-size: 10px; }
#title { width: 94px; background-color: #FFEF93; font-weight: bold;
padding: 3px; }
#content { width: 94px; background-color: #FFFFA3; height: 50px;
padding: 3px; }
```

Save this as `tooltipSelector.css` in your `css` folder. Don't forget to link to the new style sheet from the `<head>` of our page (after the link to the standard jQuery UI style sheet):

```
<link rel="stylesheet" href="css/tooltipSelector.css">
```

In this example, we're not going to use the prebuilt styling from our redmond theme, so remove the following link:

```
<link rel="stylesheet" href="development-bundle/themes/redmond/jquery.
ui.all.css">
```

We also need to remove the effects calls from the previous demonstration, so remove the following links from the `<head>` of your document:

```
<script src="development-bundle/ui/jquery.ui.effect.js"></script>
<script src="development-bundle/ui/jquery.ui.effect-bounce.js">
</script>
<script src="development-bundle/ui/jquery.ui.effect-explode.js">
</script>
```

Save our altered document as `tooltip10.html`. If we run this page in a browser, you will see the tooltip **Test tooltip** appear when hovering over a link, as shown in the following screenshot:

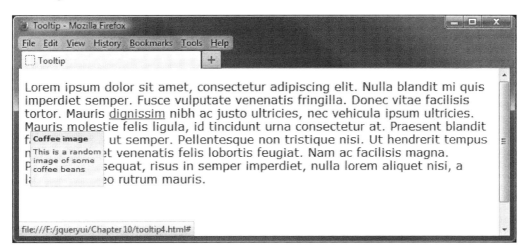

As you can see, we've completely altered the styling used on our tooltip; this method requires more work than the normal method for setting up tooltips, but it is worth the effort, provided it is done correctly!

The dangers of working with HTML

In the previous example, we looked at how you can incorporate HTML into your tooltips, which opens up some powerful opportunities in terms of what can be displayed within a tooltip. There is an inherent risk associated with using HTML in tooltips, though; in previous versions of the library, you could include HTML within the `<title>` tag, as part of setting up tooltips. However, this has been altered in UI 1.10, as a fix for the cross-site scripting (XSS) vulnerability that was present in Version 1.9, where attackers could insert (or inject) client-side script, often malicious, into the Tooltip widget on a page. You can still use HTML, but need to use the content option as outlined in the previous example. You can learn more about cross-site scripting, and how to reduce the threat, at `http://en.wikipedia.org/wiki/Cross-site_scripting`.

 As the content option overrides the default behavior, you should always ensure your content is correctly escaped (or sanitized) to minimize the risk of cross-site scripting.

Using tooltip methods

The Tooltip widget contains a handful of methods which allow us to work with it programmatically and alter its default behaviors. Let's take a look at the methods, which are listed in the following table:

Method	Used to...
close	Close a tooltip; should only be used for non-delegated tooltips.
destroy	Remove the tooltip functionality completely.
disable	Disable the tooltip.
enable	Enable the tooltip.
open	Programmatically open a tooltip. This is only intended for non-delegated tooltips.
option	Get or set the value associated with the specified optionName
widget	Return a jQuery object containing the original element.

Enabling and disabling tooltips

We can make use of the `enable` or `disable` methods to programmatically enable or disable specific tooltips. This will effectively switch on any tooltips that were initially disabled or disable those that are currently active. Let's make use of the enable and disable methods to switch on or off a tooltip, which we will configure to be disabled when the page loads in the browser.

Add the following new `<button>` elements directly after the existing markup for the Tooltip widget in `tooltip10.html`:

```
<label for="input">Please enter some text:</label>
<input type="text" id="tooltip2" title="I am a tooltip!">
<p>
  <button id="turnon">Enable Tooltip 1</button>
  <button id="turnoff">Disable Tooltip 1</button>
<p>
</body>
```

Next, change the final `<script>` element so that it appears as follows:

```
<script>
  $(document).ready(function($){
    $("#tooltip").tooltip({ disabled: true });
    $("#turnon").click(function(){
      $("#tooltip").tooltip("enable");
    })

    $("#turnoff").click(function(){
      $("#tooltip").tooltip("disable");
    })
  });
</script>
```

Save the changed file as `tooltip11.html`. On the page, we've added two new `<button>` elements. One will be used to enable the disabled tooltip and the other is used to disable it again. If we load the page into a browser, we will see something similar to the following screenshot:

Lorem ipsum dolor sit amet, consectetur adipiscing elit. Nulla blandit mi quis imperdiet semper. Fusce vulputate venenatis fringilla. Donec vitae facilisis tortor. Mauris dignissim nibh ac justo ultricies, nec vehicula ipsum ultricies. Mauris molestie felis ligula, id tincidunt urna consectetur at. Praesent blandit faucibus ante ut semper. Pellentesque non tristique nisi. Ut hendrerit tempus nulla, sit amet venenatis felis lobortis feugiat. Nam ac facilisis magna. Praesent consequat, risus in semper imperdiet, nulla lorem aliquet nisi, a laoreet nisl leo rutrum mauris.

Please enter some text: _____

[Enable Tooltip 1] [Disable Tooltip 1]

In the JavaScript, we use the `click` event of the `Enable Tooltip` button to call the `tooltip()` widget method. To do this, we pass the string `enable`, to the `tooltip()` method as the first argument. Additionally, we pass the index number of the tab we want to enable as a second argument. All methods in jQuery UI are called in this way. We specify the name of the method we wish to call as the first argument to the widget method; the `disable` method is used in the same way.

> Don't forget that if you set `$(document)` as the element upon which tooltip works, then we can use both of these methods without additional arguments, in order to enable or disable all tooltips on that page.

Displaying tooltips programmatically

As well as enabling or disabling tooltips programmatically, we can equally show or hide tooltips at will, by clicking a button or suitable link on screen. Let's use both now, to show or hide one of the tooltips at will, in our next example.

In `tooltip11.html`, alter the last lines of our existing markup as indicated:

```
<label for="input">Please enter some text:</label>
<input type="text" id="tooltip2" title="I am a tooltip!">
<p>
   <button id="showtip">Show (open) Tooltip</button>
   <button id="hidetip">Hide (close) Tooltip</button>
</p>
```

Next, let's change the final `<script>` element to include the new event handlers that will be assigned to the new buttons we've just added:

```
<script>
  $(document).ready(function($){
    $("#tooltip").tooltip();

    $("#showtip").click(function(){
      $("#tooltip").tooltip("open");
    })
    $("#hidetip").click(function(){
      $("#tooltip").tooltip("close");
    })
  });
</script>
```

Save the altered file as `tooltip12.html`. When loading the page into a browser, and clicking on the **Show (open) Tooltip** button, you will see the tooltip appear:

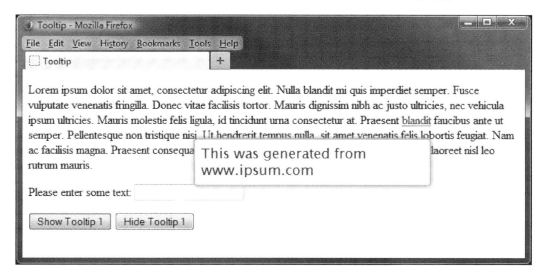

In the JavaScript, we use the click event of the **Show (open) Tooltip** button to call the Tooltip widget and display the tooltip. To do this, we only need to pass one attribute, which is the string open, to the `tooltip()` method. When we need to hide (or close) the tooltip, we can pass the string close as part of calling the Tooltip widget, in a similar manner.

Handling tooltip events

The Tooltip widget defines three events that allow you to add call back functions to perform different actions, when certain events exposed by the widget are detected. The following table lists the configuration options that are able to accept executable functions on an event:

Event	Fired when...
close	A tooltip is closed or triggered on `focusout` or `mouseleave`
create	A tooltip is created
open	A tooltip is shown or triggered on `focusin` or `mouseover`

Each component of the library has callback options (such as those in the previous table), which are tuned to look for key moments in any visitor interactions. Any functions we use within these callbacks are usually executed before the change happens. Therefore, you can return `false` from your callback and prevent the action from occurring.

In our next example, we'll look at how easy it is to react to a particular tooltip being displayed, using the standard non-bind technique. Change the final `<script>` element in `tooltip12.html` so that it appears as follows:

```
<script>
  $(document).ready(function($){
    $("#tooltip").tooltip({
      open: function(event, ui) {
        $("#console").append("Tooltip activated" + "<br>");
      },
      close: function(event, ui) {
        $("#console").append("Tooltip closed" + "<br>");
      }
    });
    $("#tooltip").tooltip();
  });
</script>
```

Save this as `tooltip13.html`. We also need to alter our markup, so remove the two buttons at the foot of our existing markup, and insert a new History `<div>` as shown:

```
<div id="history">
  <b>History:</b>
<div id="console"></div>
</div>
</body>
```

Finally, we need to add a little styling to make the display look presentable. In a new document, add the following:

```
#history { border-radius: 4px; border: 1px solid #c4c4c4; width:
250px; padding: 3px; margin-top: 15px; }
```

Save this in the `css` folder as `tooltipEvents.css`. Don't forget to link to the new style sheet from the `<head>` of our page (after the link to the standard jQuery UI stylesheet):

```
<link rel="stylesheet" href="css/tooltipEvents.css">
```

If we preview the results in a browser, then move over the tooltip link a few times. We can begin to see a history build up, as shown in this screenshot:

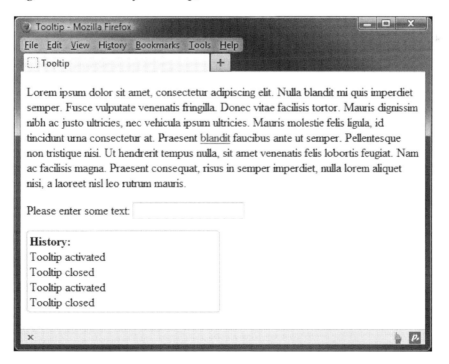

We made use of both the open and close callbacks within this example, although the principle is the same for the create custom event, that can also be fired by tooltip. The names of the callback functions are provided as the values of the open and close properties in our configuration object.

Two arguments will be passed automatically by the widget to the callback function we define, when it is executed. These are the original event object and custom ui object containing useful properties from the tooltip, which was displayed.

Binding to tooltip events

Using the event callbacks exposed by each component is the standard way of handling interactions. However, in addition to the callbacks listed in the previous table, we can also look into another set of events fired by each component at different times.

We can use the standard jQuery on() method to bind an event handler to a custom event, fired by the Tooltip widget in the same way that we could bind to a standard DOM event, such as a click.

The following table lists the Tooltip widget's custom binding events and their triggers:

Event	Fired when...
tooltipcreate	A tooltip is created
tooltipopen	A tooltip is shown or triggered on focusin or mouseover
tooltipclose	A tooltip is closed or triggered on focusout or mouseleave

The first event is fired as soon as the tooltip is created; the remaining two are fired depending on whether the tooltip has received focus.

Let's see this type of event in action; change the final <script> element in tooltip13.html to the following:

```
<script>
  $(document).ready(function($){
    $("#tooltip").tooltip();
    $("#tooltip").on("tooltipopen", function(event, ui) {
      $("#console").append("Tooltip activated" + "<br>");
    })

    $("#tooltip").on("tooltipclose", function(event, ui) {
      $("#console").append("Tooltip closed" + "<br>");
    })
  });
</script>
```

Save this change as `tooltip14.html`. Binding to the `tooltipopen` and `tooltipclose` event handlers in this way, produces the same result as the previous example, using the `open` and `close` callback functions. Like last time, the console log should be updated each time you hover over the tooltip in the text.

All of the events exposed by all of the widgets can be used with the `on()` method, by simply prefixing the name of the widget to the name of the event.

Playing videos

So far, we've covered a great deal of theory around using jQuery UI's Tooltip; in this example and the next, we will take a look at some practical uses of tooltips that you can use as a starting point for your own projects. Before continuing, make sure you have a copy of the code download available, as we will be using files from it for this exercise.

One possible use for tooltips is to mimic the like or dislike buttons you might find on social media sites, such as YouTube, where you can register your preference for videos you have enjoyed watching. Let's take a look at how you could replicate the functionality, in your own projects, but using tooltips and a number of other jQuery UI widgets that we've covered so far in this book.

 This demonstration uses a video from the open source project *The Big Buck Bunny*, created by the *Blender Foundation*, and available from `http://www.bigbuckbunny.org`.

From the code download, extract a copy of `tooltipVideo.js`; this will provide the functionality that adds the buttons and tooltips to the bottom of our video. Don't forget to link to the new JavaScript file from the `<head>` of our page (after the link to the jQuery UI button widget):

```
<script src="js/tooltipVideo.js"></script>
```

We also need to add a reference to the Button widget to the `<head>` of our page:

```
<script src="development-bundle/ui/jquery.ui.button.js"></script>
```

Next, change the `<body>` so that it contains the following elements:

```
<div class="player">
  <video controls="controls">
      <source src="video/big_buck_bunny.mp4" />
```

```
      <source src="video/big_buck_bunny.webm" />
    </video>
  </div>
  <p>
  <div class="tools">
    <span class="set">
      <button data-icon="ui-icon-circle-arrow-n" title="I like
this">Like</button>
      <button data-icon="ui-icon-circle-arrow-s">I dislike this</
button>
    </span>
    <div class="set">
      <button data-icon="ui-icon-circle-plus" title="Add to Watch
Later">Add to</button>
      <button class="menu" data-icon="ui-icon-triangle-1-s">Add to
favorites or playlist</button>
    </div>
    <button title="Share this video">Share</button>
    <button data-icon="ui-icon-alert">Flag as inappropiate</button>
  </div>
```

Last but not least, we also need to add some styling, to ensure the tooltips display correctly. Add the following to a new document in your text editor:

```
.player { width: 642px; height: 362px; border: 2px groove gray;
background: rgb(200, 200, 200); text-align: center; line-height:
300px; }
.ui-tooltip { border: 1px solid white; background: rgba(20, 20, 20,
1); color: white; }
.set { display: inline-block; }
.notification { position: absolute; display: inline-block; font-size:
2em; padding: .5em; box-shadow: 2px 2px 5px -2px rgba(0,0,0,0.5); }
```

Save this as `tooltipVideo.css`, into the `css` folder – don't forget to add a link to it from your main document, immediately after the link to the jQuery UI stylesheet:

```
<link rel="stylesheet" href="css/tooltipVideo.css">
```

Save your modified page as `tooltip15.html`. The following screenshot shows how the page should appear when previewing the video in a browser:

Using the buttons in this manner allows us to add some really powerful functionality to our sites. In our example, the buttons don't actually do anything (apart from show the tooltips), but in real-life, they would be used to maintain a running tally of those who have watched the video, and want to register their like (or dislike) for it.

Filling out and validating forms

Throughout this chapter, we've covered a lot of ground on how to implement tooltips, and configure them to our needs, within our sites. We cannot finish this chapter though, without taking a look at what is arguably the most important (or common?) use of tooltips in a site—form validation.

I am sure that over the years, you will likely have filled out forms online; perhaps as part of purchasing something, and that you will have made a mistake whilst completing it. The beauty of tooltips is that we can use them to provide some feedback to the visitor, to ensure they fill out the fields correctly, and do not enter invalid values to your form.

In your text editor, alter the final `<script>` block from `tooltip14.html`, as shown in the following code:

```
$(document).ready(function($){
  $("button").button();
  var $tooltips = $('#signup [title]').tooltip({
    position: { my: "left+15 center", at: "right center" }
  });
```

```
    $("#open").on('click', function() {
      $tooltips.tooltip('open');
    });
    $("#close").on('click', function() {
      $tooltips.tooltip('close');
    });
});
```

As we are using JQuery UI's Button widget in this example, we need to add a link to
the widget from within jQuery UI's library:

```
<script src="development-bundle/ui/jquery.ui.button.js"></script>
```

Next, we need to add in the markup for our form – remove the existing markup, and
replace it with the following:

```
<form id="signup">
  <fieldset>
    <legend>Sign Up Now</legend>
    <div>
      <label for="username">Username:</label>
      <input type="text" name="username" id="username" title="User
name must be between 8 and 32 characters."><br>
    </div>
    <div>
      <label for="password">Password:</label>
      <input type="password" name="password" title="Password must
contain at least one number.">
    </div>
    <div>
      <label for="password2">Confirm Password:</label>
      <input type="password" name="password2" title="Please re-type
your password for confirmation.">
    </div>
  </fieldset>
</form>
  <button id="open">Open Help</button>
  <button id="close">Close Help</button>
```

Save this as `tooltip16.html`. We also need a little CSS to complete this example. In
the `<head>` of the page we just created, add the following `<link>` element:

```
<link rel="stylesheet" href="css/tooltipForm.css">
```

Then in a new page in your text editor, add the following code:

```
body { font-family: verdana, sans-serif; width: 430px; }
label { display: inline-block; width: 11em; }
button { float: right; margin: 2px; }
fieldset { width: 400px; border: 3px solid black; border-radius: 4px;
margin: 3px; border-color: #7c96a9; font-size: 1.1em;}
fieldset div { margin-bottom: 1.2em; }
fieldset .help { display: inline-block; }
.ui-tooltip { width: 300px; font-size: 0.7em; }
```

Save this as `tooltipForm.css` in the `css` folder. If we preview the page in our browser, you will see each of the tooltips appear when hovering over them, or they can all be shown when clicking on the **Open Help** button, as shown in the following screenshot:

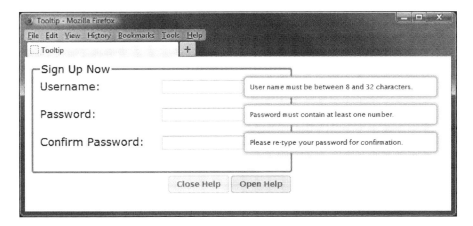

In this example, we've set jQuery UI to show the tooltips on the `[title]` attributes of each field. However, as we assigned the tooltip method handler to the `$tooltips` variable, we were able to use this to create a click handler for each of the buttons, which will either display or hide all of the tooltips, depending on which button is pressed. We can also display messages to the user, when something has gone wrong; for example, if a password has been entered incorrectly, we can use the input field's `blur` event handler to open a tooltip on screen.

Summary

Phew! For such a small widget, we certainly have covered a lot of ground!

The Tooltip widget is an excellent way to communicate short pieces of information, such as an error or alert, to the user, you can even use it as a mini help system; let's review what was covered in this chapter.

We first looked at how, with just a little underlying HTML and a single line of jQuery-flavored JavaScript, we can implement the default tooltip widget. We then saw how easy it is to style the Tooltip widget, either using a predesigned ThemeRoller theme, or one of our own; so that its appearance, but not its behavior, is altered.

We then moved on, to look at the set of configurable options exposed by the tooltip's API, and how these can be used to control the options that the widget offers. Following the configurable options, we covered the handful of methods that we can use to programmatically make the tooltip perform different actions, such as enabling or disabling specific tooltips.

We briefly looked at some of the more involved functionality supported by the tooltips widget, such as AJAX-based tooltips, and providing context to forms. Both of these techniques are easy to use and can add value to any implementation.

We have now finished our journey through the UI widgets, so let's turn our attention to looking at some of interactions available in the library, beginning with the dragging widget.

11
Drag and Drop

So far in this book, we've covered the complete range of fully released interface widgets, and over the next four chapters, we're going to shift our focus to the core interaction helpers. These are widgets that provide mouse-based interactions for widgets, where we can perform actions, such as selecting, dragging, or resizing widgets on a website. A perfect example is the resizable widget, which we will cover in *Chapter 12, The Resizable Component*. These interaction components of the library differ from those we've already looked at, in that they are not physical objects or widgets that exist on the page.

These are low-level interaction components, as opposed to the high-level widgets that we looked at in the first part of this book. They help the elements used on your pages to be more engaging and interactive for your visitors, which adds value to your site and can help make your web applications appear more professional. They also help to blur the distinctions between the browser and the desktop, and provide greater usability to make web applications more efficient, effective, and natural.

In this chapter, we'll be covering two very closely related components—**draggables** and **droppables**. The draggables API transforms any specified element into something that your visitors can pick up with the mouse pointer and drag around the page. Methods that are exposed allow you to restrict the draggables movement, make it return to its starting point after being dropped, and much more.

In this chapter, we will cover the following topics:

- How to make elements draggable
- The options available for configuring draggable objects
- How to make an element return to its starting point once the drag ends
- How to use event callbacks at different points in an interaction
- The role of a drag helper
- Containing draggables

- How to control draggability with the component's methods
- Turning an element into a drop target
- Defining accepted draggables
- Working with droppable class names
- Defining drop tolerance
- Reacting to interactions between draggables and droppables

The droppables API allows you to define a region of the page or a container of some kind for people to drop the draggables on to in order to make something else happen, for example, while adding a product to a shopping basket. A rich set of events is fired by the droppable widget that lets us react to the most interesting moments of any drag interaction.

The deal with draggables and droppables

Dragging and dropping as behaviors go hand-in-hand with each other. Where one is found, the other is invariably close by. Dragging an element around a web page is all very well and good, but if there's nowhere for that element to be dragged to, the whole exercise is usually pointless.

You can use the `draggable` class independently from the `droppable` class, as pure dragging for the sake of dragging can have its uses, such as with the dialog component. However, you can't use the `droppable` class without the `draggable` class. You don't need to make use of any of draggable's methods of course, but using droppables without having anything to drop on to them is of no value whatsoever.

Like with the widgets, it is possible, however, to combine some of the interaction helpers; draggables and droppables go together obviously. But draggables can also be used with sortables, as we'll see in *Chapter 13, Selecting and Sorting with jQuery UI,* as well as resizables.

Getting started with the draggable widget

The draggables component is used to make any specified element or collection of elements draggable, so that they can be picked up and moved around the page by a visitor. Draggability is a great effect, and is a feature that can be used in numerous ways to improve the interface of our web pages.

Using jQuery UI means that we don't have to worry about all of the tricky differences between browsers that originally made draggable elements on web pages a nightmare to implement and maintain.

Implementing a basic drag

Let's look at the default implementation by first making a simple `<div>` element draggable. We won't do any additional configuration. Therefore, all that this code will allow you to do is pick up the element with the mouse pointer and drag it around the viewport.

In a new file in your text editor, add the following code:

```
<!DOCTYPE HTML>
<html>
  <head>
    <meta charset="utf-8">
    <title>Draggable</title>
    <link rel="stylesheet" href="development-bundle/themes/redmond/
jquery.ui.all.css">
    <link rel="stylesheet" href="css/autocompleteTheme.css">
    <script src="js/jquery-2.0.3.js"></script>
    <script src="development-bundle/ui/jquery.ui.core.js"></script>
    <script src="development-bundle/ui/jquery.ui.widget.js"></script>
    <script src="development-bundle/ui/jquery.ui.mouse.js"></script>
    <script src="development-bundle/ui/jquery.ui.draggable.js "></
script>
    <script>
      $(document).ready(function($){
        $("#drag").draggable();
      });
    </script>
  </head>
  <body>
    <div id="drag"></div>
  </body>
</html>
```

Save this as `draggable1.html` in your `jqueryui` folder. As with the widget-based components of jQuery UI, the draggable component can be enabled using a single line of code. This invokes the draggable's constructor method: `draggable` and turns the specified element into a drag object.

We need the following files from the library to enable draggability on an element:

- `jquery-2.0.3.js`
- `jquery.ui.core.js`
- `jquery.ui.widget.js`

- `jquery.ui.mouse.js`
- `jquery.ui.draggable.js`

We're using a plain `<div>` element with a background image specified in the CSS file that we're linking to in the `<head>` tag of the page. Use the following stylesheet for the drag element:

```
#drag { width: 114px; height: 114px; cursor: move; background: url(../
img/draggable.png) no-repeat; }
```

Save this as `draggable.css` in the `css` folder. When you view the page in a browser, you'll see that the image can be moved around the draggable area as shown in the following screenshot:

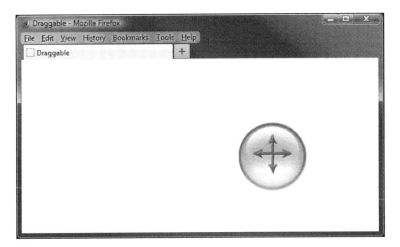

Configuring the draggable options

The draggable component has a wide range of configurable options, giving us a very fine degree of control over the behavior that it adds. The following table lists the options that we can manipulate to configure and control our drag elements:

Option	Default value	Used to...
addClasses	true	Add the ui-draggable class to the drag object. Set it to false to prevent this class being added.
appendTo	"parent"	Specify a container element for drag objects with a helper attached.
axis	false	Constrain drag objects to one axis of motion. Accepts the strings x and y as values, or the Boolean false.

Option	Default value	Used to...
cancel	":input, option"	Prevent certain elements from being dragged, if they match the specified element selector.
connectToSortable	false	Allow the drag object to be dropped on to a sortable list and become one of the sort elements.
containment	false	Prevent drag objects from being dragged out of the bounds of its parent element.
cursor	"auto"	Specify a CSS cursor to be used while the pointer is over the drag object.
cursorAt	false	Specify a default position at which the cursor appears relative to the drag object, while it is being dragged.
delay	0	Specify a time in milliseconds that the start of the drag interaction should be delayed by.
disabled	false	Disable dragging on the draggable.
distance	1	Specify the distance in pixels that the pointer should move with the mouse button held down on the drag object, before the drag begins.
grid	false	Make the drag object snap to an imaginary grid on the page. Accepts an array containing x and y pixel values of the grid.
handle	false	Define a specific area of the drag object that is used to hold the pointer on, in order to drag.
helper	"original"	Define a pseudo-drag element that is dragged instead of the drag object. Can accept the string values original or clone, or can accept a function that returns the helper element.
iframeFix	false	Stop all the <iframe> elements on the page from capturing mouse events, while a drag is in progress.
opacity	false	Set the opacity of the helper element.
refreshPositions	false	Calculate the positions of all the drop objects while the drag is in progress.
revert	false	Make the drag object return to its start position once the drag ends, when set to true. Can also accept the strings valid and invalid, where revert is only applied if the drag object is dropped on a valid drop object or vice versa, respectively.
revertDuration	500	Set the number of milliseconds it takes for the drag object to return to its starting position.

Option	Default value	Used to...
scope	"default"	Set the scope of the drag object with respect to the drop objects that are valid for it.
scroll	true	Make the viewport automatically scroll when the drag object is moved within the threshold of the viewport's edge.
scrollSensitivity	20	Define how close in pixels the drag object should get to the edge of the viewport, before scrolling begins.
scrollSpeed	20	Set the speed at which the viewport scrolls.
snap	false	Cause drag objects to snap to the edges of specified elements.
snapMode	"both"	Specify which edges of the element the drag object will snap to. Can be set to either inside, outside, or both.
snapTolerance	20	Set the distance from snapping elements that drag objects should reach, before snapping occurs.
stack	false	Ensure that the current drag object is always on top of other drag objects in the same group. Accepts an object containing group and/or min properties.
zIndex	false	Set the zIndex of the helper element.

Using the configuration options

Let's put some of these options to use. They can be configured in exactly the same way as the options exposed by the widgets that we looked at in previous chapters, and also usually have both getter and setter modes.

In the first example a moment ago, we used CSS to specify that the move cursor should be used when the pointer hovers over our draggable <div>. Let's change this and use the cursor option of the draggables component instead.

Remove cursor: move from draggable.css, and resave it as draggableNoCursor .css. Also change the <link> tag in draggable1.html, to reference the new file:

```
<link rel="stylesheet" href="css/draggableNoCursor.css">
```

Then change the final <script> element to the following one:

```
<script>
  $(document).ready(function($){
    $("#drag").draggable({
```

```
        cursor: "move"
      });
    });
  </script>
```

Save this as `draggable2.html`, and try it out in your browser. An important point to note about this option is that the move cursor that we have specified is not applied until we actually start the drag. While using this option in place of simple CSS, we should perhaps provide some other visual cue that the element is draggable.

Let's look at a few more of draggable's many configuration options. Change the configuration object in `draggable2.html` to the following one:

```
$("#drag").draggable({
  cursor: "move",
  axis: "y",
  distance: "30",
  cursorAt: { top: 0, left: 0 }
});
```

This can be saved as `draggable3.html`. The first new option that we've configured is the `axis` option, which has restricted the draggable to moving only upwards or downwards in the page, but not side to side across it.

Next, we've specified `30` as the value of the `distance` option. This means that the cursor will have to travel `30` pixels across the drag object, with the mouse button held down, before the drag begins.

The final option `cursorAt` is configured using an object literal, whose properties can be `top`, `right`, `bottom`, or `left`. The values supplied to the properties that we choose to use are the values relative to the drag object that the cursor will assume, when a drag occurs.

However, you'll notice in this example that the value for the `left` option seems to be ignored. The reason for this is that we have configured the `axis` option. When we begin the drag, the drag object will automatically move so that the cursor is at `0` pixels from the top of the element, but it will not move so that the cursor is `0` pixels from the left edge as we have specified because the drag object cannot move left.

Let's look at some more of the draggable's options in action. Change `draggable3.html` so that the configuration object appears as follows:

```
$("#drag").draggable({
  delay: 500,
  grid: [100,100]
});
```

Save the file as `draggable4.html`. The `delay` option, which takes a value in milliseconds, specifies the length of time that the mouse button must be held down with the cursor over the drag object, before the drag begins.

The `grid` option is similar in usage to the `steps` option of the slider widget. It is configured using an array of two values representing the number of pixels along each `axis` that the drag element should jump when it is dragged. This option can be used safely in conjunction with the `axis` option.

Resetting the dragged elements

It is very easy to configure drag objects to return to their original starting position on the page once they've been dropped, and there are several options that can be used to control this behavior. Change the configuration object that we used with `draggable4.html`, so that it appears as follows:

```
$("#drag").draggable({
  revert: true
});
```

Save this as `draggable5.html`. By supplying `true` as the value of the `revert` option, we've caused the drag object to return to its starting position at the end of any drag interaction. However, you'll notice that the drag element doesn't just pop back to its starting position instantly. Rather, it's smoothly animated back, with no additional configurations required.

Another revert-related option is the `revertDuration` option, which we can use to control the speed of the revert animation. Change the configuration object in `draggable5.html`, so that it appears as follows:

```
$("#drag").draggable({
  revert: true,
  revertDuration: 100
});
```

Save this as `draggable6.html`. The default value for the `revertDuration` option is `500` milliseconds, so by lowering it to `100`, the relative speed of the animation is considerably increased.

The actual speed of the animation will always be determined on the fly, based on the distance from the drop point to the starting point. The `revertDuration` option simply defines a target for the animation length in time.

Adding the drag handle support

The `handle` option allows us to define a region of the drag object that can be used to drag the object. No other areas can be used to drag the object. A simple analogy is the `dialog` widget. You can drag the dialog around only if you click and hold on the title bar. The title bar is the drag handle.

In the following example, we'll add a simple drag handle to our drag object. Put a new empty `<div>` element inside the drag element:

```
<div id="drag">
  <div id="handle"></div>
</div>
```

Then, change the configuration object to the following one:

```
$("#drag").draggable({
  handle: "#handle"
});
```

Save this as `draggable7.html`. We've given the new `<div>` an `id` attribute and then specified this `id` as the value of the `handle` option in our configuration object.

The handle is styled with a few simple style rules. Add the following new styles to `draggableNoCursor.css`:

```
#handle {
  width:30px; height:30px; border-bottom:2px solid #ff0000;
  border-left:2px solid #ff0000; position:absolute;
  right:10px; top:10px; cursor:move;
}
```

Save this as `dragHandle.css` in the `css` folder. Don't forget to link to the new stylesheet from `<head>` of `draggable7.html`:

```
<link rel="stylesheet" href="css/dragHandle.css">
```

When we preview the page in a browser, we see that the original drag object is still draggable, but only when the handle is selected with the pointer as seen in the following screenshot:

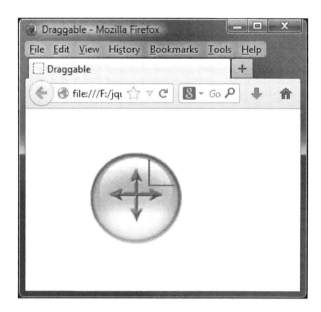

Adding the helper elements

Several configuration options are directly related to drag helpers. A helper is a substitute element that is used to show where the object is on screen, while the drag is in progress, instead of moving the actual draggable.

A helper can be a very simple object in place of the actual drag object. It can help cut down on the intensity of the drag operation, lessening the load on the visitor's processor. Once the drag is completed, the actual element can be moved to the new location.

Let's look at how helpers can be used in the following example. Remove the `<div>` element we used for `handle` and revert back to the `draggable.css` stylesheet in `draggable7.html`, and then change the configuration object to the following one:

```
$("#drag").draggable({
  helper: "clone"
});
```

Save this file as `draggable8.html`. We also need to tweak the CSS so that the cursor changes to indicate that we're moving the image at the appropriate time. Alter the CSS in `draggable.css` as follows:

```
#drag, .ui-draggable { width: 114px; height: 114px; background:
url(../img/draggable.png) no-repeat; }
.ui-draggable-dragging { cursor: move; }
```

The value `clone` for the `helper` option causes an exact copy of the original drag object to be created and used as draggable. Therefore, the original object stays in its starting position at all times. This also causes the `clone` object to revert back to its starting position, an effect that cannot be changed, even by supplying `false` as the value of the `revert` option. The following screenshot shows the `clone` option in action:

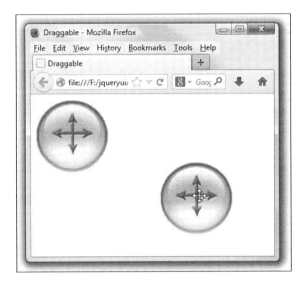

In addition to the string `clone` and the default `original`, we can also use a function as the value for this option. This allows us to specify our own custom element to use as the helper.

Change the final `<script>` element in `draggable8.html` to the following one:

```
<script>
  $(document).ready(function($){
    function helperMaker() {
      return $("<div />", {
        css: {
          border: "4px solid #ccc",
          opacity: 0.5,
          height: 110,
```

```
        width: 120
      }
    });
  }
  $("#drag").draggable({
    helper: helperMaker
  });
});
</script>
```

Save this file as `draggable9.html`. Our `helperMaker()` function creates a new `<div>` element using standard jQuery functionality, and then sets some CSS properties on it to define its physical appearance. It then, importantly, returns the new element. While supplying a function as the value of the `helper` option, the function must return an element (either a jQuery object, as in this example, or an actual DOMNode).

Now when the drag begins, it is our custom helper that becomes the drag object. Because the custom element is much simpler than the original drag object, it can help improve the responsiveness and performance of the application in which it is used.

 Make sure that when you use the helper (clone) elements that you use the element with class and not IDs, because IDs must be unique in the DOM, and the clone will duplicate it.

The following screenshot shows our custom helper:

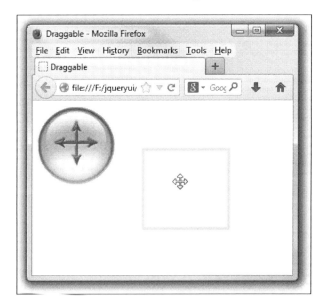

Helper opacity

We used the `css` jQuery method in this example during the creation of the custom helper. However, we can also use the `opacity` option of the drag object to set the opacity of helper elements as a cross-platform solution.

Constraining the drag

Another aspect of drag scenarios is that of containment. In our examples so far, the `<body>` element of the page has been the container of the drag object. There are also options that we can configure to specify how the drag object behaves with regards to another container element.

We'll look at these in the following examples, starting with the `containment` option, which allows us to specify a container element for the drag object. In the `<head>` tag of `draggable9.html`, add the following link to the stylesheet that we'll be using in this example:

```
<link rel="stylesheet" href="css/draggableContainer.css">
```

Then wrap the drag element within a container `<div>` as follows:

```
<div id="container">
  <div id="drag"></div>
</div>
```

Then change the configuration object to the following:

```
$("#drag").draggable({
  containment: "parent"
});
```

Save this variant as `draggable10.html`. On the page, we've added a new `<div>` element as the parent of the existing drag element. In the code, we've used the value `parent` for the `containment` option, so the element that is the direct parent of the drag object (the `<div>` element with the `id` of `container` in this example) will be used as the container.

The parent `<div>` needs some basic styling to give dimensions to it and so it can be seen on the page. Add the following code to `draggable.css` and resave the file as `draggableContainer.css`. Remember, this string is not the `id` of an element or a jQuery selector (although selectors are also supported).

```
#container { height: 250px; width: 250px; border: 2px solid #ff0000; }
```

When you run the page in your browser, you'll see that the drag object cannot exceed the boundary of its container.

Along with the string `parent` that we used in this example, we could also specify a selector, for example:

```
$("#drag").draggable({
    containment: "#container"
});
```

There are three additional options related to drag objects within containers and these are all related to scrolling. However, you should note that these are only applicable when the document is the container.

The default value of the `scroll` option is `true`, but when we drag the `<div>` element to the edge of the container, it does not scroll. You may have noticed in the previous examples, where the drag object was not within a specified container, the viewport automatically scrolled. We can fix this by setting the CSS `overflow` style to `auto` in a stylesheet if necessary.

Snapping

Drag elements can be given an almost magnetic quality by configuring snapping. This feature causes dragged elements to align themselves to specified elements, while they are being dragged.

In the next example, we'll look at the effects that snapping has on the behavior of the drag object. Get rid of the container we added in the previous example, and add a new empty `<div>` element directly after the drag element, as follows:

```
<div id="drag"></div>
<div id="snapper"></div>
```

Then, change the configuration object so that it appears as follows:

```
$("#drag").draggable({
    snap: "#snapper",
    snapMode: "inner",
    snapTolerance: 50
});
```

Save this as `draggable11.html`. We also need some additional styles; add the following code to the bottom of `draggable.css`:

```
#snapper {
   width: 300px; height: 300px; border: 1px solid #ff0000;
}
```

Save this file as `draggableSnap.css` in the `css` directory. Don't forget to add a link to the new stylesheet in the `<head>` element of the page:

```
<link rel="stylesheet" href="css/draggableSnap.css">
```

We've supplied the selector `#snapper` as the value of the `snap` option in our configuration object, and have added a `<div>` element with a matching `id` to the page. Therefore, our drag object will snap to this element on the page, while the object is being dragged.

We also set the `snapMode` option to `inner` (the other possible values are `outer` and `both`) so snapping will occur on the inside edges of our `snapper` element. If we drag the element towards the outer edge of the `snapper` element and get within the tolerance range, the element will snap to the inner edge.

Finally, we've set `snapTolerance` to `50`, which is the maximum distance (in pixels) the drag object will need to get to the `snapper` element, before snapping occurs. As soon as a drag object is within this range, it will snap to the element.

When we drag the image within `50` pixels of the edge of the snapper element, the drag object will automatically align itself to that edge, as shown in the following screenshot:

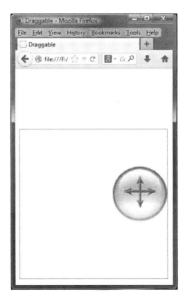

Draggable event callbacks

In addition to the options that we have already looked at, there are three more that can be used as callback functions to execute code after specific custom events occur.

These events are listed in the following table:

Event	Fired when...
drag	The mouse is moved while dragging
start	Dragging starts
stop	Dragging stops

While defining callback functions to make use of these events, the functions will always receive two arguments automatically: the original event object as the first argument, and a second object containing the following properties:

Property	Usage
helper	A jQuery object representing the helper element.
position	A nested object with properties: top and left, which is the position of the helper element relative to the original drag element.
offset	A nested object with properties: top and left, which is the position of the helper element relative to the page.

Using the callbacks and the two objects that are passed as arguments is extremely easy. We can look at a brief example to highlight their usage. Remove the snapper <div> in draggable11.html, and change the configuration object as follows:

```
$("#drag").draggable({
  start: function(e, ui) {
    ui.helper.addClass("up");
  },
  stop: function(e, ui) {
    ui.helper.removeClass("up");
  }
});
```

Save this as draggable12.html. We also need a new stylesheet for this example; add the following code to draggable.css:

```
#drag.up {
  width: 120px; height: 121px;
  background: url(../img/draggable_on.png) no-repeat;
}
```

Save this version of the stylesheet as `draggableEvents.css` in the `css` directory, and don't forget to update the link in the `<head>` element of the page to point to the new stylesheet.

In this example, our configuration object contains just two options—the `start` and `stop` callbacks. We set literal functions as the values of these options. What all the functions do in this example is add or remove a class name respectively.

The class name adds a slightly different background image to the draggable element, which when applied appears as shown in the following before and during screenshot:

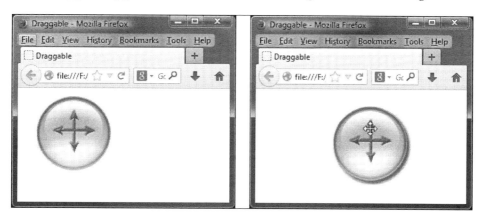

Let's move on to a slightly more complex example where we can make use of the second object passed to our callbacks. We need a couple of new elements on the page; change the `<body>` element of the page so that it contains the following elements:

```
<div id="container">
  <div id="drag"></div>
</div>
<div id="results"></div>
```

Then change the final `<script>` element, so that it appears as follows:

```
<script>
  $(document).ready(function($){
    $("#drag").draggable({
      stop: function(e, ui) {
        var rel = $("<p />", {
          text: "The helper was moved " + ui.position.top +
          "px down, and " + ui.position.left + "px to the
          left of its original position."
        }),
        offset = $("<p />", {
```

```
               text: "The helper was moved " + ui.offset.top + "px
               from the top, and " + ui.offset.left + "px to the
               left relative to the viewport."
             });
             $("#results").empty().append(rel).append(offset);
          }
       });
    });
</script>
```

Save this as `draggable13.html`. We've defined a callback function as the value of the `stop` option, so it will be executed each time a drag interaction stops. Our callback function receives the event object (which we don't need but must specify in order to access the second object) and a `ui` object containing useful information about the draggable helper.

All our function needs to do is create two new `<p>` elements, concatenating the values found in the `ui` object: `ui.position.top`, `ui.position.left`, `ui.offset.top`, and `ui.offset.left`. It then inserts the new elements into the results `<div>`.

Here's how the page should look after the draggable has been dragged:

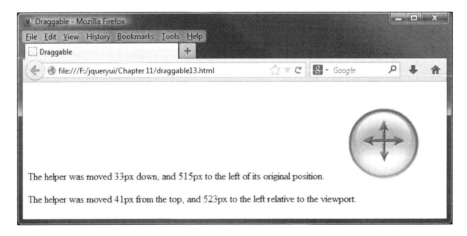

Draggable's methods

The draggable interaction helper does not expose any unique methods of its own, only the common API methods, which are `destroy`, `disable`, `enable`, `option`, and `widget`.

Getting started with the droppable widget

In a nutshell, the droppables component of jQuery UI gives us a place for the drag objects to be dropped. A region of the page is defined as a droppable, and when a drag object is dropped onto that region, something else is triggered. You can react to drops on a valid target very easily using the extensive event model exposed by this component.

Let's start with the default droppable implementation. In a new file in your text editor, add the following page:

```
<!DOCTYPE HTML>
<html>
  <head>
    <meta charset="utf-8">
    <title>Droppable</title>
    <link rel="stylesheet" href="development-bundle/themes/redmond/
jquery.ui.all.css">
    <link rel="stylesheet" href="css/droppable.css">
    <script src="http://code.jquery.com/jquery-2.0.3.js"></script>
    <script src="development-bundle/ui/jquery.ui.core.js"></script>
    <script src="development-bundle/ui/jquery.ui.widget.js"></script>
    <script src="development-bundle/ui/jquery.ui.mouse.js"></script>
    <script src="development-bundle/ui/jquery.ui.draggable.js"></
script>
    <script src="development-bundle/ui/jquery.ui.droppable.js"></
script>
    <script>
        $(document).ready(function($){
        $("#drag").draggable();
        $("#target").droppable();
        });
    </script>
  </head>
  <body>
    <div id="drag"></div>
    <div id="target"></div>
  </body>
</html>
```

Save this as `droppable1.html`. The extremely basic stylesheet that is linked to, in this example, is simply an updated version of `draggable.css`, and appears as follows:

```
#drag { width:114px; height:114px; margin-bottom:5px; z-index:2;
cursor:move; background:url(../img/draggable.png) no-repeat; }
#target { width:200px; height:200px; border:3px solid #000;
position:absolute; right:20px; top:20px; z-index:1; }
```

Save this as droppable.css in the css folder. When the page runs in a browser, it should look like the following screenshot:

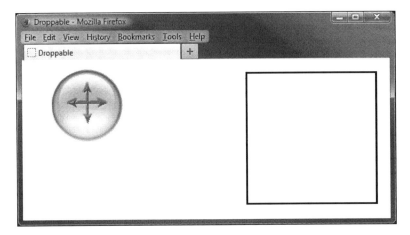

In this example, the droppable is created; we can see this with the class name ui-droppable, which is added to the specified element when the page loads.

Even though we haven't added any additional logic to our script, events are firing throughout the interaction on both the drag object and the drop target. A little later in the chapter, we'll look at these events in more detail to see how we can hook into them, to react to successful drops.

The files we used for this basic droppable implementation are as follows:

- jquery-2.0.3.js
- jquery.ui.core.js
- jquery.ui.widget.js
- jquery.ui.mouse.js
- jquery.ui.draggable.js
- jquery.ui.droppable.js

As you can see, the droppables component is an extension of draggables, rather than a completely independent component. Therefore, it requires the jquery.ui.draggable.js file in addition to its own source file. The reason our droppable does nothing is because we haven't configured it, so let's do that next.

Configuring droppables

The `droppable` class is considerably smaller than the `draggable` class, and there are fewer configurable options for us to play with. The following table lists those options available to us:

Option	Default	Used to...
accept	"*"	Set the draggable element(s) that the droppable will accept.
activeClass	false	Set the class that is applied to the droppable, while an accepted drag object is being dragged.
addClasses	true	Add the `ui-droppable` class to the droppable.
disabled	false	Disable the droppable.
greedy	false	Stop drop events from bubbling when a drag object is dropped onto nested droppables.
hoverClass	false	Set the class that is applied to the droppable, while an accepted drag object is within the boundary of the droppable.
scope	"default"	Define sets of drag objects and drop targets.
tolerance	"intersect"	Set the mode that triggers an accepted drag object being considered over a droppable.

Configuring accepted draggables

In order to get a visible result from the droppable, we're going to use a couple of the configurable options together in the following example, which will highlight the drop target when an accepted drag object is interacted with. Change the elements on the page in `droppable1.html` so that they appear as follows:

```
<div class="drag" id="drag1"></div>
<div class="drag" id="drag2"></div>
<div id="target"></div>
```

Next, change the final `<script>` element to the following one:

```
<script>
  $(document).ready(function($){
    $(".drag").draggable();
    $("#target").droppable({
      accept: "#drag1",
      activeClass: "activated"
    });
  });
</script>
```

Save this as `droppable2.html`. The `accept` option takes a selector. In this example, we've specified that only the drag object that has `id` of `drag1` should be accepted by the droppable.

We've also specified the class name activated as the value of the `activeClass` option. This class name will be applied to the droppable when the accepted drag object starts to be dragged. The `hoverClass` option can be used in exactly the same way to add styles, when an accepted drag object is over a droppable.

We need a new stylesheet for this example; modify `droppable.css` so that it appears as follows:

```
.drag { width: 114px; height: 114px; margin-bottom: 5px; z-index:2;
cursor: move; background: url(../img/draggable.png) no-repeat; }
#target { width: 200px; height: 200px; border: 3px solid #000;
position: absolute; right: 20px; top: 20px; z-index: 1; }
.activated { border: 3px solid #339900; background-color: #fe2e2e; }
```

Save this file as `droppableActive.css` in the `css` folder, and link to it in the `<head>` element of the page:

```
<link rel="stylesheet" href="css/droppableActive.css">
```

When we view this page in a browser, we should find that when we move the first drag object, which is defined as accepted, the droppable picks up the `activated` class and turns red. However, when the second drag object is moved, the drop target does not respond. The following screenshot shows how the page should look, while the first drag object is being dragged over the square:

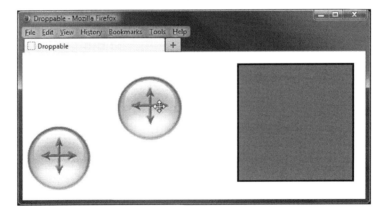

In addition to a string value, the `accept` option can also take a function as its value. This function will be executed once for every drag object that is on the page. The function must return either `true`, to indicate that the drag object is accepted, or `false` to indicate that it's not.

To see the function value of the `accept` option in action change the final `<script>` element in `droppable2.html` to the following one:

```
<script>
  $(document).ready(function($){
    $(".drag").draggable();
      function dragEnrol(el) {
        return (el.attr("id") === "drag1") ? true : false;
      }
      $("#target").droppable({
        accept: dragEnrol,
        activeClass: "activated"
      });
    });
  });
</script>
```

Save this variation as `droppable3.html`. On the surface, the page works exactly the same as it did in the previous example. But this time, acceptability is being determined by the JavaScript ternary statement within the `dragEnrol` function, instead of a simple selector.

Note that the function we use with the `accept` option has automatically passed a jQuery object representing the drag object as an argument, so we can call the jQuery methods on this object. This makes it easy to obtain information about it, such as its `id` as in this example. This callback can be extremely useful when advanced filtering beyond a selector is required.

Configuring drop tolerance

Drop tolerance refers to the way a droppable detects whether a drag object is over it or not. The default value is `intersect`. The following table lists the modes that this option may be configured with:

Mode	Implementation
fit	The drag object must be completely within the boundary of the droppable for it to be considered over it.
intersect	At least 25 percent of the drag object must be within the boundary of the droppable before it is considered over it.
pointer	The mouse pointer must touch the droppable boundary before the drag object is considered over the droppable.
touch	The drag object is over the droppable as soon as an edge of the drag object touches an edge of the droppable.

So far, all of our droppable examples have used intersect, which is the default value of the `tolerance` option. Let's see what difference the other values for this option make to an implementation of the component. Revert to the `#drag` and `#target` IDs from their respective elements in `droppable2.html`, and then use the following configuration object:

```
$("#target").droppable({
    hoverClass: "activated",
    tolerance: "pointer"
});
```

Save this as `droppable4.html`. This time we use the `hoverClass` option to specify the class name that is added to the droppable. We then use the `tolerance` option to specify which tolerance mode is used.

The part of the drag object that is over the droppable is irrelevant in this example; it is the mouse pointer that must cross the boundary of the droppable while a drag is in progress for our `activated` class to be triggered:

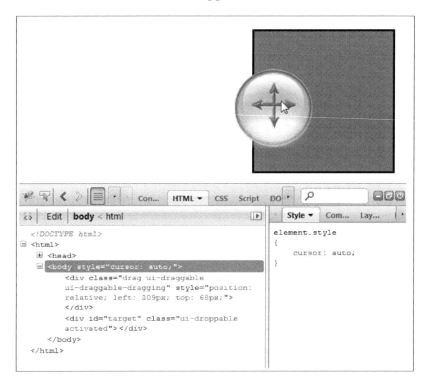

Understanding the droppable callback options

The options that we've looked at so far configure various operational features of the droppable. In addition to these, there are almost as many callback options so that we can define functions that react to different things occurring to the droppable and its accepted drag objects. These options are listed in the following table:

Callback option	Invoked when...
activate	An accepted drag object begins dragging.
deactivate	An accepted drag object stops being dragged.
drop	An accepted drag object is dropped onto a droppable.
out	An accepted drag object is moved out of the bounds (including the tolerance) of the droppable.
over	An accepted drag object is moved within the bounds (including the tolerance) of the droppable.

Let's put together a basic example that makes use of these callback options. We'll add a status bar to our droppable that reports the status of different interactions between the drag object and the droppable. In droppable4.html, add the following new element directly after the target element:

```
<div id="status"></div>
```

Then, change the final <script> element to this:

```
<script>
  $(document).ready(function($){
    $("#drag").draggable();
    $("#target").droppable({
      accept: "#drag",
      activate: eventCallback,
      deactivate: eventCallback,
      drop: eventCallback,
      out: eventCallback,
      over: eventCallback
    },
      eventMessages = {
      dropactivate: "A draggable is active",
      dropdeactivate: "A draggable is no longer active",
      drop: "An accepted draggable was dropped on the droppable",
      dropout: "An accepted draggable was moved off the droppable",
      dropover: "An accepted draggable is over the droppable"
```

```
    });
    function eventCallback(e) {
      var message = $("<p />", {
        id: "message",
        text: eventMessages[e.type]
      });
      $("#status").empty().append(message);
    }
  });
</script>
```

Save this file as `droppable5.html`. We also need some new styles for this example. Create a new stylesheet in your text editor, and add to it the following selectors and rules:

```
#drag { width: 114px; height: 114px; margin-bottom: 5px; z-index: 2;
cursor: move; background: url(../img/draggable.png) no-repeat; }
#target { width: 250px; height: 200px; border: 3px solid #000;
position: absolute; right: 20px; top: 20px; z-index: 1; }
#status { width: 230px; padding: 10px; border: 3px solid #000;
position: absolute; top: 223px; right: 20px; color: #000; }
#message { margin: 0px; font-size: 80%; }
```

Save this file as `droppableEvents.css` in the `css` directory. Don't forget to update `<link>` in the `<head>` element of the page to point to the new stylesheet:

```
<link rel="stylesheet" href="css/droppableEvents.css">
```

The `<body>` element of the page contains, along with the droppable, a new status bar, which in this case is a simple `<div>` element. In the script, we define our configurable options, specifying that the function `eventCallback` should be executed when each of the events are detected.

Next, we define an object literal, in which the key for each property is set to one of the event types that may be triggered. The value of each property is the message that we want to display for any given event.

We then define our callback function. Like other components, the callback functions used in the droppables component automatically pass two objects: the `event` object and an object representing the drag element.

We use the `type` property of the `event` object to retrieve the appropriate message from the `eventMessages` object. We then use standard jQuery element creation and manipulation methods to add the message to the status bar.

Here's how the status bar will look following an interaction:

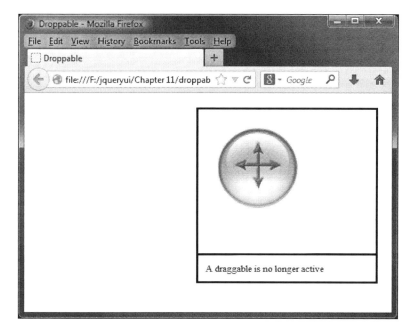

After playing around with the page, it may appear that one of our messages is not being displayed. When the drag object is dropped onto the droppable, our drop message is not shown.

Actually, the message is shown, but because the deactivate event is fired immediately after the drop event; the drop message is overwritten right away. There are a number of ways we could work around this; the simplest, of course, would be not to use the drop and deactivate options together.

Although we only make use of the event object (e) in this example, a second object is also passed automatically to any callback functions we use with the event options.

This object contains information relevant to the droppable such as the following:

Property	Value
ui.draggable	The current drag object.
ui.helper	The current drag helper.
ui.position	The current relative position of the helper.
ui.offset	The current absolute position of the helper.

Setting the scope options for droppable

Both the draggables and droppables feature the scope configuration option that allows us to easily define groups of drag objects and drop targets. In this next example, we can look at how these options can be configured and the effect it has by configuring them. We'll link to another new stylesheet in this example so in the `<head>` element of `droppable5.html`, change the `<link>` element so that it appears as follows:

```
<link rel="stylesheet" href="css/droppableScope.css">
```

We need a number of new elements for this example. Change the `<body>` element of the page in `droppable5.html` so that it contains the following elements:

```
<div id="target_a">A</div>
<div id="target_b">B</div>
<div id="group_a">
  <p>A</p>
  <div id="a1" class="group_a">a1</div>
  <div id="a2" class="group_a">a2</div>
  <div id="a3" class="group_a">a3</div>
</div>
<div id="group_b">
  <p>B</p>
  <div id="b1" class="group_b">b1</div>
  <div id="b2" class="group_b">b2</div>
  <div id="b3" class="group_b">b3</div>
</div>
```

To make these elements behave correctly, change the final `<script>` element to the following one:

```
<script>
  $(document).ready(function($){
    var dragOpts_a = { scope: "a" },
    dragOpts_b = { scope: "b" },
    dropOpts_a = { hoverClass: "over", scope: "a" },
    dropOpts_b = { hoverClass: "over", scope: "b" };
    $(".group_a").draggable(dragOpts_a);
    $(".group_b").draggable(dragOpts_b);
    $("#target_a").droppable(dropOpts_a);
    $("#target_b").droppable(dropOpts_b);
  });
</script>
```

Save this file as `droppable6.html`. Next, we need to create a new CSS file; in a new page in your text editor add the following code:

```
#target_a, #target_b, #group_a, #group_b { width: 150px; height:
150px; padding: 50px; margin: 0 20px 20px 0; border: 2px solid black;
float: left;
font-family: Georgia; font-size: 100px; color: red; text-align:
center; }
#group_a, #group_b { width: 518px; height: 115px; padding: 5px 0 5px
5px; margin-bottom: 20px; clear: both; }
p { float: left; margin: 0 20px 0; }
.group_a, .group_b { width: 94px; height: 94px; padding: 20px 0 0
20px;
.group_a, .group_b { width: 94px; height: 94px; padding: 20px 0 0
20px; margin-right: 20px; float: left; font-family: arial; font-size:
14px; color: red; text-align: left;
background: url(../img/draggable.png) no-repeat; }
.over { background-color: #fe2e2e; }
```

Save this as `droppableScope.css` in the `css` folder.

The page has two drop targets and two groups of three drag objects, all of which are labeled to show the group they belong to. In the script, we define two configuration objects for the two groups of draggables, and two configuration objects for the drop targets. Within each configuration object we set the `scope` option.

The values we set for the `scope` option of each drop target matches `scope` of each drag object. Therefore, if we want to use the `scope` option, it must be defined for both the drag object and drop target. If we try to set `scope` of a droppable, but don't give at least one drag object to the same `scope`, an error is thrown.

Setting the `scope` option gives us another technique for defining which drag objects are accepted by which drop targets, but it is provided as an alternative to the `accept` option; the two options should not be used together.

The following screenshot shows how the page will appear:

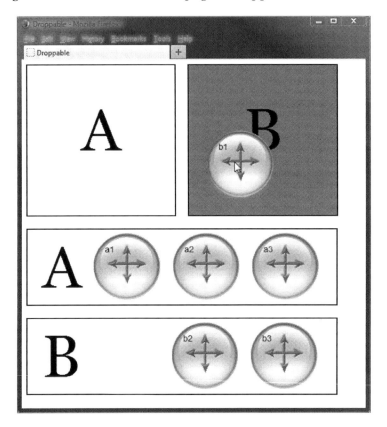

Configuring the greedy option

The final option that we are going to look at in connection with the droppable component is the greedy option. This option can be useful in situations where there is a droppable nested within another droppable. If we don't use this option, both droppables will fire events during certain interactions.

The greedy option is an easy way to avoid event-bubbling problems in an efficient and cross-browser manner. Let's take a closer look at this option with an example.

Change the `<link>` element in `droppable6.html` so that it links to a new stylesheet:

```
<link rel="stylesheet" href="css/droppableNesting.css">
```

Then change <body> so that it contains the following elements:

```
<div id="drag"></div>
  <div class="target" id="outer">
  <div class="target" id="inner"></div>
</div>
<div id="status"></div>
```

Finally, change the last <script> element so that it appears as follows:

```
<script>
  $(document).ready(function($){
    $(".target").css({ opacity:"0.5" });
    $("#drag").draggable({ zIndex: 3 });
    $(".target").droppable({
      drop: dropCallback,
      greedy: true
    });
    function dropCallback(e) {
      var message = $("<p></p>", {
        id: "message",
        text: "The firing droppable was " + e.target.id
      });
      $("#status").append(message);
    }
  });
</script>
```

Save this example as `droppable7.html`. The CSS for this example is simple and builds on the CSS of previous examples.

```
#drag { width: 114px; height: 114px; margin-bottom: 5px; cursor: move;
background: url(../img/draggable.png) no-repeat; float: left; }
#outer { width: 300px; height: 300px; border: 3px solid #000; float:
right; background-color: #fe2e2e; }
#inner { width: 100px; height: 100px; border: 3px solid #000;
position: relative; top: 100px; left: 100px; background-color:
#FFFF99; }
#status {width: 280px; padding: 10px; border: 3px solid #000; float:
right; clear: right; color: #000; }
#message { margin: 0px; font-size: 80%; }
```

Save this as `droppableNesting.css` in the `css` folder.

In this example, we have a smaller droppable nested in the center of a larger droppable. Their opacity is set using the standard jQuery library's `css()` method.

In this example, this is necessary because if we alter the `zIndex` option of the elements, so that the drag object appears above the nested droppables, the target element is not reported correctly.

In this example, we use the `zIndex` option of the draggables component to show the drag object above the droppables, while a drag is in progress. The `dropCallback` function is used to add a simple message to the status bar, notifying us which droppable was the target of the drop.

Our droppables configuration object uses the `drop` option to wire up our callback function. However, the key option is the `greedy` option that makes whichever target the draggable is dropped on to stop the event from escaping into other targets.

If you run the page and drop the drag object onto one of the droppables, you should see something like what's shown in the following screenshot:

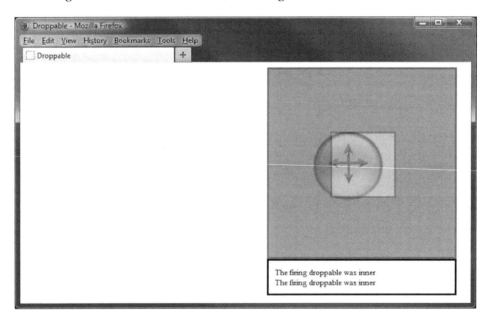

The net effect of setting the `greedy` option to `true` is that the inner droppable prevents the event from propagating into the outer droppable and firing again.

If you comment out the `greedy` option and drop the draggable onto the inner droppable, the status message will be inserted twice, once by the inner droppable and once by the outer droppable.

Droppable methods

Like the draggable component, droppable has only the common API methods shared by all the library components. This is another component that is primarily option driven. The methods available to us are the same ones exposed by draggable, namely the standard methods shared by all the library components, which are `destroy`, `disable`, `enable`, `option`, and `widget`.

Creating a maze game using the widgets

We've now reached the point where we can have a little fun by putting what we've learned about these two components into a fully working example. In our final drag-and-drop example, we're going to combine both of these components to create a simple maze game.

The game will consist of a draggable marker that will need to be navigated through a simple maze to a specified droppable at the other end of the maze. We can make things a little more challenging so that if any of the maze walls are touched by the marker, it will return to the starting position.

The following screenshot shows what we're going to build:

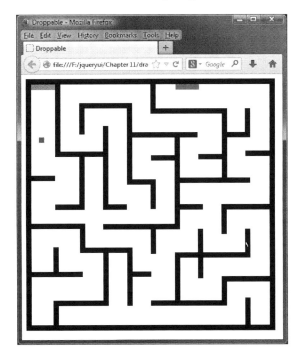

Let's start with the markup. In a new page in your text editor, add the following code:

```html
<!DOCTYPE HTML>
<html>
  <head>
    <meta charset="utf-8">
    <title>Droppable</title>
    <link rel="stylesheet" href="development-bundle/themes/redmond/
jquery.ui.all.css">
    <script src="http://code.jquery.com/jquery-2.0.3.js"></script>
    <script src="development-bundle/ui/jquery.ui.core.js"></script>
    <script src="development-bundle/ui/jquery.ui.widget.js"></script>
    <script src="development-bundle/ui/jquery.ui.mouse.js"></script>
    <script src="development-bundle/ui/jquery.ui.draggable.js" ><//
script>
    <script src="development-bundle/ui/jquery.ui.droppable.js" ><//
script>
    <script>
    </script>
  </head>
  <body>
    <div id="maze">
      <div id="drag"></div>
      <div id="start"></div>
      <div id="end"></div>
    </div>
  </body>
</html>
```

Save this file as `dragMaze.html`. On the page, we have our outer container that we've given `id` of maze. We have `<div>` elements for the starting and ending positions, as well as for the drag marker. Our map will need walls. Rather than hand coding the 46 required walls for the map pattern that we're going to use, I thought we could use jQuery to do this for us.

We left an empty `<script>` element at the bottom of our page. Let's fill that up with the following code:

```javascript
$(document).ready(function($){
  var dragOpts = {
    containment: "#maze"
  },
  dropOpts = {
    tolerance: "touch",
```

```
        over: function(e, ui) {
          $("#drag").draggable("destroy").remove();
          $("<div />", {
            id: "drag",
            css: {
              left: 0,
              top: 0
            }
          }).appendTo("#maze");
          $("#drag").draggable(dragOpts);
        }
      },
      endOpts = {
        over: function(e, ui) {
          $("#drag").draggable("destroy").remove();
          alert("Woo! You did it!");
        }
      };
      for (var x = 1; x < 47; x++) {
        $("<div />", {
          id: "a" + x,
          class: "wall"
        }).appendTo("#maze");
      }
      $("#drag").draggable(dragOpts);
      $(".wall").droppable(dropOpts);
      $("#end").droppable(endOpts);
    });
```

We also need to style up the walls of the maze, but we can't use any simple JavaScript pattern for this. Unfortunately, we have to hardcode them. In another new file in your text editor, add the following selectors and rules:

```
#maze { width: 441px; height: 441px; border: 10px solid #000000;
position: relative; background-color: #ffffff; }
#drag { width: 10px; height: 10px; z-index: 1; background-color:
#0000FF; }
#start { width: 44px; height: 10px; background-color: #00CC00;
position: absolute; top: 0; left: 0; z-index: 0; }
#end { width: 44px; height: 10px; background-color: #FF0000; position:
absolute; top: 0; right: 130px; }
.wall { background-color: #000000; position: absolute; }
#a1 { width: 10px; height: 133px; left: 44px; top: 0; }
#a2 { width: 44px; height: 10px; left: 0; top: 167px; }
#a3 { width: 44px; height: 10px; left: 44px; top: 220px; }
```

```
#a4  { width: 89px;  height: 10px;  left: 0;      bottom: 176px;  }
#a5  { width: 94px;  height: 10px;  left: 0;      bottom: 88px;   }
#a6  { width: 10px;  height: 41px;  left: 40px;   bottom: 0;      }
#a7  { width: 10px;  height: 48px;  left: 88px;   top: 44px;      }
#a8  { width: 78px;  height: 10px;  left: 54px;   top: 123px;     }
#a9  { width: 10px;  height: 97px;  left: 88px;   top: 133px      }
#a10 { width: 10px;  height: 45px;  left: 40px;   bottom: 98px;   }
#a11 { width: 88px;  height: 10px;  left: 89px;   bottom: 132px;  }
#a12 { width: 10px;  height: 97px;  left: 132px;  bottom: 35px;   }
#a13 { width: 10px;  height: 44px;  left: 89px;   bottom: 142px;  }
#a14 { width: 92px;  height: 10px;  left: 40px;   bottom: 35px;   }
#a15 { width: 89px;  height: 10px;  left: 88px;   top: 34px;      }
#a16 { width: 10px;  height: 145px; left: 132px;  top: 76px;      }
#a17 { width: 44px;  height: 10px;  left: 132px;  top: 220px;     }
#a18 { width: 133px; height: 10px;  left: 132px;  bottom: 175px;  }
#a19 { width: 10px;  height: 107px; left: 176px;  bottom: 35px;   }
#a20 { width: 10px;  height: 150px; left: 176px;  top: 34px;      }
#a21 { width: 35px;  height: 10px;  left: 186px;  top: 174px      }
#a22 { width: 35px;  height: 10px;  left: 186px;  bottom: 88px;   }
#a23 { width: 122px; height: 10px;  left: 186px;  top: 88px;      }
#a24 { width: 10px;  height: 44px;  left: 220px;  top: 0px;       }
#a25 { width: 10px;  height: 55px;  left: 220px;  top: 174px;     }
#a26 { width: 10px;  height: 45px;  left: 220px;  bottom: 130px;  }
#a27 { width: 133px; height: 10px;  right: 88px;  top: 44px;      }
#a28 { width: 10px;  height: 168px; right: 166px; top: 98px;      }
#a29 { width: 44px;  height: 10px;  right: 176px; top: 130px;     }
#a30 { width: 10px;  height: 98px;  right: 166px; bottom: 35px;   }
#a31 { width: 133px; height: 10px;  right: 88px;  bottom: 35px;   }
#a32 { width: 10px;  height: 133px; right: 78px;  top: 44px;      }
#a33 { width: 44px;  height: 10px;  right: 88px;  top: 128px;     }
#a34 { width: 131px; height: 10px;  right: 35px;  top: 171px;     }
#a35 { width: 43px;  height: 10px;  right: 123px; top: 220px;     }
#a36 { width: 10px;  height: 91px;  right: 123px; bottom: 85px;   }
#a37 { width: 131px; height: 10px;  right: 35px;  bottom: 123px;  }
#a38 { width: 10px;  height: 55px;  right: 79px;  top: 220px;     }
#a39 { width: 44px;  height: 10px;  right: 0;     top: 122px;     }
#a40 { width: 10px;  height: 54px;  right: 79px;  bottom: 35px;   }
#a41 { width: 79px;  height: 10px;  right: 0;     bottom: 79px;   }
#a42 { width: 10px;  height: 45px;  right: 35px;  top: 44px;      }
#a43 { width: 43px;  height: 10px;  right: 35px;  top: 88px;      }
#a44 { width: 79px;  height: 10px;  right: 0;     top: 220px;     }
#a45 { width: 10px;  height: 44px;  right: 35px;  bottom: 132px;  }
#a46 { width: 10px;  height: 50px;  right: 35px;  bottom: 0;      }
```

Save this file as `dragMaze.css` in the `css` folder.

Let's review what the new code does. First, we define a simple configuration object for the drag object. The only option we need to configure is the `containment` option that constrains the draggable marker element within the maze.

Next, we define the configuration object for the walls. Each wall is treated as a droppable. We specify `touch` as the value of the `tolerance` option, and add a callback function to the `over` option. Therefore, whenever the drag object touches a wall, the function will be executed.

All we do in this function is destroy the current drag object and remove it from the page.

We then create a new drag object back at the starting position and make it draggable once more. There is no `cancelDrag` method that causes the drag object to act as if it had been dropped and revert to its starting position, but we can easily replicate this behavior ourselves.

Now, we add another droppable configuration object that configures the ending point of the maze. All we configure for this droppable is a function to execute when the draggable is over this droppable. In this function, we remove the drag object again and present the user with an alert congratulating them.

We then use a simple `for` loop to add the walls to our maze. We use the plain vanilla `for` loop in conjunction with jQuery to create 46 `<div>` elements, and add `id` and `class` attributes to each one, before appending them to the `maze` container. Finally, we make the drag object draggable and the walls and the end target droppables.

We can now attempt to navigate the marker from the starting point to the finish by dragging it through the maze. If any wall is touched, the marker will return to the starting point. We could make it harder (by adding additional obstacles to navigate), but for the purpose of having fun with jQuery UI draggables and droppables, our work here is complete.

Summary

We looked at two very useful library components in this chapter—the draggable and droppable components. Draggables and droppables, as we saw, are very closely related and have been designed to be used with each other, allowing us to create advanced and highly interactive interfaces.

We've covered a lot of material in this chapter, so let's recap what we have learned. We saw that the draggable behavior can be added to any element on the page with zero configurations. There may be implementations where this is acceptable, but usually we'll want to use one or more of the component's extensive range of configurable options.

In the second part of this chapter, we saw that the droppables class allows us to easily define areas on the page that draggables can be dropped onto, and can react to things being dropped on them. We can also make use of a smaller range of configurable droppable options to implement more advanced droppable behavior.

Both components feature an effective event model for hooking into the interesting moments of any drag-and-drop interaction. Our final example showed how both the draggables and droppables components can be used together to create a fun and interactive game. Although the game was very basic by modern gaming standards, it nevertheless provides a sound base that we can easily build upon to add features.

In the next chapter, we'll take a look at the resizable component, which allows users to resize selected elements using a familiar drag-based interface.

12
The Resizable Component

We have already seen resizables in action briefly when we looked at the dialog widget, earlier in the book. In this chapter, we're going to focus on it directly. However, the dialog is a perfect example of how useful the resizable component can be in a real-world implementation.

The resizable widget adds the same functionality that is automatically added to `<textarea>` elements in WebKit browsers such as Safari or Chrome, or newer versions of Firefox. In these browsers, a resize handle is added to the bottom-right corner, which allows the element to be resized. With the jQuery UI resizable component, we can add this behavior to almost any element on the page.

In this chapter, we'll be looking at the following aspects of the component:

- Implementing basic resizability
- The configurable options available for use
- Specifying which resize handles to add
- Managing the resizable's minimum and maximum sizes
- The role of resize helpers and ghosts
- A look at the built-in resize animations
- How to react to resize events
- Determining the new size of a resizable
- Using a resizable with other library widgets

The resizable widget is a flexible component that can be used with a wide range of different elements. Throughout the examples in this chapter, we'll mostly be using simple `<div>` elements so that the focus remains on the component and not on the underlying HTML. We will also look at some brief examples using `<img>` and `<textarea>` elements, towards the end of the chapter.

The resizable component works well with other components and is very often used in conjunction with draggables. However, while you can easily make draggable components resizable (think dialog), the two classes are in no way related.

Implementing a basic resizable widget

Let's implement the basic resizable so we can see how easy making elements resizable is, when you use jQuery UI as the driving force behind your pages. In a new file in your text editor add the following code:

```
<!DOCTYPE HTML>
<html>
  <head>
    <meta charset="utf-8">
    <title>Resizable</title>
    <link rel="stylesheet" href="development-bundle/themes/redmond/
jquery.ui.all.css">
    <link rel="stylesheet" href="css/resize.css">
    <script src="js/jquery-2.0.3.js"></script>
    <script src="development-bundle/ui/jquery.ui.core.js"></script>
    <script src="development-bundle/ui/jquery.ui.widget.js"></script>
    <script src="development-bundle/ui/jquery.ui.mouse.js"></script>
  <script src="development-bundle/ui/jquery.ui.resizable.js"></script>
  </head>
  <script>
    $(document).ready(function($){
      $("#resize").resizable();
    });
  </script>
  <body>
    <div id="resize"></div>
  </body>
</html>
```

Save this as `resizable1.html`. The basic widget method used with no arguments for the default implementation uses the same simplified syntax as the rest of the library. This requires just one line of code for the example to work.

Along with the CSS framework files that we need for any resizable implementations, we also use a custom stylesheet to add basic dimensions and borders to our resizable `<div>`. Use the following CSS in a new file in your text editor:

```
#resize { width: 200px; height: 200px; margin: 30px 0 0 30px;
border: 1px solid #7a7a7a; }
```

Save this file as `resize.css` in the `css` folder. We've specified the dimensions of our resize `<div>` in the CSS, as without them the `<div>` element will stretch the width of the screen. We've also specified a border to clearly define it, as the default implementation only adds a single resize handle to the bottom-right corner of the targeted element. The following screenshot shows how our basic page should look after the `<div>` element has been resized:

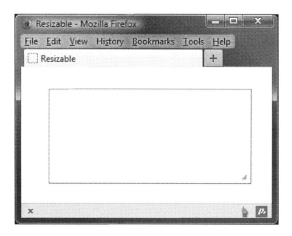

The files required for the resizable component are as follows:

- `jquery-2.0.3.js`
- `jquery.ui.core.js`
- `jquery.ui.widget.js`
- `jquery.ui.mouse.js`
- `jquery.ui.resizable.js`

The component automatically adds the three required elements for the drag handles. Although the only visible resize handle is the one in the bottom-right corner, both the bottom and right edges can be used to resize the widget.

Listing the resizable options

The following table lists the configurable options that we have at our disposal while working with the resizable component:

Option	Default value	Used to...
`alsoResize`	`false`	Automatically resize specified elements in sync with the resizable.
`animate`	`false`	Animate the resizable element to its new size.
`animateDuration`	`slow`	Set the speed of the animation. Values can be integers, specifying the number of milliseconds, or one of the string values `slow`, `normal`, or `fast`.
`animateEasing`	`swing`	Add easing effects to the resize animation.
`aspectRatio`	`false`	Maintain the aspect ratio of the resize element. Accepts numerical custom aspect ratios in addition to Boolean values.
`autoHide`	`false`	Hide the resize handles until the resizable is hovered over with the mouse pointer.
`cancel`	`':input, option'`	Stop specified elements from being resizable.
`containment`	`false`	Constrain the resizable within the boundary of the specified container element.
`delay`	`0`	Set a delay in milliseconds from when the pointer is clicked on a resizable handle to when the resizing begins.
`disabled`	`false`	Disable the component at page load.
`distance`	`1`	Set the number of pixels the mouse pointer must move with the mouse button held down before the resizing begins.
`ghost`	`false`	Show a semi-transparent helper element while the resizing is taking place.
`grid`	`false`	Snap the resize to imaginary grid lines while resizing is taking place.

Option	Default value	Used to...
handles	'e, se, s'	Define which handles to use for resizing. Accepts a string containing any of the following values: n, ne, e, se, s, sw, w, nw, or all. The string could also be an object where the properties are any of the preceding values and the values are jQuery selectors matching the elements to use as handles.
helper	false	Add a class name to the helper element that is applied during resizing.
maxHeight	null	Set the maximum height the resizable may be changed to.
maxWidth	null	Set the maximum width the resizable may be set to.
minHeight	null	Set the minimum height the resizable may be changed to.
minWidth	null	Set the minimum width the resizable may be set to.

Configuring the resize handles

Thanks to the `handles` configuration option, specifying which handles we would like to add to our target element is exceptionally easy. In `resizable1.html`, change the final `<script>` element so that it appears as follows:

```
<script>
  $(document).ready(function($){
    $("#resize").resizable({ handles: "all" });
  });
</script>
```

Save this as `resizable2.html`. When you run the example in a browser, you'll see that although the component looks exactly as it did before, we can now use any edge or corner to resize the `<div>` element.

Adding additional handle images

One thing you'll notice straight away is that although the element is resizable along any axis, there's no visual cue to make this obvious; the component will automatically add the resize stripes to the bottom-right corner, but it's up to us to add the rest.

There are several different ways to do this. Although the method doesn't add images to the other three corners, it does insert DOM elements with class names, so we can easily target these with CSS and provide our own images. This is what we'll do next.

In a new page in your text editor, add the following style rules:

```
#resize {width: 200px; height: 200px; margin: 30px 0 0 30px; border:
1px solid #7a7a7a;}
.ui-resizable-sw, .ui-resizable-nw, .ui-resizable-ne {width: 12px;
height: 12px; background: url(../img/handles.png) no-repeat 0 0;}
.ui-resizable-sw {left: 0; bottom: 0;}
.ui-resizable-nw {left: 0; top: 0; background-position: 0 -12px;}
.ui-resizable-ne {right: 0; top: 0; background-position: 0 -24px;}
```

Save this file in the css folder as resizeHandles.css. We provide our own image for this example, which is a single image containing copies of the standard bottom-right image flipped and reversed (this can be found in the code download). We can then reference them by setting the background-position attribute in our CSS style rules. Use of a single image or sprite reduces the need to cache multiple images; all of the individual images we've used are actually segments from a single, larger file.

Chris Coyier has written a useful article, explaining how to implement sprites, that can be found at http://css-tricks.com/css-sprites/.

Our selectors target the class names that are automatically added to the handle elements by the control. Link to the new stylesheet in the <head> element of resizable2.html and resave it as resizable3.html:

```
<link rel="stylesheet" href="css/resizeHandles.css">
```

The new stylesheet should give our element the following appearance:

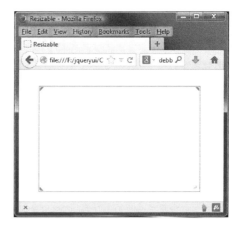

Another configuration option related to resize handles and how they are displayed is `autoHide`. Let's take a quick look at this option next. Change the configuration object in `resizable3.html` to the following:

```
$("#resize").resizable({
  handles: "all",
  autoHide: true
});
```

Save this version as `resizable4.html`. We've added the `autoHide` option and set its value to `true` in this example. Configuring this option hides all of the resize handles until the mouse pointer moves onto the resizable element. This is great for a minimal intrusion of the additional DOM elements when there is pictorial content inside the resizable element.

Defining size limits

Restricting the minimum or maximum sizes that the target element can be resized to is made exceptionally easy with four configurable options. They are `maxWidth`, `maxHeight`, `minWidth`, and `minHeight`. We will see in action in the next example. It's better to have some content in the container for this example, so add some layout text in a `<p>` element within our resizable `<div>` in `resizable4.html`:

```
<p>Lorem ipsum etc, etc...</p>
```

Change the configuration object that we used in `resizable4.html` to as follows:

```
$("#resize").resizable({
  maxWidth: 500,
  maxHeight: 500,
  minWidth: 100,
  minHeight: 100
});
```

Save this as `resizable5.html`. This time, the configuration object uses the dimension-boundary options to specify the minimum and maximum height and width that the resizable may be adjusted to. These options take simple integers as their values.

As we can see when we run this example, the resizable now adheres to the sizes we have specified, whereas in previous examples, the resizable element's minimum size was the combined size of its resize handles, and it had no maximum size.

So far, our resizable has been an empty `<div>` element and you may be wondering how the resizable handles minimum and maximum sizes when there is content within the target element. The restrictions are maintained, but we'll need to add `overflow: hidden` to the CSS. Otherwise, the content may overflow the resizable if there is too much for the minimum size to handle.

Of course, we can also use `overflow: auto` as well to add a scroll bar when there is too much content, which can sometimes be the desired behavior.

Resizing ghosts

Ghost elements, which are semi-transparent helper elements, are very similar to the proxy element that we used when we looked at the draggables component in the previous chapter. A ghost element can be enabled with the configuration of just one option. Let's see how this is done.

Change the configuration object we used in `resizable5.html` to the following:

```
$("#resize").resizable({ ghost: true });
```

Save this file as `resizable6.html`. All that is needed to enable a resize ghost is to set the `ghost` option to `true`. The effect of the resizable ghost is very subtle. It is basically a clone of the existing resizable element, but is only a quarter of the opacity. This is why we've left the layout text from the previous example within the resizable element.

We're also linking to a new stylesheet in this example, which is exactly the same as `resize.css` with a background color specified:

```
#resize { width: 200px; height: 200px; margin: 30px 0 0 30px;
border: 1px solid #7a7a7a; overflow: hidden; background-color: #999; }
```

Save this as `resizeGhosts.css` in the `css` folder. The next screenshot shows how the resizable ghost will appear while it is visible when being dragged:

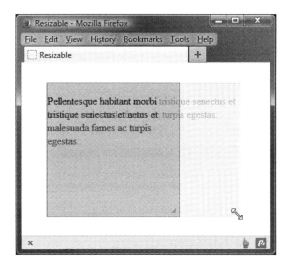

In some versions of Internet Explorer, ghost elements may cause issues when transparent PNGs are within the resizable. If you find this is the case, there is a useful article available at `http://www.pixelthemestudio.ca/news-and-updates/156-fixing-that-png-image-optimization-for-ie` that details how to fix these issues using TweakPNG.

The ghost element is just a helper element that has been made semitransparent. If this is not suitable and further control over the appearance of the helper element is required; we can use the `helper` option to specify a class name to be added to the helper element, which we can then use to style it. Change the configuration object in `resizable6.html`, so that it appears as follows:

```
$("#resize").resizable({
  ghost: true,
  helper: "my-ui-helper"
});
```

Save this revision as `resizable7.html`. We've simply specified the class name that we'd like to be added as the value of the `helper` option. We can target the new class name from a CSS file. Open `resize.css` and add the following code to it:

```
.my-ui-helper { background-color:#FFFF99; }
```

Save the new stylesheet as `resizeHelper.css` and don't forget to link it at the top of `resizable7.html`:

```
<link rel="stylesheet" href="css/resizeHelper.css">
```

The only thing we do in this example is give the helper a simple background color, which in this case is yellow. This is how it looks when the new page is run and a resize is in action:

The `ghost` and `helper` options don't have to be used together; we can use either one separately, but if we use the `helper` option without the `ghost` option, we do not get the semi-transparent content within the resize helper.

Containing the resize

The resizable component makes it easy to ensure that a resized element is contained within its parent element. This is great if we have other content on the page that we don't want moving around all over the place during a resize interaction. In `resizable7.html`, change the elements on the page so that they appear as follows:

```
<div class="container">
  <img id="resize" src="img/moon.jpg" alt="Moon Landing">
</div>
```

Finally, change the `configuration` object to use the `containment` option:

```
$("#resize").resizable({
  containment: ".container"
});
```

Save this as `resizable8.html`. On the page, we've added a container element for the resizable and have switched from using a `<div>` element to an image as the resizable element.

Once again, we need some slightly different CSS for this example. In a new file in your text editor, add the following code:

```
.container { width: 600px; height: 600px; border: 1px solid #7a7a7a;
padding: 1px 0 0 1px; }
#resize { width: 300px; height: 300px; }
```

Save this as `resizeContainer.css` in the `css` folder and change the `<link>` in the `<head>` element of the page from `resizeHelper.css` to the new stylesheet:

```
<link rel="stylesheet" href="css/resizeContainer.css">
```

The `containment` option allows us to specify a container for the resizable, which will limit how large the resizable can be made, forcing it to stay within its boundaries.

We specify a jQuery selector as the value of this option. When we view the page, we should see that the image cannot be resized to larger than its container.

Handling aspect ratio

In addition to maintaining the aspect ratio of the resizable element, we can also define it manually. Let's see what control this interaction gives us over the resize. Change the configuration object used in `resizable8.html` to the following:

```
$("#resize").resizable({
  containment: ".container",
  aspectRatio: true
});
```

Save this file as `resizable9.html`. Setting the `aspectRatio` option to `true` ensures that our image will maintain its original aspect ratio. So in this example, the image will always be a perfect square.

For a greater degree of control, we can instead specify the actual aspect ratio that the resizable should maintain:

```
$("#resize").resizable({
  containment: ".container",
  aspectRatio: 0.5
});
```

By specifying the floating-point value of `0.5`, we're saying that when the image is resized, the x-axis of the image should be exactly half of the y-axis.

 Care should be taken when deviating from the aspect ratio of any images; it is wise to try to keep the element and container sizes in proportion, otherwise you may find an object doesn't resize to the full extent of its container, as happened in our example. If you change `aspectRatio` to 1, you will find that it resizes to the full size of our container correctly.

Resizable animations

The resizable API exposes three configuration options related to animations: `animate`, `animateDuration`, and `animateEasing`. By default, animations are switched off in resizable implementations. However, we can easily enable them to see how they enhance this component.

In this example, change the markup from the previous couple of examples so that the resizable element goes back to a plain `<div>`:

```
<div id="resize"></div>
```

We should also switch back to the `resizeGhosts.css` stylesheet:

```
<link rel="stylesheet" href="css/resizeGhost.css">
```

Now, change the configuration object to use the following options:

```
$("#resize").resizable({
  ghost: true,
  animate: true,
  animateDuration: "fast"
});
```

Save this as `resizable10.html`. The configuration object we use in this example starts with the `ghost` option.

While using animations, the resizable element is not resized until after the interaction has ended, so it's useful to show the ghost as a visual cue that the element will be resized.

All we need to do to enable animation is set the `animate` option to `true`. That's it; no further configuration is required. Another option we can change is the speed of the animation, which we have done in this example by setting the `animateDuration` option. This accepts any of the standard values that can be used with jQuery's `animate()` method.

When we run this page in a browser, we should find that the `resize` div will smoothly animate to its new size, once we let go of the mouse button.

Simultaneous resizing

We can easily make several elements on the same page individually resizable by passing references to them to the resizable widget method. But, in addition to doing this, we can make use of the `alsoResize` property to specify additional elements that are to be resized together as a group, whenever the actual resizable element is resized. Let's see how.

First, we'll need to reference to a new stylesheet once again:

```
<link rel="stylesheet" href="css/resizeSimultaneous.css">
```

Next, we'll need to change the elements in `<body>` of the page as follows:

```
<div id="mainResize">
  <p>I am the main resizable!</p>
</div>
<div id="simultaneousResize">
  <p>I will also be resized when the main resizable is resized!</p>
</div>
```

Then change the configuration object to the following:

```
$("#resize").resizable({
  alsoResize: "#simultaneousResize"
});
```

Save this file as `resizable11.html`. We provide a selector as the value of the `alsoResize` option, in order to target the second `<div>` element. The secondary element will automatically pick up the resizable attributes of the actual resizable.

So, if we limit the resizable to having just an e handle, the secondary element will also only resize in this direction.

The new stylesheet referenced in this example should contain the following code:

```
#mainResize { width: 100px; height: 100px; margin: 0 0 30px;
border: 2px solid #7a7a7a; text-align: center; }
#simultaneousResize { width: 150px; height: 150px; border: 2px solid
#7a7a7a; text-align: center; }
p { font-family: arial; font-size: 15px; }
```

Save this file as resizeSimultaneous.css in the css folder. When we run the file, we should see that the second <div> element is resized at the same time as the first:

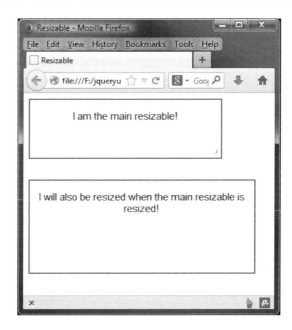

Preventing unwanted resizes

There may be times when we'd like to make an element resizable, but it also has other functionality, perhaps it listens for click events too. In this situation, it may be desirable to prevent the resize unless it is definitely required, enabling us to easily differentiate between clicks and true drags. We can use two options to achieve this.

First, in resizable10.html, revert to the original stylesheet resize.css:

```
<link rel="stylesheet" href="css/resize.css">
```

We can also return to the simple empty resizable `<div>`:

```
<div id="resize"></div>
```

Then change the configuration object to the following:

```
$("#resize").resizable({
  delay: 1000
});
```

Save this version as `resizable12.html`. The `delay` option accepts an integer that represents the number of milliseconds that need to pass with the mouse button held down after clicking on a resize handle before the resize will begin.

We've used `1000` as the value in this example that is equal to one second. Try it out and you'll see that if you click on a resize handle and release the mouse button too soon, the resize won't take place.

Along with delaying the resize, we could also use the `distance` option instead to specify that the mouse pointer must move a certain number of pixels, with the button held down after clicking on a resize handle, before the resize occurs.

Change the configuration object in `resizable12.html`, so that it appears as follows:

```
$("#resize").resizable({
  distance: 30
});
```

Save this as `resizable13.html`. Now when the page runs, instead of having to wait with the mouse button held down, the mouse pointer will need to travel `30` pixels with the mouse button held down, before the resize occurs.

Both of these options present certain usability issues, especially when set to `high` as in these examples. They both make it harder to resize an element along more than one axis at a time. They should be used sparingly, with as low values as possible.

Defining resizable events

Like other components of the library, resizable defines a selection of custom events, and allows us to easily execute functions when these events occur. This makes the most of interactions between your visitors and the elements on your pages.

Resizable defines the following callback options:

Option	Triggered when...
create	The resizable is initialized
resize	The resizable is in the process of being resized
start	A resize interaction begins
stop	A resize interaction ends

Hooking into these custom methods is just as easy for resizables as it has been for the other components of the library we have looked at.

Let's explore a basic example to highlight this fact the following screenshot shows how our page will look before <div> fades away:

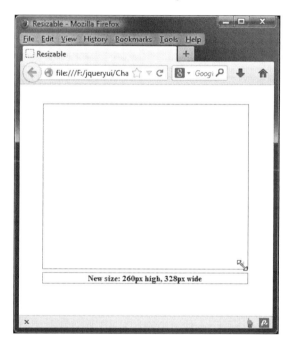

In resizable13.html, change the second <link> to point to a new stylesheet as follows:

```
<link rel="stylesheet" href="css/resizeStop.css">
```

Then change the final `<script>` element so that it appears as follows:

```
<script>
  $(document).ready(function($){
    function reportNewSize(e, ui) {
      var width = Math.round(ui.size.width),
      height = Math.round(ui.size.height);
      $("<div />", {
        "class": "message",
        text: "New size: " + height + "px high, " + width + "px wide",
        width: width
      }).appendTo("body").fadeIn().delay(2000).fadeOut();
    }
    $("#resize").resizable({
      stop: reportNewSize
    });
  });
</script>
```

Save this as `resizable14.html`. In `resize.css`, add the following selector
and rules:

```
.message { display: none; border: 1px solid #7a7a7a; margin-top: 5px;
position: absolute; left: 38px;fontSize: 80%; font-weight: bold; text-
align: center; }
```

Save this as `resizeStop.css` in the `css` folder.

We define a function called `reportNewSize`; this function (along with all of the other
event handlers) is automatically passed two objects. The first is the event object and
the second is an object containing useful information about the resizable.

We can use the `size` property of the second object to find out what the `width` and
`height` the resizable has been changed to. These values are stored as variables within
the function. We use the JavaScript `Math.round()` function to make sure that we end
up with an integer.

We then create a new `<div>` element and give it a class name for styling. We also set
the text of the new element to display the `width` and `height` variables along with
a brief message. We also set the width of the new element to match the resizable.
Once created, we append the message to the page and then fade it in with jQuery's
`fadeIn()` method. We then use the `delay()` method to pause for 2 seconds before
fading the message out again.

Looking at the resizable methods

This component comes with the four basic methods found with all of the interaction components of the library, namely the `destroy`, `disable`, `enable`, and `option` methods. Unlike most of the other components, the resizable component has no custom methods unique to it. For clarification on these basic API methods, see the API introduction section in *Chapter 1, Introducing jQuery UI*.

Creating resizable tabs

In our final resizable example, let's look at combining this component with one of the widgets that we looked at earlier. This will help us see how compatible it is with the rest of the library. We'll be working with the tabs component in the following example. The following screenshot shows the page we will end up with:

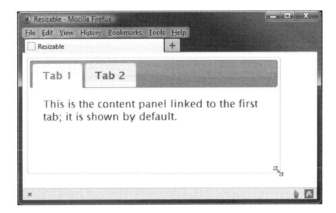

In your text editor, add the following CSS style to a new file, and save it as `resizeTabs.css`:

```
#resize { width: 200px; height: 200px; margin: 30px 0 0 30px; border:
1px solid #7a7a7a; }
#myTabs { width: 400px; height: 170px; }
```

Next, add the following code to a new file:

```
<!DOCTYPE HTML>
<html>
  <head>
    <meta charset="utf-8">
    <title>Resizable</title>
    <link rel="stylesheet" href="development-bundle/themes/redmond/
jquery.ui.all.css">
```

```
<link rel="stylesheet" href="css/resizeTabs.css">
<script src="js/jquery-2.0.3.js"></script>
<script src="development-bundle/ui/jquery.ui.core.js"></script>
<script src="development-bundle/ui/jquery.ui.widget.js"></script>
<script src="development-bundle/ui/jquery.ui.tabs.js"></script>
<script src="development-bundle/ui/jquery.ui.mouse.js"></script>
<script src="development-bundle/ui/jquery.ui.resizable.js"></script>
<script>
  $(document).ready(function($){
    var tabs = $("#myTabs").tabs(), resizeOpts = {
      autoHide: true,
      minHeight: 170,
      minWidth: 400
    };
    tabs.resizable(resizeOpts);
  });
</script>
</head>
<body>
  <div id="myTabs">
    <ul>
      <li><a href="#a">Tab 1</a></li>
      <li><a href="#b">Tab 2</a></li>
    </ul>
    <div id="a">
      This is the content panel linked to the first tab; it is
        shown by default.
    </div>
    <div id="b">
      This content is linked to the second tab and will be shown
        when its tab is clicked.
    </div>
  </div>
</body>
</html>
```

Save this as `resizable15.html`. Making the tabs widget resizable is extremely easy and only requires calling the resizable method on the tab's underlying `<ul>`.

We're using a single configuration object in this example. The tabs component can be initialized without the need for any configuration. Apart from setting the `autoHide` option for the resizable in our configuration object to `true`, we also define `minWidth` and `minHeight` values for usability purposes.

Summary

In this chapter, we covered the resizable. This is a component that allows us to easily resize any on-screen element. It dynamically adds resize handles to the specified sides of the target element and handles all of the tricky DHTML resizing for us, neatly encapsulating the behavior into a compact, easy-to-use class.

We then looked at some of the configurable options that we can use with the widget, such as how to specify which handles to add to the resizable, and how the minimum and maximum sizes of the element can be limited.

We briefly looked at how to maintain an image's aspect ratio, or how to work with custom ratios, while it is being resized. We also explored how to use ghosts, helpers, and animations to improve the usability and appearance of the resizable component.

We also looked at the event model exposed by the component's API and how we can react to elements being resized in an easy and effective way. Our final example explored resizable's compatibility with other components of the library. In the next chapter, we'll look at how you can select, filter, and sort objects with the Selectable and Sortable widgets.

13

Selecting and Sorting with jQuery UI

If you spend any time working with lists (in an application such as Microsoft Excel), then it is possible that you will need to select and sort items into some logical order, in a similar fashion to selecting and ordering icons on your computer's desktop.

The selectable and sortable interaction helpers in jQuery UI allow you to define a series of elements that can be chosen by dragging a selection square around them, and then reordered into a new order.

Topics that will be covered in this section include:

- Creating the default selectable implementation
- How selectable class names reflect the state of selectable elements
- Filtering selectable elements
- Working with selectables' built-in callback functions
- A look at selectables' methods
- Creating a default sortable widget
- Basic configurable properties
- Sortables' wide range of built-in event handlers and methods
- Submitting the sorted result to a server
- Adding drag elements to a sortable

Selecting and sorting has been a standard part of modern operating systems for a long time. For example, if you wanted to select and sort some of the icons on your desktop, you could hold the mouse button down on a blank part of the desktop and drag a square around the icons you wanted to select, or select the **Auto arrange icons** option from your desktop.

The selectable and sortable interaction helpers add this same functionality to our web pages, which allows us to build more user-friendly interfaces without needing to use external environments, such as Flash or Silverlight.

Introducing the selectable widget

The first thing we should do is invoke the default implementation to get a glimpse of the basic functionality provided by this component.

In a new file in your text editor, add the following code:

```
<!DOCTYPE HTML>
<html>
  <head>
    <meta charset="utf-8">
    <title>Selectable</title>
    <link rel="stylesheet" href="development-bundle/themes/redmond/jquery.ui.all.css">
    <script src="js/jquery-2.0.3.js"></script>
    <script src="development-bundle/ui/jquery.ui.core.js"></script>
    <script src="development-bundle/ui/jquery.ui.widget.js"></script>
    <script src="development-bundle/ui/jquery.ui.mouse.js"></script>
    <script src="development-bundle/ui/jquery.ui.selectable.js">
</script>
    <script>
      $(document).ready(function($){
        $("#selectables").selectable();
      });
    </script>
  </head>
  <body>
<ul id="selectables">
  <li> This is selectable list item 1</li>
  <li> This is selectable list item 2</li>
  <li> This is selectable list item 3</li>
  <li> This is selectable list item 4</li>
  <li> This is selectable list item 5</li>
</ul>
  </body>
</html>
```

Save this as `selectable1.html` in the `jqueryui` folder. We simply call the `selectable` widget method on the parent `<ul>` element and then all of its child `<li>` elements are made selectable. This allows selection by clicking on them or using the selection square (like you would do on your desktop).

Note that there is no styling associated with the selectable component. Default behavior includes clicking on individual elements, causing them only to be selected, and clicking on one of the selected elements to deselect them. Holding down the *Ctrl* key will enable multiselect. The following screenshot shows the selection square enclosing the list items:

The minimum set of library files we need for a selectable implementation is as follows:

* `jquery-2.0.3.js`
* `jquery.ui.core.js`
* `jquery.ui.widget.js`
* `jquery.ui.mouse.js`
* `jquery.ui.selectable.js`

Along with building selectables from list items, we can also build them from other elements, such as a collection of `<div>` elements. Add the following link to the `<head>` of the `selectable1.html` file:

```
<link rel="stylesheet" href="css/selectable.css">
```

Also, replace the list elements in `selectable1.html` with the following code:

```
<div id="selectables">
  <div>This is selectable list item 1</div>
  <div>This is selectable list item 2</div>
  <div>This is selectable list item 3</div>
```

```
    <div>This is selectable list item 4</div>
    <div>This is selectable list item 5</div>
  </div>
```

Save this as `selectable2.html`. Everything is essentially the same as before.

We're just basing the example on different elements. However, due to the nature of these elements, we should add a little basic styling so that we can see what we're working with.

In a new file in your text editor, add the following code:

```
#selectables div { width: 170px; height: 25px; padding: 5px 0 0 10px;
margin: 10px 0 0 10px; border: 1px solid #000; }
```

Save this as `selectable.css` in the `css` folder. It's not much, but it helps to clarify the individual selectables in the example, as shown in the following screenshot:

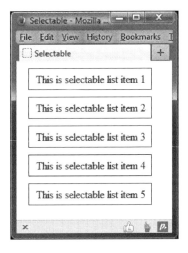

Introducing the Selectee class names

The elements that are made selectable are all initially given the `ui-selectee` class, and the parent element that contains them is given the `ui-selectable` class. While elements are selected, they are given the `ui-selected` class.

While the selecting square is around selectable elements, they are given the `ui-selecting` class, and whilst an element is being deselected it is given the `ui-unselecting` class. These classnames are added purely for our benefit, so that we can highlight different states that the selectable may be in.

This extensive class system makes it very easy to add custom styling to show when elements are either in the process of being selected or have been selected. Let's add some additional styling now to reflect the selecting and selected states. Add the following new selectors and rules to `selectable.css`:

```
#selectables div.ui-selecting { border: 1px solid #fe2f2f; }
#selectables div.ui-selected { background: #fe2f2f; color: #fff; }
```

Save this `selectableStates.css` in the `css` folder. Change the link to the stylesheet reference in the `<head>` of `selectable2.html`, then save this file as `selectable3.html`:

```
<link rel="stylesheet" href="css/selectableStates.css">
```

With the addition of this very simple CSS, we can add visual cues to elements that are part of the current selection, both during and following a select interaction. The following screenshot shows some elements in the process of being selected on the left, and the same elements having been selected on the right:

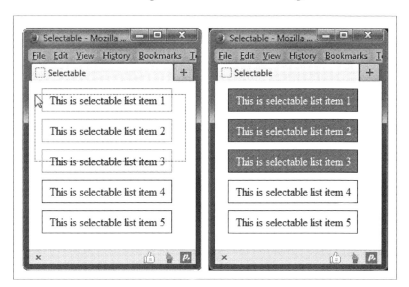

Configuring the selectable component

The `selectable` class is quite compact, with relatively few configurable options compared to some of the other components that we've looked at.

The following options are available for configuration:

Option	Default value	Used to...
autoRefresh	True	Automatically refresh the size and position of each selectable at the start of a select interaction.
cancel	":input, option"	Prevent the specified elements from being selected with a click. The default string contains the :input jQuery filter, which matches all <input>, <textarea>, <select>, and <button> elements along with the standard option element selector.
delay	0	Set the delay in milliseconds before the element is selected. The mouse button must be held down on the element before the selection will begin.
disabled	false	Disable selection when the page initially loads.
distance	0	Set the distance the mouse pointer must travel, with the mouse button held down, before selection will begin.
filter	"*"	Specify child elements to make selectable.
tolerance	"touch"	Set the tolerance of the selection square. Possible values are touch or fit. If fit is specified the element must be completely within the selection square before the element will be selected.

Filtering selectables

There may be situations when we don't want to allow all of the elements within the targeted container to be made selectable. In this situation we can make use of the filter option to nominate specific elements, based on a CSS selector, that we want selecting to be enabled on. In selectable3.html, change the collection of <div> elements so that it appears as follows:

```
<div id="selectables">
  <div> This is unselectable list item 1</div>
  <div> This is unselectable list item 2</div>
  <div class="selectable">This is selectable list item 3</div>
  <div class="selectable">This is selectable list item 4</div>
  <div class="selectable">This is selectable list item 5</div>
</div>
```

Then change the final <script> element to the following:

```
<script>
  $(document).ready(function($){
    $("#selectables").selectable({
```

```
        filter: ".selectable"
    });
  });
</script>
```

The width of each selectable needs to be increased, so in `selectableStates.css`, change the `#selectables div` rule to have a width of 190 px.

Save this version as `selectable4.html`. In the underlying markup, we have given a class to each element except for the first. In the JavaScript, we define a configuration object containing the `filter` option. The value of this option is the class selector of the elements that we want to be selectable; elements without this class name are filtered out of the selection:

As shown in the previous screenshot, the selection square is over the unselectable element, but it's not picking up the `ui-selecting` class like the others. The component completely ignores the filtered selectable and it does not become part of the selection.

Canceling the selection

Along with indirectly making elements unselectable using the `filter` option, we can also directly make elements unselectable using the `cancel` option. This option was also exposed by the interaction helper we looked at in *Chapter 12, The Resizable Component*, although we didn't look at it in any detail. Now is the perfect opportunity to play with it.

Add the class name `unselectable` to the first and second elements in the container in `selectable4.html`:

```
<div class="unselectable"> This is unselectable list item 1</div>
<div class="unselectable">This is unselectable list item 2</div>
```

Change the configuration object from the last example so that it uses the `cancel` option:

```
$("#selectables").selectable({
    cancel: ".unselectable"
})
```

Save this as `selectable5.html`. Instead of passing the class name of the selectable elements to the configuration object, we pass the class name of the unselectable element to it. When we run the example, we can see that the first element, with the class name `unselectable`, is still given the class `ui-selectee`. However, it is only selectable with the selection square; it cannot be selected by clicking, even with the *Ctrl* key held down.

Handling selectable events

In addition to the standard configurable options of the selectable API, there are also a series of event callback options that can be used to specify functions that are executed at specific points during a select interaction. These options are listed in the following table:

Option	Triggered when
selecte	The select interaction ends and each element added to the selection triggers the callback.
selecting	Each selected element triggers the callback during the select interaction.
start	A select interaction begins.
stop	A selection operation ends.
unselected	Any elements that are part of the selectable, but are not selected during the interaction will fire this callback.
unselecting	Unselected elements will fire this during the select interaction.

Selecting really only becomes useful when something happens to the elements once they have been selected, which is where this event model comes into play. Let's put some of these callbacks to work so that we can appreciate their use.

Replace the configuration object in `selectable5.html` so that it contains the following code:

```
$("#selectables").selectable({
  selected: function(e, ui) {
    $(ui.selected).text("I have been selected!");
  },
  unselected: function(e, ui) {
    $(ui.unselected).text("This div was selected");
  },
  start: function(e) {
    if (!$("#tip").length) {
      $("<div />", {
        "class": "ui-corner-all ui-widget ui-widget-header",
        id: "tip",
        text: "Drag the lasso around elements, or click to select",
        css: {
          position: "absolute",
          padding: 10,
          left: e.pageX,
          top: e.pageY - 30,
          display: "none"
        }
      }).appendTo("body").fadeIn();
    }
  },
  stop: function(e) {
    $("#tip").fadeOut("slow", function() {
      $(this).remove();
    });
  }
});
```

Save this as `selectable6.html`. In the `<script>`, we've added functions to the selected, unselected, start, and stop options. These will be executed at the appropriate times during an interaction.

As with other components, these functions are automatically passed two objects. The first is the original browser event object (typically called `e`) and the other is an object containing useful properties of the selected element (often referred to as `ui`). However, not all callbacks can successfully work with the second object—start and stop, for example. In our example, we've left out the `ui` object; there is no need to include it, as it will be empty.

When a `<div>` is selected, we change its inner text to reflect the selection using the `selected` event callback. We can use the `selected` property to get the element that was selected in order to change its text content to a new message. When an element is deselected, we set the text to `The div was selected` using the same technique.

We can also alter the text of any selectable that was previously selected using the `unselected` event.

At the start of any interaction, we create a tooltip that is appended to the `<body>` of the page, slightly offset from the mouse pointer, using the `start` event. We use a basic conditional to check that the tool tip does not already exist to prevent duplicate tips. We can make use of the framework classes `ui-corner-all`, `ui-widget`, and `ui-widget-header` to do most of the styling for us. The few styles we require that are not provided by the theme are added using the `css()` method. We can get the pointer coordinates using the `e` (event) object, which is passed as the first argument to our callbacks, in order to position the tool tip. At the end of the selection, we remove the tool tip using the `stop` property. The following screenshot shows the results of different interactions:

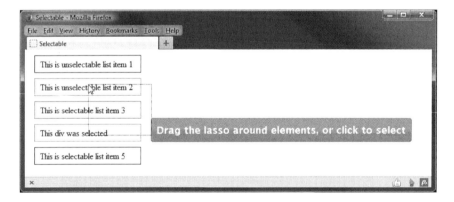

The `selecting` and `unselecting` callback options work exactly the same way as those we have just looked at, but are fired as elements are added or removed to the selection. To see those in action, replace the `selected` and `unselected` options in the configuration object in `selectable6.html` with the following:

```
selecting: function(e, ui) {
  $(ui.selecting).text("I am part of the selection");
},
unselecting: function(e, ui) {
  $(ui.unselecting).text("I was part of the selection");
},
```

Save your work as `selectable7.html`. This time we use the `selecting` and `unselecting` properties to specify callback functions, which again change the text content of the elements at certain times during an interaction. We repeat the procedure from the last example, this time we're just using different callbacks and properties of the objects passed to them.

The second object passed to any of the selectable callbacks contains a property relating to the type of custom event. For example, the selected callback receives an object with a `selected` property, which can be used to gain information about the element that was added to the selection. All callbacks have a matching property that can be used in this way.

Working with vast amounts of selectables

The jQuery UI library, such as jQuery itself, is already extremely efficient. It uses the ultra-effective **Sizzle selector engine** (via jQuery) and each component has been optimized as much as possible.

> Sizzle is a pure JavaScript CSS Selector engine, used by jQuery, which allows you to use JavaScript on CSS selectors, such as `$("<div>")`. If you would like to learn more, you can visit the project site at `http://sizzlejs.com/`.

However, there is only so much that the creators of the library can do. In our examples so far, we've used a maximum of five selectable elements, which aren't really many at all. What if we were to use 500 instead?

When working with great numbers of selectables there is still something we can do to make sure that the select interactions are as efficient as possible. The `autoRefresh` option is set to `true` by default, which causes the sizes and positions of all selectable elements on the page to be recalculated at the beginning of every interaction.

This can cause delays on pages with many selectable elements on it, so the `autoRefresh` option can be set to `false` when dealing with large collections of elements. We can also use the `refresh` method to manually refresh the selectables at appropriate times in order to improve the speed and responsiveness of the interactions. On most pages we would not need to worry about configuring this option and can leave it at its default setting.

Let's take a look at how this option can help our pages in certain situations. In the `<head>` of `selectable7.html` change the `<link>` for the custom stylesheet to the following:

```
<link rel="stylesheet" href="css/selectableMany.css ">
```

Then change the selectables container element so that it appears as follows:

```
<div id="selectables" class="ui-helper-clearfix">
  <div class="selectable">Selectable</div>
</div>
```

We're going to use a little jQuery to create our selectable elements automatically, so replace the existing script in `document.ready()` block with the following code:

```
var $selectable = $(".selectable");
for(var I = 0; I < 100; i++) {
  $selectable.parent().append($selectable.clone());
}
$("#selectables").selectable({
  autoRefresh: false
});
```

Save this page as `selectable8.html`. Our page should now contain 100 individual selectables within the selectables container. We've also added a class name to the outer container so that the container is cleared properly when we float our selectables (which we will do in a moment). If the container is not cleared correctly, the selection square will not work. We added the `.ui-helper-clearfix` class to our selectables `div` to help cure this issue.

We also need a new stylesheet in this example that consists of the following code:

```
#selectables div { width: 70px; height: 25px; padding: 5px 0 0 10px;
border: 1px solid #000; margin: 10px 0 0 10px; float: left; }
.ui-selected { background-color: #fe2f2f; }
```

Save this in the `css` folder as `selectableMany.css`. It's purely for layout purposes, so we don't need to discuss it further.

We can use something like Chrome's Developer Tools to profile a selection of all 100 selectables with and without the `autoRefresh` option enabled; it's enabled by default, so our example will disable it. The results will probably vary between tests, but you should find that the profile (in both milliseconds and the number of calls) is consistently lower with `autoRefresh` set to disabled.

How do I profile JavaScript performance?

For details of how to perform profiling in a browser such as Chrome, you can view a useful tutorial at `https://developers.google.com/chrome-developer-tools/docs/cpu-profiling`.

Working with selectable methods

The methods that we can use to control the selectables component from our code are similar to the methods found in other interaction helpers and follow the same pattern of usage. The only unique method exposed by the selectables component is listed as follows:

Method	Usage
Refresh	Manually refreshes the positions and sizes of all selectables. Should be used when autoRefresh is set to false.

In addition to this unique method, the selectables component (like every other component) makes use of the common API methods destroy, disable, enable, option, and widget.

Refreshing selectables

Setting the autoRefresh property to false can yield performance gains when there are many selectables on the page, especially in Internet Explorer. However, there will still be times when you will need to refresh the size and positions of the selectables, such as when this component is combined with the draggables component.

Let's take a look at the refresh method as it leads on perfectly from the last example. Add the following new <button> element directly after the selectables container:

```
<button id="refresh">Refresh</button>
```

We'll also need to link to the draggable source file for this example:

```
<script src="development-bundle/ui/jquery.ui.draggable.js">
</script>
```

Then change the final <script> element so that it appears as follows:

```
<script>
  $(document).ready(function($){
    var $selectable = $(".selectable");
    for(var i = 0; i < 100; i++) {
      $selectable.parent().append($selectable.clone());
    }
    $("#selectables").selectable({
      autoRefresh: false
    });
    $("#selectables div").draggable();
    $("#refresh").click(function() {
```

```
                $("#selectables").selectable("refresh");
            });
        });
    </script>
```

Save this as `selectable9.html`. We've added a new `<button>` to the page and we now link to the draggable source file as well as the selectable's. Each of the 100 elements is made both draggable and selectable.

Our click handler that is attached to the `<button>` will simply call the `refresh` method manually on the selectables container. When we run the page in a browser we should first select some, but not all, of the selectable widgets. We should then deselect the elements and move some of them around. We can move other elements that weren't selected into the selection group as well. Really shuffle them up!

When we try to select the same group again, we find that the wrong elements are being selected:

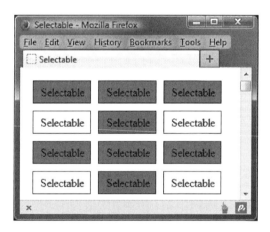

The component hasn't refreshed the positions of the selectables, so it still thinks that all of the selectables are in the same place as they were when the first selection was made. If we click on the **refresh** button and make a third selection, the correct elements will now be selected.

Creating a selectable image viewer

In our final selectable example, we're going to make a basic image viewer. Images can be chosen for viewing by selecting the appropriate thumbnail. Although this sounds like a relatively easy achievement, in addition to the actual mechanics of displaying the selected image, we'll also need to consider how to handle multiple selections.

The following screenshot shows an example of what we'll end up with:

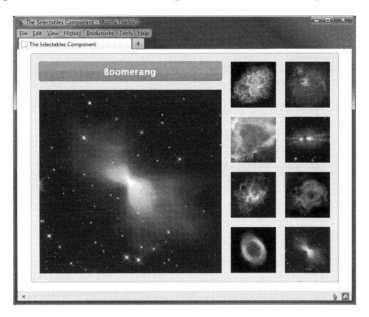

Let's get started with the code. In a fresh page in your text editor, add the following page:

```
<!DOCTYPE HTML>
<html>
  <head>
    <meta charset="utf-8">
    <title>The Selectables Component</title>
    <link rel="stylesheet" href="development-bundle/themes/redmond/
jquery.ui.all.css">
    <link rel="stylesheet" href="css/selectableViewer.css">
    <script src="js/jquery-2.0.3.js"></script>
    <script src="development-bundle/ui/jquery.ui.core.js"></script>
    <script src="development-bundle/ui/jquery.ui.widget.js"></script>
    <script src="development-bundle/ui/jquery.ui.mouse.js"></script>
    <script src="development-bundle/ui/jquery.ui.selectable.js">
</script>
    <script src="development-bundle/ui/jquery.ui.tabs.js"></script>
    <script>
    </script>
  </head>
  <body>
    <div id="imageSelector"
```

```
        class="ui-widget ui-corner-all ui-helper-clearfix">
        <div id="status" class="ui-widget-header ui-corner-all">Crab</
  div>
        <div id="viewer"><img src="img/crab.jpg"></div>
        <div id="thumbs">
          <img class="ui-selected" id="crab" src="img/crab.jpg">
          <img class="right" id="orion" src="img/orion.jpg">
          <img id="omega" src="img/omega.jpg">
          <img class="right" id="egg" src="img/egg.jpg">
          <img id="triangulum" src="img/triangulum.jpg">
          <img class="right" id="rosette" src="img/rosette.jpg">
          <img id="ring" src="img/ring.jpg">
          <img class="right" id="boomerang" src="img/boomerang.jpg">
        </div>
      </div>
    </body>
  </html>
```

Save this as `imageSelector.html`. On the page, we have a parent `<div>` with an `id` of `imageSelector` into which all of our other elements go.

Within the parent, we have a `<div>` that will act as a status bar to display the names of individually selected images, and a `<div>` that will act as the viewing panel and will display the full-sized version of the image. Finally, we have our thumbnail images, which will be made selectable.

Adding the behavior

Next we need to add the script that makes the image selector work, so directly after the final `<script>` element add the following code; throughout this section, we'll walk through the code block by block, beginning with the configuration object for the selectables:

```
$(document).ready(function($){
  $("#thumbs").selectable({
    stop: function(e, ui) {
      $("#imageSelector").children().not("#thumbs")
.remove();
        $("<div />", {
          id: "viewer"
        }).insertBefore("#thumbs");
        if ($(".ui-selected", "#thumbs").length == 1) {
          singleSelect();
        } else {
```

```
            multiSelect();
        }
    }
});
```

We use the `stop callback` function to do some prep work, such as removing the contents of the image selector container (except for the thumbnails) and creating an empty viewer container. We then use an `if` conditional to call either the `singleSelect()` or `multiSelect()` functions.

```
function singleSelect() {
    var id = $(".ui-selected", "#thumbs").attr("id");
    $("<div />", {
      id: "status",
      text: id,
      "class": "ui-widget-header ui-corner-all"
    }).insertBefore("#viewer");
      $("<img />", {
        src: "img/" + id + ".jpg",
        id: id
      }).appendTo("#viewer");
}
```

We then define the first of two functions, which is `singleSelect()`. This will be invoked every time a single thumbnail is selected. We first cache the `id` of the selected element; we'll be referring to this several times, so it's more efficient to store it in a variable.

Next we create a new status bar and set its `innerText` to the `id` value that was cached a moment ago, which will be the `id` attribute of whichever thumbnail is selected. We give the new element some of the framework classes to style the element and then insert it into the image selector container.

The last thing we do in this function is to create the full-sized version of the thumbnail. To do this, we create a new image and set its `src` attribute to match the large version of the thumbnail that was selected (both the large and thumbnail versions of each image have the same filename). The full-size image is then inserted into the viewer container.

```
function multiSelect() {
    $("<div />", {
      id: "tabs"
    }).insertBefore("#viewer");
    var tabList = $("<ul />", {
      id: "tabList"
    }).appendTo("#tabs");
```

Next we define the `multiSelect()` function, which is called when multiple thumbnails are selected. This time we start by creating a new `<div>` element, give it an `id` of tabs and insert it before the viewer container. Following this, we create a new `<ul>` element, as this is a required component of the tabs widget (which we looked at in *Chapter 3, Using the Tabs Widget*). This element is appended to the tabs container we created a moment ago.

```
$(".ui-selected", "#thumbs").each(function() {
    var id = $(this).attr("id"),
        tabItem = $("<li />").appendTo(tabList),
        tabLink = $("<a />", {
            text: id,
            href: "#tabpanel_" + id
        }).appendTo(tabItem),
        panel = $("<div />", {
            id: "tabpanel_" + id
        }).appendTo("#viewer");
        $("<img />", { src: "img/" + id + ".jpg",
            id: id
        }).appendTo(panel);
    });
    $("#viewer").css("left", 0).appendTo("#tabs");
    $("#tabs").tabs();
    }
});
```

We then use jQuery's `each()` method to iterate over each of the thumbnails that were selected. For each item we create a series of variables, which will hold the different elements that make up the tab headings. We cache the `id` attribute of each image and create a new `<li>` and a new `<a>` element. The link will form the clickable tab heading and is given the `id` of the thumbnail as its text content.

We then create the new tab panel that will match the tab heading that we just created. Notice that we create a unique `id` for the content panel based on the thumbnail's `id` attribute and some hardcoded text. Note that the `id` will precisely match the `href` attribute that we set on the `<a>` element. Each new image is created in the same way as in the `singleSelect()` function.

After the `each()` method, we set a CSS property on the viewer container to tidy up its appearance and then append it to the tabs container. Finally the `tabs()` method is called on the tabs container, transforming it into the tabs widget. At the end of the script the thumbnails are made selectable.

Styling the image selector

Our example is also heavily reliant on CSS to provide its overall appearance. In a new file in your text editor, create the following new stylesheet:

```
#imageSelector { width: 676px; height: 497px; border: 1px solid
#adadad; margin: 0 auto; position: relative; background-color:
#dfdede; }
#status { width: 380px; height: 21px; padding: 10px; position:
absolute; left: 17px; top: 17px; font-size: 19px; text-align: center;
background-color: #adadad; border: 1px solid #adadad; text-transform:
capitalize; }
#viewer { width: 400px; height: 400px; border: 1px solid #fff;
position: absolute; left: 17px; top: 78px; }
#thumbs { width: 222px; height: 460px; position: absolute; right:
17px; top: 17px; }
#thumbs img { width: 100px; height: 100px; float: left; margin: 0 18px
18px 0; cursor: pointer; border: 1px solid #fff; }
#thumbs img.right { margin-right: 0; }
#thumbs img.ui-selected { border: 1px solid #99ff99; }
#tabs { padding: 0; border: none; position: absolute; left: 17px;
background: none; }
#tabs .ui-tabs-panel { padding: 0; }
#tabs .ui-tabs-nav { padding: 0; border: none; position: relative;
top: 54px; background: none; }
#tabs .ui-tabs-nav li { margin: 0; }
#tabs .ui-tabs-nav li a { padding: 5px 4px; font-size: 11px; text-
transform: capitalize; }
#tabs .ui-tabs-nav li.ui-tabs-selected a,
#tabs .ui-tabs-nav li.ui-state-disabled a,
#tabs .ui-tabs-nav li.ui-state-processing a { font-weight: bold; }
```

Save this in the `css` folder as `selectableViewer.css`. Most of the styles are arbitrary and are required purely for layout or visual appearance. We're using some of the framework classes in our mark up in order to add the rounded corners, so the amount of CSS we need to write is minimal. The last few selectors are required in order to override some of the tab widget's default styling.

When we run the example in a browser, we should see something similar to what is shown in the previous screenshot. When a single thumbnail is selected the full-size version of the image will be displayed. When multiple images have been selected, tabs are recreated at the top of the viewer, which allow all of the selected images to be shown:

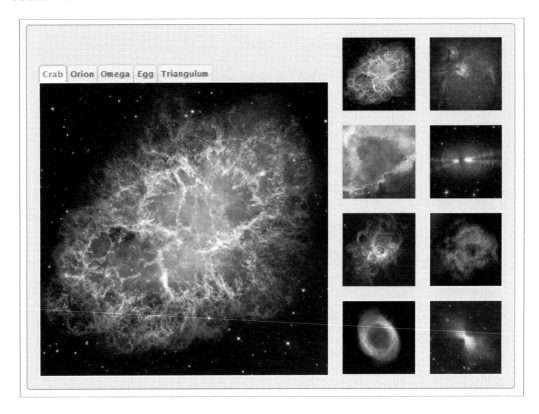

Getting started with the sortable widget

The final interaction helper that we're going to look at is the sortables component. This component allows us to define one or more list of elements (not necessarily actual `<ul>` or `<ol>` elements), where the individual items in the list(s) can be reordered by dragging. The sortables component is like a specialized implementation of drag-and-drop, with a very specific role. It has an extensive API, which caters for a wide range of behaviors.

A basic sortable list can be enabled with no additional configuration. Let's do this first, so that you can get an idea of the behavior enabled by this component. In a new file in your text editor, add the following code:

```
<!DOCTYPE HTML>
<html>
  <head>
    <meta charset="utf-8">
    <title>Sortable</title>
    <link rel="stylesheet" href="development-bundle/themes/redmond/
jquery.ui.all.css">
    <script src="js/jquery-2.0.3.js"></script>
    <script src="development-bundle/ui/jquery.ui.core.js"></script>
    <script src="development-bundle/ui/jquery.ui.widget.js"></script>
    <script src="development-bundle/ui/jquery.ui.mouse.js"></script>
    <script src="development-bundle/ui/jquery.ui.sortable.js">
</script>
    <script>
    $(document).ready(function($){
      $("#sortables").sortable();
    });
    </script>
  </head>
  <body>
    <ul id="sortables">
    <li>Sortable 1</li>
    <li>Sortable 2</li>
    <li>Sortable 3</li>
    <li>Sortable 4</li>
    <li>Sortable 5</li>
    </ul>
  </body>
</html>
```

Save this as `sortable1.html`. On the page, we have a simple unordered list with five list items. Thanks to the sortables component, we should find that the individual list items can be dragged to different positions in the list, as shown in the following screenshot:

Code-wise, the default implementation is the same as it has been for each of the other components. We simply call the sortable widget method on the parent `<ul>` element of the list items that we want to make sortable.

A lot of behaviors are added to the page to accommodate this functionality. As we drag one of the list items up or down in the list, the other items automatically move out of the way, creating a slot for the item that is currently being sorted to be dropped on.

Additionally, when a sortable item is dropped, it will slide quickly, but smoothly into its new position in the list. The library files that were needed for the basic implementation are as follows:

- `jquery-2.0.3.js`
- `jquery.ui.core.js`
- `jquery.ui.widget.js`
- `jquery.ui.mouse`
- `jquery.ui.sortable.js`

As I mentioned earlier, the sortables component is a flexible addition to the library that can be applied to many different types of elements. For example, instead of using a list, we could use a series of `<div>` elements as the sortable list items, in place of the `<ul>` element in the previous example:

```
<div id="sortables" class="ui-widget">
    <div class="ui-widget-header ui-corner-all">Sortable 1</div>
    <div class="ui-widget-header ui-corner-all">Sortable 2</div>
    <div class="ui-widget-header ui-corner-all">Sortable 3</div>
    <div class="ui-widget-header ui-corner-all">Sortable 4</div>
    <div class="ui-widget-header ui-corner-all">Sortable 5</div>
</div>
```

This can be saved as `sortable2.html`. As you can see, the behavior exhibited by this version is exactly the same as it was before. All that's changed is the underlying markup. We've added some of the CSS framework classes in order to add some basic styling to our elements, and we can also use a custom stylesheet to add a few extra styles.

Create a new file and add the following styles:

```
#sortables { width: 300px; }
#sortables div { padding: 2px 0 2px 4px; margin-bottom: 8px; }
```

Save this in the `css` folder as `sortable.css`. Link to the CSS file in the `<head>` of `sortable2.html`:

```
<link rel="stylesheet" href="css/sortable.css">
```

With our new stylesheet, the page should now appear as follows:

Styling the sortable widget

Now that we have styled our first set of sortable elements, it's a good point in journey at which to examine the style classes used by the sortable widget.

The sortable widget uses a number of styles. They are shown in the following table:

Class name	Used to...
ui-widget ui-sortable	Used on the container element; this first sets the generic classes from ui-widget, followed by those in ui-sortable.
ui-widget-header	Style each sortable element; this is by default with rounded corners, using the ui-corner-all style.
ui-sortable-helper –	Show a clone of the element being sorted, during the dragging process.
ui-sortable-placeholder –	Act as the placeholder element, ready to accept the element being sorted. This is hidden by default, but can be changed, as we will see later in the chapter.

Configuring sortable options

The sortables component has a huge range of configurable options, much more than any of the other interaction components (but not as many as some of the widgets).

The following table shows the range of options at our disposal:

Option	Default value	Used to...
appendTo	"parent"	Set the element that helpers are appended to, during a sort.
axis	false	Constrain sortables to one axis of movement. Possible values are the strings x or y.
cancel	":input, button"	Specify elements that cannot be sorted, if they are the elements being sorted.
connectWith	false	Enable one-way sorting from the current list to the specified list.
containment	false	Constrain sortables to their container while they are being sorted. Values can be the string's parent, window, or document, or can be a jQuery selector or element node.

Option	Default value	Used to...
cursor	"auto"	Define the CSS cursor to apply while dragging a sortable element.
cursorAt	false	Specify the coordinates that the mouse pointer should be at, while a sort is taking place. Accepts an object with the keys top, right, bottom, or left with integers as the values.
delay	0	Set the time delay in milliseconds before the sort begins, once a sortable item has been clicked (with the mouse button held down).
disabled	false	Disable the widget on page load.
distance	1	Set how far in pixels the mouse pointer should move, while the left button is held down before the sort begins.
dropOnEmpty	true	Allow linked items from linked sortables to be dropped onto empty slots.
forceHelperSize	false	Force the helper to have a size when set to true.
forcePlaceholderSize	false	Force the placeholder to have a size when set to true. The placeholder is the empty space that a sortable can be dropped on to.
grid	false	Set sortables to snap to a grid while being dragged. Accepts an array with two items—the x and y distances between gridlines.
handle	false	Specify an element to be used as the drag handle on sortable items. Can be a selector or an element node.
helper	original"	Specify a helper element that will be used as a proxy, while the element is being sorted. Can accept a function that returns an element.
items	">*"	Specify the items that should be made sortable. The default makes all children sortable.

Option	Default value	Used to...
opacity	false	Specify the CSS opacity of the element being sorted. Value should be an integer from 0.01 to 1, with 1 being fully opaque.
placeholder	false	Specify a CSS class to be added to empty slots.
revert	false	Enable animation when moving sortables into their new slots, once they have been dropped.
scroll	true	Enable page scrolling when a sortable is moved to the edge of the viewport.
scrollSensitivity	20	Set how close a sortable must get, in pixels, to the edge of the viewport, before scrolling should begin.
scrolSpeed	20	Set the distance in pixels that the viewport should scroll, when a sortable is dragged within the sensitivity range.
tolerance	"intersect"	Control how much of the element being sorted must overlap other elements, before the placeholder is moved. Another possible value is the string pointer.
zIndex	1000	Set the CSS zIndex of the sortable or helper, while it is being dragged.

Let's work some of these properties into our previous example to get a feel for the effect they have on the behavior of the component. First wrap the #sortables container in a new <div>:

```
<div id="container">
  <div id="sortables" class="ui-widget">
    <div class="ui-widget-header ui-corner-all">Sortable 1</div>
    <div class="ui-widget-header ui-corner-all">Sortable 2</div>
    <div class="ui-widget-header ui-corner-all">Sortable 3</div>
    <div class="ui-widget-header ui-corner-all">Sortable 4</div>
    <div class="ui-widget-header ui-corner-all">Sortable 5</div>
  </div>
</div>
```

Then change the final `<script>` element in `sortable2.html`, so that it appears as follows:

```
<script>
  $(document).ready(function($){
    $("#sortables").sortable({
      axis: "y",
      containment: "#container",
      cursor: "ns-resize",
      distance: 30
    });
  });
</script>
```

Save this as `sortable3.html`. We also need to add a little padding to our new container element. Update `sortable.css`, so that it contains the following new code:

```
#container { padding: 10px 0 20px; }
```

Resave this file as `sortableContainer.css` and update the `<link>` in the `<head>` of `sortable3.html`, so that it points to the new stylesheet.

We use four options in our configuration object: `axis`, `containment`, `resize`, and `distance`. Let's take a look at the role they perform:

- The `axis` option is set to `y`, to constrain the motion of the sortable currently being dragged to just up-and-down.

- The `containment` option specifies the element that the sortables should be contained within, to limit the bounds of their movement.

- The `cursor` option that automatically adds the CSS `ns-resize` cursor. In a similar fashion to the draggable component that we looked at in *Chapter 11, Drag and Drop*, the cursor is not actually displayed until the sort begins.

- The `distance` option is configured with a value of `30`, which specifies that the mouse pointer should move `30` pixels before the sort begins. It works in the same way with sortables as it did with draggables, and is great for preventing unwanted sorts, but in practice, we'd probably use a much lower threshold than 30 pixels.

Sortable spacing

Care should be taken when using the `containment` option. This is specifically why we added some padding to the container element in our stylesheet. Without this padding, the first sortable element is flushed against the top of the container and the last element is flushed against the bottom. In order to be able to push a sortable element out of the way, there must be some space above or below it.

Let's look at some more options. In this next example, we'll adapt the code from `sortable3.html` to restrict the handle of each item to a specific part of the item. We will also prevent jQuery UI from allow sorting until a certain time has passed.

Change the underlying `<div>` elements in `sortable3.html`, so that they appear as follows:

```
<div id="sortables" class="ui-widget">
  <div class="ui-widget-header ui-corner-all">Sortable 1
    <span class="ui-icon ui-icon-triangle-2-n-s"></span>
  </div>
  <div class="ui-widget-header ui-corner-all">Sortable 2
    <span class="ui-icon ui-icon-triangle-2-n-s"></span>
  </div>
  <div class="ui-widget-header ui-corner-all">Sortable 3
    <span class="ui-icon ui-icon-triangle-2-n-s"></span>
  </div>
  <div class="ui-widget-header ui-corner-all">Sortable 4
    <span class="ui-icon ui-icon-triangle-2-n-s"></span>
  </div>
  <div class="ui-widget-header ui-corner-all">Sortable 5
    <span class="ui-icon ui-icon-triangle-2-n-s"></span>
  </div>
</div>
```

We can get rid of the `#container` element for this example. We also need a modified stylesheet for this example. Change `sortable.css`, so that it includes the following new styles:

```
#sortables span { margin: 2px 2px 0 0; float: right; }
```

Save the new stylesheet as `sortableHandles.css` in the `css` folder and update the `<link>` element to point to the new stylesheet.

Finally, change the configuration object as follows:

```
$("#sortables").sortable({
  revert: "slow",
  handle: "span",
  delay: 1000,
  opacity: 0.5
});
```

Save this as `sortable4.html`. We've made a slight change to the page. Within each sortable element is a new `<span>` element that will be used as the sort handle. We give this element some CSS Framework classes in order to reduce the CSS we need to add manually.

The `revert` option has a default value of `true`, but can also take one of the speed integer or string values (`slow`, `normal`, or `fast`) that we've seen in other animation options in other components.

The `delay` option accepts a value in milliseconds that the component should wait, before allowing the sort to begin. If the mouse pointer is moved away from the handle while the left-button is held down, the sort will still occur after the specified time. If the mouse-button is released, however, the sort will be canceled.

The value of the `opacity` option is used to specify the CSS opacity of the element that is being sorted, while the sort takes place. The value should be a floating-point number between `0` and `1`, with `1` corresponding to full opacity and `0` specifying no opacity.

Another option we've used is the `handle` option, which allows us to define a region within the sortable that must be used to initiate the sort. Dragging on other parts of the sortable will not cause the sort to begin.

You can see how the handle will appear in the following screenshot:

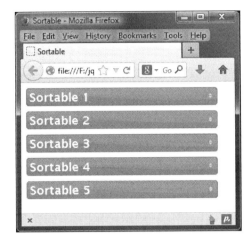

Make my handles bigger

For usability reasons, we should probably use a bigger handle than the one used in the previous example.

Placeholders

A placeholder defines the empty space or slot that is left, while one of the sortables is in the process of being moved to its new position. The placeholder isn't rigidly positioned. It will dynamically move to whichever sortable has been displaced by the movement of the sortable that is being sorted.

There are two options that are specifically concerned with placeholders the very aptly named `placeholder` option and the `forcePlaceholderSize` option. Let's take a look at these two options in action. Remove the `<span>` elements from the sortable `<div>` elements in `sortable4.html` and then change the configuration object, so that it appears as follows:

```
$("#sortables").sortable({
  placeholder: "empty ui-corner-all",
  forcePlaceholderSize: true
});
```

Save this as `sortable5.html`. Next, we should add the new selector and rules to a CSS file. Change `sortable.css`, so that it contains the following styles:

```
.empty {border: 1px solid #4297D7; background-color: #c5dbec;}
```

Save this as `sortablePlaceholder.css` in the `css` folder.

The `placeholder` option allows us to define a CSS class that should be added to the placeholder element. This is a useful property that we can use often in our implementations. Remember this is a class name, not a class selector, so no period is used at the start of the string. It can accept multiple classnames.

The `forcePlaceholderSize` option ensures that the placeholder is the same size as the actual sortables. If we left this option at its default value of `false`, in this example, the placeholder would just be a thin line made up of the padding that we applied to the sortable `<div>` elements.

When we run the new HTML file in a browser, we should be able to see the specified styles applied to the placeholder, while the sort is taking place:

Sortable helpers

We looked at helper/proxy elements back when we looked at the draggables component earlier in the book. Helpers can also be defined for sortables that function in a similar way to those of the draggable component, although there are some subtle differences in this implementation.

With sortables, the original sortable is hidden when the sort interaction begins, and a clone of the original element is dragged instead. So with sortables, helpers are an inherent feature.

Like with draggables, the `helper` option of sortables may take a function as its value. The function, when used, will automatically receive the `event` object and an object containing useful properties from the sortable element as arguments.

The function must return the element to use as a helper. Although it's very similar to the draggable helper example, let's take a quick look at it when used in conjunction with sortables. In `sortable5.html`, change the last `<script>` block, so that it appears as follows:

```
<script>
  $(document).ready(function($){
    var buildHelper = function(e, ui) {
      return $("<div />", {
        text: $(ui).text(),
        "class": "ui-corner-all",
        css: {
          opacity: 0.5,
          border: "4px dashed #cccccc",
          textAlign: "center"
        }
      });
    },
    $("#sortables").sortable({
      helper: buildHelper
    });
  });
</script>
```

Save this file as `sortable6.html`. We define a `helperMaker` function that creates and returns the element to be used as the helper, while the sort is in progress. We set some basic CSS properties on the new element, so that we don't need to provide additional rules in the stylesheet.

The following screenshot shows how the helper will appear while a sort is taking place:

Sortable items

By default, all children of the element that the method is called on are turned into sortables. While this is a useful feature of the component, there may be times when we don't necessarily want all child elements to become sortable.

The `items` option controls which child elements of the specified element should be made sortable. It makes all child elements sortable using the string `>*` as its default value, but we can alter this to specify only the elements we want. Change the sortable `<div>` elements in `sortable6.html`, so that the last element has a new class name:

```
<div class="ui-widget-header ui-corner-all unsortable">
  Sortable 5
</div>
```

Then, change the configuration object to make use of the `items` option:

```
$("#sortables").sortable({
  items: ">:not(.unsortable)"
});
```

Save this as `sortable7.html`. In the `<script>`, we've specified the selector `">:not(.unsortable)"` as the value of the `items` option, so the element with the classname `unsortable` will not be made sortable, while the rest of the `<div>` elements will.

When we run the page in a browser, we should find that the last item in the collection cannot be sorted, and other sortable items cannot be moved into the space that the last item occupies.

Connecting lists

So far, the examples that we have looked at have all centered on a single list of sortable items. What happens when we want to have two lists of sortable items, and more importantly, can we move items from one list to another?

Having two sortable lists is of course extremely easy and involves simply defining two containers and their child elements, and then passing a reference to each container to the `sortable()` method.

Allowing separate lists of sortables to exchange and share sortables is also extremely easy. This is thanks to the `connectWith` option, which allows us to define an array of sortable containers, who can share their sortable contents.

Let's look at this in action. Change the underlying markup on the page, so that it appears as follows:

```
<div id="sortablesA" class="ui-widget">
  <div class="ui-widget-header ui-corner-all">Sortable 1A</div>
  <div class="ui-widget-header ui-corner-all">Sortable 2A</div>
  <div class="ui-widget-header ui-corner-all">Sortable 3A</div>
  <div class="ui-widget-header ui-corner-all">Sortable 4A</div>
  <div class="ui-widget-header ui-corner-all">Sortable 5A</div>
</div>
<div id="sortablesB" class="ui-widget">
  <div class="ui-widget-header ui-corner-all">Sortable 1B</div>
  <div class="ui-widget-header ui-corner-all">Sortable 2B</div>
  <div class="ui-widget-header ui-corner-all">Sortable 3B</div>
  <div class="ui-widget-header ui-corner-all">Sortable 4B</div>
  <div class="ui-widget-header ui-corner-all">Sortable 5B</div>
</div>
```

Everything on the page is pretty similar to what we have worked with before. We also need a new stylesheet for this example. In a new file, add the following styles:

```
#sortablesA, #sortablesB { width: 300px; margin-right: 50px; float:
left; }
.ui-widget div { padding: 2px 0 2px 4px; margin-bottom: 8px; }
```

Save this as `sortableConnected.css` in the `css` folder. Don't forget to point to the new stylesheet in the `<head>` of the new page. Finally, change the last `<script>` element, so that it appears as follows:

```
<script>
  $(document).ready(function($){
    $("#sortablesA, #sortablesB").sortable({
      connectWith: ["#sortablesA", "#sortablesB"]
    });
  });
</script>
```

Save this as `sortable8.html`. We still define a single configuration object, which can be shared between both sets of sortable elements. The `connectWith` option is able to accept multiple selectors if they are passed in as an array, and it's this option that allows us to share individual sortables between the two sortable containers.

This configuration option only provides a one-way transmission of sortables, so if we were to only use the configuration object with `sortablesA` and specify just the selector `#sortablesB`, we would only be able to move items from `sortablesA` to `sortablesB`, not the other way.

Specifying both sortables' `id` attributes in the option and selecting both of the containers when calling the `sortable()` method allows us to move items between both elements, and allows us to cut down on coding.

When we run the page in a browser, we find that not only can the individual items be sorted in their respective elements, but that items can also be moved between elements, as shown in the following screenshot:

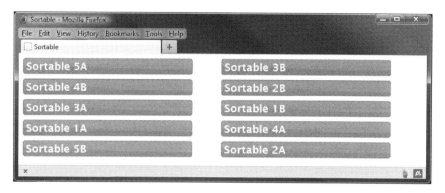

Reacting to sortable events

In addition to the already large list of configurable options defined in the sortables class, there are also a whole lot more in the form of event callbacks, which can be passed as functions to execute at different points during a sortable interaction. These are listed in the following table:

Event	Fired when...
activate	Sorting starts on a connected list.
beforeStop	The sort has stopped, but the original slot is still available.
change	The DOM position of a sortable has changed and the sort is still in progress.
create	The widget is initialized.
deactivate	Sorting stops on a connected list.
out	A sortable is moved out of a connected list.
over	A sortable is over a connected list. This is great for providing visual feedback while a sort is taking place.
receive	A sortable is received from a connected list.
remove	A sortable is moved from a connected list.

Event	Fired when...
sort	A sort is taking place.
start	A sort starts.
stop	A sort ends.
update	The sort has ended and the DOM position has changed.

Each of the components that we've looked at in the preceding chapters has defined its own suite of custom events, and the sortables component is no exception.

Many of these events will fire during any single sort interaction. The following list shows the order in which they will fire:

- start
- sort
- change
- beforeStop
- stop
- update

As soon as one of the sortables is picked up, the start event is triggered. Following this, on every single mouse move, the sort event will fire, making this event very intensive.

As soon as another item is displaced by the current sortable, the change event is fired. Once the sortable is dropped, the beforeStop and stop events fire, and if the sortable is now at a different position, the update event is fired last of all.

For the next few examples, we'll work some of these event handling options into the previous example, starting with the start and stop events. Change the configuration object in sortable8.html, so that it appears as follows:

```
var sortOpts = {
  connectWith: ["#sortablesA", "#sortablesB"],
  start: function(e, ui) {
    $("<p />", {
      id: "message",
      text: ui.helper.text() + " is active",
      css: { clear:"both" }
    }).appendTo("body");
  },
  stop: function() {
    $("#message").remove();
  }
};
```

Save this as `sortable9.html`. Our event usage in this example is minimal. When the sort starts, we simply create a new paragraph element and add some text to it, including the text content of the element that is being sorted. The text message is then duly appended to the `<body>` of the page. When the sort stops, we remove the text. Using the second object passed to the callback function is very easy, as you can see. The object itself refers to the parent sortables container, and the `helper` property refers to the actual item being sorted (or its helper). As this is a jQuery object, we can call jQuery methods, such as `text`, on it.

When we run the page, the message should appear briefly until the sort ends, at which point it's removed.

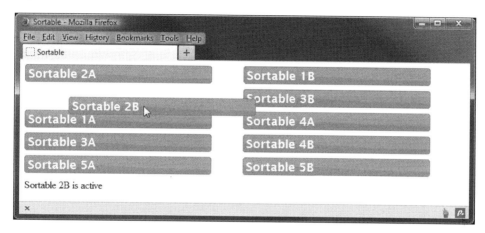

Let's look at one more of these simple callbacks, before we move on to look at the additional callbacks used with connected sortables. In our next example, we will take a look at how we can track movement of sortable items between lists, and use a callback function to display the results on screen.

Change the final `<script>` element in `sortable9.html` to the following:

```
<script>
    $(document).ready(function($){
        var getPlaces = function(e, ui) {
            var extraMessage = (e.type === "sortreceive") ? " in a new
list" : "";
            $("#message").remove();
            $("<p />", {
              id: "message",
              text: [
                "Item now at position ",
                (ui.item.index() + 1).toString(),
                extraMessage
```

```
      ].join(" "),
      css: {
        clear: "both"
      }
    }).appendTo("body");
  };
  $("#sortablesA, #sortablesB").sortable({
    connectWith: ["#sortablesA", "#sortablesB"],
    beforeStop: getPlaces,
    receive: getPlaces
  });
});
</script>
```

Save this as `sortable10.html`. In this example, we work with the `receive` and `beforeStop` callbacks to provide a message, indicating the position within the list that any sortable is moved to, as well as which list it is in. We also make use of the `ui.item` property from the object, which is automatically passed to any callback functions used by the events.

We first define a variable called `extraMessage`, which is initially set to an empty string. We then define a function called `getPlaces`. This function will be used as a callback function for sortable events and will, therefore, automatically receive `e` and `ui` objects.

Within the function, we first check whether the event object's type property has a value of `sortreceive`; if it does, we know that a sortable has moved lists and can, therefore, set the extra part of the message.

We then remove any pre-existing messages, before creating a new `<p>` element and setting a message, indicating its new position in the list. We can obtain the new position of the element that was sorted using the `item` property of the second object passed to our callback in conjunction with jQuery's `index()` method, which we convert to a string and concatenate into a message.

In our configuration object, we connect the two lists using the `connectWith` option as before, and make use of both the `receive` and `beforeStop` options, which both point to our `getPlaces` function.

The `receive` event is fired whenever a sortable container receives a new sortable element from a connected list. The `beforeStop` event is fired just before the sort interaction ends. In terms of event order, in this example the `beforeStop` event is fired first, followed by the `receive` event.

The `receive` event will only be fired if a sortable element moves to a new sortable container. The following screenshot shows how the page should look following a sort interaction:

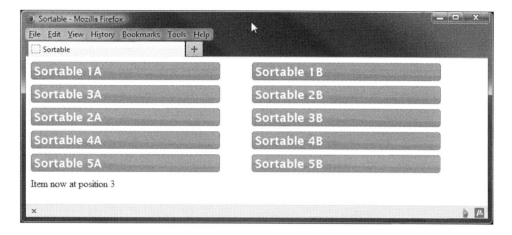

Connecting callbacks

Six of the available callbacks can be used in conjunction with connected sortables. These events fire at different times during an interaction, alongside the events that we have already looked at.

Like the standard unconnected events, not all of the connected events will fire in any single interaction. Some events, such as `over`, `off`, `remove`, and `receive` will fire only if a sort item moves to a new list.

Other events, such as `activate` and `deactivate`, will fire in all executions, whether any sort items change lists or not. Additionally, some connected events, such as `activate` and `deactivate`, will fire for each connected list on the page. Provided at least one item is moved between lists, events will fire in the following order:

1. start
2. activate
3. sort
4. change
5. beforeStop
6. stop
7. remove

8. update

9. receive

10. deactivate

Let's now see some of these connected events in action. Change the final <script> element in sortable10.html, so that it appears as follows:

```
<script>
  $(document).ready(function($){
    var activateSortable = function() {
      $("<p />", {
        text: $(this).attr("id") + " has been activated",
        css: { clear:"both" }
      }).appendTo("body");
    }

    var deactivateSortable = function() {
      $("<p />", {
        text: $(this).attr("id") + " has been deactivated",
        css: { clear:"both" }
      }).appendTo("body");
    }

    var receiveSortable = function(e, ui) {
      var senderAttr = ui.sender.attr("id");
      var receiverAttr = $(this).attr("id");
      $("<p />", {
        text: [ ui.item.text(), "was moved from", senderAttr, "into",
receiverAttr ].join(" "),
        css: { clear:"both" }
      }).appendTo("body");
    }

    $("#sortablesA, #sortablesB").sortable({
      connectWith: ["#sortablesA", "#sortablesB"],
      activate: activateSortable,
      deactivate: deactivateSortable,
      receive: receiveSortable
    });
  });
</script>
```

Save this as `sortable11.html`. The `activate` and `deactivate` events are fired for each connected list at the start of any sort interaction. Within our callback functions, `$(this)` refers to each sortable container. We can easily determine which sortable list the item originated in using the `sender` property of the second object, passed to our function.

When we run the page in a browser, we see that as soon as a sort begins, both of the sortables are activated, and when the sort ends, both of them are deactivated. If an item is moved between lists, the message generated by the `receive` callback is shown in the following screenshot:

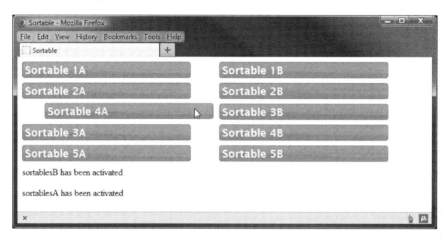

Listing the sortable methods

The sortables component exposes the usual set of methods for making the component perform actions. Like the selectables component that we looked at before, it also defines a couple of unique methods not seen in any of the other components. The following table lists sortables' unique methods:

Method	Used to...
cancel	Cancel the sort and cause elements to return to their original positions.
refresh	Reload the set of sortables.
refreshPositions	Trigger a cache refresh of the set of sortables.
serialize	Construct a query string that can be used to send a new sort order to the server, for further processing or storage.
toArray	Serialize the sortables into an array of strings.

Serializing

The `serialize` and `toArray` methods are great for storing the new order of the sortables. Let's see this in action. We will create a series of sortable elements, and then set Sortable to display their order. This will be updated on screen each time you move one of the elements around.

Change the underlying markup on the `<body>` of the page in `sortable11.html` to as follows:

```
<div id="sortablesA" class="ui-widget">
  <div id="sortablesA_1" class="ui-widget-header ui-corner-
all">Sortable 1A</div>
  <div id="sortablesA_2" class="ui-widget-header ui-corner-
all">Sortable 2A</div>
  <div id="sortablesA_3" class="ui-widget-header ui-corner-
all">Sortable 3A</div>
  <div id="sortablesA_4" class="ui-widget-header ui-corner-
all">Sortable 4A</div>
  <div id="sortablesA_5" class="ui-widget-header ui-corner-
all">Sortable 5A</div>
</div>
```

Then change the final `<script>` element, so that it appears as follows:

```
<script>
  $(document).ready(function($){
    $("#sortablesA").sortable({
      stop: function(e, ui) {
        var order = $("#sortablesA").sortable("serialize");
        $("#message").remove();
        $("<p />", {
          id: "message",
          text: order,
          css: { clear:"both" }
        }).appendTo("body");
      }
    });
  });
</script>
```

Save this as `sortable12.html`. We've dropped the second set of sortables for this example and have added `id` attributes to each of the sortable items in the format of the name of the parent sortable and a number, separated by an underscore.

We use the `stop` event to execute an anonymous function, after each sort interaction.

Within this function, we store the result of the `serialize` method in the `order` variable, and then display this variable in a new `<p>` element on the page:

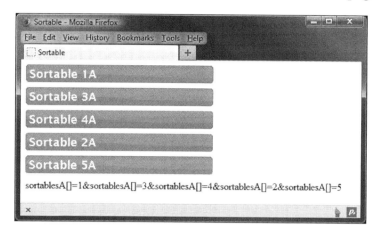

As you can see, the format of the serialized string is quite straightforward. The sortable items appear in the order that the items appear on the page, and are separated by an ampersand. Each serialized item is made up of two parts: a hash of the `id` attribute of each sortable item followed by an integer representing the item's new order.

In the previous example, all we do is display the serialized string on the page, but the string is in the perfect format for use with jQuery's `ajax` method to pass to a server for further processing.

The `serialize` method is also able to accept a configuration object to tailor how the serialization occurs. The options we can configure are listed in the following table:

Option	Default value	Used to...
`attribute`	`id`	Specify the attribute to use when parsing each item in the list of sortables and generating the hash.
`connected`	`false`	Include all connected lists in the serialization.
`expression`	`"(.+)[-=_] (.+)"`	Specify the `regexp` to use to parse the sortable list.
`key`	`The first part of the id attribute of each sortable item`	Specify the string to be used as the first part of each item in the serialized output.

The `toArray` method works in a similar way to serialize, except that with `toArray`, the output is not a string, but an array of strings.

Exploring widget compatibility

In the previous chapter, we saw that both the resizable and the selectable components worked well with the tabs widget (and we already know how well the dialog and resizables components go together). The sortable component is also highly compatible with other widgets. Let's look at a basic example. In a new file in your text editor, add the following code:

```
<!DOCTYPE HTML>
<html>
  <head>
    <meta charset="utf-8">
    <title>Sortable Tabs</title>
    <link rel="stylesheet" href="development-bundle/themes/redmond/
jquery.ui.all.css">
    <script src="js/jquery-2.0.3.js"></script>
    <script src="development-bundle/ui/jquery.ui.core.js"></script>
    <script src="development-bundle/ui/jquery.ui.widget.js"></script>
    <script src="development-bundle/ui/jquery.ui.mouse.js"></script>
    <script src="development-bundle/ui/jquery.ui.sortable.js">
</script>
    <script src="development-bundle/ui/jquery.ui.tabs.js"> </script>
    <script>
      $(document).ready(function($){
        $("#tabs").tabs().sortable({
          axis: "x",
          items: "li"
        });
      });
    </script>
  </head>
  <body>
    <div id="tabs">
      <ul>
        <li><a href="#0"><span>Sort Tab 1</span></a></li>
        <li><a href="#1"><span>Sort Tab 2</span></a></li>
        <li><a href="#2"><span>Sort Tab 3</span></a></li>
      </ul>
      <div id="0">The first tab panel</div>
      <div id="1">The second tab panel</div>
```

```
        <div id="2">The third tab panel</div>
    </div>
  </body>
</html>
```

Save this page as `sortable13.html`. There is nothing in the code that we haven't seen before, so we won't go into any great detail about it. Note that only the `tabs()` and `sortable()` methods are called on the same element—the outer containing the `<div>` element.

When we run the page in a browser, we should find that the components work in exactly the way that we want them to. The tabs can be sorted horizontally to any order, but as the tabs are linked to their panel by `href`, they will still show the correct panel, when selected.

Sorting the tabs works on the `mousedown` event and selecting the tabs works on the `mouseup` event, so there are no event collisions and no situations arising where you want to select a tab, but end up sorting it. The following screenshot shows how the tabs may appear after sorting:

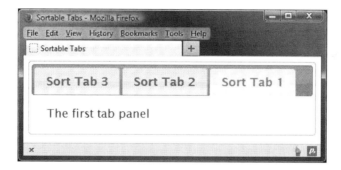

Adding draggables

When we looked at draggables and droppables, earlier in the book, we saw that there was a configuration option for draggables called `connectToSortable`. Let's take a look at that option now that we've been introduced to the fundamentals of the sortables component. In this example, we'll create a sortable task list that can have new tasks dragged into it.

The resulting page will appear as follows:

In a new file in your text editor, add the following code:

```
<!DOCTYPE HTML>
<html>
  <head>
    <meta charset="utf-8">
    <title>Sortable</title>
    <link rel="stylesheet" href="development-bundle/themes/redmond/
jquery.ui.all.css">
    <link rel="stylesheet" href="css/sortableTasks.css">
    <script src="js/jquery-2.0.3.js"></script>
    <script src="development-bundle/ui/jquery.ui.core.js"></script>
    <script src="development-bundle/ui/jquery.ui.widget.js"></script>
    <script src="development-bundle/ui/jquery.ui.mouse.js"></script>
    <script src="development-bundle/ui/jquery.ui.sortable.js">
</script>
```

```
        <script src="development-bundle/ui/jquery.ui.draggable.js">
</script>
    </head>
    <body>
      <ul id="drag">
        <li>Click here to add a new task...</li>
      </ul>
      <a id="add" href="#"></a>
      <div id="taskList">
        <ul id="tasks">
          <li>Design new site</li>
          <li>Call client</li>
          <li>Order pizza</li>
        </ul>
      </div>
    </body>
</html>
```

Save this as `sortable14.html`. On the page, we have a couple of `<ul>` elements: the first contains a single item that provides an instruction to the visitor and the second is the task list. The second list is wrapped in a container `<div>`, mostly for styling purposes.

We also use a new stylesheet for this example. Add the following code to a new page in your text editor:

```
#drag { padding: 0 0 0 11px; margin: 0; float: left; }
#drag li { font-style: italic; color: #999; }
#drag li input { width: 175px; }
#taskList { width: 250px; height: 400px; clear: both; background:
url(../img/paper.jpg) no-repeat; }
#tasks { width: 170px; padding: 89px 0 0; margin: 0; float: right; }
#tasks li, #drag li { height: 28px; padding-top: 5px; list-style-type:
none; }
#add { display: none; width: 24px; height: 24px;  position: absolute;
left: 218px; top: 13px; background: url(../img/add.png) no-repeat; }
#add.down { background: url(../img/down.png) no-repeat; }
```

Save this as `sortableTasks.css` in the `css` folder. Mostly this is just decorative, superficial stuff for the purposes of the example.

Finally, we can add the script that wires it all up. Add the following `<script>` element, after the library resources:

```
<script>
    $(document).ready(function($){
```

We first cache a couple of selectors that we'll be using frequently throughout the script:

```
var dragItem = $("#drag li"), addButton = $("#add"), taskItems =
$("#tasks");
```

We then define and initialize the configuration object for the sortables. Sorting is restricted to the vertical axis and a callback function specified for the stop event.

Within this function, we hide the add button and reset any text that has been added to the draggable, then use the option method of the draggable to disable dragging on the element, so that the text label cannot be dragged into the task list.

Additionally, when we set the disabled option of the draggable, it adds a CSS framework class that reduces the opacity of the draggable. This is not necessary for our example, so we also remove this class name:

```
taskItems.sortable({
  axis: "y",
  stop: function() {
    addButton.css("display", "none");
    dragItem.text("Click here to add new task...");
    dragItem.draggable("option", "disabled", true);
    dragItem.removeClass("ui-state-disabled");
  }
});
```

Following this, we define and initialize the draggable configuration object and set the connectToSortable option to an id selector that matches the parent sortables container, and the helper option to clone. The dragging is initially disabled:

```
dragItem.draggable({
  connectToSortable: "#tasks",
  helper: "clone",
  disabled: true
});
```

We need to create two helper functions: the first to count the number of items in the list, and the second to work out if the <input> field has any content:

```
function countItems(x) {
  return x === taskItems.children().length;
}

function addNewItem(y) {
  return y === $("#drag input").val();
}
```

We add a click handler to the draggable element using jQuery's on() method. When the draggable <li> is clicked, it checks that there aren't too many tasks in the list already, and if not, it will create a new <input> field and append it to the <li> in the first <ul>. The hidden add button is also displayed. The visitor can then enter a new task and make the new task draggable, by clicking on the button:

```
dragItem.on("click", function() {
  if (countItems(7)) {
    $("#drag").tooltip({
      content: "too many tasks already!",
      items: "ul"
    });
  } else {
    var input = $("<input />", { id: "newTask" });
    $(this).text("").append(input);
    input.focus();
    addButton.removeClass("down").css("display", "block");
  }
});
```

We also add a click handler for the add button that we create, again using jQuery's on() method. This function checks that the <input> contains some text, and provided it does, it then gets the text and then removes the text field. The text is then added to the draggable <li> element, and the <li> is made draggable by setting the disabled option to false. Finally, the <input> is removed, and the message and button are set back to their original state.

```
addButton.on("click", function(e) {
  e.preventDefault();
  if (!addNewItem("")) {
    dragItem.text($("#newTask").val())
      .draggable("option", "disabled", false);
    $("#drag input").remove();
    addButton.addClass("down").
      attr("title", "drag new task into the list");
  }
});
});
</script>
```

The text box and icon will appear as shown in the following screenshot:

We also add a click handler for the add button that we create, again using jQuery's on() method. This function checks that the <input> contains some text, and provided it does, it then gets the text and then removes the text field. The text is then added to the draggable <li> element, and the <li> is made draggable by setting the disabled option to false. Finally, the <input> is removed, and the message and button are set back to their original state.

Summary

We've finished our tour of the interaction components of the library, by looking at the selectable and sortable components. Similar to the other modules that we looked at before, both have a wide range of properties and methods that allow us to configure and control their behavior and appearance in both simple and more complex implementations.

We started off the chapter with a look at a simple, default implementation of the selectable with no configuration to see the most basic level of functionality added by the component.

We first looked at the default implementation of a selectable and then moved on to look at the configurable options, along the numerous callback properties, which can be used to perform different actions at different points in an interaction.

Next we looked at how the performance of a page can be improved when there are a large number of selectables on the page, and how the single unique method exposed by the component, refresh, is used.

Lastly we looked at a fun example that brought together what we had learned throughout the chapter and combined the selectables component with the tabs component to create an image viewer capable of handling single or multiple selections.

We then moved on to look at some of the different elements that can be made sortable and added some basic styling to the page.

Following this, we looked at the range of configurable options that are exposed by the sortable API. The list is extensive and provides a wide range of functionality that can be enabled or disabled with ease.

We moved on to look at the extensive event model used by this component that gives us the ability to react to different events, as they occur in any sort operation, initiated by the visitor.

Connected lists offer the ability to be able to exchange sortable items between lists or collections of sortables. We saw the additional options and events that are used specifically with connected sortable lists.

In the last part of the chapter, we looked at the methods available for use with the sortables component, and focused on the highly useful `serialize` method, and also had a quick look at its compatibility with other members of the jQuery UI library in the form of the sortable tabs example. We've now looked at all of the current interaction components found in the library. In the next and final chapter, we'll look at all of the different animation effects that jQuery UI brings to the table.

14
UI Effects

We've so far looked at a range of incredibly useful widgets and interaction helpers. All are easy to use, but at the same time are powerful and highly configurable. Some have had their subtle nuances, which have required consideration and thought during their implementation.

The effects provided by the library, on the other hand, are for the most part extremely compact, with very few options to learn and no methods at all. We can use these effects quickly and easily, with minimum configuration.

The effects that we'll be looking at in this chapter are as follows:

- Highlight
- Bounce
- Shake
- Transfer
- Scale
- Explode
- Puff
- Pulsate
- Slide
- Blind
- Clip
- Fold

Using the core effects file

Like the individual components themselves, the effects require the services of a separate core file. It provides essential functionality to the effects, such as creating wrapper elements and controlling the animations. Most, but not all, of the effects have their own source files, which build on the core foundation to add functionality specific to the effect.

All we need to do to use an effect is include the core file (`jquery.ui.effect.js`) in the page, before the effect's source file. However, unlike the `jquery.ui.core.js` file, the `jquery.ui.effect.js` file has been designed to be used, in part, completely standalone.

Using color animations

If we use the core effect file on its own, we can take advantage of the color animations. This includes changing the background color of an element to another color (and not just a snap change, but a smooth morphing of one color into another), class transitions, and advanced easing animations.

 jQuery UI 1.10 uses Version 2.0.0 of the jQuery Color library as the basis for much of the color support in the library. If you would like to learn more about jQuery Color, then visit the project page at `https://github.com/jquery/jquery-color`.

The core effects plugin within jQuery UI adds the ability to animate color properties using `rgb()`, `rgba()`, hex values, or even color names such as aqua to jQuery Core. All we need to do is include the jQuery UI effects core file and jQuery's `.animate()` will gain support for colors.

Let's take a look at how to create color animations. First, create the following new page:

```
<!DOCTYPE HTML>
<html>
  <head>
    <meta charset="utf-8">
    <title>Color Animations</title>
    <link rel="stylesheet" href="css/effectColor.css">
    <script src="js/jquery-2.0.3.js"></script>
    <script src="development-bundle/ui/jquery.ui.effect.js"></script>
  </head>
  <script>
  <body>
```

```
<form action="#">
  <div>
    <label for="name">Name: </label>
    <input id="name" type="text">
  </div>
  <div>
    <label for="age">Age: </label>
    <input id="age" type="text">
  </div>
  <div>
    <label for="email">Email: </label>
    <input id="email" type="text">
  </div>
  <button type="submit">Submit</button>
</form>
</body>
</html>
```

Save the page as `effectColor.html`. In the last `<script>` block, add the following code, which will provide the visual feedback for each field:

```
$(document).ready(function($){
  function Validate(fieldname, response)    {
    var bgColor, brdrColor;

    switch(response) {
      case "invalid" :
        bgColor = "#ff9999";
        brdrColor = "#ff0000";
        break;
      case "valid" :
        bgColor = "#ccffcc";
        brdrColor = "#00ff00";
        break;
    }

    fieldname.animate({
      backgroundColor: bgColor,
      borderTopColor: brdrColor,
      borderRightColor: brdrColor,
      borderBottomColor: brdrColor,
      borderLeftColor: brdrColor
    });
  }

  $("form").submit(function() {
    ($("#name").val().length == 0) ? Validate($("#name"),
"invalid") : Validate($("#name"), "valid");
```

```
          ($("#age").val().length == 0) ? Validate($("#age"), "invalid")
    : Validate($("#age"), "valid");
          ($("#email").val().length == 0) ? Validate($("#email"),
    "invalid") : Validate($("#email"), "valid");
        });
      });
```

As you can see, all we need is jQuery and the `jquery.ui.effect.js` file to create attractive color transitions. On the page, we have a simple `<form>` element enclosing three container elements and three sets of the `<label>` and `<input>` elements. The `animate` method is a part of jQuery rather than jQuery UI specifically, but the `jquery.ui.effect.js` file extends jQuery's `animate` method by allowing it to specifically work with colors and classes.

When the **Submit** button is clicked, we simply use the `animate` method to apply a series of new CSS properties to the target elements based on whether the text inputs have been filled out or not. If they have been completed, we color them green, and if not, we color them red. We also use a basic stylesheet in this example. In another new page in your text editor, add the following basic selectors and rules:

```
div { margin-bottom: 5px; }
label { display: block; width: 100px; float: left; }
input { border: 1px solid #000000; }
```

Save this as `effectColor.css` in the `css` folder. When we view this page in our browser, we should see that any fields that are left blank smoothly turn red when the **Submit** button is clicked, while fields that are not empty smoothly turn green. However, it's most attractive when a field changes from red to green.

The following screenshot shows the page once the **Submit** button has been clicked:

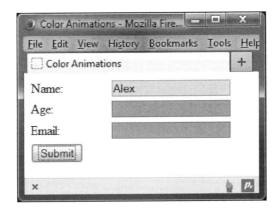

A key point to note is that we've used `backgroundColor` as the attribute in our code; the reason for this is that jQuery is not able to animate the `background-color` CSS style by default, unless we use the jQuery Color plugin. Let's take a look at these attributes in more detail.

The style attributes that color animations can be used on are as follows:

- `backgroundColor`
- `borderTopColor`
- `borderRightColor`
- `borderBottomColor`
- `borderLeftColor`
- `color`
- `outlineColor`

Colors may be specified using either RGB, hexadecimal (in the format `#xxx[xxx]`), or even standard color names. It is recommended that RGB or hexadecimal colors be used where possible, as browsers do not always recognize color names consistently.

The default build of the Color plugin only includes support for basic color names. If you need to use other color names, you can download a version that includes support for this from `https://github.com/jquery/jquery-color#readme`.

Using class transitions

In addition to animating individual color attributes, `jquery.ui.effect.js` also gives us the powerful ability to animate between entire classes. This allows us to switch styles smoothly and seamlessly without sudden jarring changes. Let's look at this aspect of the file's use in the following example.

Change the `<link>` tag in the `<head>` element of `effectColor.html` to point to a new stylesheet:

```
<link rel="stylesheet" href="css/effectClass.css">
```

Then change the final `<script>` element so that it appears as follows:

```
<script>
  $(document).ready(function($){
    var obj;

    function showValid(obj) {
       (obj.val().length == 0) ? null : obj.switchClass("error",
"pass", 2000);
    }

    function showInvalid(obj) {
       (obj.val().length != 0) ? null : obj.switchClass("pass",
"error", 2000);
    }

    function showEither(obj) {
       (obj.val().length == 0) ? obj.addClass("error", 2000) : obj.
addClass("pass", 2000);
    }

    $("form").submit(function(e) {
      $("input").each(function() {
        var cssStyle = $(this).attr('class');
        if (cssStyle == "error") { showValid($(this)); };
        if (cssStyle == "pass") { showInvalid($(this)); }
        if (cssStyle == null) { showEither($(this)); }
      })
    });
  });
</script>
```

Save this as `effectClass.html`. The `jquery.ui.effect.js` file extends the jQuery class API by allowing us to specify a duration over which the new classname should be applied, instead of just switching it instantly. We can also specify an easing effect.

The `switchClass` method of the `jquery.ui.effect.js` file is used when the fields already have one of the classnames and need to change to a different classname. The `switchClass` method requires several arguments; we specify the classname to be removed, followed by the classname to be added. We also specify duration as the third argument.

Essentially, the page functions as it did before; although, using this type of class transition allows us to use non-color-based style rules as well, so we can adjust widths, heights, or many other style properties if we want to. Note that background images cannot be transitioned in this way.

As in the previous example, we have a stylesheet attached. This is essentially the same as in the previous example, except with some styles for our two new classes.

Add the following selectors and rules to the bottom of `effectColor.css`:

```
.error { border: 1px solid #ff0000; background-color: #ff9999; }
.pass { border: 1px solid #00ff00; background-color: #ccffcc; }
```

Save the updated file as `effectClass.css` in the `css` folder.

Advanced easing

The `animate` method found in standard jQuery has some basic easing capabilities built in, but for more advanced easing, you have to include an additional easing plugin (ported to jQuery by GSGD).

 See the easing plugin's project page for further information at `http://gsgd.co.uk/sandbox/jquery/easing/`.

The `jquery.ui.effect.js` file has all of these advanced easing options built in, so there is no need to include additional plugins. We won't be looking at them in any real detail in this section; however, we will be using them in some of the examples later on in the chapter, in the section, *Scaling elements on a page*.

Highlighting specified elements

The highlight effect temporarily applies a light-yellow coloring to any element that it's called on (the effect is also known as **Yellow Fade Technique (YFT)**). Let's put a simple example together, so we can see the effect in action:

```
<link rel="stylesheet" href="css/effectHighlight.css">
```

The `<script>` element refers to the effect's source file so that it uses the `jquery.effects.highlight.js` file:

```
<script src="development-bundle/ui/jquery.ui.effect-highlight.js">
</script>
```

Then remove the `<form>` element from the `<body>` element of the page and replace it with the following markup:

```
<h1>Choose the correct download below:</h1>
<a id="win" href="#"><img src="img/iconWin.png"></a>
<a id="mac" href="#"><img src="img/iconMac.png"></a>
<a id="linux" href="#"><img src="img/iconLinux.png"></a>
<button id="hint">Hint</button>
```

Lastly, change the final `<script>` element so that ends up as follows:

```
<script>
  $(document).ready(function($){
    var ua = navigator.userAgent.split(" ");
    $("#hint").click(function() {
      var el = ua[1].toLowerCase().substring(1);
      $("#" + el).effect("highlight");
    });
  });
</script>
```

Save this page as `effectHighlight.html`. The code that invokes the highlight effect takes the same familiar form as other library components. The `effect` method is called and the actual effect is specified as a string argument to the method.

We simply sniff the `userAgent` string and see if a search for Windows, Mac, or Linux returns a positive integer. If a positive integer is found, the `userAgent` string contains the search word; if `-1` is returned, the search term was not found.

We also need to create the new stylesheet, not for the effect to work, but just tidy things up a little. In a new page in your text editor, add the following selectors and rules:

```
a { padding: 10px; float: left; }
a img { display: block; border: none; }
button { display: block; position: relative; top: 10px; clear: both; }
```

Save this file as `effectHighlight.css` in the `css` folder.

View the example and click the **Hint** button. The icon for whichever operating system you are using should be highlighted briefly:

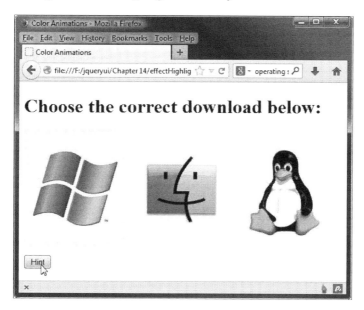

While our example may seem a little contrived, it is easy to see the potential for this effect as an assistance tool on the frontend. Whenever there is a sequence of actions that needs to be completed in a specific order, the highlight effect can instantly give the visitor a visual cue as to the step that needs to be completed next.

Adding additional effect arguments

Each of the `effect` methods, as well as the argument that dictates which effect is actually applied, can take up three additional arguments that control how the effect works. All of these arguments are optional, and consist of the following (in the listed order):

- An object containing additional configuration options
- An integer representing in milliseconds, the duration of the effect, or a string specifying one of `slow`, `normal`, or `fast`
- A callback function that is executed when the effect ends

The `highlight` effect has only one configurable option that can be used in the object passed as the second argument, and that is the highlight color.

Let's add some of these additional arguments into our highlight example to clarify their usage. Change the call to the `effect` method in the final `<script>` element in `effectHighlight.html` so that it appears as follows:

```
$(el).effect("highlight", {}, function() {
  $("<p />", {
    text: "That was the highlight"
  }).appendTo("body").delay(2000).fadeOut();
});
```

Save this as `effectHighlightCallback.html`. Perhaps the most striking feature of our new code is the empty object passed as the second argument. In this example, we don't use any additional configurable options, but we still need to pass in the empty object in order to access the third and fourth arguments.

The callback function, passed as the third argument, is perhaps the least useful callback in the history of JavaScript, but it does serve to illustrate how easy it is to arrange additional post-animation code execution following an effect.

Bouncing

Another simple effect we can use with little configuration is the bounce effect. To see this effect in action change the contents of the `<body>` element in `effectHighlight.html` to the following:

```
<div id="ball">
  <img src="img/ball.png">
</div>
```

We also need to use the source file for the bounce effect; change the reference to the `jquery.ui.effect-highlight.js` file, so that it points to the `bounce.js` source file:

```
<script src="development-bundle/ui/jquery.ui.effect-bounce.js">
</script>
```

Save this as `effectBounce.html`. We need to add a tiny bit of styling to really see the effect in full, but it's probably not worth creating a whole new stylesheet so simply replace the `<link>` element in the `<head>` element of the page with the following:

```
<style>
  #ball { position: relative; top: 150px; }
</style>
```

Finally, change the final `<script>` element so that it appears as follows:

```
<script>
  $(document).ready(function($){
    $("#ball").click(function() {
      $(this).effect("bounce", { distance: 140 });
    });
  });
</script>
```

Using the bounce effect in this example shows how easy it is to add this simple but attractive effect. We configure the `distance` option to set how far the element travels. Other options that can be configured are listed in the following table:

Option	Default value	Use
direction	"up"	Sets the direction of the bounce
distance	20	Sets the distance in pixels of the first bounce
times	5	Sets the number of times the element should bounce

When you run the example you will notice that the bounce effect has an ease-out easing feature built into it so the distance of the bounce will automatically decrease as the animation proceeds.

> The default easing effect used here is `swing`; this is one of many easings features that are available for use within the library. Easing functions control the speed at which an animation proceeds at different points within the animation; you can see the full list of easings features available at `http://api.jqueryui.com/easings/`.

One thing to note is that with most of the different effects, including the bounce effect (but not the highlight effect we looked at earlier), the effect is not actually applied to the specified element. Instead a wrapper element is created and the element targeted by the effect is appended to the inside of the wrapper. The actual effect is then applied to the wrapper.

This is an important detail to be aware of, because if you need to manipulate the element that has the effect applied to it in mid-animation, then the wrapper will need to be targeted instead of the original element. Once the effect's animation has completed, the wrapper is removed from the page.

Shaking an element

The shake effect is very similar to the bounce effect, but with the crucial difference of not having any built-in easing. So, the targeted element will shake the same distance for the specified number of times, instead of lessening each time (although it will come to a smooth stop at the end of the animation).

Let's change the previous example so that it uses the shake effect instead of the bounce effect. Change `effectBounce.html` so that it uses the `shake.js` source file instead of the bounce source file:

```
<script src="development-bundle/ui/jquery.ui.effect-shake.js">
</script>
```

Then change the click-handler in the final `<script>` element at the bottom of the `<body>` element so that it appears as follows:

```
$("#ball").click(function() {
  $(this).effect("shake", { direction: "up" }, 100);
});
```

Save this as `effectShake.html`. This time we've made use of the `direction` configuration option and the duration argument. The configuration option controls the direction of the shake. We set this to override the default setting for this option, which is `left`. The duration we use speeds up the animation.

This effect shares the same options as the bounce effect, although the defaults are set slightly differently. The options are listed in the following table:

Option	Default value	Uses
direction	"left"	Sets the direction of the shake
distance	20	Sets the distance of the shake in pixels
times	3	Sets the number of times the element should shake

Transferring an element's outline

The transfer effect is different from others, in that it doesn't directly affect the targeted element. Instead, it transfers the outline of a specified element to another specified element. To see this effect in action, change the `<body>` element of `effectShake.html` so that it contains the following elements:

```
<div id="container">
  <div id="basketContainer">
    <div id="basket"></div>
    <p>Basket total: <span id="total">0</span></p>
```

```
    </div>
    <div id="productContainer">
      <img alt="GTX 280" src="img/gcard.png"></img>
      <p>BFG GTX 280 OC 1GB GDDR3 Dual DVI HDTV Out PCI-E Graphics
Card</p>
      <p id="price">Cost: $350</p>

    </div>
    <div id="purchase"><button id="buy">Buy</button></div>
  </div>
```

Save this as `effectTransfer.html`. We've created a basic product listing; when the **Buy** button is clicked, the transfer effect will give the impression of the product being moved into the basket. To make this happen, change the final `<script>` element so that it contains the following code:

```
<script>
  $(document).ready(function($){
    $("#buy").click(function() {
      $("#productContainer img").effect("transfer", {
        to:"#basket"
      }, 750, function() {
        var currentTotal = $("#total").text(),
        numeric = parseInt(currentTotal, 10);
        $("#total").text(numeric + 1);
      });
    });
  });
</script>
```

Of course, a proper shopping cart application would be exponentially more complex than this, but we do get to see the transfer effect in all its glory. Don't forget to update the effect's source file:

```
<script src="development-bundle/ui/jquery.effects.transfer.js">
</script>
```

We also need some CSS for this example, so create the following new stylesheet:

```
body { font-family: "Lucida Grande",Arial,sans-serif; }
#container { width: 707px; margin: 0 auto; }
#productContainer img { width:  92px; height: 60px; border: 2px solid
#000000; position: relative; float: left; }
#productContainer p { width: 340px; height: 50px; padding: 5px;
border: 2px solid #000; border-left: none; margin: 0; font-family:
Verdana; font-size: 11px; font-weight: bold; float: left; }
```

```
p#price { height: 35px; width: 70px; padding-top: 20px; float: left; }
#purchase { height: 44px; width: 75px; padding-top: 16px; border: 2px
solid #000; border-left: none; float: left; text-align: center; }
#basketContainer { width: 90px; margin-top: 100px; float: right; }
#basketContainer p { width:  100px; }
#basket { width: 65px; height: 50px; position: relative; left: 13px;
background: url(img/shopping.png) no-repeat; }
.ui-effects-transfer { border: 2px solid #66ff66; }
```

Save this as `effectTransfer.css` in the `css` folder. The key rule in our new stylesheet is the one that targets the element which has the class as `ui-effects-transfer`.

This element is created by the effect and together with our styling produces the green outline that is transferred from the product to the basket.

Run the file in your browser. I think you'll agree that it's a nice effect which would add value to any page that it was used on. Here's how it should look while the transfer is occurring:

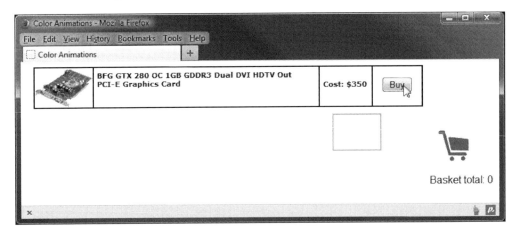

The transfer effect has just two configurable options, one of which is required and that we have already seen. For reference, both are listed in the following table:

Option	Default value	Use
className	"ui-effects-transfer"	Applies a custom classname to the effect helper element.
to	"none"	Sets the element the effect will be transferred to. This property is mandatory.

The four effects that we've looked at so far all have one thing in common–they can only be used with the `effect` method. The remaining effects can be used not only with the `effect` method, but also with jQuery's toggle and the `show`/`hide` methods.

Let's take a look.

Scaling elements on a page

The scale effect is highly configurable and is used to shrink an element. It is very effective when used to hide elements. In this example we'll use the `hide()` method to trigger the effect, instead of using the `effect` method.

We'll use a few of the CSS framework classes in this example, as well as a few custom styles; so add two new `<link>` elements to the `<head>` element of `effectTransfer.html`:

```
<link rel="stylesheet" href="development-bundle/themes/redmond/jquery.
ui.all.css">
<link rel="stylesheet" href="css/effectScale.css">
```

Then, replace the underlying markup in the `<body>` element with the following:

```
<div class="ui-widget ui-widget-content ui-corner-all">
  <div class="ui-widget-header ui-corner-all">
    A dialog box
    <a id="close" class="ui-icon ui-icon-closethick" href="#">
    Close
    </a>
  </div>
  <div class="content">Close the dialog to see the scale effect</div>
</div>
```

Don't forget to change the `<script>` element for the effect, to the scale effect's source file:

```
<script src="development-bundle/ui/jquery.ui.effect-scale.js">
</script>
```

Finally, replace the last `<script>` element, so that it appears as follows:

```
<script>
  $(document).ready(function($) {
    $("#close").click(function(e) {
      $("#close").click(function(e) {
        e.preventDefault();
        $(this).closest(".ui-widget").hide("scale", {}, 900);
```

```
        });
      });
    });
  </script>
```

Save the new page as `effectScale.html`. The custom stylesheet we use is as follows:

```
.ui-widget { padding: 3px; width: 300px; }
.ui-widget-header, .content { padding: 5px 10px; }
.ui-widget-header a { margin-top: 2px; float: right; }
```

Save this file as `effectScale.css` in the `css` folder. These styles are used to give the example a vaguely dialog-like appearance.

In the script, we simply add a click handler for the close icon and call the `effect()` method on the outer container of the dialog box. An empty object is passed as the second argument to the method, and a relatively long duration is passed as the third argument, as this effect proceeds quite rapidly. The following screenshot shows the effect in action:

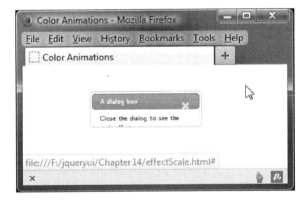

Using the `hide()` method instead of the `effect()` method is advantageous to us in this example, because we want the dialog box to remain hidden after the effect has completed. When the `effect()` method is used instead, bits of the widget remain visible at the end of the animation.

When should the percent option be configured?

The `percent` configuration option must be configured when using the `effect()` method in conjunction with the scale effect.

There are several configuration options which can be used with scale; these are as listed in the following table:

Option	Default value	Use
direction	"both"	Sets the direction to scale the element in. May be a string specifying horizontal, vertical, or both.
from	{}	Sets the starting height and width of the element to be scaled.
origin	["middle","center"]	Sets the vanishing point, used with show / hide animations.
percent	0	Sets the end size of the scaled element.

Exploding elements on a page

The explosion effect is truly awesome. The targeted element is literally exploded into a specified number of pieces, before disappearing completely. It's an easy effect to use and has few configuration properties, but the visual impact of this effect is huge, giving you a lot of effect in return for very little code. Let's see a basic example.

Create the following new page:

```
<!DOCTYPE HTML>
<html>
  <head>
    <meta charset="utf-8">
    <title>Explode</title>
    <link rel="stylesheet" href="development-bundle/themes/redmond/jquery.ui.all.css">
    <style>
      body { width: 200px; margin-left: auto; margin-right: auto; }
    </style>
    <script src="js/jquery-2.0.3.js"></script>
    <script src="development-bundle/ui/jquery.ui.effect.js"></script>
    <script src="development-bundle/ui/jquery.ui.effect-explode.js"></script>
  </head>
  <script>
    $(document).ready(function($){
      $("#theBomb").click(function() {
        $(this).hide("explode");
      });
    });
```

```
    </script>
    <body>
        <p>Click the grenade to pull the pin!</p>
        <img id="theBomb" src="img/nade.jpg">
    </body>
</html>
```

Save this as `effectExplode.html`. As you can see, the code is extremely simple and can be used completely out of the box with no additional configuration. This effect has only one configurable property, which is the `pieces` property, and it determines how many pieces the element is exploded into. The default is nine. The effect works equally as well with the `effect()` method as it does with the `hide()` method.

Once the specified element has been exploded, it will be hidden from view by having its `style` attribute set to `display: none`. This is the default behavior. However, it will still remain in the DOM of the page. The following screenshot shows the explosion in progress:

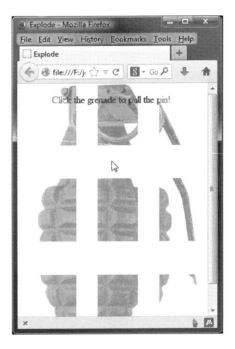

Physicists sometimes speculate as to why the arrow of time seems to only point forward. They invariably ask themselves philosophical questions like "Why do we not see grenades spontaneously forming from a large cloud of debris?" (Actually the object is usually an egg, but I don't think an egg-based example would have had quite the same impact!)

jQuery UI cannot help our understanding of entropy, but it can show us what spontaneously reassembling of a grenade might look like. We'll need to hide the `<img>` tag in order to show it. The easiest way to do this is with an inline `style` attribute:

```
<img id="theBomb" src="img/nade.jpg" style="display:none">
```

Then, change the final `<script>` element so that it appears as follows:

```
<script>
  $(document).ready(function($){
    $("#theBomb").show("explode");
  });
</script>
```

Save this variant as `effectExplodeShow.html`. This time we use the `show()` method instead of the `hide()` method to trigger the animation, which occurs once the page has loaded.

The animation is the same, except that it is shown in reverse and this time the grenade is not hidden from view once the animation ends. Like other effects, explode can also make use of specific durations and callback functions.

Creating a puff effect

Similar to the explode effect, but slightly more subtle is the puff effect, which causes an element to grow slightly before fading away. Like explode, there are few configuration options to concern ourselves with.

Consider a page that has AJAX operations occurring on it. It's useful to provide a loading image that shows the visitor that something is happening. Instead of just hiding an image like this when the operation has completed, we can puff it out of existence instead.

Remove the `<p>` element and change the `<img>` element from the previous example, so that it points to a new image:

```
<img id="loader" src="img/ajax-loader.gif">
```

Then change the effect's source file to the scale effect:

```
<script src="development-bundle/ui/jquery.ui.effect-scale.js">
</script>
```

Finally, change the last `<script>` element, so that it appears as follows:

```
<script>
  $(document).ready(function($){
    $("#loader").click(function() {
      $(this).hide("puff");
    });
  });
</script>
```

Save this as `effectPuff.html`. We're actually not detecting whether a given process has finished loading in this example. It would require too much work just to see the effect we're looking at. Instead, we tie the execution of the effect into a simple click-handler.

You'll notice that we used the `jquery.ui.effect-scale.js` source file for this effect.

The puff effect is the only effect that does not have its own source file, and instead it's a part of the very closely related scale effect's source file.

Like the explode effect that we looked at in the last section, this effect has just one configuration option that can be passed in an object as the second argument of the `effect` method. This is the `percent` option and controls the size the image is scaled up to. The default value is 150 percent. Like the explode effect, the target element is hidden from view once the animation ends. This happens whether `effect()` or `hide()` is used.

The effect stretches the targeted element (and its children, if it has any), while at the same time reducing its opacity. It works well on proper images, background colors, and borders, but you should note that it does not work so well with background images specified by CSS. Nevertheless, it's a great effect.

The following screenshot shows it in action:

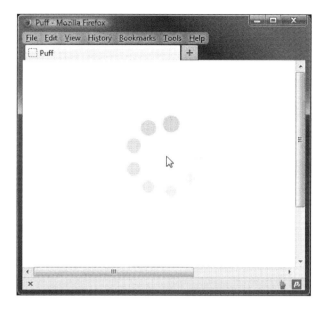

Working with the pulsate effect

The pulsate effect is another effect that works with the opacity of a specified element. This effect reduces the opacity temporarily, a specified number of times, making the element appear to pulsate.

In the following basic example, we'll create a simple countdown time that counts down from 15. When the display reaches 10 seconds, it will begin to flash red. In `effectPuff.html`, change the link in the `<head>` element of the page to point to a new stylesheet:

```
<link rel="stylesheet" href="css/effectPulsate.css">
```

Then remove the loading `<img>` element from the page and add the following element in its place:

```
<div id="countdown">15</div>
```

Next, change the source file of the effect so that the `jquery.ui.effect-pulsate.js` file is used:

```
<script src="development-bundle/ui/jquery.ui.effect-pulsate.js">
</script>
```

Finally, remove the existing last `<script>` element, and replace it with the following:

```
<script>
  $(document).ready(function($){
    var age = 15, countdown = $("#countdown"),
      adjustAge = function() {
        countdown.text(age--);
        if (age === 0) {
          clearInterval(timer);
        } else if (age < 10) {
          countdown.css({
          backgroundColor: "#ff0000",
          color: "#fff"
        }).effect("pulsate", { times: 1 });
      }
    },
    timer = setInterval(function() { adjustAge() }, 1000);
  });
</script>
```

Save this as `effectPulsate.html`. The page itself contains just a simple `<div>` element with the text 15 inside it. The code first sets a counter variable and then caches a selector for the `<div>` element. We then define the `adjustAge()` function.

This function first decreases the text content of the countdown element and at the same time reduces the value of the counter variable by one. It then checks whether the counter variable has reached zero yet; if yes, it clears the interval we are about to set.

If the counter variable is greater than 0 but less than 11, the function applies a background color of red to the element and white to the element's text content, and then runs the pulsate effect.

We use the `times` configuration option to specify how many times the element should pulsate. As we'll be executing the method once every second, we can set this to just pulsate once each time. This is the only configurable option.

After our `adjustAge` function, we start the interval using JavaScript's `setInterval` function. This function will repetitively execute the specified function after the specified interval, which in this example is 1000 milliseconds, or 1 second. We avoid using the `window` object by using an anonymous function to call our named function.

The new stylesheet is very simple and consists of the following code:

```
#countdown { width: 100px; border: 1px solid #000; margin: 10px auto
0; font-size: 60px; text-align: center; }
```

Save this in the `css` folder as `effectPulsate.css`.

Adding the drop effect to elements

The drop effect is simple. Elements appear to drop off (or onto) the page, which is simulated by adjusting the element's `position` and `opacity` values.

This effect exposes the following configurable options:

Option	Default value	Use
direction	"left"	Sets the direction of the drop
distance	The outer width or height of the element (depending on the direction) divided by 2	Sets the distance the element drops
easing n	one	Sets the easing function used during the animation
mode	"hide"	Sets whether the element is hidden or shown

There are many situations in which the drop effect would be useful, but the one that instantly springs to mind is when creating custom tooltips. We can easily create a tooltip that appears when a button is clicked, but instead of just showing the tooltip, we can drop it onto the page. We'll use the button widget and the `position` utility in this example, as well as the effect.

Add a link to the CSS framework file and change the stylesheet link in the `<head>` element of `effectPulsate.html`:

```
<link rel="stylesheet" href="development-bundle/themes/redmond/jquery.
ui.all.css">
<link rel="stylesheet" href="css/effectDrop.css">
```

Remove the countdown `<div>` element from the page and add the following element instead:

```
<a id="button" href="#" title="This button does nothing">
  Click me!
</a>
```

Now we need to change the effect's source file and add the source files for the position and button widgets:

```
<script src="development-bundle/ui/jquery.ui.effect-drop.js">
</script>
<script src="development-bundle/ui/jquery.ui.core.js">
</script>
<script src="development-bundle/ui/jquery.ui.widget.js">
</script>
<script src="development-bundle/ui/jquery.ui.position.js">
</script>
<script src="development-bundle/ui/jquery.ui.button.js">
</script>
```

Lastly, change the final `<script>` element, so that it appears as follows:

```
<script>
  $(document).ready(function($){
    $("#button").button().click(function() {
      var button = this, tip = $("<span />", {
        id: "tip",
        text: button.title
      }),
      tri = $("<span />", {
        id: "tri"
      }).appendTo(tip);
      tip.appendTo("body").position({
        of: button,
        my: "right-35 center",
        at: "left center",
        offset: "-30 0"
      });
      tip.show("drop", { direction: "up" }, function() {
        $(this).delay(1000).fadeOut();
      });
    });
  });
</script>
```

Save this file as `effectDrop.html`. When the button is clicked, we first store a reference to the DOM node of the button. We then add a configuration object for the `position` utility, in order to position our tooltip to the right of the button.

We then create a new `<span>` element to use as the tooltip, which has its text content set to the title text of the button. We also create another element used to create a triangular CSS shape to give the tooltip a pointer. This element is appended to the tooltip.

Once created, the tooltip is appended to the `<body>` element of the page and is then shown using the drop effect. The `direction` configuration option is used to make the tooltip appear to drop down; we have to specify the opposite direction here, because our tooltip is absolutely positioned.

There is also some minimal CSS required for this example, in addition to the styles provided by the CSS framework, to style the tooltip. Create the following stylesheet:

```
#tip { display: none; padding: 10px 20px 10px 10px;
position: absolute; background-color: #cecece; }
#tri { border-top: 20px solid transparent; border-right: 30px solid
#cecece; border-bottom: 20px solid transparent; position: absolute;
left:- 30px; top: 0; }
```

Save this in the `css` folder as `effectDrop.css`. The styling here is purely for aesthetics.

When you run the file in your browser, you should see your tooltip, as in the following screenshot:

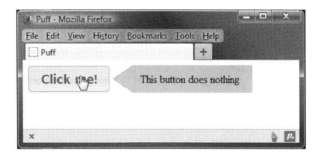

Implementing the sliding effect

The remaining effects of the jQuery UI library all work by showing and hiding elements in different ways, rather than using opacity like most of the effects we have already looked at.

The slide effect is no exception and shows (or hides) an element by sliding it into (or out of) view. It is similar to the drop effect that we just looked at. The main difference is that it does not use opacity.

The slide effect contains the following configuration options:

Option	Default value	Use
direction	"left"	Sets the direction of the slide
distance	The outer width or height of the element (depending on the direction)	Sets the distance the element slides
easing	none	Sets the easing function used during the animation
mode	"show"	Sets whether the element is hidden or shown

These are the same configuration options used by the drop effect that we looked at in the previous example, except that some of the default values are different.

For our next example, we can create exactly this kind of functionality. In effectDrop.html, change the <link> element in the <head> element of the page from effectDrop.css to effectSlide.css:

```
<link rel="stylesheet" href="css/effectSlide.css">
```

Then remove the <a> element from the <body> element of the page and add the following HTML in its place:

```
<aside id="basket" class="ui-widget">
  <h1 class="ui-widget-header ui-corner-all">
    Basket
    <a id="toggle" title="Show basket contents" class="ui-icon ui-icon-circle-triangle-s" href="#">
      Open
    </a>
  </h1>
  <div class="ui-widget-content ui-corner-bottom">
    <ul>
      <li>
        <img src="img/placeholder.gif">
        <h2>Product name</h2>
        <h3>Brief descriptive subtitle</h3>
        <span>£xx.xx</span>
      </li>
      <li>
        <img src="img/placeholder.gif">
        <h2>Product name</h2>
        <h3>Brief descriptive subtitle</h3>
        <span>£xx.xx</span>
```

```
        </li>
        <li>
          <img src="img/placeholder.gif">
          <h2>Product name</h2>
          <h3>Brief descriptive subtitle</h3>
          <span>£xx.xx</span>
        </li>
      </ul>
    </div>
  </aside>
```

The outer element in this collection is `<aside>`, which is the perfect element for a mini-basket widget that sits in the right column of a site. Within this element, we have a `<h1>` element that serves as the heading for the basket. The heading contains a link, which will be used to show or hide the contents of the basket. The contents of the basket will consist of an unordered list of products within a container `<div>`.

Don't forget to change the `<script>` element for the effect's source file to use `jquery.ui.effect-slide.js`, and remove the `<script>` files for `jquery.ui.core.js`, `jquery.ui.widget.js`, `jquery.ui.position.js`, and `jquery.ui.button.js`:

```
<script src="development-bundle/ui/jquery.ui.effect-slide.js">
</script>
```

The final `<script>` element will need to be changed to the following code:

```
<script>
  $(document).ready(function($){
    $("#toggle").on("click", function(e) {
      var slider = $("#basket").find("div"),
        header = slider.prev();
      if (!slider.is(":visible")) {
        header.addClass("ui-corner-top")
          .removeClass("ui-corner-all");
      }
      slider.toggle("slide", {
        direction: "up"
      }, "slow", function() {
        if (slider.is(":visible")) {
          header.find("a").switchClass("ui-icon-circle-triangle-s",
"ui-icon-circle-triangle-n");
        } else {
          header.switchClass("ui-corner-all", "ui-corner-top");
          header.find("a").switchClass("ui-icon-circle-triangle-n",
"ui-icon-circle-triangle-s");
```

```
            }
        });
     });
   });
</script>
```

Save this as `effectSlide.html`. All of the functionality resides within a clickhandler, which we attach to the icon in the basket header. When this element is clicked, we first initialize the `slider` and `header` variables, as these are the elements that we will be manipulating.

We then check whether the `slider` (which is the basket contents container) is hidden; if it is hidden, we know that it is about to be opened and so remove the rounded corners from the bottom of the `header`. This is so that the slider element sits flush up to the bottom of the `header`, even while it is sliding open.

We then use jQuery's `toggle()` method to call the effect, which we specify using the first argument of the method. We then set the configuration option, `direction`, in an object passed as the second argument. The duration of the animation is lengthened using the string `slow` as the third argument, and an anonymous callback function is used as the fourth argument. This function will be executed at the end of the slide animation.

Within this function, we check the state of the `slider` to see if it is hidden or open. If it is open at the end of the animation, we remove the border from the bottom of the `header` and then change the icon in the `header`, so that it points up to indicate that the basket can be closed by clicking on the icon again.

If the `slider` is now closed, we add the bottom border and rounded corners to the `header` once again, and change the icon back to an arrow pointing down.

We also use a little CSS in this example. Create the following stylesheet:

```
#basket { width: 380px; float: right; }
#basket h1 { padding: 5px 10px; margin: 0; }
#basket h1 a { float: right; margin-top: 8px; }
#basket div { display: none; }
#basket ul { margin: 0; padding: 0; list-style-type: none; }
#basket li { padding: 10px; border-bottom: 1px solid #aaa; }
#basket li:last-child { border-bottom: none; }
#basket li:after { content: ""; display: block; width: 100%; height:
0; visibility: hidden; clear: both; }
#basket img { float: left; height: 75px; margin: 2px 10px 0; width:
105px; }
#basket h2 { margin: 0 0 10px; font-size: 14px; }
#basket h3 { margin: 0; font-size: 12px; }
#basket span { margin-top: 6px; float: right; }
```

Save this as `effectSlide.css` in the `css` folder. We don't need much CSS in this example, because we are using the CSS framework classes.

The effect in progress should appear as in the following screenshot:

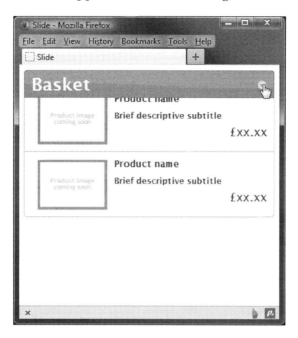

In this example, we could easily just use jQuery's native `slideToggle()` method; the main benefit of using jQuery UI's slide effect is that we can also slide left or right.

Using easing

As mentioned earlier that the `jquery.ui.effect.js` file had the built-in ability to seamlessly use easing with the effects. Let's see how easy this is to achieve. Change the last `<script>` element in `effectSlide.html`, so that it appears as follows:

```
<script>
  $(document).ready(function($){
    $("#toggle").on("click", function(e) {
      var slider = $("#basket").find("div"),
        header = slider.prev(),
        easing = (slider.is(":visible")) ?
          "easeOutQuart" :
          "easeOutBounce";
        if (!slider.is(":visible")) {
```

```
            header.addClass("ui-corner-top")
              .removeClass("ui-corner-all");
          }
          slider.toggle("slide", {
            direction: "up",
            easing: easing
          }, "slow", function() {
          if (slider.is(":visible")) {
            header.find("a").switchClass("ui-icon-circle-triangle-s",
  "ui-icon-circle-triangle-n");
          } else {
            header.switchClass("ui-corner-all", "ui-corner-top")
            header.find("a").switchClass("ui-icon-circle-triangle-n",
  "ui-icon-circle-triangle-s");
          }
        });
      });
    });
  </script>
```

Save this as `effectsSlideEasing.html`. See how easy that was? All we need to do is add the `easing` option within the effect's configuration object and define one or more of the easing methods as the option value.

In this example, we specify a different easing method for each toggle state by setting a variable which uses the JavaScript ternary condition to set an easing function, depending on whether the slider is visible or not.

When the basket slides down, it bounces slightly at the end of the animation with `easeOutBounce`. When it slides back up, it will gradually slow down over the course of the animation using `easeOutQuart`.

> The full range of easing methods, which we can use with any of the effects are shown on an excellent page on the jQueryUI site and can be seen at `http://jqueryui.com/demos/effect/easing.html`.

Understanding the blind effect

The blind effect is practically the same as the slide effect. Visually, the element appears to do the same thing, and the two effects' code files are also extremely similar. The main difference between the two effects that we need to worry about is that with this effect we can only specify the axis of the effect, not the actual direction.

The blind effect has the following configuration options:

Option	Default value	Use
direction	"vertical"	Sets the axis of motion
easing	none	Sets the easing function used during the animation
mode	"hide"	Sets whether the element is hidden or shown

The `direction` option that this effect uses for configuration only accepts the values `horizontal` or `vertical`. We'll build on the last example to see the blind effect in action. Change the `<script>` resource for the blind effect in `effectSlide.html`, so that it refers to the `jquery.ui.effect-blind.js` file:

```
<script src="development-bundle/ui/jquery.ui.effect-blind.js">
</script>
```

Now change the `toggle()` method, so that it uses the blind effect, and change the value of the `direction` configuration option:

```
slider.toggle("blind", {
  direction: "vertical"
}, "slow", function() {
  if (slider.is(":visible")) {
    header.css("borderBottomWidth", 0).find("a")
      .addClass("ui-icon-circle-triangle-n")
      .removeClass("ui-icon-circle-triangle-s");
  } else {
    header.css("borderBottomWidth", 1)
      .addClass("ui-corner-all")
      .removeClass("ui-corner-top").find("a")
      .addClass("ui-icon-circle-triangle-s")
      .removeClass("ui-icon-circle-triangle-n");
  }
});
```

Save this as `effectBlind.html`. Literally, all we've changed is the string specifying the effect, in this case to `blind`, and the value of the `direction` property from `up` to `vertical`. Notice the subtle difference when we view the file between sliding the element and blinding it up.

When the login form slides up, the bottom of the element remains visible at all times, as if the whole basket is moving up into or out of the header. However, with the blind effect, the element is shown or hidden, starting with the bottom first, just like a window blind opening or closing.

Clipping elements

The clip effect is very similar to the slide effect. The main difference is that instead of moving one edge of the targeted element towards the other, to give the effect of the element sliding out of view, the clip effect moves both edges of the targeted element in towards the center.

The clip effect has the same configuration options as the blind effect and these options have the same default values.

At the end of *Chapter 5, The Dialog*, we created an example that showed a full-size image in a dialog when a thumbnail image was clicked. When the close button on the dialog was pressed, the dialog was simply removed from the page instantly.

We could easily use the clip effect to close our dialog instead.

In `dialog14.html`, add the source files for the clip effect after the existing library files:

```
<script src="development-bundle/ui/jquery.ui.effect.js"></script>
<script src="development-bundle/ui/jquery.ui.effect-clip.js"></script>
```

Then, change the dialog configuration object so that it appears as follows:

```
dialogOpts = {
  modal: true,
  width: 388,
  height: 470,
  autoOpen: false,
  open: function(event, ui) {
  $("#dialog").empty();
    $("<img>").attr("src", filename).appendTo("#dialog");
    $("#dialog").dialog("option", "title", titleText);
  },
  hide: {
    effect: "clip"
  }
};
```

Save this as `effectClip.html`. In this simple addition to the existing file, we use the clip effect in conjunction with the `close` event callback to hide the dialog from view. The default configuration value of `vertical` for the `direction` option and the default speed of normal are both fine, so we just call the `hide` method, specifying clip with no additional arguments.

The following screenshot shows the dialog being clipped:

Folding elements

Folding is a neat effect that gives the appearance that the element it's applied to is being folded up like a piece of paper. It achieves this by moving the bottom edge of the specified element up to 15 pixels from the top, then moving the right edge completely over towards the left edge.

The distance from the top that the element is shrunk to in the first part of this effect is exposed as a configurable property by the effect's API. So, this is something that we can adjust to suit the needs of our implementation. This property is an integer.

We can see this effect in action by modifying the dialog example once again. In effectClip.html, change the effect source file for clip to fold:

```
<script src="development-bundle/ui/jquery.ui.effect-fold.js"></script>
```

Then change the `hide` event callback to the following:

```
hide: {
  effect: "fold",
  size: 200,
  duration: 1000
}
```

Save this as `effectFold.html`. This time we make use of the size configuration option to make the effect stop in the first fold, 200 pixels before the top of the dialog. We also slow the animation down a little, by setting the duration to 1000 milliseconds. It's a really nice effect; the following screenshot shows the second part of the animation:

Summary

In this chapter, we've covered the complete range of UI effects available in the jQuery UI library. We've seen how easy it is to use the `jquery.ui.effect.js` base component to construct attractive color animations and smooth class transitions.

We also saw that the following effects can be used in conjunction with the simple effect API:

- Bounce
- Highlight
- Shake
- Transfer

An important point is that most of the individual effects can be used not only with the effect API but can also make use of `show`/`hide` and `toggle` logic, making them incredibly flexible and robust. The following effects can be used with this advanced API:

- Blind
- Clip
- Drop
- Explode
- Fold
- Puff
- Pulsate
- Scale
- Slide

We also saw that the jQuery UI effects' core files also include all of the easing functions used in the `jquery.easing.js` plugin that must be used with jQuery when we are not using jQuery UI.

This now brings us to the end of this chapter. There is a saying that I'm sure almost all of you will have heard before. It's the "Give a man a fish..." saying. I hope that during the course of this book, I've taught you how to fish, instead of just giving you a fish.

Help and Support

Throughout this book, you will have noticed that we've concentrated on using jQuery Version 2.0 as the most recent version available for use with jQuery UI. However, jQuery UI 1.10 comes bundled with jQuery 1.9.1 by default—why should we use Version 2.0, if Version 1.9.1 is bundled with jQuery UI 1.10?

The reason for this is simple, and relates to an important change made with Version 2.0, where support for Internet Explorer (IE) 6-8 has been removed. Removing support for these older browsers has allowed the jQuery team to remove significant parts of the library, as these were only included to provide workarounds for browsers!

While there has been a big push to retire IE 6 because of the security vulnerabilities, there is still an element of need to support it; with this in mind, the jQuery team are still producing and supporting versions of jQuery under the 1.x branch, for as long as these older browsers are still used.

Downloading jQuery

Each chapter's exercise folder in the code download will come with both versions of jQuery included—copies of Version 2.0.3 have been added to the JS folder that comes as part of the normal download of jQuery (and which contains 1.9.1).

If you need to obtain fresh copies of Version 2.x of jQuery, you can do so by browsing to `http://www.jquery.com/download`. Here you will find links for both the uncompressed and compressed versions of jQuery 2.x. For the purposes of the exercises, I would recommend using the uncompressed version. You will need to right-click on the link, and choose **Save target as...** (or your browser's equivalent), in order to save the file into the JS sub-folder.

Updating the code samples

All of the code samples are already set to use jQuery 2.0.3 by default. If we look at an example using the Tabs widget, we should see something like this, at the head of our example:

```
<!DOCTYPE html>
<html>
<head>
  <meta charset="utf-8">
  <title>Tabs</title>
  <link rel="stylesheet" href="development-bundle/themes/base/
  jquery.ui.all.css">
  <script src="js/jquery-2.0.3.js"></script>
  <script src="development-bundle/ui/jquery.ui.core.js"></script>
  <script src="development-bundle/ui/jquery.ui.widget.js">
  </script>
  <script src="development-bundle/ui/jquery.ui.tabs.js"></script>
...
```

Here the highlighted line is important to us; you will need to ensure that the file you have just downloaded has been saved with the filename of `jquery-2.0.3.js`, in order for each sample to work correctly.

Getting help

Getting to know a new library can be daunting sometimes, particularly one the size of jQuery UI—let's go through some of the options available, where you can get hints, tips, help, and support for your endeavors with the library.

Changing themes

At various points throughout the book, we covered the use of themes within jQuery UI—a useful tool you can incorporate into your pages, is the Super Theme Switcher (STS) plugin, available from `https://github.com/harborhoffer/Super-Theme-Switcher`. Once implemented, you can use it to switch between themes at will; it's a great way to see how your site's widgets will look when a theme is changed, before making that change permanent.

This is particularly useful if you need to edit an existing theme; it is better practice to place your edits into an override file, and call this separately; editing the core UI CSS files means that you may face issues when upgrading to the next version of jQuery UI, as customizations could be lost.

Getting help from the community

jQuery UI has a wide range of demos where you can see elements of what each plugin provides. This is accompanied by extensive API documentation that covers the widgets, effects, methods, and selectors provided by jQuery UI. You can view this documentation from `http://api.jqueryui.com`; another good location to browse is the documentation available at `http://learn.jquery.com/jquery-ui/getting-started/`.

Need to ask a question?

This isn't a problem either; there are a number of public forums available for jQuery UI:

- **Using jQuery UI**: For everyone using jQuery UI, the best place to ask questions and advice regarding the use of all UI components, including Themeroller, visit `http://forum.jquery.com/using-jquery-ui`.

- **Developing jQuery UI**: For more advanced developers who want to work on developing the jQuery UI library and websites, you can get help from `http://forum.jquery.com/developing-jquery-ui`.

- **jQuery Accessibility**: For anyone that is unable to use the normal forums due to accessibility issues, there is an alternative forum available at `https://groups.google.com/forum/#!forum/jquery-a11y`.

Getting help via IRC chat

You can even get help through IRC chat, the official IRC support channel is `#jquery` on `irc.freenode.net`. For discussions about development of jQuery UI, join the `#jqueryui-dev` channel.

Asking at Stack Overflow

You can even get help on the questions and answers site for jQuery (and jQuery UI) at Stack Overflow, available at `http://stackoverflow.com/tags/jquery/info`. This is a large site where people can ask questions, seek advice, and general help with any questions relating to jQuery UI.

Reporting a bug in the library

Software isn't perfect; it's often down to the help of contributors that developed libraries, such as jQuery UI, are still actively used today. Should you find a bug, you can report it at `http://bugs.jqueryui.com`.

> It is strongly recommended that you read the notes and browse through the bugs already recorded, just in case someone has already reported the same issue!

Index

W

weekHeader option 187
widget factory 57
widget method 72, 130, 302
widgets
  components 19
width option 117

X

XMLHttpRequest parameter 175

Y

yearRange option 187
yearSuffix option 204
Yellow Fade Technique (YFT) 431

Z

zIndex option 320, 398
z-index order, dialog
  focus, controlling 126, 127
  setting 125, 126
z-index value
  overriding 126

Thank you for buying
jQuery UI 1.10:
The User Interface Library for jQuery

About Packt Publishing

Packt, pronounced 'packed', published its first book "*Mastering phpMyAdmin for Effective MySQL Management*" in April 2004 and subsequently continued to specialize in publishing highly focused books on specific technologies and solutions.

Our books and publications share the experiences of your fellow IT professionals in adapting and customizing today's systems, applications, and frameworks. Our solution based books give you the knowledge and power to customize the software and technologies you're using to get the job done. Packt books are more specific and less general than the IT books you have seen in the past. Our unique business model allows us to bring you more focused information, giving you more of what you need to know, and less of what you don't.

Packt is a modern, yet unique publishing company, which focuses on producing quality, cutting-edge books for communities of developers, administrators, and newbies alike. For more information, please visit our website: www.packtpub.com.

About Packt Open Source

In 2010, Packt launched two new brands, Packt Open Source and Packt Enterprise, in order to continue its focus on specialization. This book is part of the Packt Open Source brand, home to books published on software built around Open Source licences, and offering information to anybody from advanced developers to budding web designers. The Open Source brand also runs Packt's Open Source Royalty Scheme, by which Packt gives a royalty to each Open Source project about whose software a book is sold.

Writing for Packt

We welcome all inquiries from people who are interested in authoring. Book proposals should be sent to author@packtpub.com. If your book idea is still at an early stage and you would like to discuss it first before writing a formal book proposal, contact us; one of our commissioning editors will get in touch with you.

We're not just looking for published authors; if you have strong technical skills but no writing experience, our experienced editors can help you develop a writing career, or simply get some additional reward for your expertise.

Learning jQuery *Fourth Edition*

ISBN: 978-1-782163-14-5   Paperback: 444 pages

Better interaction, design, and web development with simple JavaScript techniques

1. An introduction to jQuery that requires minimal programming experience

2. Detailed solutions to specific client-side problems

3. Revised and updated version of this popular jQuery book

jQuery UI Cookbook

ISBN: 978-1-782162-18-6   Paperback: 290 pages

70 recipes to create responsive and engaging user interfaces in jQuery

1. Packed with recipes showing UI developers how to get the most out of their jQuery UI widgets

2. Solutions to real-world development issues distilled down in a reader-friendly approach

3. Code examples written in a concise and elegant format making it easy for the reader to adapt to their own style

Please check **www.PacktPub.com** for information on our titles

jQuery Game Development Essentials

ISBN: 978-1-849695-06-0   Paperback: 244 pages

Learn how to make fun and addictive multi-platform games using jQuery

1. Discover how you can create a fantastic RPG, arcade game, or platformer using jQuery!

2. Learn how you can integrate your game with various social networks, creating multiplayer experiences and also ensuring compatibility with mobile devices

3. Create your very own framework, harnessing the very best design patterns and proven techniques along the way

Instant jQuery 2.0 Table Manipulation How-to

ISBN: 978-1-78216-468-5   Paperback: 56 pages

Enhance and add functionality with interactivity to your HTML tables with jQuery

1. Learn something new in an Instant! A short, fast, focused guide delivering immediate results

2. Use simple jQuery functions to enhance your HTML tables

3. Demonstrate client-side functionality and add AJAX for server-side integration

4. Modify your tables without editing your HTML

Please check **www.PacktPub.com** for information on our titles

Made in the USA
San Bernardino, CA
28 September 2017